Medical Malpractice

Medical Malpractice

Frank A. Sloan and Lindsey M. Chepke

The MIT Press
Cambridge, Massachusetts
London, England

First MIT Press paperback edition, 2010

For information about special quantity discounts, please email special_sales @mitpress.mit.edu

This book was set in Sabon by SNP Best-set Typesetter Ltd., Hong Kong. Printed and bound in the United States of America.

Library of Congress Cataloging-in-Publication Data

Sloan, Frank A.
Medical malpractice / Frank A. Sloan and Lindsey M. Chepke.
    p. ; cm.
Includes bibliographical references and index.
ISBN 978-0-262-19572-0 (hardcover : alk. paper)
        978-0-262-51516-0 (paperback : alk. paper)
    1. Medical personnel–Malpractice–United   States. 2. Insurance, Liability–Malpractice–United   States. I. Chepke, Lindsey M. II. Title.
[DNLM: 1. Insurance, Liability–legislation & jurisprudence–United States. 2. Malpractice–legislation & jurisprudence–United   States. 3. Insurance, Liability–economics–United   States. 4. Malpractice–economics–United   States. W 33 AA1 S6m 2007]
KF2905.3.S66   2007
344.7304′11–dc22   2007019119

Contents

Preface

For more than three decades, medical malpractice has been at the top of the U.S. policy agenda from time to time. Medical malpractice crises begin when medical malpractice premiums spike and some insurers withdraw from the market. Major changes in the price and availability of coverage in turn lead to pressures on public policymakers for relief. Policymakers are pressured to implement quick solutions, typically on the basis of little objective information. After a few years, premiums stabilize and insurers return to the market. The disruptions, both real and imagined, are clearly unfortunate. But there is also a benefit. Although the controversies and many of the solutions do not seem to vary much, with each crisis we learn more about how the system really operates. The "system" reflects the actions of citizens as patients (more frequently) and plaintiffs (much less frequently), physicians, hospitals, and other health care providers, lawyers for plaintiffs and defendants, judges, insurers, and governments.

This book is about what we do and do not know about the ways in which this complex system operates, the important lessons to be learned from the past, and recommended policies for the future. We have written the book for a broad readership, ranging from individuals (as patients and voters), physicians, hospital administrators, attorneys, and insurers to state legislators, as well as the advocates for the various policy positions on medical malpractice. Scholars in the various disciplines will find a lot of material on medical malpractice, with documentation, in the endnotes. Although the authors are an economist and a lawyer, respectively, we have tried to write this book in nontechnical language. Some issues, such as those pertaining to insurance, are inherently technical.

Major funding for this research is from an Investigator Award from the Robert Wood Johnson Foundation to Frank Sloan. The Investigator Award program is a very valuable source of research support. Even investigator-initiated research grants do not generally give scholars the scope to explore paths totally unanticipated at the time the grant proposal is written, as the Investigator Awards do.

A purpose of these awards is to give scholars the time to think broadly about health care issues. In this spirit, we have ventured into methods of paying professionals in chapter 6, and no-fault insurance as applied to areas outside of personal health care services, such as for motor vehicle liability and workers' compensation, in chapter 11. The material on insurance cycles and reinsurance in chapters 2 and 10 applies much more broadly than only to medical malpractice. We cite experience with specialized courts from other fields, such as family and bankruptcy courts, in our analysis of the desirability and feasibility of health courts in chapter 7. This analysis also draws on evidence from product liability.

Our research also benefited from a grant from the Pew Charitable Trust and help from the principal investigator of the Pew grant, William Sage, who was on the faculty of Columbia Law School when the funding was active. Parts of the chapters on reinsurance and medical no-fault programs come from work funded by the Pew grant.

Kenneth Morris, senior vice president, chief financial officer, and treasurer of the Duke University Health System, provided helpful perspectives on Duke's approach to and experiences with its hospitals and physicians, as well as important details on how reinsurance markets function in practice.

Medical Malpractice

1

Introduction

Focus of the Book

In the first years of this century, for the third time in three decades, the United States faced a crisis over medical malpractice. Each crisis has had its unique features, but each crisis shares important attributes with its predecessors as well. In large part because there are always new persons in the policy arena, old discussions and experiences tend to be forgotten, and the same old questions are asked anew. Since each crisis stimulates new research, we know increasingly more about medical malpractice and medical malpractice insurance. In fact, we know much more than is commonly acknowledged—not that we have all the answers. For example, we do not know precisely why insurance crises reoccur, except that it is inevitable that they will. Also, evidence on the effects of past reforms, other than the ones that have been implemented repeatedly by state legislatures since the mid-1970s, is limited.

Interestingly, there is little fundamental disagreement among most researchers active in this field about the nature and extent of the "medical malpractice problem" and even about many of the solutions. However, there are some important differences in emphasis in policy recommendations. Virtually all experts would agree that the current system is "ill-suited" for deterring injuries and compensating injury victims efficiently. These same experts would agree that the issues in medical malpractice are at a crossroads, in that the policy responses to previous crises have not altered the fundamental incentives of the participants in the care, claiming, claims resolution, and insurance processes.

By contrast, there are substantial differences in views among the public at large, health professionals who are on the front line but seldom conduct quantitative analysis, medical malpractice insurers, large businesses in general, trial lawyers, and consumer groups. In large part, these differences in perceptions and recommendations for reform reflect the adage "Where you stand depends on where you sit." In addition, to a considerable extent these differences reflect reliance on personal experiences versus reliance on information assembled and analyzed by methods generally accepted by the scientific community.

While we identify deficiencies of the existing system, we do not propose sweeping reforms. Rather, our emphasis is on *achievable* reforms, although achieving *any* meaningful reform is admittedly not an easy task. In deciding what is and what is not achievable, it is essential to consider the institutional and political context which has guided how health care is financed and delivered in the United States. The experiences of other parts of the U.S. economy or of other countries are important to consider, but it is doubtful that these experiences would be replicated by the U.S. health care system, at least without substantial modifications.

An objective of this book is to make empirical evidence available, in a balanced fashion, to readers who do not typically read scholarly journals or attend academic conferences. Several books have been written on medical malpractice. Most are now over one or even two decades old. In addition, there has been much empirical research and writing since about 2000 which is reflected in this book for the first time.

Our evaluation of current practices is based on a substantial amount of empirical evidence and several premises. First, considerable research has been conducted on many aspects of medical malpractice, such as the claims resolution process, juries, defensive medicine, and the effects of tort reforms, especially those termed "first-generation tort reforms."[1] The research consistently indicates that rhetoric of the stakeholders on both sides of the debate has been highly exaggerated.

Second, the approach taken here is centrist. Some of the findings and our proposals will not be readily embraced by either organized medicine or the organized trial bar. For example, we are highly critical of flat caps on nonmonetary or total loss, which has been advocated by organized medicine. On the other hand, we find flaws with the existing method of assessing damages and recommend that alternative approaches for scheduling damages be considered. The organized trial bar has consistently opposed legislation that would constrain the latitude that juries now have to make such determinations.

Third, for any program of reform to succeed, the financial interests of health care providers must be aligned with the social objective of injury prevention and claims prevention. The financial incentives that providers have to engage in error reduction and quality improvement currently are insufficient. Under the best of circumstances, medical malpractice alone cannot succeed in encouraging implementation of all desirable quality improvements. Yet, rather than be an ineffective or even a negative force, medical malpractice can have a productive role in deterring iatrogenic injuries and in quality improvement.[2]

Fourth, the states have been laboratories for tort reform, whereas the U.S. government has been inactive.[3] Most of the recommendations in this book can be implemented by individual states.

Fifth, especially when empirical evidence on effects of some promising reforms is lacking or inconclusive, the law should permit health care organizations to implement reforms. That is, in general, voluntary approaches are to be favored over legislating broad "one size fits all" packages.

Medical Malpractice and Tort Law

Tort law has several important goals, among the most important of which are deterring misconduct (and hence injury) and compensating injury victims.[4] Other goals of tort include meting out justice and providing a safety valve for airing victims' grievances. These latter objectives are important to maintaining a civil society. While concerns arise more frequently during times of rising insurance premiums, there are standing concerns among scholars of tort law in general and of medical malpractice in particular. Specifically, how successful is tort in attaining the above objectives?

To date, there is no evidence that the threat of tort deters medical injuries, although such evidence exists for other applications of tort law, such as dram shop for alcohol sellers[5] and automobile liability.[6] Why the threat of a civil lawsuit is effective under some circumstances and not under others is not entirely clear. A possible explanation is that the underlying technology of injury prevention is easier in some areas than it is in others. Having a bartender call a taxicab for a patron who has consumed too many beers involves a simpler technology than is necessary for preventing a mishap in transplanting an organ.

Indicators of a Broken System

A logical first step in the public policy process is to assess "what works" and "what is broken" and needing change. Diagnosis is an essential first step in the policy process, and much of our attention is devoted to diagnosis, especially on the empirical evidence required for a good diagnosis.

The above rationale for tort, as embodied in such goals as injury deterrence and compensation, assumes that the legal system is efficient and accurate in adjudicating claims. At some point, inefficiencies and inaccuracies tip the balance against use of tort liability. Critics often cite the inefficiencies and inaccuracies of tort liability in general and of medical malpractice in particular. For example, legal disputes, especially those involving medical malpractice, can take years to resolve, requiring substantial use of legal resources on both sides of the dispute. Overall, the medical malpractice process is a slow and expensive approach for compensating persons who are injured as a result of receiving (or not receiving) medical care.

Compensation under tort is indeed very expensive—when measured in terms of the legal fees incurred by plaintiffs and defendants, court costs, and insurer overhead.[7] For tort liability as a whole (not just for medical malpractice), between 40 and 50 cents on the dollar is returned to plaintiffs as compensation for their injuries, which is much lower than the share of the premium dollar returned to insured individuals in other contexts, such as private health insurance, Medicare, and Social Security.

Even though the current system has these very negative attributes, it also has some important positive ones. For one, being able to sue in combination with the contingent fee method for paying plaintiffs' attorneys gives patients who are unsatisfied with outcomes of care a mechanism for addressing their grievances that would not be possible through other channels. The regulatory apparatus, in principle designed to serve the public interest, is sometimes controlled or substantially influenced by the parties it is designed to regulate. Because of health care provider influence or for some other bureaucratic reason, regulatory agencies may be unresponsive to patients' complaints. Ironically, one reason that medical malpractice is so aggravating to the health care provider community is that patients' ability to file a tort claim empowers patients to obtain justice and compensation when other systems, likely to be more subject to providers' influence, fail. Not all patients' complaints prove to be meritorious in the end, but some do.

Advocates for tort see it as an effective private mechanism for meting out justice, especially when other systems, such as public regulation and self-regulation by hospitals and physicians, fail to achieve their stated purposes. Moreover, defenders of the current system argue that individualized justice is costly to achieve and hence is inherently expensive.

Fortunately, there is now a large body of empirical evidence on the performance of tort in general and of medical malpractice in particular. Unfortunately, much of the public discourse continues to be based on anecdotes, which may be valid in isolated cases but do not generalize.

The rising cost of medical malpractice insurance premiums is cited in public discourse as an indicator that the medical malpractice system is "broken." While complaining about spending more money for insurance is certainly understandable—no one feels good about spending more for insurance—rising premiums, numbers of medical malpractice claims, and payments per paid claim are not in themselves valid social indicators that the system is broken. In a dynamic economy, expenditures on some goods and services rise and expenditures on others fall. There have been attempts to link trends in medical malpractice to increased spending on personal health services and reduced patient access to care.[8] But the empirical evidence indicates that medical malpractice is a factor of second- or even of third-order importance among determinants of increases in health care spending and of decreases in patient access to care.

If one views secular trends in medical malpractice payments and premiums, adjusted for general price changes, increases in payments and premiums have actually been quite modest, only slightly higher than the changes in prices overall. It is the substantial increase in premiums and withdrawal of medical malpractice insurance at the onset of "hard markets" that have attracted widespread attention. These premium shocks as well as shocks to availability of insurance have indeed been substantial, but sharply contrast with secular trends which have been much more moderate.

Levels, trends, and cycles in premiums, claims, and payments are invalid indicators that the system is functioning or is failing and badly in need of repair. But, as documented below, one reason that the threat of medical malpractice litigation fails to deter medical injuries is that there are too few rather than too many lawsuits, at least meritorious ones. If the state police went on strike, it would seem unlikely that the accident rate on highways would fall. In fact, having fewer troopers patroling the roads would reduce the probability of being apprehended for speeding and drunk driving. Thus, drivers might be inclined to be less cautious. Most commentators tend to be unwilling to make a parallel inference about too few medical malpractice suits—that more suits might make operating rooms safer places for patients under the knife.

Further, if medical malpractice litigation were serving a useful role, one would expect to observe situations in which more beneficial care is given and greater precautions are taken in providing such care than would occur in the absence of the threat of tort. The lack of empirical demonstration that the threat of medical malpractice has improved the quality of care, and hence has deterred iatrogenic injuries, is much more troubling. Yet some elected officials gauge the success of statutory changes, called "tort reform," in terms of their effects on claims frequency (box 1.1).

Not only is the number of claims no indication of success, but such reforms have often not had lasting effects, even on claims frequency. State courts have found some of the changes to be unconstitutional. Most of the changes may have appeared to be likely to reduce claims, payments per claim, and premiums at the time they were enacted but, as documented in chapter 4, for various reasons they did not have this effect.

Box 1.1
Court Statistics as an Indicator of Success of State Policy

"Citing data released from the state Supreme Court as "proof that our reforms are making a difference," Governor Edward G. Rendell proposed a series of immediate and long-term proposals to address Pennsylvania's medical malpractice situation. The proposals supplement those offered by the Governor in June 2003.

"Court statistics released last week showing a 30 percent decrease in the number of malpractice suits filed in 2004 are great news and a tribute to the reforms enacted by Governor Schweiker, the General Assembly and Supreme Court prior to my tenure as Governor," Governor Rendell said. "They confirm what I've said for more than a year—the reforms are good ones and will have an impact on the medical malpractice situation in Pennsylvania."

Pennsylvania has experienced much higher rates of claims, payouts, and premiums than other states, especially in Philadelphia and Pittsburgh (Bovbjerg and Bartow 2003).

Source: "Governor Rendell Announces Medical Malpractice Liability Proposals," *PAPowerPort* (March 2004). (http://www.state.pa.us/papower/cwp/view.asp?A=11&Q=436418 (accessed Dec. 30, 2004).

History Repeats Itself

During each crisis, as the medical malpractice issue gains steam, experts receive the same types of inquiries from the media. Questions include: Has this happened before? Why are malpractice premiums and losses skyrocketing? Where is the primary source of the problem—insurance markets, dispute resolution, medical errors, failure of government oversight, some other factor, or a combination of these factors? Which solutions have been tried and "work"? One's definition of "work" depends, of course, on one's perspective. Those who believe that premiums are too high define "work" as a reduction in insurers' losses and in premiums. For the victim of a medical injury, the concept of "work" is quite different.

There are also questions of fact relating to specific consequences of a medical malpractice crisis. For example, are physicians really relocating because of rising premiums? Is statistical evidence from past years still relevant? The growth of managed care and fixed physician fee schedules, which make it much more difficult for physicians to pass higher premiums forward to patients and health insurers in the form of higher fees, inform the responses to these questions. The responses from the early twenty-first century may differ considerably from those in the 1970s and 1980s.

Four Markets

Medical malpractice is a complex topic in large part because its effects are so far-reaching. It is not only about physicians and patients, not only about lawyers, not only about insurers, and not only about governments which are cajoled into responding in times of medical malpractice insurance crisis. It is really about them *all*—each with different objectives, constraints, and cultures. Outcomes are determined in four conceptually distinct markets—legal, medical malpractice insurance, medical care, and government activity (not stated in any particular order). The simultaneous operation of these four markets is largely what makes the issue of medical malpractice as complex as it is. Though each market is discrete in theory, in practice they interact. Most previous studies have focused on one aspect (or one market). In this book, we analyze them all.

The Legal Market

In the legal market, injury victims and physicians as defendants demand legal services, supplied by lawyers and the courts. In theory, lawyers are to be perfect agents for their clients. But in practice, this may not occur for financial and nonfinancial reasons. For instance, choice of compensation method—paying lawyers on a contingent fee or hourly basis—may make a difference in attorney willingness to represent a client or on lawyer effort on behalf of clients, as well as certain decisions, such as whether and on what terms the dispute is resolved.[9] In discussing lawyer compensation, a report from a state governor alleged lawyer fee-splitting, noting, "It is common practice for lawyers who do not handle medical malpractice cases to refer these cases to lawyers who do specialize in this area. For simply referring a case a lawyer will negotiate a fee agreement with the other lawyer, which range[s] from 25 to 50 percent of any fee for a settlement or judgment. The referring attorney is not obligated to perform any actual work on the case."[10] Courts have expressed concerns that juries' decisions are unduly swayed by the severity and circumstances of the plaintiff's injury, but this is disputed by other studies.[11] In spite of some limitations in the judicial process, the American jury gives ordinary citizens, in their roles as jurors, a part in the dispute resolution process.

While insurers who engage lawyers for the defense are obligated to act in the interest of the physicians they insure, they also have their own interests, such as seeking to minimize total expense per case, which do not take account of unquantifiable losses, such as the loss of a physician defendant's reputation. Market failures would occur if, for example, (1) claimants consistently file nonmeritorious claims and obtain settlements, (2) payments to claimants systematically exceed injury cost, or (3) courts often make legal errors in determining liability and damages.

The Medical Malpractice Insurance Market

Another market is for medical malpractice insurance.[12] Medical malpractice insurance is part of a larger market—the market for property-casualty insurance. This market is competitive but subject to a considerable amount of state regulation. In the medical malpractice insurance market, physicians and other health professionals are the consumers and medical malpractice insurers are the suppliers. Insurers decide which physicians to insure (whom to underwrite) and at what premium. Physicians have an underlying suspicion that they may not be well represented by commercial insurers. This is due, in part, to the fact that an individual physician, whose business is not insurance, may be no match for a large insurer whose business is insurance. For this reason, as well as the exit of many commercial insurers from the medical malpractice insurance line, physician-sponsored medical malpractice insurers were formed in many states in the mid-1970s. Many of these insurers survive today.

Embedded in the premium-setting decision is the issue of risk classification,[13] the process of placing insured individuals into separate groups for purposes of assigning a premium to each group. At first glance, this seems like a purely technical decision, of interest only to the experts. In general, there is an important trade-off between the goal of risk-sharing which insurance provides and maintaining an incentive for policyholders to exercise due care.

However, hospital liability insurance is another matter. Many hospitals self-insure for much of their coverage and buy excess insurance to cover catastrophic risk. Excess insurance is highly experienced-rated.

If a careless policyholder, or one who works in an area in which injuries are more likely to occur, pays the same premium as one who exercises due care or works in an area in which injuries are less likely to occur, there are two potentially adverse consequences. First, the incentive for physicians to exercise due care may be reduced. Second, the insured physician with a low claims risk subsidizes the physician with a high claims risk. Thus, risk classification has important practical implications, not only for the premiums that insured individuals pay, but also for any effects medical malpractice insurance may have on deterring injuries.

As already noted, there are no documented deterrent effects of medical malpractice. This may partly reflect the broad risk classes commonly employed in the medical malpractice insurance field. Experience rating is used far less in medical malpractice than in other lines of property-casualty insurance, such as automobile liability insurance.[14]

For example, drivers with prior accidents or traffic violations routinely pay higher premiums. The reason for the lack of experience rating in medical malpractice may be a common perception that outcomes of the claims are random, and hence physicians should not be made to pay higher premiums after payments are made on their behalf. Charging higher premiums for physicians who engage in risky practices, such as delivering babies, may cause physicians to stop such practices—an adverse reaction from a societal point of view.[15] Rather than charge higher premiums, insurers may refuse to underwrite high-risks, leaving high-risk physicians without coverage or having to purchase coverage from "surplus line carriers," insurers which specialize in hard-to-insure risks.[16]

Insurers also make decisions about which markets to enter, how aggressively to defend claims, and about the amounts of reserves to set aside for future losses incurred during a particular year in which they insure risks (policy year). Physicians decide how much coverage to purchase and from whom. Rising premiums and exits of insurers are the *immediate* causes of crisis, but these decisions plausibly reflect more complex underlying factors.

The Medical Care Market

The third market is for medical care. Here, consumers are patients, and physicians, hospitals, and others are suppliers. Higher premiums may lead to increased medical fees. In theory, medical malpractice would lead to provision of optimal levels of care,[17] but for various reasons, there may be under- or overdeterrence (the latter called "defensive medicine"). Underdeterrence may arise from the asymmetric relationship between patients and physicians. For example, patients may fail to request certain types of care because they do not have advance knowledge that such care would potentially benefit them. In principle, imposing liability on physicians is a method for preventing underdeterrence. However, overdeterrence could arise if the liability threat is excessive and/or imposed arbitrarily. As a result of overdeterrence, physicians may overprescribe diagnostic tests or therapeutic procedures, or avoid certain types of procedures or practice locations associated with higher probabilities of lawsuits.

Critics often use such presumed effects as a pretext for public intervention. However, it is difficult for physicians to argue for government assistance because higher medical malpractice premiums have depressed physicians' incomes. It is much more persuasive for physicians adversely affected by premium increases to argue that this will reduce provision of highly beneficial medical services, such as obstetrical and emergency room care. This is not to deny the validity of such arguments, only to admit to the possibility that such arguments may be self-serving.

The Market for Government Activity

Finally, there is the market for government activity. The law-as-market view asserts that legislation (and government activity more generally) is a good demanded and supplied much like other goods.[18] Legislative protection flows to groups obtaining the greatest value from public sector decisions, irrespective of their impact on social welfare. Citizens are on both sides of the market, benefiting and paying taxes. Those benefiting more from a type of decision form special interest groups to advocate for it (in this context, physician, lawyer, and insurer groups). The cost of the policy is much more widely shared, mainly by taxpayers who do not enjoy a direct benefit and who have an insufficient incentive to inform themselves about policies in advance and act in their self-interest.

Political officials maximize the aggregate political support they receive from all interest groups.[19] In the context of medical malpractice, these officials are associated with executive or administrative, legislative, and judicial branches of state government. They regulate the solvency, premiums, and marketing practices of insurers. Legislatures enact laws affecting claims resolution. They create special organizational forms (e.g., mutual insurers). In addition, in some states, the state is a medical malpractice insurer, providing no-fault coverage and public reinsurance. Operated on an actuarially sound basis, publicly supplied reinsurance has much to recommend it,[20] but even so, such programs have been subject to manipulation (see e.g., box 1.2). Empirical evidence on prior effects of government intervention is often cited in debates, albeit selectively.

What Is Known and Unknown About the Four Markets?

At one end of the continuum, there is the view that nothing is known about medical malpractice, so it is necessary to resort to anecdotes. At the other extreme is the view that everything is known, so public policy remedies are obvious. Neither of these views is accurate. From an optimistic or "cup half full" perspective, scholars have presented an enormous amount of information about medical malpractice and tort liability, and insurance more generally.

On the legal market, there are research findings, both theoretical and empirical, on why injury victims file claims.[21] There are studies about the universe of injuries relative to claims frequency,[22] determinants of award sizes,[23] and comparisons of injury cost with compensation.[24] In addition, scholars have researched the relative awards when claimants use a specialist lawyer versus when they do not,[25] the choice made by injury victims between tort and no-fault when they have a choice,[26] and the outcomes in medical no-fault versus tort and in other contexts (auto

Box 1.2
"Raiding" the Medical Malpractice Patient Compensation Fund

Physicians in Wisconsin feel that their low medical liability insurance rates are being jeopardized by the governor's plan to deal with the state budget deficit.

Wisconsin Gov. Jim Doyle has proposed taking $200 million from the state's Patient Compensation Fund to help offset a $454 million budget deficit. Physicians, hospitals and other health care professionals have paid into the fund annually for more than 25 years. The money is used to pay damages that exceed the coverage of medical liability insurance policies.

The governor says the fund has money to spare, but physicians and some lawmakers say it doesn't and that it would be irresponsible to use the money for other budget expenses.

"They are trying to plug a hole in one situation, but are creating a permanent problem in another area," said Mark L. Adams, general counsel for the Wisconsin Medical Society.

In addition to worrying that injured patients won't be fairly compensated, physicians and some lawmakers say that the fund, as part of extensive tort reform efforts in Wisconsin, has helped keep medical liability insurance rates low, even as they have soared in much of the rest of the country. Wisconsin is one of only six states that the AMA says is not showing signs of being in the midst of a medical liability crisis.

Source: Tanya Albert, AMEDNews.com. (Apr. 7, 2003). http:www .ama-assn.org/amednews/2003/04/07/prsd0407.htm (accessed Dec. 30, 2004).

no-fault).[27] Finally, scholars have studied the effects of contingent fees on legal outcomes, and on jury behavior in tort litigation in general.[28] Although much evidence suggests well-functioning legal markets, there is recent evidence, not specifically in regard to medical malpractice, that courts located in areas with high proportions of minorities and low-income households award higher amounts of compensation than in other areas.[29] Also, medical malpractice appears to pay higher compensation to injury victims than in other contexts (e.g., auto liability).[30]

In addition to research findings, there is much literature on markets for medical malpractice insurance and other relevant work on property-liability insurance. There is general literature on insurance cycles and their causes.[31] To preserve a deterrent incentive in the presence of complete insurance, experience rating is desirable.[32] Although experience rating is feasible in medical malpractice,[33] it is rare.[34] Even so, surplus line carriers insure some physicians not able to obtain coverage from standard insurers.[35] There is some empirical evidence on exit/entry, loss reserving, investment, premium-setting practices, and profitability of medical malpractice insurers,[36] and general findings on loss prevention practices.[37] Research exists on malpractice insurers' decisions to reinsure,[38] but we know relatively little about how reinsurer premium increases and stricter underwriting practices affect primary insurers. The literature misses some of the more recent developments.

Less is known about effects of medical malpractice on the market for medical care. Some important theoretical work on the effects of alternative liability regimes on physician decisions has been conducted.[39] We know that in the past, premium increases have been shifted forward to consumers in the form of higher fees,[40] but this may not be possible now, given the growth of fixed fee schedules (e.g., under Medicare Part B) and the growth of managed care.

The effect of the threat of tort liability on physician care levels has been studied.[41] Medical errors remain frequent, even with the threat of tort claims.[42] Also, one study[43] found that prior claims experience is unrelated to subsequent technical quality of care. Although often asserted, there is no conclusive evidence that physicians are leaving practice on account of high medical malpractice premiums or altering product mixes (e.g., dropping obstetrics). On the contrary, in one study based on data from the 1970s and 1980s,[44] physicians who had experienced high frequency of claims were less likely to change their practices (e.g., leave the state or retire). The potential deterrent benefit of liability may be greater under capitation than under fee-for-service,[45] but there is no empirical evidence on this.

Conceptual research in economics, political science, and law has described the government market in terms quite similar to any private market. In this context, with strong, well-organized stakeholders advocating for and against change, this analogy appears to be particularly apt. Empirically, we know a lot about effects of tort reform on medical malpractice premiums, claims frequency and severity, and total loss.[46] Much less is known about why states implement specific statutory changes in medical malpractice or property-casualty more generally.[47]

Crises in premiums and availability of insurance appear to be leading precipitators of change. There is no quantitative evidence on the effect of lobbies on legislative decisions affecting medical malpractice. Regulatory practices of state departments of insurance have been described.[48]

Government decisions ideally would be guided by both empirical evidence and well-articulated social objectives. Economic analysis of tort liability has been excellent in conceptually describing how alternative legal rules may produce socially optimal levels of care.[49] The level of care that is optimal from society's vantage point is one at which the marginal social benefit of care equals the marginal social cost of providing it. For example, if the total cost of conducting and interpreting a diagnostic test is $1,000 per test, society's welfare is maximized if tests are conducted only on persons for whom the benefit of the test is also at least $1,000. If the test is conducted on persons for whom the benefit is only $10, this is a waste of society's scarce resources.

Such benefits reflect both the effectiveness of care in producing better health outcomes and the society's willingness to pay for such better outcomes. Such cost reflects resource outlays for care borne by all payers as well as nonmonetary costs. For example, the price of a colonoscopy is not the only out-of-pocket cost for the procedure. There are also other costs, including transportation, the opportunity cost of the patient and a family member taking time from work or other pursuits, and the pain and suffering from preparing for the procedure and possible rare adverse outcomes from the procedure itself.

Discussing the socially optimum level of care conceptually is one thing. Determining what the marginal social benefit and marginal social cost curves look like in practice is quite another matter. A major reason that the calculation is so complicated is that benefits and costs differ substantially among individuals.[50] "Defensive medicine" presumably occurs to the extent that the legal system causes too much care to be provided— that is, care for which the marginal social cost exceeds the marginal social benefit. What this means, for example, is that if there is a one-in-a-hundred chance of a person having a disease and the loss incurred if the disease goes undetected is $100,000, then the test should be conducted if its cost is $1,000 or less. Otherwise, the test should not be conducted. Defensive medicine occurs in the latter case. Although defensive medicine is said to be a major driver of health care cost growth, there really is no evidence of how much it is.[51] And health care cost growth is the wrong metric in any case. The correct method applies the principle of cost versus benefit.

The effects of various statutory changes on the well-being of injury victims, individuals as patients, physician defendants, and attorneys ultimately always involve equity issues. These issues, although considered in the political process and by the popular media, have received little attention from scholars in any discipline, with a very few notable exceptions.[52] Statutory changes in tort liability inevitably involve trade-offs. For example, implementing limits on contingent fees has potential effects on the levels of care doctors provide to patients, since the threat of being sued may decline after the fee limits are imposed,[53] but also may raise barriers for injury victims in obtaining legal representation. Lawyers, for both the plaintiff and the defense, are made worse off, the latter because legal effort is roughly equivalent on both sides of the dispute.[54] A priori, the net effect of this statutory change on societal well-being is not clear, although the well-being of particular types of individuals is clearly affected, either positively or negatively.

There are trade-offs among categories of injured persons. For example, is a person who is the victim of medical negligence more worthy of compensation than a person injured in a natural disaster, such as a hurricane or an earthquake? Currently, in a comparison of victims of medical malpractice and hurricanes, the former would generally receive higher compensation than the latter would. In the end, when there are two groups that stand to gain or lose from a public policy decision, political officials must make the trade-off decision in the well-being between the two groups. The best an analyst can do is identify the nature of the trade-off.

Five Myths of Medical Malpractice

Any discussion of malpractice would be incomplete without acknowledging the myths associated with medical malpractice. In some lectures and in the first author's undergraduate class on health economics, the first author states and discusses five myths of medical malpractice. The purpose of the discussion of the myths is not only to present empirical evidence demonstrating that the statements are myths, but also to be provocative and elicit interest in the topic (though hopefully not too provocative). The five myths are the following:

Myth 1. There are too many medical malpractice claims.

Myth 2. Only "good" doctors are sued.

Myth 3. Dispute resolution in medical malpractice is a lottery.

Myth 4. Medical malpractice claimants are overcompensated for their losses.

Myth 5. Medical care is costly because of medical malpractice.

Myths 2–5 will be discussed at greater length in subsequent chapters. Thus, only a very brief preview is provided here.

Doctors who are sued for medical malpractice are neither of higher nor of lower quality, on average, than those who are not sued (myth 2). Some critics of medical malpractice contend that being at the cutting edge technologically makes a physician more vulnerable to being sued. There is no empirical evidence that being sued is an indicator of superior performance, as is sometimes alleged. There is some empirical evidence about differences in physician–patient relationships between those physicians with adverse medical malpractice claims histories and physicians with no claims, the latter rated by their patients as being, or at least appearing to be, more understanding, more caring, more available, and a good communicator. A more patient-oriented practice style is good defensive medicine, a point rarely mentioned in public discourse on medical malpractice.

There is a definite relationship, albeit an imperfect one, between independent assessments of liability and of injury cost and outcomes of legal disputes alleging medical malpractice (myth 3). Assertions that medical malpractice outcomes as a general matter are random or a lottery are not supported by the empirical evidence. Based on available evidence comparing the costs of injuries of medical malpractice claimants and compensation actually received, such claimants are, on average, undercompensated, not overcompensated (myth 4). In the one study that has compared injury cost versus compensation, compensation exceeded cost by 22 percent for claimants who received compensation at verdict. The 22 percent included payment for pain and suffering.

Practice decisions attributable to the threat of a medical malpractice suit may have raised spending on personal health services above what it would have been absent the threat, but threats of a medical malpractice suit are not a major cause of rising expenditures on personal health services (myth 5). In addition, any reduction in spending that would occur if the threat were eliminated or appreciably reduced would inevitably lead to a decline in physician and hospital revenue. For example, if 15–20 percent of personal health expenditures were eliminated due to "effective" tort reform, the health care sector would fall into a deep recession or even a depression, and depending on how funds released from the health care sector were reallocated, Gross Domestic Product for the economy as a whole might suffer more than a blip as well. Physicians would leave practice in large numbers, and many hospitals would close. Although expenditures on personal health services would probably fall, patient access to physicians and hospitals would be much worse than it is now.

Myth 1 deals with the excess number of medical malpractice claims. As background for discussing this myth, two pathbreaking studies are especially pertinent. The first was conducted in California in 1974.[55] The second was conducted in New York in 1984.[56] In both studies, surveys of medical records of hospitalized patients were conducted to ascertain (1) rates of injury ("adverse events") attributable to provision of medical care to these patients and (2) rates of adverse events due to provider negligence, termed "negligent adverse events." Follow-up studies to the New York study were conducted in Colorado and Utah.

In the California study, records of 20,864 randomly selected patients at twenty-three hospitals were reviewed. Records were abstracted according to a protocol and then analyzed by medical and legal experts to determine whether the injury occurred while the patient was receiving medical care and whether or not the injury could be attributed to provider negligence.

In the New York study, 31,429 records of patients were reviewed. The data collection, abstraction process, and medical and legal expert review were patterned after the process used in California a decade earlier. The

California study revealed that 5 percent of patients experienced an adverse health event while in the hospital, and 17 percent of *these patients* suffered a negligent adverse event. In New York, the corresponding rate was 4 percent for adverse events, and of those, 28 percent were classified as due to negligence.

The authors of the New York study and the Institute of Medicine of the U.S. National Academy of Sciences used estimates from the New York study to compute the annual number of deaths due to iatrogenic injuries in the United States and the number of such injuries for which providers were at fault. These estimates have been criticized on grounds that the implied number of deaths due to iatrogenic injuries is too high.[57] Like any research, these studies have strengths and weaknesses; they will be discussed in detail in a later chapter. But the exact number of deaths is really unimportant. The number is large, and this should suffice for private and public decision-making. It is a bit like the critiques of the estimates that six million Jews died in the Holocaust—not that we wish to compare those who deny that there are numerous medical errors with those who deny that the Holocaust occurred, but our example does make an important point. Suppose the true number of Holocaust deaths were four million. Would this change the analysis in any important way?

The New York researchers obtained data on medical malpractice claims filed on behalf of the injury victims identified in their study. The authors found "invalid" claims—those not matching the study's determination of liability from raters' evaluations of the medical records—outnumbered valid claims by a ratio of three to one—providing empirical support to myth 1.[58] However, it is not appropriate to stop here. They also found that only 2 percent of negligent adverse events resulted in medical malpractice claims. There were 7.6 times as many negligent injuries as there were claims. Thus, there were errors in both directions: individuals filed too many invalid claims and not enough valid claims.

Do these results serve to strike down myth 1? In two important senses, the answer is no. First, many valid claims are not filed. What is filed is the tip of the iceberg of potentially valid claims. Second, the raters viewed only medical records for the patients when they were hospitalized.[59] In addition, the litigation process involves accumulating much more information than is contained in a single medical record. It is quite possible that with the additional information, the expert findings could have been reversed. Of course, the reversal could be in both directions. Yet it seems highly likely that the true percentage of negligent adverse events resulting in claims is somewhere between 0 and 4 percent. The percentage of negligent adverse events resulting in claims is very, very unlikely to be in, say, the 50 to 80 percent range of negligent adverse events.

Then how does the large number of invalid claims affect the validity of myth 1? At least at first glance, there appears to be support for the allegation that there are too many lawsuits. The measurement error in estimating the number of negligent adverse events that result in claims is plausibly relevant here as well. Applying the same logic, the true ratio of invalid claims to valid claims could be much higher than three to one. Further, medical malpractice plaintiffs lose the overwhelming majority of suits for which a verdict is reached.[60] Thus, the system does weed out many invalid claims.

From another perspective, litigation can be viewed as an information-gathering process; many claims that are filed are dropped by claimants after initial investigation reveals that the claim has little or no legal merit.[61] Would we want to say that the large number of negative test results provides conclusive evidence of overtesting, even when the tests are justifiable ex ante on a clinical basis? The fact that the person in the above example had a negative test result even though the ex ante chance of having the disease was one in one hundred does not imply that the test was unnecessary. This is not to assert that there are no frivolous claims, but rather that not every claim that turns out to have been "invalid" is frivolous. The term "frivolous lawsuits" has been used much too loosely in public discourse about medical malpractice.

At a superficial level, the New York study offers "good news" for advocates on both sides of the medical malpractice debate. In the end, myth 1 is partially valid; there are both too many invalid claims and too few valid claims. The system, in sum, is imperfect.

Chapter Roadmap

The intended audience for this book is nonspecialists. With this in mind, the text unites several areas of academic research in medical malpractice.

It is difficult to be well versed in all of the topics presented, and for that reason we aim to provide a text useful for anyone interested in medical malpractice. A reader who is familiar with the legal issues will be made aware of the political issues. In the same way, a reader who is familiar with the political issues may not have previously understood how insurance works.

This chapter and the next three chapters describe what is known about the functioning of medical malpractice insurance, defensive medicine, and the effects of tort reforms implemented to date. Chapter 2 describes why insurance cycles arise. "Hard markets" characterized by sharply rising medical malpractice premiums and withdrawal of insurers from the market have led to much political pressure for policy changes. Further, advocates for particular statutory changes base their arguments for change on their theories of the origins of cycles.

Chapter 3 analyzes *effects* of rising medical malpractice premiums and the threat of lawsuits. Arguments for change are often linked to the concepts of positive and negative defensive medicine. Positive defensive medicine involves the use of diagnostic and therapeutic procedures in excess of levels that physicians would recommend solely on the basis of their professional clinical judgments. Negative defensive medicine involves withdrawal of care because of high premiums and/or the threat of lawsuits.

Chapter 4 describes tort reforms and their effects. Reflecting the goals of the stakeholders who promote tort reforms and reflected in the term "tort reform," success has been gauged in terms of whether or not, and the extent to which, specific tort reforms reduce medical malpractice claims frequency, insurance payments, and premiums. The "prizewinners" to date are caps on nonmonetary loss and on total loss. A large body of evidence is generally consistent with the view that caps reduce payments of insurers, and also decrease the variance in anticipated loss, and lead to lower medical malpractice premiums.

Some tort reforms in effect transfer money from injury victims and their attorneys to health care providers. Flat caps on damages, the overwhelming favorite of the lobbies for provider organizations, particularly since 2000, fall in this category. Placing a cap on damages has no potential for improving patient safety. In addition, this policy disproportionately makes plaintiffs with severe injuries worse off. A stronger argument for limits on awards is that there is considerable variation in awards, limiting, among other things, the injury deterrent signal. As an alternative to flat caps, chapter 5 examines proposals to fully schedule damages for nonmonetary loss rather than just place limits on the high payments. Another alternative to fixed lump-sum payments, periodic payments, or even a complement to scheduled damages, is service benefit insurance contracts to cover medical, custodial, educational, and rehabilitative services. Chapter 5 also describes a proposal for service benefit contracts.

Damage caps do reduce medical malpractice premiums and are favored for this reason, but again, they disproportionately disadvantage claimants with severe injuries. We propose more equitable methods for limiting damages and providing more consistent compensation, both horizontally (for plaintiffs with similar injuries) and vertically (for plaintiffs with more severe or less severe injuries and loss).

Much of this book is about avoiding misguided reforms. Limitations on lawyers' contingent fees are a case in point, for reasons described in chapter 6. Such limitations represent a partial incomes policy, one which redistributes income from plaintiffs' lawyers to physicians and perhaps to others as well. The data that have been presented to show that plaintiffs' attorneys have excessive earnings are seriously flawed. Moreover, if there is concern about earnings inequality, this should be addressed by a broad policy change, not by concentrating on a single occupation, such as plaintiffs' lawyers. Even if the data on plaintiff lawyers' earnings were accurate, such lawyers are not the only persons to enjoy high earnings. Defendants' lawyers are likely to have similar earnings, on average. Moreover, some insurance executives are very well compensated, as are physicians in some specialties. As much as fee limits bar access to legal representation, they do this indiscriminately, affecting access to legal representation of potential claimants with and without meritorious claims.

Chapter 6, which describes empirical evidence on this issue, as well as some prominent policy proposals, concludes that no change is warranted in this area. Aside from the lack of empirical support for arguments supporting change, in terms of horizontal equity (equal treatment of equals) it seems imprudent to impose constraints on fees of attorneys who represent claimants without likewise imposing constraints on individuals in other highly compensated professions.

Chapter 7 examines empirical evidence on jury behavior, finding that "runaway juries" perhaps appear in a few highly publicized cases and more generally make good fiction, but do not apply to the typical jury. One solution to a "runaway jury" problem, thought in part to stem from jurors' inability to process relevant scientific information and in part due to jurors' alleged sympathy with injury victims, is to shift medical malpractice cases to specialized health courts. Regulatory agencies and even judges may not be equally sensitive to consumer interests, although, after considerable discussion in this book, we leave as an open question whether or not health courts should be implemented. The pros and cons of this policy option are evaluated in chapter 7.

Existing tort reforms do not make care safer. There has been much discussion of patient safety, especially since around 2000, including the high rates of medical errors that occur. As chapter 8 indicates, in spite of all the national attention the issue of medical errors has received, surprisingly little progress has been made in implementing error reduction systems. This is partly because meaningful financial incentives for health care providers to adopt patient safety measures have been lacking.

In principle, tort liability could provide such incentives, but not as it is currently structured in the medical field. And under the best of circumstances, tort liability is only one of several policy instruments that can be applied to make medical care safer than it is now. The threat of a lawsuit would presumably deter such errors, but (1) there is empirical evidence that such errors are widespread (although there is some disagreement about how widespread they are), and (2) some experts even argue that medical malpractice has been counterproductive in achieving the objective of reducing medical error rates.

One impediment appears to be the lack of a financial incentive to implement such systems. Not only is there a general lack of a market incentive, but medical liability is not playing a positive role. Physicians practicing alone or in small groups may not be well positioned to make major investments in error reduction approaches. This suggests that hospitals may be in a relatively good position to do this; there is a good case for enterprise liability at the hospital level. Physicians would be included for the care they provide within the walls of the hospital, in both inpatient and outpatient settings.

Following chapter 2's discussion of insurance cycles, chapters 9 through 11 discuss medical malpractice insurance. Chapter 9 focuses on the lack of experience rating of medical malpractice, insurance regulation, the various alternative ownership forms that insurance companies can and do take, and government interventions to assure health care providers access to medical malpractice insurance coverage and to cover losses in the event of insurer bankruptcy.

Chapter 10 discusses private markets for reinsurance and the rationale for and experience with government provision of such insurance. Volatility in reinsurance markets is one cause of cycles in markets for primary medical malpractice insurance. One approach for reducing the amplitudes of cycles, which can be quite disruptive, especially in some geographic locations and physician specialties, is to substitute publicly provided for privately provided reinsurance, an option considered in chapters 10 and 12.

Chapter 11 focuses on provision of medical no-fault insurance as a substitute for standard third-party medical malpractice (or professional liability) insurance. A voluntary no-fault plan in which hospitals and patients can elect no-fault has attractive features. However, no-fault insurance for iatrogenic injuries, such as exists in Sweden and New Zealand, is not an achievable alternative in the United States. The experiences with medical no-fault in Florida and Virginia, and of the federal Vaccine Injury Compensation Program, demonstrate limitations of medical no-fault, U.S.-style. While there are some advocates of substantial expansions in no-fault coverage among academic experts, the proof of the pudding is in actual implementation. The successes of no-fault in some other countries have been impossible to replicate in the United States. Therefore, the recommendation in chapter 11 is to expand voluntary, hospital-based, no-fault insurance as a substitute for tort liability/insurance and to do this by contract.

In the concluding chapter, chapter 12, the focus is on public policy reforms that have promise in terms of improving quality of care and determining injuries in health care settings. The chapter recommends locating insurance coverage with the hospital as the insuring unit for all care delivered within its walls. Much of the loss is incurred in hospital settings. Certainly the high premiums in such specialties as obstetrics/ gynecology and neurosurgery reflect the medical malpractice risk from care delivered at hospitals. Nevertheless, even though physicians would be covered for care they deliver in hospital inpatient and outpatient facilities, they would still purchase medical malpractice coverage for services delivered in their own practices. Enterprise liability with the hospital as the enterprise is also an attractive option, but it is a somewhat more radical change that may face greater resistance. Under enterprise liability, only the enterprise (the hospital) would be sued.

In sum, in terms of the four markets, chapters 6 and 7 are most directly about the legal market; chapters 2 and 9–11, about the medical malpractice insurance market; chapters 3 and 8, mostly about the medical care market; and chapters 4, 5, and 12 mostly about the government market and public policy.

2
Why the Crises in Medical Malpractice?

Most industries experience business cycles, yet it is not clear why the property-casualty insurance industry, of which medical malpractice insurance is part, has such prominent cycles. The property-casualty industry's cycle, termed more generally "insurance cycle" or "underwriting cycle," is characterized by periods of "soft" and "hard" market conditions. Cycles in medical malpractice insurance are important because they can be at least temporarily disruptive to health care delivery (at a minimum, this is a widespread perception), and they elicit strong demands for change in the political arena.

This chapter has three purposes: (1) to examine how deeply entangled medical malpractice is with the insurance cycle; (2) to provide insight into the functioning of the medical malpractice insurance business; (3) to explore the dynamics of the cycle by looking at both internal and exogenous causes. The description of the insurance industry requires a look into the frequency and severity of claims; reserves and premium-setting; the insurer's income statement and balance sheet; and their relationship with each other. Discussion of internal and external, largely exogenous causes reflects the true complexity of the insurance industry and requires attention to several factors: inflation shocks; capacity constraints; the oligopolistic (few firms in a market with each firm taking into account the actions of its competitors—in pricing, for example) structure of the property-casualty insurance industry; and price and availability of reinsurance. This chapter provides context essential for understanding the nature of the crisis.

The Nature of Insurance Cycles

Before beginning a scrutiny of the insurance cycle, some background is necessary. To start with, a major feature of insurance cycles is the intensity of competition among insurers during one phase and the seeming lack of sellers during another. After the hard market subsides, premiums decline as insurers compete to increase their individual market shares. As the soft phase of the market matures, and losses on previously sold, underpriced insurance policies mount, profits decline, often to the point of insurers experiencing losses. Competition among insurers becomes far less intense, and underwriting standards[1] become more stringent. The supply of insurance decreases because of a decrease in capital available to underwrite insurance, and premiums rise. Then, improved profitability attracts more capital to the industry from external sources, and a new soft phase with increased competition begins, eventually leading to another hard market. Interestingly, the periods during which the property-casualty insurance industry has experienced hard markets since 1970—1975–1978, 1984–1987, and 2001–2004—coincide with the periods of crisis in medical malpractice insurance.[2]

Widespread media and public policy interest mainly exists only in times of crisis.[3] Insurance cycles are not an important issue on many politicians' agenda, absent pressure from stakeholders. However, political pressures for legislative change rise markedly during hard markets. Sharply rising premiums and nonavailability of insurance coverage provide the immediate impetus.

Even the frequency of published research papers on medical malpractice per year varies with the cycle, more articles appearing after the onset of hard markets. During periods of soft markets (e.g., 1988–2000), analogies to Rip van Winkle and the title (but not the plot) of the 1946 Humphrey Bogart movie *The Big Sleep* are apt. This is not to say that individuals are unconcerned about medical malpractice issues during the quiescent periods. Rather, political activity is much lower, because either the stakeholders' organizations are focused on other issues, or individuals are not sufficiently riled up about medical malpractice to compel their leaderships to act. During a quiescent period for medical malpractice insurance during the 1990s, for example, organized medicine was preoccupied with mounting a campaign for patient protection laws to combat managed care's alleged excesses.

The dynamics of the insurance cycle are not fully understood. Two features of cycles are prominent. Premium increases are in excess of increases in costs incurred by insurers, and there is a lack of supply of insurance at the beginning of hard markets.

Absent some external interference, such as government controls over prices, lack of supply is an anomaly in markets. Even though Picasso paintings are no longer produced, there is no shortage of such paintings. Rather, if there is increased demand, the price of such artwork rises. At higher prices, some potential purchasers of Picasso paintings drop out of the market. Nonavailability of such paintings is at most a very short-term phenomenon. In the longer run, the paintings are available but at higher prices than before.

In the context of medical malpractice insurance—in sharp contrast to the market for Picasso artwork, not being able to obtain insurance at any price, even for weeks or months, can be highly disruptive for physicians. In addition, the premium increases lead to a great deal of complaining in public forums, especially when the victims are as politically influential as physicians.

Medical Malpractice Insurance and the Cycle

The cycle is inextricably linked to medical malpractice insurance for several reasons. First, "crisis" is a by-product of cycles, not of secular trends. The trend in losses from medical malpractice claims does not exceed the trend in the medical Consumer Price Index (CPI), at least when viewed over several decades. Certainly the trend in the medical CPI has not produced a "crisis." In other contexts, price spurts are seen as predictors of adverse future trends, as was the case with the increase in oil prices following the oil embargo of the 1970s and the "stagflation" that ensued. A similar example is the concerns about $100 or even $300 per barrel oil prices that followed the substantial increase in oil prices in 2005–2006. Clearly, medical malpractice is not the only subject area in which cycles and trends are confused.

Second, advocates on both sides of the medical malpractice issue make their cases for change or preserving the status quo based on whom they identify as the "culprits"—those who are allegedly responsible for the crisis. On the one side there are those who link the crisis to "runaway juries"[4] and "greedy lawyers."[5] On the other side are those who blame interest rates, and possibly insurer pricing practices, for the crisis. If one attributes the crisis to falling interest rates and bad investments in the stock market, the policy implications are markedly different than if softhearted and cognitively limited juries and ambulance-chasing lawyers are to blame.

Third, cycles are here to stay. In the mid-1960s, some advocates of Keynesian macroeconomic policies[6] thought that business cycles had been eliminated because governments knew precisely when and how to apply fiscal policies. History proved them wrong. The same goes for insurance cycles.

Inept juries and greedy lawyers cannot explain cycles, unless one argues that there are cycles in softheartedness, ineptness, and ambulance chasing. Poor investments in the stock market are not a plausible reason. Property-casualty insurers have the bulk of their investments in interest-bearing securities, not in equity. Furthermore, insurers could not recoup losses from bad investments by charging more to current customers. Another insurer, which had been a prudent investor, could sell insurance at a lower price, and the insurer with imprudent past investments would lose market share. Or an insurer with neither a good nor a bad investment history could enter the market and attract business from the imprudent insurer. There are cycles in interest rates, but only *anticipated*, not prior interest rates, are relevant for insurers' premium-setting decisions.

Another argument is that increased premiums are due to insurers' exploiting their market power in setting premiums. This argument can be rejected for three reasons. First, one would have to argue that there are cycles in insurers' pursuit of their profit-maximizing objectives, which seems implausible. Second, many of the medical malpractice insurers are sponsored by medical societies. It is doubtful that such organizations would exploit their own sponsors. Third, there is empirical evidence for the period including the first two crises that, at least in the long run, medical malpractice premiums are actuarially fair.[7] Thus, the above arguments can be rejected as causes of insurance cycles; to find likely causes, it is necessary to look elsewhere.

Background Pertinent to Analysis of Cycles

Frequency and Severity

Unlike most insurance, medical malpractice is a low claims frequency and high severity line of insurance. Health and automobile liability claims are much more frequent than medical malpractice insurance claims; and earthquake and life insurance claims are much less frequent. Severity refers to the size of paid claims. Malpractice claims are relatively high in mean payment, and the distribution of such payments is highly skewed, with a few very large payments, reflecting a few very severe injuries, at the high end of the frequency distribution. Low claims frequency makes actuarial predictions more difficult; high-dollar severity, especially when coupled with a few very large paid claims, increases the importance of reinsurance.[8]

Tail of an Insurance Policy

Premiums for all types of insurance are received *before* claims are paid. The mean lag between the date of the occurrence of an insurable event, the date the claim is filed, and the date the claim is paid differs appreciably among lines of insurance. This lag is called the "tail" of an insurance policy. Thus, the "claims tail" is the length of time from filing to resolution of a claim.

Claims on health insurance are paid relatively quickly.[9] The fact that a covered expense occurred is easily documented, and improvements in electronic transmission have reduced the delay even further.[10] Since the insurance is taken out on oneself, there is no opposing party to dispute the validity of the claim, which applies to all first-party insurance in general.

Demonstrating negligence in a line of third-party insurance, such as medical malpractice insurance, can be a lengthy process. For some injuries, such as from automobile accidents, the injury is documented at the site of the accident and rapidly confirmed—say, when the injured person is transported to a hospital emergency room. In contrast, some medical malpractice injuries take years to be identified (e.g., delayed development in a child attributed to an injury the child suffered at birth), leading to a long delay between the injury date and the date the claim is eventually resolved. To shorten this time period, many medical malpractice insurers switched from occurrence to claims-made insurance during the 1970s, but some occurrence policies continue to be written three decades later.

Occurrence policies cover liability from the date of occurrence. Claims-made policies cover liability from the date the claim is filed.[11] Nevertheless, in spite of this change in much of insurance practice, the claims tail remains unusually long for medical malpractice insurance.

Based on a conversation its personnel had with a national association of insurers, the U.S. General Accounting Office (June 2003, p. 8) reports that many medical malpractice claims take five years to resolve, including discovering the malpractice, filing a claim, determining payment responsibilities, and paying the claim. Some claims can take as long as eight to ten years to resolve.[12]

Insurer's Income Statement

A company's income statement records its revenue, expenses, and profits (losses) for a particular period, its fiscal year. In the context of insurance, there are essentially two revenue streams—revenue from the sale of insurance and revenue from investments. Expenses consist of payments to policyholders, other expenses attributable to individual claims, "adjusted loss expense" (ALE, which includes payments for defending cases, such as attorneys' fees), and expenses for marketing, managing investments, and general overhead. The difference between total revenue and total expenses is total profit. The core of the insurance business is assuming (or underwriting) the risk of uncertain future events in exchange for a premium. Underwriting profits are the difference between premiums and *paid losses* and ALE in a fiscal year. Premium income is invested from the time it is received to the time that payments for loss and ALE are made.

Insurer's Balance Sheet

A firm's balance sheet lists assets, liabilities, and equity, the latter being the difference between assets and liabilities. Because of government regulation of insurer solvency and their own decisions to avoid bankruptcy, insurers are generally very conservative investors. With some exceptions,[13] the major part of their portfolios is invested in interest-bearing securities.[14] These investments were estimated by the U.S. General Accounting Office (June 2003) to account for 79 percent of medical malpractice insurers' portfolios of the fifteen largest medical malpractice insurers nationally, which consisted of both commercial stock and medical society-sponsored mutuals and reciprocals. In other words, insurance companies have relatively little common stock in their portfolios, and thus are not greatly affected by the performance of stock markets—to a far lesser extent than for most personal investors.

More important to an insurer's bottom line is its liabilities, which consist of its reserves on the insurance policies it issues. When an insurer issues an insurance policy, it incurs a dollar obligation that must be backed by assets of corresponding size. Losses are incurred throughout the policy year, not on the date the premium is received (or day 1 of the policy year). With some exceptions, insurers do not immediately know that a potential loss has been incurred. Further, there is a distinction between unearned and earned premiums. Premiums switch from unearned to earned as the policy year evolves. For earned premiums, there are two types of loss, reserves—incurred but not reported (IBNR)—and case reserves.

As the name suggests, IBNR reserves are set to cover losses that have occurred but have not yet been reported to the insurer. Once the report is made and the insurer has determined the most likely loss from the specific claim, some part of IBNR reserves converts to a case reserve on that claim. The case reserve reflects the insurer's best estimate of the loss that will ultimately result from that claim. The case reserve or, equivalently, the anticipated loss on the claim, is not set in stone; rather, it is adjusted periodically as new information pertinent to the claim is revealed to the insurer. New information could include a previously unseen transcript of a deposition, a communication by an attorney of the opposing party, or a jury verdict in a similar case.

When an insurer sells a policy before the policy year begins, the entire reserve is unearned. The anticipated loss, especially in a long-tail line, such as medical malpractice insurance, is best seen as an educated guess. It reflects the insurer's view of trends in claims frequency and severity, which in turn reflects anticipated inflation, trends in legal decisions, and so on. Some premiums may be ceded to a reinsurer.[15] In this transaction, a primary insurer exchanges money (pays a premium) for a promise by the reinsurer to cover a specific expense, should the criteria for payment warrant this. Reinsurance is insurance for the primary insurer. By reinsuring, the primary insurer reduces its liabilities and its risk of insolvency, but it sacrifices some revenue in return.

The term used in the insurance industry for the difference between total assets and total liabilities is the surplus. The surplus for some single-line medical malpractice insurers is often quite small relative to the potential loss on a handful of claims, exposing these insurers to substantial bankruptcy risk, absent some action, such as reinsuring to reduce such risk.

Setting Premiums
Premiums are set on the basis of forecasts of future losses from insurance written in a particular policy year, an adjustment for risk, the tail, and the anticipated returns to be earned on investments from the premium funds collected for the policy year, as well as market factors. Because it can earn investment return on premiums, the insurer can charge a premium that is below the anticipated loss on the insurance policy. Higher risk tends to result in higher premiums. A longer tail and higher *anticipated* returns tend to result in lower premiums. When an insurer computes a premium for a future period, it takes account of expected returns from investing money it collects as premiums that it will retain until payments on losses are made. The potential return is positively related to the length of the time period that elapses from the date the claim is filed until payment is actually made.

When considering returns on investments, insurance companies look forward, not backward. As explained earlier, in a competitive insurance market, no one should be willing to pay a higher premium to a company just to allow the company to recover losses from errors in its past investments. Forecasting future returns is fraught with uncertainty. Interest rates reflect many factors, including inflationary expectations and monetary policies of central banks. If insurers forecast higher real returns on investments, premiums can be lowered, and conversely.

Adjusting for risk is both a complex and a not fully resolved issue (at least to scholars). At the most basic level, insurers diversify the risk of loss by pooling uncorrelated risks of individual insureds. By pooling, what is a risk of loss to an individual is a much smaller risk to the members of the pool. In any period, most insureds are fortunate not to incur losses. Others are not so fortunate, and incur losses. But as long as losses are uncorrelated, risk pooling works.

However, losses may be correlated. Outcomes at verdict/appeal may be correlated. A particular judicial decision, for example, may be precedent-setting. Juries and others may hear about a large award, and a string of experts may be unduly influenced by a scientific theory that carries over to a number of legal disputes. Or a state supreme court may find a particular statute to be unconstitutional, and its decision in turn may affect a number of pending cases. For any of these reasons for correlated loss on the underwriting side of the insurer's business, risk may not be diversified away by insuring additional individuals or organizations.

In principle, diversification of assets on the investment side of the insurer's business should eliminate much market risk, and holding a large number of assets should reduce credit risk.[16] Insurers can hold shorter-term securities and engage in various types of hedging activities to reduce some risk. However, for various reasons, diversification will not eliminate all such risk, and higher "nondiversifiable" risk is expected to be reflected in higher premiums as well.

Another nondiversifiable risk relates to the relationship between the variability of underwriting results and the variability of returns on a well-diversified portfolio of securities. If returns on the sale of insurance and on investments are negatively correlated (as in personal portfolios, bonds tend to increase in price during recessions as interest rates fall while stock prices tend to decrease), then selling insurance reduces the overall nondiversifiable risk, and conversely if there is a positive relationship. If losses fall when the economy is depressed, insurers' underwriting losses and performance of the general economy are negatively correlated.

This implies that adding policyholders with uncorrelated risks reduces overall nondiversifiable risk. Adding uncorrelated risks would in turn increase the insurance firm's share value and decrease the cost of raising equity capital from external sources.

On the other hand, if underwriting losses rise when the general economy is depressed, losses on the underwriting and investment sides of the business are positively correlated. Then, following the same reasoning, adding policyholders increases the insurer's cost of external equity capital (the return investors demand for investing in the company).

Some types of insurance are likely to be correlated with the business cycle—for example, disability claims rise with the unemployment rate. Medical malpractice payments do not seem to vary *systematically* with or counter to the business cycle.[17] Thus, although underwriting risks may be correlated, overall underwriting losses and investment losses appear to be uncorrelated. This suggests why a prudent insurer would be cautious of putting all of its eggs in the medical malpractice insurance underwriting basket, although many insurers, by specializing in a single line—medical malpractice insurance—largely do this.

Dynamics of the Cycle

Before delving into explanations of cycles, it is important to have a picture of changes in losses from underwriting, as well as in profits, as the cycle progresses. This discussion and the accompanying figure (figure 2.1) are adapted from T. Baker (2005a), who presents a very clear account of the dynamics of the cycle.

There are three lines in figure 2.1: operating profit, which is akin to underwriting profit; initial incurred losses; and developed losses for medical malpractice insurers (1980–2003). The period covered by figure 2.1 (1) follows the hard market that ended in 1978, (2) includes the entire hard market of 1984–1987, and (3) includes part of the hard market of 2001–2005.

Operating profit (from the income statement), reflecting underwriting losses, becomes negative before the onset of the hard market, but reaches its low around the beginning of the hard market, reflecting outlays on

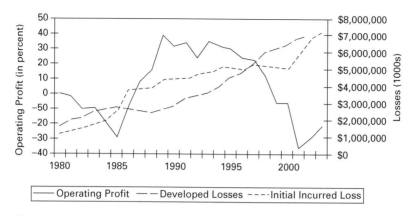

Figure 2.1
U.S. Medical Malpractive Insurers' Operating Profit and Loss Experience, 1980–2003. Source: Baker (2005a).

previously underpriced insurance policies. Poor profit performance is expected to be reflected in declines in the insurance companies' share prices.

Initial incurred losses are losses projected at the time the insurance policy is sold. As figure 2.1 shows, initial losses (in nominal terms) increase throughout the period, except briefly during the late 1990s, when there is a decrease. There are substantial increases in such losses during hard markets. What this means is that insurers substantially increased their initial loss projections at these times. These are *antici-pated*—not actual or realized losses—losses reported at the end of the year during which the policies for the policy year were sold.[18]

The third line is for developed losses. These are calculated at ten years after the policies were sold or as of the end of 2003, whichever is earlier, and are assigned to the year in which the policies were sold. Developed losses represent revisions based on "development" of losses for the policy year, as well as other information revealed after the policy year, such as changes in inflation rates and judicial decisions most relevant to the insurance sold during a policy year. The beginning and the end points of the two loss series are nearly identical. Prior to the hard market of the 1980s, developed losses exceeded initial incurred losses, implying that insurers were increasing their estimates of loss on policies they had previously sold. From 1986 to 1998, initial incurred losses exceeded developed losses. Insurers then believed that they had been too pessimistic about losses on these policies when the policies were sold, and they subsequently revised their projections downward. In 1998, developed losses again exceeded initial incurred losses, implying that insurers increased anticipated losses after the policies were sold. This is not surprising in view of the increase in the real value of paid claims that were occurring then.[19] The pattern from the 1980s shown in figure 2.1 is not exactly repeated during the 2001–2004 hard market, but this could reflect the lack of a ten-year follow-up for computing developed losses for this period.

When insurers are revising their loss projections upward, the funds to cover their additional losses have to come from somewhere. More specifically, the funds have to come from revenue from other lines of insurance sold by the company for which the initial incurred loss proved to be too pessimistic—from surplus and/or from additional cash flows obtained from higher insurance premiums on policies from subsequent policy years. The data in figure 2.1 are for the medical malpractice insurance industry. All, or virtually all, firms were being similarly affected. Deteriorating financial performance is not an isolated case of mismanagement by a single insurer, but rather of simultaneous, similar decisions by many insurers.

Explanations of Insurance Cycles: Factors Internal to the Companies and the Industry versus Factors External or Exogenous to the Companies and the Industry

Overview

The above description of changes in losses in the balance sheet and in profit as reflected in the companies' income statements reveals nothing about the *causes* of these changes. The trends in losses say nothing about why sharp increases in premiums occurred, although higher premiums are reflected in higher operating profits. For purposes of this discussion, it is useful to distinguish internal factors from external factors accounting for insurance cycles, the latter including changes in interest rates, changes in the relationship between investment returns and underwriting returns, depletion of capacity to write insurance, and changes in the relationship between return.[20] The external factors are typically exogenous (not influenced by) to the insurance industry. These exogenous factors reflect developments in the national or global economy as a whole, weather, war, and so on.

Competition Among Oligopolists: An Internal Factor

The recurrent crises in medical malpractice insurance have been attributed to an oligopolistic structure of the medical malpractice insurance market.[21] In oligopoly[22] there is a very small number of firms competing in the same product market, with each firm taking into account the actions and reactions of its competitors in setting its price. Each firm's demand curve is kinked at the current price, with demand being elastic above and inelastic below the current price. Demand is elastic for price increases because each firm assumes that competitors will not follow a price increase; thus, raising price will result in large decreases in the firm's market share. Decreases in price, by contrast, will be matched by competitors, with the consequence that the firm will not gain market share by reducing price. Because of these demand conditions, oligopolists often engage in nonprice competition rather than compete on price. Nonprice competition is designed to establish consumer loyalty. In the medical malpractice market, there might be competition on service following the filing of a claim. Or the medical society-sponsored medical malpractice insurers might hypothetically be able to convince some physicians that they are more loyal to the medical profession than their commercial competitors.

In their account of oligopolistic behavior as a reason for medical malpractice insurance cycles, Nye and Hofflander (1987) begin with the observation that physician demand for malpractice insurance across the entire industry is not very sensitive to its price (i.e., is highly inelastic). However, the authors' demand for an *individual* insurer's product may be very sensitive to price changes. Some doctors may be very quick to switch to a different company if their current insurer raises premiums. In such a situation, an insurer cannot charge a substantially higher premium than its competitors. Further, the authors assert that insurers face constant returns to scale, meaning that much larger firms do not inherently have a proportionally greater competitive (cost) advantage than smaller firms. Although existing firms in a market may be in a price equilibrium, a new entrant can rapidly build its market share by under-pricing existing firms in the market. Relative ease of entry means that it would be relatively easy for any single firm to dominate a given market with a low-price strategy unless other firms follow its lead in pricing.

With these conditions established, the authors make the argument that any price cut in premiums by one insurer, such as a new market entrant, would result in price decreases by its competitors in an effort to avoid losing customers and market share. The result would be a reduction in premium levels but no change in the number of physicians insured. However, eventually the insurers in the market would realize they are verging on bankruptcy and raise premiums nearly simultaneously.

One would think that the consequences of a price reduction would be anticipated in advance, and no single company would begin the price reduction process. But a new entrant into the market needs to have a way of enticing physicians in the market to switch insurers, and having the new entrant brag about its great service or loyalty to the medical profession may not be enough to induce physicians to switch. A price incentive may be just what is needed.

Even without entry, an existing insurer in a market may become myopic (see box 2.1). Under one scenario, a combination of entry and myopic behavior occurs. A firm with poor management enters a market, underestimates future losses, and sets premiums below the actuarial value of the losses. Some of this does occur, as the PHICO experience, described more fully in Chapter 8, illustrates. PHICO entered new insurance markets and underpriced its medical malpractice insurance product, which led to its demise. St. Paul, the largest seller of national medical malpractice insurance, did not go bankrupt but may have seen itself as a victim of price-cutting, and as a result dropped the medical malpractice insurance line at the beginning of the 2001–2005 hard market (box 2.2).

As described in box 2.1, myopia may reflect internal conflict within insurance companies.[23] Fitzpatrick (2003–2004) discusses the interplay of forces within insurance companies during various phases of the cycle. During downturns in the cycle, when the companies are losing money

Box 2.1
The Price War of 1979–1981

Nye, Gifford, Webb, et al. (1988) describe a price war in the medical malpractice insurance market during 1979–1981. At the time, nominal returns on Treasury bills were very high (15.5 percent in 1981). With interest rates on riskless securities this high, insurers aggressively reduced premiums to gain market share. They expected to offset any underwriting losses by increased investment income. According to the authors, this practice, called cash-flow underwriting, is not necessarily unsound or imprudent business practice. It represents a legitimate and desirable response from insurers that benefits insurance buyers in the form of reduced rates.

During 1979–1981, however, excesses of cash-flow underwriting occurred, and virtually all insurers reduced premiums to preserve their market shares. The result, in many instances, was cutthroat price competition. Insurance companies' chief executives were faced with pleas from heads of their marketing departments that unless prices were reduced, the company would lose market share. Such claims, in most instances, prevailed over the protests of actuaries that the premiums in 1981 were not actuarially sound. This intense price competition resulted in premiums well below actuarially sound premiums. The inevitable upward pressure on insurance rates as a result of increasing paid claims was delayed and obscured. In other words, in hindsight, premium rates for physicians and others in 1981 were lower than they should have been (p. 1526).

and are under pressure to restore profitability, actuaries, who tend to be conservative in premium-setting, become relatively influential in company decision-making, and their advice, particularly in setting premiums, is followed. By contrast, during prosperous times, underwriters, who may be compensated on the basis of the volume of business they attract to the organization, are relatively more influential.[24] Underwriters often lobby for lower premiums with the objective of expanding market share. Their arguments are more persuasive in times of good financial performance. Following this type of reasoning, we might observe substantial increases in premiums as companies pay less attention to the opinions of their underwriters and more attention to their actuaries, who tend to be more concerned about the adequacy of insurance premiums as the companies move in the direction of restoring profitability from the bottom of the cycle.

Box 2.2
St. Paul Stops Selling Medical Malpractice Insurance in 2001

During the hard market of the 1980s, St. Paul increased its reserves. But by decade's end, claims frequency and severity had leveled, and the company concluded that it had overreserved. The company released $1.1 billion in reserves during 1992–1997. According to a newspaper report (Zimmerman and Oster 2002), "The money flowed through its income statement and boosted its bottom line. St. Paul stated clearly in its annual reports that excess reserves had enlarged its net income. But that part of the message didn't get through to some insurers—especially bedpan mutuals—dazzled by St. Paul's bottom line, according to industry officials. In the 1990s, some bedpan mutuals began competing for business beyond their original territories. . . . With St. Paul seeming to offer a model for big, quick profits, 'no one wanted to sit still in their own backyard, says Scipie's [a California-based physician-sponsored medical malpractice mutual] Mr. Zuk. The boards of directors said, 'We've got to grow.' Scipie expanded into Connecticut, Florida, and Texas, among other states, starting in 1997. . . . The newer competitors soon discovered, however, that 'the so-called profitability of the '90s was the result of those years in the mid-'80s when the actuaries were predicting the terrible trend, says Donald J. Fager, president of Medical Liability Mutual Insurance Co. [New York]. . . . The competition intensified, even though some insurers 'knew rates were inadequate from 1995 to 2000' to cover malpractice claims, says Bob Sanders, an actuary. . . . In the late 1990s, the size of payouts for malpractice awards increased, carriers say. . . . St. Paul's malpractice business sank into the red. The new Chief Executive announced that the company would drop the coverage line. St. Paul reported a $980 million loss on the [malpractice] business for 2001" (p. A1).

Some studies have focused on errors in loss reserving as a cause of insurance cycles. If companies act rationally, but face chance variation in losses for reasons beyond their control, there will be errors in loss reserving; however, these errors should also be random. Using the loss reserve errors shown in figure 2.1, the differences between initial incurred losses and developed losses seem serially correlated, not random.

Such nonrandom variation could reflect several types of behavior. First, loss forecasts could be based on past losses rather than on a full consideration of factors likely to occur in the future.[25] Any changes in initial incurred loss, which has increased sharply at the beginning of hard markets in medical malpractice, should have much greater effects on premiums in a long-tail line, such as medical malpractice, than in lines with shorter tails. An increase in anticipated inflation from 2 percent to 3 percent will have a larger effect on future anticipated losses if the payout period is seven years than if it is two years due to compounding.

Second, because stockholders desire stability in earnings, firms could manipulate losses to reduce the volatility in earnings.[26] However, this second explanation encounters two problems of its own. First, many malpractice insurers, organized as mutuals, reciprocals, or some alternative to the stock company form, have no stockholders. In recent years there has been substantial growth of self-insured plans run by large hospitals and large groups of physicians.[27] These organizations have no incentive to manipulate their losses either. Second, profits are volatile, and hardly seem to have been substantially smoothed. A succession of inflation shocks or adverse (to companies) judicial decisions could also generate serial correlation in loss reserve errors.

In sum, competitive behavior among companies in the industry can account for some aspects of the cycle but not for others. It potentially describes pricing behavior. *Nominal* prices of medical malpractice insurance fall in some areas during soft markets.[28] Whether or not nominal prices decrease, insurers interested in gaining market share offer insurance at premiums below the actuarial value (expected value) of the loss. Price wars and below actuarially fair pricing may result as a response to an entrant's low price and/or to high profitability, as was the case with St. Paul before it exited (box 2.2).

Such price wars could in principle be prevented by state insurance regulation. Although insurance regulation is found in some form in all U.S. states, not all states regulate premiums. And even when they do, a small line of insurance, such as medical malpractice insurance, may be below state regulators' radar in states where the focus is on much larger lines of insurance. Moreover, state regulation of premiums may itself be a cause of insurance cycles. Insurance regulators may be too slow to approve justifiable premium increases.[29]

The notion that there are internal conflicts about pricing within firms, and that the relative influence of marketing personnel and actuaries within companies in premium decisions is cyclical, is plausible, especially since the same story comes from several different sources.[30] This is a hard topic to study quantitatively since discussions within firms are private information. It also seems plausible that publicly traded companies are sensitive to the effects of company earnings reports on short-run fluctuations in the share price, a type of thinking that is not unique to insurance. However, many medical malpractice companies are not publicly traded. Thus, the importance to be attached to this latter explanation of company behavior is correspondingly smaller.

Industry pricing dynamics do not explain withdrawal of coverage at the beginning of hard markets. In addition, it seems a bit of a stretch that the large changes in loss reserves associated with cycles merely reflect efforts to reduce the volatility in reported earnings. Under the rational expectations hypothesis, an insurer's predictions of future losses should be unbiased.[31] Thus, although the ex ante forecasts would not coincide with the realized losses, taken over a number of years, the difference between realized and anticipated losses should be small. This is true especially for the industry as a whole, since decision makers use all available information in making decisions, and errors made by individuals are offset by errors by other individuals in the opposite direction, which is the "wisdom of crowds."[32]

Finally, increases in payments to policyholders and for ALE do not explain short-run fluctuations. While increases in such payments should be fully reflected in higher premiums in the long run, the cycle is about the short run.

Exogenous Factors: Changes in Returns on Interest-Bearing Securities

Part of the premium-setting process involves anticipating the pattern of future interest rates over time. Even if insurers' expectations of future interest rates are unbiased, they may make major mistakes in estimating future interest rates after the fact. For example, Harrington and Litan (1988) contend that in the early 1980s, insurers did not anticipate the substantial decrease in interest rates that occurred later in the decade. As a result, premiums were set too low, and were raised after the substantial decrease in interest rates became apparent.

Real interest rates were declining before each of the three hard markets since 1970. However, nominal interest rates[33] increased before the hard market of the 1970s, the difference between trends in nominal and real rates reflecting high inflation during this period.[34] Nominal rates decreased before the onset of the other two hard markets. It seems unlikely that insurers overpriced medical malpractice insurance on the basis of falling interest rates, since, with history as a guide, they almost certainly would have increased within a few years. Interest rates at best explain only part of cyclical underpricing of insurance premiums.

Exogenous Factors: Unanticipated Inflation Shocks

In principle, anticipated losses would be revised upward in response to anticipated increases in prices, particularly in medical prices. Here again, there is no consistent pattern. The late 1990s and early 2000s, for example, were years of relative price stability, including medical prices.[35]

Exogenous Factors: Capacity Constraints

Financial models of insurance pricing based on various standard frameworks[36] link premiums to the present value of expected claims expense plus a loading factor.[37] In these models, the cost of capital to the insurer does not vary with the amount of insurance the company sells.

A separate group of models embodies capital constraints.[38] In these, the cost of raising a dollar of capital (marginal cost of capital) rises with the amount of insurance sold. To the extent that the cost rises steeply or is vertical at a certain threshold of insurance sales (i.e., at a specific level of underwriting volume, no extra capital is forthcoming at any price) this places an effective limit on the amount of insurance that will be sold. Capacity constraints may go at least partway to explaining a puzzle about cycles, namely, the refusal of insurers to offer coverage at any premium.[39]

Insurance contracts represent liabilities of insurers. As a matter of prudence of the companies and a requirement of state insurance regulators, companies need assets to match the liabilities. A problem arises if the insurer lacks assets to back the sale of insurance policies. Because companies have made upward revisions on policies sold in prior years or for some other reason, they may lack internally generated funds to back the sale of insurance policies.

The capacity constraint explanation begins with the notion that a dollar of externally generated capital may be more expensive than a dollar of internally generated capital. For insurers that are not organized as stock companies, such as mutuals and reciprocals, and certainly for self-insured plans, there is practically no recourse at all to equity supplied by investors. These organizations must fully rely on internally generated capital, such as profits derived from premium income.

To see how the capacity constraint works, suppose that the firm is initially at the equilibrium P_0 and q_0 (figure 2.2). In the short run, the firm would issue more insurance policies, but along the supply curve of insurance S_0. While in the long run the firm can expect growth in internally generated capital at a constant (opportunity) cost—hence the curve S_{LR}—in the short run, extra capital could be obtained only at relatively unfavorable rates, which is reflected in S_0. Now suppose the firm experiences a loss shock due, for example, to a string of adverse judicial decisions,[40] reflected in increased developed losses. Then, even if the demand for insurance curve (D) is stable, the equilibrium price of insurance will increase in the short run. For other types of insurance, such shocks may be the result of natural disasters or terrorism.

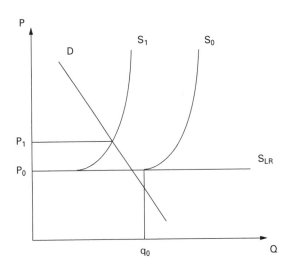

Figure 2.2
Insurance Market Equilibrium.

In lines of insurance in which losses from underwriting are relatively volatile, underwriting must be covered by relatively large amounts of surplus. When insurers' capacity is high, relatively volatile lines are allocated comparatively more surplus in relation to premium volume. However, when capacity is low, the uncertain or capacity-using lines are allocated the least capacity. At the same time, one observes withdrawal from those lines or less withdrawal coupled with steep premium increases. In lines with more predictable losses, such as automobile liability, availability of insurance is not curtailed as much and premiums remain relatively stable.

Using aggregate time series data on stock property-casualty insurers for the years 1935–1997, Choi, Hardigree, and Thistle (2002) report evidence that an increase in surplus or surplus growth leads to lower premiums in the short run. Doherty and Posey (1987) likewise find support for an effect of surplus on insurance availability, using a sample of stock general liability insurers from A. M. Best for 1979–1989. However, applying these results to medical malpractice insurance should be done with some caution, since stock companies are declining in market share in the medical malpractice line. Also, although the capacity constraint explanation seems plausible, and some evidence supports the capacity constraint hypothesis, other evidence does not, or provides weak support.[41]

Exogenous Factors: Role of Reinsurance in Cycles

Another factor exogenous to primary medical malpractice insurers and self-insuring organizations in the United States is the price and availability of reinsurance. As explained more fully in Chapter 10, insurers purchase reinsurance, termed excess loss insurance when purchased by a self-insured organization, such as a hospital, to protect itself against large, unpredictable losses. Medical malpractice insurers, especially small single-line insurers, are highly dependent on reinsurance as a hedge against risk.[42] According to interviews conducted with reinsurers described by the U.S. General Accounting Office (June 2003), reinsurance premiums increased at the beginning of the hard market of 2001–2005 for two reasons. First, there was a general increase in reinsurance premiums following the terrorist acts of September 11, 2001. This may have reflected a combination of reinsurers' reassessment of their exposure to serially correlated losses following this event and the loss of surplus. Second, for medical malpractice insurance in particular, reinsurers had experienced increased loss payments since about 1998, and for this reason raised reinsurance premiums to customers in this line of insurance substantially, with increases ranging from 50 to 100 percent. Higher reinsurance premiums were in turn passed forward to medical malpractice insurers and then to their customers. To hold premium increases down, some insurers raised the dollar threshold of loss before reinsurance coverage applied.

Many of the reinsurers are not domiciled in the United States, but rather in Caribbean countries, where they are not subject to corporate taxation and much insurance regulation, or in Europe (e.g., Swiss Re, Münchener Rückversicherung). Insurers and self-insured groups contract with several reinsurers which cover various levels of loss ("layers"). Insurance brokers often serve as intermediaries in developing reinsurance packages for clients—primary insurers and self-insuring organizations. Unlike many primary medical malpractice insurers, reinsurers are involved in multiple lines of insurance. They are also subject to the shocks (losses attributable to natural disasters, terrorism) described above. However, primarily because of state regulation of insurance, the market area for medical malpractice insurance in the U.S. is limited to individual states, whereas the market for reinsurance is global.

A reinsurer/excess insurer similarly faces risks from insuring against large claims. By definition, large claims are rare. When claims are infrequent, it is more difficult to judge whether an individual claim is a random event or represents an underlying change in claiming; the latter, but not the former, would require a change in the premium.

The fact that claims are resolved in the far distant future is problematic for the reinsurer/excess insurer because it increases the likelihood that events affecting claim resolution will intervene. For example, a high jury verdict in a jurisdiction may be precedent-setting, affecting how juries decide other claims as well as settlements which mirror jury verdicts. To the extent that the precedent affects all large claims in the jurisdiction (i.e., the correlation in claims outcomes increases), the price of coverage is likely to increase to reflect this risk. In fact, in markets for coverage of catastrophic risk, the premium may be several times the expected value of the loss for the policy year.[43] For these reasons, a few large payouts may lead to substantial increases in reinsurance/excess insurance premiums. These, in turn, are paid directly by self-insured entities or are shifted forward by primary insurers in the premiums they charge physicians and other primary insurance premiums.

Particularly because many reinsurers are not subject to the same extent of public regulation as other insurers, and many reinsurers are not public corporations, much less is known about reinsurers than about primary insurers. There is virtually no academic literature on the subject of reinsurance. Froot (2001) provides the most in-depth analysis of reinsurance markets in general. His article does not specifically deal with reinsurance for medical malpractice, however. Nor does it consider events that have occurred since 2000. Froot examined several nonmutually exclusive hypotheses to explain why reinsurance premiums were a multiple of expected loss, even prior to 2000. As discussed in Chapter 10, Froot does not reach a definitive conclusion as to why premiums are so high. Although he does not discuss reinsurance after the year 2000, a combination of shocks to capacity from natural disasters and 9/11, and some unanticipated payments on medical malpractice claims, seems like the most plausible reason for the withdrawal of coverage and substantial reinsurance premiums charged to malpractice insurers and the self-insured for medical malpractice in hospitals that occurred after 2000.

Conclusion

Insurance cycles reflect a number of factors. Several conclusions can be reached with near certainty. Others are much more uncertain.

First, insurance cycles, like business cycles and cycles in weather, clearly are here to stay. There may be changes in amplitude, but we can expect cycles to reoccur with certainty. Second, it is far easier to say what are not causes of cycles than to say definitively what causes them.

Prominent among the *noncauses* are (1) attempts of insurers to recoup losses on poorly performing investments by raising premiums and (2) exercise of market power by insurers to raise premiums well above actuarially fair values. On the former, the market for medical malpractice insurance is too competitive to allow for such actions. Even in markets with a single seller, entry of other sellers is always a possibility. On the latter, in many states there is more than one insurer competing for the business of physicians and hospitals which do not self-insure for medical malpractice. There is no evidence that insurers collude. In fact, the notion that a medical society-sponsored mutual medical malpractice insurer would collude with a for-profit insurer, such as St. Paul when it was in the medical malpractice insurance market, is implausible on its face.

Having eliminated the noncauses, we are left with considering possible causes. Underpricing of insurance is a common phenomenon leading up to crises. Shocks are also factors, even though the shocks pertinent to each cycle differ. Substantial changes in interest rates and prices that characterized the 1970s and 1980s did not reoccur after 2000. In contrast, the massive shocks from natural disasters and 9/11 were more likely factors after 2000.

The relative importance of precipitating causes of cycles may well differ among cycles. Similar to motor vehicle fatalities, we can be sure that they will occur in the future. In some seasons, they may be predominantly due to slick roads. In others, they may be due to heavy drinking and driving on holidays, reflecting fewer police patrols.

If there is nothing to be done about preventing cycles, what can be done to reduce their amplitude and disruptive effects? Among the possibilities discussed in later chapters are public provision of reinsurers—public reinsurers being much less likely to withdraw coverage during hard markets—and hospital provision of medical malpractice insurance for all care provided within the walls of the hospital. Hospitals would cover much primary insurance on a self-insured basis with reinsurance for the large losses. Here, too, the hospital would be far less likely to withdraw coverage during hard markets. However, it should be clear that there is no free lunch. Each proposal has its own pluses and minuses.

3

An Increased Threat of Lawsuits and Higher Premiums: The Consequences

Is there a doctor in the house? Increasingly, in Florida and around the country, the answer is no—not in the house, not in the doctor's office, and not in the hospital. Many physicians are choosing to retire early or to practice in other states because medical malpractice insurance in Florida has become unaffordable and, in some, cases, unavailable.

Thus begins the Executive Summary of the report of the Governor's Select Task Force on Healthcare Professional Liability Insurance, State of Florida, submitted to Governor Jeb Bush in early 2003.[1] The same report finds that "The concern over litigation and the cost and lack of medical malpractice insurance have caused doctors to discontinue high-risk procedures, turn away high-risk patients, close practices, and move out of the state. In some communities, doctors have ceased delivering babies and discontinued hospital care."[2] The report concludes that previous tort reforms have failed and that limitation of damages, the only provision proven to be effective in reducing the severity of judgments, was struck down by the Florida Supreme Court.[3]

In the political debate about tort reform during 2000–2005, the high cost of personal health services in the United States was frequently attributed to litigation and the high cost of medical malpractice insurance. For example, President George W. Bush explained in a speech delivered on January 5, 2005, "Many of the costs we are talking about don't start in an examining room or an operating room, they start in a courtroom."[4]

A decade and a half earlier, Danzon, Pauly, and Kingston[5] made the following observation in response to similar assertions: "Although malpractice insurance is still less than 2 percent of total health care expenditures, many observers argue that medical malpractice is a major factor contributing to rising health care costs. One implication of such arguments is that virtually all the cost is borne by patients. This seems at odds with arguments, made by others, that a significant fraction of physicians are giving up practice, or at least high-risk procedures, because of liability."

This chapter presents evidence on two of the five myths of medical malpractice listed in chapter 1. First, myth 2—Only "good" doctors are sued. We will see that both high- and low-quality physicians are sued for medical malpractice. Second, myth 5—Medical care is costly because of medical malpractice. At most, only a small part of the growth in real expenditures on personal health services in the United States can be attributed to medical malpractice. A focus of this chapter is whether there is empirical evidence that medical malpractice is to blame for creating access barriers to health care services, and has increased the cost of such services. Much of the conventional wisdom is that there is clearly a link of sufficient importance to require statutory changes. The effects of damage caps will be discussed in the next two chapters.

In a democracy such as ours, each of us has a right to pursue our private interest in a public forum. Throughout history, farmers have lobbied for price supports; the steel industry has argued for tariffs on foreign steel. Domestic automobile manufacturers have sought to restrain others who would impose more stringent gasoline mileage standards on the automobiles that they manufacture. Pursuit of private interest is not necessarily contrary to the public interest, but the two frequently do not coincide. Lower medical malpractice premiums and lower probabilities of being sued are certainly in the private interest of those who advocate tort reform. However, these policies may or may not serve the public well.

Lobbying on the basis that physicians have suffered reductions in their net income because premiums have risen is not likely to be popular with voters since physicians earn relatively high incomes. Therefore, the rationale for policy intervention is often cast as a need to help the public; assertions that patients have been disadvantaged by medical malpractice are common.

A major question this chapter addresses is whether the empirical evidence establishes a link between rising premiums and claim severity, on the one hand, and patient access to medical services and spending on personal health care services, on the other. The issue is not whether there is *ever* a link. For example, some physicians may have left practice for reasons at least partly related to medical malpractice. Rather, it is important to know whether there is evidence of widespread access barriers the existence of which can be attributed to rising premiums and threat of litigation. Further, the issue is not whether there are access barriers; the existence of access barriers has been amply documented. The issue is, compared to other causes of access barriers to patient care, how important medical malpractice is as a cause. All of the discussion assumes that premiums and outlays for awards have risen appreciably. The data presented below, however, do not show appreciable increases over long time periods.

Another potential impact is on spending for personal health care services. Such expenditures have clearly increased, but how much of the increase can be attributed to medical malpractice, including the threat of being sued?

The public discussion of the issue of defensive medicine has been particularly confused. Any increase in spending on personal health care services attributable to the threat of litigation is often considered wasteful. However, a well-functioning tort liability system would encourage physicians to order procedures for which benefit exceeds cost. As effective diagnostic tests and procedures are developed, their use should be encouraged, not discouraged. A malfunctioning tort system would encourage the use of procedures for which cost falls short of benefit. Thus, it is not enough to demonstrate that expenditures have risen as a consequence of medical malpractice; it is also necessary to document that such expenditures were wasteful, measured in cost/benefit terms. Such documentation is very rarely provided.

Referring back to an example provided in chapter 1, if the cost of a diagnostic test (to all parties, not just the out-of-pocket cost to the patient) is $1,000 per test, this test is appropriately provided to all patients for whom the benefit is $1,000 or more (again considering all benefits when benefits accrue to persons other than the patient, as would be the case, for example, in testing for AIDS). In the case in which the benefit is $1 and the cost is $1,000, the test should not be conducted.

This is an admittedly economic viewpoint. In what some describe as a medical model, a test should be provided if the benefit is positive. Thus, the test would be provided in cases in which the benefit is $1 and the cost is $1,000. When one describes this "medical model" in abstract terms, it seems to makes sense. Few, however, would recommend testing when the benefit versus cost is as stark as our $1 versus $1,000 example. Perhaps a fully insured patient would demand this, but few would support such decision criteria as sound public policy.

Benefit includes nontangible benefits, such as relief of pain and suffering, and of anxiety, which are very real and sometimes avertable costs. For example, people spend a great deal of money for painkillers and for anxiety relief. These costs are very real.

Often physicians are quoted as stating that they order tests and procedures in excess of what they would order in the absence of a threat of being sued. This could be so in a well-functioning system as well as a dysfunctional one, since an objective of tort is to provide an incentive to use tests and procedures for which benefit exceeds cost in an economist's sense. There is undoubtedly a lot of waste (care for which cost exceeds benefit or even care for which the benefit is zero) in the U.S. health care system. Nevertheless, allegations that health care spending is high because of medical malpractice generally do not include an accompanying analysis of the effects of *other* factors on such spending. Waste would almost surely exist even if there were no threat of lawsuits.

A distinction is made between "positive" and "negative defensive medicine." Positive defensive medicine refers to increases in the cost of personal health care services attributable to the threat of being sued. Negative defensive medicine applies to withdrawal of care due to retirements, changes in physician location, and dropping of particular procedures which often lead to lawsuits, such as obstetrical care. A rigorous definition of positive defensive medicine should be limited to provision of services for which the added cost is less than the anticipated benefit, not to increased cost per se.

If only premiums are considered, it is difficult to make a case that tort liability has had a major impact on the cost of medical care.[6] As documented below, U.S. health expenditures exceed medical malpractice premiums by a factor of 50 or more. The trend in the rate of growth in premiums relative to inflation has been modest. In addition, about half of a premium goes to pay injury victims and involves a transfer of income, not the use of scarce resources. For this reason, to obtain a large effect of medical malpractice on health care spending, one must incorporate the cost of positive defensive medicine *in addition to* higher premiums. By creating access barriers, negative defensive medicine may actually reduce health care spending.

The next section discusses what economic theory has to say about effects of increased medical malpractice premiums on physicians' fees and incomes; this is followed by a description of trends in medical malpractice premiums, claims frequency, payment per paid claim, and an empirical evaluation of the effects of increased medical malpractice premiums on physicians' fees and incomes. The next three sections are organized according to the trilogy often used to assess health care: access, cost, and quality or injury deterrence. We then review evidence on the association between a physician's claims history and indicators of quality. The final section summarizes the empirical evidence and implications based on the findings.

Effects of Premium Increases on Physicians' Fees and Incomes: Theory and Empirical Evidence

Economic theory offers predictions about price and output responses to an increase in the price the firm pays for an input used to produce its output, but the predictions depend on the underlying assumptions. As a practice expense, medical malpractice premiums are an input, as are expenses on aides and medical supplies, in the production of practice outputs.

Premiums as a Fixed Cost to a Physician's Practice

Premiums do not typically vary with physician hours of work or the volume of services delivered, and hence are plausibly viewed as a fixed cost to the physician's practice. The obstetrician who delivers five babies a year pays the same premium as a colleague in the same geographic location who delivers 150 annually.

A lesson from the microeconomics[7] of the firm, at least at its most basic level, is that an increase in the price of fixed input reduces the firm's profit, but does not affect the firm's product price or its output (sales). For physicians, a reduction in profit is typically equivalent to a reduction in net physician income.[8]

Although premiums do not reflect physician hours of work or practice volume, they do reflect the types of services a physician provides. For example, medical malpractice premiums can be reduced appreciably if a physician drops obstetrical deliveries from his or her practice. Thus, one would expect that raising premiums for physicians who deliver obstetrical care would reduce the number of physicians who provide such care. The decrease in supply should be particularly concentrated among those physicians with low obstetrical caseloads prior to the increase in the premiums among physicians who deliver such care.

Premium Changes as Physician Supply in a Market Changes

Immediately following an increase in the premium, physicians may make some alterations in their practices, but they are unlikely to move or quit practice. Such changes become more likely over time. To the extent that increased premiums reduce net incomes of physicians, the supply of physicians in the area experiencing the premium increase may fall in the long run. A drop in net income can induce older physicians to retire, and younger physicians may be less prone to enter practice in locations with high premiums. Other physicians may migrate to areas with relatively smaller premium increases. Physicians' fees may increase as the number of physicians in an area decreases. For example, a managed care organization (MCO) is likely to be in a poor bargaining position vis-á-vis a physician who is the only physician performing obstetrical deliveries in a geographic area. Women do not want to drive long distances when in labor, and MCOs unable to include an obstetrician in their local networks can expect to lose market share.

To the extent that the amount the insurer pays physicians eventually rises to reflect increased medical malpractice premiums, the increased premiums would lead to higher fees actually paid to physicians. This seems rather unlikely in markets in which there are many physicians and relatively few MCOs, but may occur in areas in which physicians have more bargaining power due, for example, to their relative scarcity. In addition, some insurers, most notably Medicare, base fee schedules in part on medical malpractice premiums in the geographic area and the specialty. Medicare fee schedules change slowly in response to changes in medical malpractice premiums.[9]

Premiums as a Variable Cost to a Physician's Practice

Physicians, however, may not view increased premiums simply as an increase in fixed cost. Rather, they may view the premium increase as a signal that the probability of being sued, or being sued for a lot of money, has risen. Each additional patient seen represents another chance to be sued. And when premiums grow, that chance of being sued increases. In contrast, if premiums are seen as a fixed cost, seeing another patient does not increase the malpractice cost. But if each additional patient adds to the overall risk of being sued, then seeing additional patients does add to the malpractice cost, and doctors will reduce practice volume and raise price, if they have the market power to do this.

With the growth of managed care and changes in physician reimbursement, such as Medicare's change in its method of paying physicians in the late 1980s, individual physicians have lost a great deal of power to set prices for their services. To the extent that this has occurred, physicians may wish to raise their fees in response to a medical malpractice premium increase, but be unable to do so. Rather, they must wait for offers from insurers to raise their fees in response to changes in practice expense.

Effects of Premium Changes on Positive Defensive Medicine

The above simple framework can explain fee changes that mirror changes in premiums. The model is equally appropriate for analyzing visits to the barber and barbers' fees.

With positive defensive medicine, the physician orders more tests, more surgical procedures, and more follow-up care than the patient would if he or she was fully knowledgeable about the efficacy of the tests, procedures, and follow-up care in the same situation. Models that allow for such physician-induced demand are necessarily more complex, and a detailed discussion of these models would take us far afield.[10]

While less specific models seem more realistic, the cost of adding generality is that even some of the above predictions no longer hold. For example, an increase in a fixed practice expense leading to decrease in practice income could cause physicians to supply more rather than less output.

Summary of Theoretical Results

If the discussion of theory to this point seems like another product of a two-armed economist, weighing options on the one hand as well as the other hand, this is not a false impression. Theories are useful for providing a conceptual framework for analysis, but predictions are sensitive to the assumptions underlying the analysis. Using one set of assumptions, an increase in medical malpractice premiums will have no effect on physicians' fees or on positive defensive medicine, but will increase negative defensive medicine. Under alternative assumptions, a rise in premiums will increase fees and positive defensive medicine. To the extent that these increase, there would be less of a tendency to leave practice. In other words, negative defensive medicine would decrease.

There is a limit to how far logic, economic or noneconomic, can take us. Logic does, however, suggest there are trade-offs between positive and negative defensive medicine. A physician who orders many tests because the threat of lawsuits has increased, and for which he or she is compensated, is not as likely to experience a major loss of income and leave practice. Economic theory is often good for generating hypotheses about relationships between variables, but the proof of the pudding is in the empirical evidence.

Empirical Evidence: Trends in Premiums, Claims Frequency, and Payment per Paid Claim

Actual trends in medical malpractice premiums have been more moderate than much of the rhetoric asserts. Using data from national surveys of physician practice conducted by the American Medical Association during 1970–2000, Rodwin et al. (2006) document trends in self-employed physicians' mean malpractice premiums, total practice expenses, and net income. Mean medical malpractice premiums were

$18,400 in 2000, which amounted to 7.5 percent of total practice expenses and 3.8 percent of gross physician revenue. Three decades earlier, before any of the major crises in medical malpractice, medical malpractice premiums as percentages of total practice expenses and gross physician revenue were 5.5 percent and 2.0 percent, respectively.

In 1975, liability costs were 0.91 percent of U.S. health care spending. In 2002, liability cost as a share of health care spending had risen to 1.58 percent. In 1975, physicians paid 50.7 percent of liability cost in premiums, and hospitals paid 41.0 percent. By 2002, the shares were 57.7 and 30.2 percent, respectively.[11]

These changes hardly seem dramatic, raising the question "Where's the beef?" Following spikes in premiums, physicians, hospitals, and other health care providers have sought relief, pointing fingers at others, the alleged culprits, while making widespread appeals to politicians.

Admittedly, as Rodwin and his coauthors acknowledge, these estimates obscure areas of medical practice and specialties in which premium growth was more substantial. On the other hand, there are areas and specialties for which premium growth was less than average. Further, because the AMA discontinued its surveys of physician practice after 2000, these estimates exclude the premium growth that occurred after 2000. Between 2000 and 2004, according to data from the *Medical Liability Monitor*, mean premiums paid by obstetrician/gynecologists increased by about 70 percent in real terms (2004 dollars). General surgeons' mean premiums about doubled. However, the increase for specialists in internal medicine was much lower, about 50 percent (figure 3.1).

Nevertheless, as already noted, it seems likely the "beef" is really about more than the increase in premiums. Even though medical malpractice insurance covers the dollar loss of the claim and the associated legal expense, there are other costs to physicians and hospitals, such as stress and loss of time in defending the cases.

Medical malpractice claims frequency spiked in 1975 and 1985, both crisis years, but claims frequency has increased slowly since the mid-1990s. The crisis that occurred in the early 2000s was associated with a modest increase in claims frequency at most. In some states, claims frequency declined.[12]

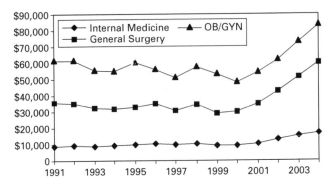

Figure 3.1
Mean Insurance Premiums in Three Specialties, 1991–2004 (2004 $). Source: Medical Liability Monitor surveys (1991–2004).

However, payment per claim has increased substantially since the mid-1990s (figure 3.2). Relationships between medical malpractice premiums, claims frequency, mean payment size, and total payments are complex. In particular, payments in a particular year come from insurance policies sold in the past, not from policies sold in the same year. The more fundamental relationship is between the premiums set in a particular year and anticipated losses in future years on claims filed in the policy year.

Empirical Evidence on Effects of Changes in Premiums

Danzon et al. (1990) report results of cross-sectional and time series analyses on the effects of changes in premiums on physicians' fees. Using cross-sectional data from the 1970s, they find that premium increases boosted fees by more than can be explained solely by the effect of the increase on overall practice expense. In other words, there was more than 100 percent forward shifting of the burden of the premium increase onto patients and insurers. If more than a full pass-through of the additional cost occurred, physician incomes would have *risen* as a consequence of premium increases. However, the authors' time series analysis of effects of premium changes during 1976–1983 reveals that the increased premiums had no impact on physicians' incomes.

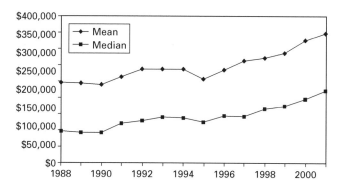

Figure 3.2
Claims Payouts, 1988–2002 (2004 $). Source: PIAA Data Sharing Project, in Smarr (2003).

Danzon et al. explore several possible reasons for the lack of change in incomes, the most plausible of which is that insurers increased reimbursements to physicians by the amount of the premium increase. Moreover, physicians could have increased fees for reasons besides the reimbursement increase, which led to a compounding effect. But given the important changes in insurer payment practices that have occurred since the early 1980s, it is not at all certain their results would generalize to the post-2000 period.[13]

Only one study has updated Danzon et al.'s (1990) analysis. This study, described in Pauly (2006), covering the years 1994, 1998, and 2002, reached essentially the same conclusion as Danzon et al. (1990), a rather surprising finding, given the changes in insurer payment practices that have occurred since the early 1980s. The bottom line is that the empirical evidence indicates that increases in medical malpractice premiums lead to physician fee increases. Patients, taxpayers, and premium payers—and not physicians—ultimately bear the burden of malpractice premium increases.

Pauly adds a cautionary note, however, that *on average,* the conclusion that physicians do not bear the financial burden of increased premiums appears to hold. It is quite possible that when premiums increase, some physicians lose, and others gain, income. Perhaps those physicians who lose financially are the most vocal in demanding relief from the burden of medical malpractice.

Data collected by the American Medical Association indicate that physicians' incomes rose in real terms over the period 1970–1996, but declined between 1996 and 2000, just before the most recent sharp rise in medical malpractice premiums occurred.[14] The decline in real income between 1996 and 2000 did not result from a rise in premiums, as premiums remained constant in real terms during these years. As of 2000, medical malpractice premiums were 7.5 percent of total practice expenses, up from 5.5 percent in 1970.[15]

Does Medical Malpractice Reduce Patient Access to Care? Physician Supply

Aggregate Trends and Disparities by Physician Specialty and Geographic Location

Starting about the late 1960s, the number of physicians relative to the to U.S. population increased appreciably. Between 1980 and 2003, for example, the number of physicians in the United States nearly doubled.[16] Supply has grown even faster in some states, such as Florida, which seems inconsistent with the quotations at the beginning of this chapter.

In 1980, the U.S. Graduate Medical Education National Committee released a report concluding that the United States faced a massive physician surplus by the year 2000. Although by various indicators this surplus did not materialize,[17] there were no widespread policy concerns that the supply in the aggregate was insufficient. Concerns have been expressed about excess supply in some physician fields, especially surgery.[18] Disparities in the geographic distribution of physicians have been long-standing,[19] predating public awareness of a medical malpractice issue.

Studies Linking Medical Malpractice to Physician and Hospital Supply: Anecdotes and Evidence from Two Surveys of Physicians

There is considerable anecdotal evidence that physicians and hospitals have reduced availability of medical care in response to higher medical malpractice premiums. The anecdotes based on newspaper stories in box 3.1 illustrate this point. Not only do they add color; the anecdotes also serve to personalize the problems. They say nothing about the effect of a rise in premiums on availability of care for the population as a whole

Box 3.1
Anecdotal Evidence on the Impact of Higher Medical Malpractice Premiums and Availability of Medical Malpractice Insurance on the Availability of Medical Care

- *Arizona* The city of Bisbee, along the Mexican border, lost the maternity ward at its local hospital when malpractice rate increases led to four of the city's six obstetricians to stop delivering babies.
- *Florida* The number of insurers offering medical malpractice coverage dropped in half (from forty to twenty) over the past decade, pushing premiums up and reducing the availability of coverage. Malpractice insurance premiums in 2002 averaged $201,376 for ob/gyns, while the average was $174,268 for general surgeons. The Orlando Regional Medical Center is currently at risk of closing its trauma center due to the lack of neurosurgeons willing to work the emergency room.
- *Georgia* A recent study of Georgia physicians projected that 2,800 doctors in the state (or about one in five) would stop providing higher-risk procedures in order to reduce their liability exposure. One in three ob/gyns said they would limit their services (including delivering babies), and 11 percent would stop working in emergency rooms. Four percent of the state's doctors reported that high malpractice premiums have led them to retire early or leave the state. Overall, the study reported that malpractice premiums increased between 11 percent and 30 percent in the state.
- *Nevada* It has been reported that dozens of doctors have stopped practicing in the state due to the medical malpractice crisis. The decision by St. Paul Companies to cease writing malpractice insurance left 60 percent of Las Vegas doctors seeking new insurers, and 10 percent of the city's doctors are expected to quit or relocate as a result. The crisis in Nevada was made particularly clear when the state's only Level 1 trauma center closed for ten days in July 2002, during which time the hospital's CEO warned the public to "Drive home carefully."
- *New Jersey* Medical liability premiums have been increasing 20 percent to 25 percent annually, and the Medical Society of New Jersey estimates that 3,000 physicians in the state are at risk of losing coverage due to reduced coverage by insurers. Over a period of less than a year, three insurers—the MIXX Group, PHICO, and St. Paul Companies—covering 55 percent of the state's doctors stopped writing coverage for malpractice, leaving doctors rushing to find new sources of insurance.
- *Pennsylvania* The state's largest malpractice insurer, the PHICO Group, has been placed in liquidation, and the MIXX Group and Princeton Insurance have ceased writing new policies. Rising malpractice costs have induced doctors to leave the state, retire early, or stop performing certain procedures. Difficulty obtaining malpractice coverage caused Abington Memorial Hospital outside Philadelphia to close its trauma center for almost two weeks. Among doctors hit the hardest, according to Pennsylvania Hospital, are radiologists specializing in mammography. The loss of radiologists in the state has resulted in waiting periods for routine mammograms of up to eight months.

Box 3.1
(continued)

• *Texas*   Doctors along the Rio Grande River have experienced significant increases in malpractice premiums, with neurosurgeons paying up to $120,000 a year and ob/gyns paying up to $100,000 for coverage. Numerous surgeons, internists, and the only pediatric surgeon in El Paso left the city. According to one physician, "The physicians along the Mexican border have a lower percentage of patients who are privately insured, and to have a line item like medical liability insurance go up 100 percent to 300 percent in a year's time is a lot for some practices to swallow."

• *West Virginia*   Higher malpractice rates have contributed to about 5 percent of the state's doctors either retiring early or leaving the state. The Charleston Area Medical Center had to pay $2,000 daily in malpractice premium subsidies in order to retain the doctors necessary to keep its trauma center open. After the last emergency room neurosurgeon left Wheeling, the local hospital had to transport trauma patients by helicopter to other emergency rooms. The departure of St. Paul Companies from the malpractice insurance market has forced two-thirds of the state's doctors to seek coverage from other sources.

• *Washington*   Increased losses forced Washington Casualty Co., the state's largest provider of malpractice coverage to rural hospitals, into receivership. The firm provided coverage to forty-six hospitals and twenty community health clinics in the state, and covered 75 percent of the state's rural hospitals. PedMac, which provides health care services to the poor, reported that its annual malpractice insurance costs increased by 150 percent, and the average cost for malpractice coverage for hospitals increased 60 percent statewide. A survey by the state medical association found that obstetricians have been hit hard, with 19 percent reporting that they have already stopped practicing obstetrics and 8 percent saying they plan to stop in the near future.

Source: Saxton, U.S. Congress, Joint Economic Committee (2003), pp. 15–17.

---

or even for segments of the population. Many of the accounts speak in terms of "up to." Minimum, mean, and median values, however, are not presented.

The brief examples in box 3.1 may be oversimplifications of reality. For example, when Bisbee, Arizona, lost its maternity ward at the local hospital, where were did residents of Bisbee go for obstetrical services? Did the ward reopen later? Did the two obstetricians remaining in Bisbee increase their capacity? Were new obstetricians recruited to the community? If there was no entry and if residents of the community had no nearby alternative, the situation would be far more serious than if the example describes only a very temporary event.

Surveys of physicians in Pennsylvania and in Florida were conducted in 2003[20] and 2004,[21] respectively. Both surveys were conducted by mail, with response rates of 65 percent and 40 percent. Seven percent of specialist respondents to the Pennsylvania survey said that they would definitely retire in the next two years because of liability costs, and another 32 percent said that they would be very likely or somewhat likely to retire for this reason. Surgeons were more inclined to state that they would retire early than were other specialists. Four percent said that they would definitely relocate to another state for this reason in the next two years, and another 29 percent said that they were very likely or somewhat likely to do so. Surgeons (general surgeons, neurosurgeons, and orthopedic surgeons) were more likely to say that they were apt to relocate in the future than were other specialists. Twelve percent of specialists had reduced or eliminated "high-risk aspects of their practices," which included delivering babies, performing back surgery, and avoiding high-risk patients, such as the obese and high-risk pregnancies, because of liability costs, and another 38 percent stated that they were very likely or somewhat likely to do so.

The format of the questions about future retirement and practice location intentions in the Florida survey differed from that of its Pennsylvania counterpart. When asked about how long the physician respondents intended to stay in their current practice, 11.2 percent said "less than two years." These responses included retirements, relocations to other geographic areas, and relocations within the same area. Retirements accounted for about two-fifths of the decisions regarding planned changes. Among those planning to leave their current practices within two years, 61.6 percent said that "inability to find medical liability insurance played a role" in their plans. An even larger share of respondents, 77.8 percent, said that "inability to pay for medical liability insurance played a role."

Much of the Florida survey focused on changes in availability of specific services attributable to the medical liability insurance market. The most commonly eliminated services were nursing home coverage (42.1 percent of respondents), vaginal deliveries (29.1 percent), cesarean deliveries (26.0 percent), emergency department coverage (22.8 percent), and mental health services (21.2 percent). There were no statistically significant differences between rural and suburban/urban physicians in these assessments.

These types of survey findings can be influential in the legislative decision-making process. Not only are physicians in a financial position to contribute to political campaigns, but they are also on the front line and, therefore, presumably are "in the know." Nevertheless, such survey findings are subject to several important limitations.

First, response rates to physician surveys tend to be low, especially to mail questionnaires, as was the case with these two surveys, especially the Florida survey. This raises the possibility that those physicians who were most upset about recent events in the market for medical malpractice insurance would be overrepresented among respondents.

Second, the surveys measured *planned* exits, but not planned entry. If physicians stay in practice, they have to move somewhere. No state, to the authors' knowledge, has acknowledged that it has benefited from receiving many expatriates from other states because of high medical malpractice insurance costs in these other states. If, following a decrease in supply, payments from insurers eventually rise to cover at least part of the physician income initially lost due to the increase in premiums, this will provide opportunities for physicians to locate to these states.

An immediate response to a substantial increase in premiums may be to contemplate retirement or moving to another state. But after two years during which premiums do not increase further, with increases in insurer payments to partly offset the premium increase, and when malpractice insurance again becomes widely available, many physicians are likely to change their plans. Added to this are uncertainties associated with retirement and the appreciable cost and uncertainty of moving to another state and establishing practice there. For these latter reasons as well, many physicians who planned to leave are likely to decide to stay put.

Also, moving to another state for reasons of medical malpractice is a risky undertaking. Such states as West Virginia were "crisis states" for the first time in the post-2000 crisis. A physician could have moved there from Florida, only to find that West Virginia was just as bad or even worse. Actual changes may differ from planned ones. In one study based on data from the 1970s and 1980s,[22] physicians who had previously experienced high frequency of claims were less likely to actually change their practice status (e.g., leave the state or retire).

Key informant interviews used to help design the mail questionnaire for the Pennsylvania survey revealed that "Physician migration particularly affected hospitals located near Pennsylvania's borders, because physicians could easily commute across state lines."[23] However, at about the same time, the New Jersey Hospital Association reported impacts of the medical malpractice crisis that threatened New Jerseyans' access to health care services. This included a group of seven New Jersey retinal specialists who stopped providing care to premature infants, a community that lost its only neurosurgeon to New York, and reductions in access to obstetrical care.[24] It might be advisable for the tort reform advocates in both states to coordinate their public relations activities.

Third, the decreases in services may seem alarming, but no information was provided on the actual volume of the reductions in services. For example, for obstetrical deliveries, the physician may have performed very little obstetrical care before quitting the performance of deliveries. Cutbacks in service provision may sometimes be desirable. Low-volume providers tend to provide lower-quality care, holding other factors constant.[25] Another concern has been that rates of cesarean sections are too high. Some declines in these rates may be a welcome outcome.

Fourth, some physicians may view surveys of impacts of medical malpractice on their practices as political tools, and the responses may have been strategic to elicit legislative changes favorable to physicians. Fortunately, some researchers have studied the relationship between medical malpractice and physician supply, using multivariate analysis. Medical malpractice is certainly not the only determinant of physician supply. Using multivariate analysis, researchers can ascertain the contribution of changes in medical malpractice variables to changes in physician supply, while accounting for other determinants of physician supply.

Studies Linking Medical Malpractice to Physician Supply: Results of Multivariate Analysis

Baicker and Chandra (2004) assess changes in physician supply by state between 1992 and 2001, using several alternative measures of the threat of medical malpractice, premiums, frequency of paid claims, severity of paid claims, and a measure of the loading factor on medical malpractice insurance,[26] and holding several other potential determinants of physician supply constant in their analysis. They conclude that medical malpractice has no effect on physician location.

Hellinger and Encinosa (2003) study physician location patterns in selected years from 1985 to 2000. Rather than use a measure of medical malpractice cost or threat, the authors assessed the impact of dollar limits on damages in medical malpractice cases as the key variable explaining the geographic distribution of physicians. Among all statutory changes involving tort liability of physicians, limits on damages have been shown to be the most effective in terms of reducing medical malpractice payments and premiums.[27] Hellinger and Encinosa conclude that (1) states with caps on nonmonetary damages had about 12 percent more physicians than states without caps and (2) states with relatively high caps were *less likely* to experience an increase in numbers of physicians during the observational period than were states with lower caps.

The Hellinger-Encinosa study differs from Baicker and Chandra's in several respects, including the definition of the physician supply, the dependent variable, the other explanatory variables included in the analysis, and the measure of medical malpractice threat. Perhaps some other factor, not included, such as a favorable political climate for physicians, was responsible both for the passage of damage caps and for physician entry into the state. Baicker and Chandra report no effect of medical malpractice on supply, and another study, by Kessler et al. (2005), described more fully in a later chapter, finds a much smaller effect (2.9 percent) than did Hellinger and Encinosa.

The most appropriate conclusion seems to be that there may be a link between a state's medical malpractice climate and its supply of physicians. The effect is probably not large, especially when compared with the difference in supply among geographic areas that persists, and relative to the growth in aggregate physician supply that occurred in the U.S. during the latter part of the twentieth century.

Patient Access to Medical Care: Qualitative Evidence of Access Problems

Like the quantitative evidence, qualitative evidence on the relationship between the medical malpractice environment and physician location is ambiguous. The U.S. General Accounting Office (GAO) conducted case studies in five states (Florida, Mississippi, Nevada, Pennsylvania, and West Virginia).[28] Medical malpractice crises were reported in all of these states during this period.[29] The GAO reports some examples of reduced access to services, such as lack of full orthopedic surgeon coverage in an emergency room. However, it also finds that some reports of physicians relocating to other states, retiring, or closing practices were either inaccurate or involved relatively few physicians.[30]

The American Medical Association was asked to comment on a preliminary report of GAO's research. The point-counterpoint (as described by the GAO) is interesting since it mirrors the general tenor of the debate between groups advocating tort reform and evidence assembled by independent organizations with no particular stake in the outcome.

The AMA had several criticisms of the GAO's analysis of access. First, the AMA criticized the limited scope of the study, in particular its covering only five states. The GAO responded that reports from other sources had indicated that the five states were experiencing medical malpractice crises. Second, the AMA criticized the GAO for failing to cover two specialties in which problems with medical malpractice were most acute, obstetrics-gynecology and emergency room medicine. These are indeed specialties which have experienced problems with litigation from time to time over decades. Yet they are not the only specialties to have been adversely affected in this way.

Third, the AMA said that the GAO's aggregate analysis obscured access problems in particular specialties and localities. Among its responses to this criticism, the GAO noted that it had conducted some specialty and state-specific analysis. It cited cases in which results from its detailed investigation contradicted prior reports of access problems that had been attributed to medical malpractice.

Fourth, the AMA commented that some of the GAO's analysis was not sufficiently recent. The GAO responded that its analysis of 2000–2002 data included a period during which medical malpractice premiums rose appreciably.

Patient Access to Medical Care: The Relationship between Medical Malpractice and Patient Travel Time

To the extent that hospitals are closing units at their facilities, one would expect to observe increases in patient travel time to the facilities that remain open. Using hospital inpatient utilization data from Florida for the years 1997, 2000, and 2003, Dranove and Gron (2005) assess utilization of inpatient procedures that would normally be performed by obstetricians and neurosurgeons, two high-risk specialties in a high-risk state. From the data, they could determine the distance between the patient's place of residence and the hospital at which the procedure was performed. The most notable finding on travel time for craniotomies is an increase in travel time from home to hospital of from thirty-seven to forty-two minutes between 2000 and 2003—before and during the medical malpractice crisis in that state. Although the travel times were more than twenty minutes longer for rural craniotomy patients than for similar patients statewide, there was no differential change in travel times for such patients between 2000 and 2003. For high-risk obstetrical deliveries, travel time increased by less than half a minute, on average, between 2000 and 2003.

Access to Care: Implications

Overall, the empirical evidence suggests that reports of physicians leaving practice because of the professional liability crisis are overstated, as are statements that the crisis is causing problems of patient access. Lack of health insurance, which has not received nearly as much political support from the advocates of tort reform as has tort reform, has been clearly established as a barrier to care. "Negative defensive medicine" undoubtedly exists at some times and in some places. However, if the policy intent is to improve access to care, a *much* broader strategy is warranted.

The Rising Cost of Medical Care: Is Medical Malpractice the Culprit? Positive Defensive Medicine

Lack of Adequate Definition
Given that medical malpractice premiums are a small fraction of total personal health care spending, rising premiums per se cannot be a major driver of the increased cost of personal health services. Those who see medical malpractice as the culprit point to the effects of the threat of lawsuits on decisions of physicians and other providers. Providers practice "defensively" to avoid litigation.

The vast majority of providers carry medical malpractice insurance, which tends to cover all payments to claimants as well as the legal expense of defending such cases. Since medical malpractice insurance premiums are not generally experience-rated,[31] insured providers face very little direct financial risk from medical malpractice litigation. However, there is a substantial uninsured expense in terms of the value of time and the emotional burden on parties accused of medical malpractice, as well as possible loss of reputation. Thus, even insured physicians and other providers may have an incentive to practice defensively.

The lack of an adequate definition for defensive medicine has led to much confusion; the vast majority of assertions have not been based on a precise definition of defensive medicine, nor has quantification of the extent of this practice been attempted. As explained above, to the extent that the threat of medical malpractice litigation increases provision of care for which marginal benefit exceeds marginal cost, then such litigation serves its desired purpose, and conversely. Thus, not all additional services attributable to the threat are "defensive" or unproductive. Any effort to measure the effect of defensive medicine should start with an operational definition of the term.

The U.S. Office of Technology Assessment (OTA) defined defensive medicine in the following way: "Defensive medicine occurs when doctors order tests, procedures, or visits, or avoid high-risk patients or procedures, primarily (but not necessarily solely) to reduce their exposure to malpractice liability. When physicians do extra tests or procedures primarily to reduce malpractice liability, they are practicing positive defensive medicine. When they avoid certain patients or procedures, they are practicing negative defensive medicine."[32] The OTA definition, based on a view shared by the vast majority of health professionals, starts from a very different premise. Medical liability has little or nothing to do with optimal care. Rather, the threat of being sued is a disruption, and any changes in resource allocation attributable to the threat are wasteful.

In contrast to the OTA definition, the law and economics tradition starts with the concept of optimal care, the level that would maximize consumer well-being, given available scarce resources. Health professionals are called upon to serve as the patient's agent in deciding on which care is expected to yield a benefit in excess of cost. According to this view, only care for which expected cost exceeds expected benefits is excessive and defensive. There may be uncertainty about the anticipated benefit, but the expectation is that the parties act on the best information they have to achieve the objective.

Quantifying the Cost of Medical Malpractice: The Role of Positive Defensive Medicine

Reynolds et al. (1987) estimate the net impact of medical malpractice on the cost of physicians' services in 1985. These costs include malpractice insurance premiums, the costs of defending claims, and the costs of practice changes made in response to increasing medical liability risk. The authors used two methods. Their first approach used statistical techniques to assess the relationship between medical malpractice premiums and the price and volume of services provided, an approach followed in most subsequent studies of defensive medicine.

Their second approach utilized a survey of physicians. The authors questioned physicians about how they have responded to the threat of medical liability. The physicians stated that they gave more detailed documentation of patient encounters in medical records and took more time to discuss care with patients. To the extent that good documentation leads to better care, this is something that patients are likely to value. At least some patients are likely to want to discuss their diagnoses and therapies with physicians. As some of the physician responses to the threat of medical malpractice litigation are desirable, those desirable responses should not contribute to the *cost* of medical liability unless there is a separate calculation for the benefit as well.

Payments to claimants as reflected in premiums are not a social cost of medical malpractice. Social costs reflect use of scarce resources. The resources are used up and are not available for another purpose. Instead, such payments represent *transfer payments* from defendants to claimants. Such payments are a private cost to defendants and private revenue to claimants.

For these reasons, Reynolds and his coauthors plausibly overestimate the cost of medical malpractice. They report that in 1985 in the U.S., physicians paid $3.7 billion in premiums. The value of physicians' time in litigation was $100 million. The cost of defensive medicine in that year was $11.7 billion, for a total cost of medical malpractice of $15.4 billion. This was relative to an expenditure of $82.8 billion on physicians' services. Thus, their conclusion is that premiums, defensive medicine, and the total cost of professional liability were, respectively 4.5, 14.1, and 18.6 percent of spending on physicians' services in that year.

Because the $11.7 billion figure includes additional resources associated with *desirable* responses by physicians (a benefit of the threat of lawsuits, not a cost), and the $3.7 billion figure includes transfer payments to injury victims, the estimated total cost of professional liability is probably too high. One component, the $100 million estimate for time in litigation, is too low. Physicians (like the vast majority of defendants in litigation) plausibly would place a value on time spent in litigation at far more than their hourly wage. (We admit that we would!) And the number of hours in litigation excludes all the time defendants are likely to spend fretting about the case. But even if the $100 million figure were multiplied by a factor of 5 or even 10, it seems unlikely that a more accurate estimate of the total cost of professional liability would be anywhere near 18.6 percent of spending on physicians' services in a year.

Quantifying the Cost of Medical Malpractice from Clinical Scenarios

Other approaches used more recently are clinical scenario surveys and case studies describing the impact of malpractice liability concerns on the use of specific medical technologies. In clinical scenario surveys, physicians were asked by the OTA to say how they would respond in various situations and to rate the relative importance of various reasons for the physicians' stated choices.[33] The list of reasons included the threat of medical malpractice. A positive aspect of this method is that the scenarios represent clinically relevant situations and choices that physicians often make in practice. There is a risk, however, that respondents might tailor responses to help achieve a political outcome that they desire.

Based on a review of existing studies, the OTA reports no convincing previous empirical evidence on defensive medicine at the time it conducted its own research on the topic. The OTA administered scenarios to physicians practicing in states with different liability climates. Based on its findings, the OTA report concludes that defensive medicine raises the use of diagnostic procedures by less than 8 percent, and the effect varies substantially by clinical situation.

Quantifying the Cost of Medical Malpractice: Kessler and McClellan's Analysis of Positive Defensive Medicine in Cardiac Care

The most cited scholarly paper[34] on the topic of defensive medicine and one that is often used to support the case for tort reform in recent years is by Kessler and McClellan (KM).[35] KM used longitudinal data on all elderly (aged sixty-five and over). Medicare beneficiaries who were hospitalized for a new acute myocardial infarction (AMI) or a new episode of ischemic heart disease (IHD) in 1984, 1987, and 1990. Like subsequent studies by Hellinger-Encinosa (2003) and Kessler, Sage, and Becker (2005), KM's measures of the medical malpractice threat are variables reflecting tort reforms implemented in the state in which the beneficiary was admitted for treatment. KM assessed the effect of the statutory changes on total hospital Medicare payments made during the year following admission for the AMI or IHD. These data were used to measure the effect of the statutory changes on intensity of treatment. KM also studied the impact of the tort reforms on patient outcomes.

According to KM's methodology, defensive medicine is reduced if the reforms (1) reduced treatment intensity *and* (2) did not adversely affect patient outcomes. Their outcome measures are mortality within one year of admission for the index event (admission to a hospital for AMI or IHD) and whether or not the patient experienced a subsequent AMI or heart failure, measured by admission for either condition in the year following the index event. Rather than analyze effects of tort reforms individually, KM combine reforms into two variables: "direct" and "indirect." The direct reforms are caps on damage awards,[36] abolition of punitive damages,[37] no mandatory prejudgment interest,[38] and collateral source rule reform.[39] KM define indirect reforms as other reforms that may affect pressure from tort on care provision, but affect awards only indirectly. An example of an indirect reform is limitations on the plaintiff's attorney's contingency fees, because it makes it more difficult for injury victims to file medical malpractice claims. Indirect reforms include limits on contingent fees,[40] mandatory periodic payments,[41] joint and several liability reform,[42] and the availability of a patient compensation fund.[43] The study controlled for the effects of other factors' heterogeneity by including explanatory variables for state and year.

KM find that in states adopting direct reforms (relative to states without direct reforms), Medicare payments for hospital care during the first year following the index admission declined by from 5 percent to 9 percent; for the indirect reforms, the decline was 1.8 percent. Mortality was virtually the same in reform and nonreform states. Since the reforms reduced cost of care, while not adversely affecting outcomes, KM conclude that liability reforms can reduce defensive medicine practices.

The KM study has several important strengths. It assesses both cost and outcomes. It is national in scope and uses a large sample (200,000+ hospital admissions). KM acknowledge that elderly persons are less likely to file medical malpractice claims than others.[44] However, as KM argue, results from analysis of a group that is not suit-prone provides a conservative estimate of the extent of defensive medicine.

The study also has some weaknesses. The most important deficiency is its possible lack of generalizability. While some proponents of tort reform have used the paper to make generalizations about the effects of tort reform, in fact, admissions for AMI and IHD (although an important category of admissions) constitute only a small part of Medicare hospital admissions. Implementation of tort reforms may reduce the cost of care without adversely affecting mortality for AMI and IHD, but *on average* it does not reduce the cost of care when elderly persons are admitted to the hospital for other reasons.

This deficiency is remedied at least in part by a later study by Kessler and McClellan (1997), which uses national data to study effects of direct and indirect reforms with a national survey of physician data from the American Medical Association. That study focuses on effects of reforms on claims frequency and premiums, finding some evidence that direct reforms affected both, but with a lag.[45] Further, they find that a variable for direct *and* indirect reforms reduced referrals for consultation and time spent with patients.[46]

Quantifying the Cost of Medical Malpractice: Studies of Positive Defensive Medicine in Obstetrics

Several studies have assessed the effect of the threat of medical malpractice lawsuits on the probability that a cesarean section rather than a vaginal delivery would be performed. Birth injuries are a major allegation in medical malpractice suits, far more frequent than suits involving failure to perform a cardiac procedure.[47]

Sloan, Entman, Reilly, et al. (1997), using data from Florida, find no effect of malpractice pressures on the method of obstetrical delivery (cesarean versus vaginal delivery). An earlier study of the effect of the threat of tort on the probability of cesarean section, using data from New York State, also reports no effect.[48]

More recently, Dubay et al. (1999) have used national data from birth certificates from 1990 thorough 1992 to assess the impact of medical malpractice risk on cesarean rates and infant health. They find that a $10,000 reduction in malpractice premiums would result in a 1.4–2.4 percent decline in the cesarean section rate for some mothers, but not for women with the highest socioeconomic status. The authors conclude that a total cap on damages would reduce the number of cesarean sections by 3 percent and total obstetrical charges by 0.27 percent.

Bottom Line on Positive Defensive Medicine

In the end, this review of studies goes to show how hard it is to find evidence that the threat of tort alters practice patterns in an important way. In spite of its limitations, the KM study is well executed. And with the limitations noted, it does provide empirical evidence for positive defensive medicine in a much more rigorous fashion than the anecdotal accounts and the studies based on surveys of physician opinion. On the other hand, the evidence on cesarean sections is mixed. Placed in context, even if direct reforms reduce the cost of care by 5–9 percent, real spending on personal health services increases by about this much in a two-to-three-year period. These reforms are not a panacea for reducing the growth in such expenditures.

The potential effect of the threat of liability may interact with how the physician is paid. For example, any deterrent benefit of liability may be greater under capitation, since providers have a greater incentive to reduce services for financial reasons independent of the threat of lawsuits. Perhaps facing the threat of lawsuits, physicians would be more reluctant to cut services. On the other hand, under fee-for-service, physicians may have a strong incentive to provide tests and perform surgery. The threat of being sued may reinforce this incentive to provide services. However, there is no reliable empirical evidence on this issue.[49]

Good "Bedside Manner" as a Defense Against Lawsuits

Finally, one method of fending off claims has received some, but insufficient, attention. Having a good relationship with patients might be a productive defense against being sued.

In 1992 Hickson et al. (1994) surveyed 963 women who had given birth in Florida in 1987. The identities of the patients' obstetricians were obtained from the vital statistics files. Information on claims and loss experience of these obstetricians was obtained from closed medical malpractice claims information filed with the Florida Department of Insurance. Although mothers with adverse birth outcomes were oversampled, none of the 963 women filed a medical malpractice claim, though twenty-four had spoken with an attorney about this. Women seeing physicians who had the greatest numbers of claims were more likely to complain that they felt rushed, never received explanations for tests, and were ignored. In response to the open-ended question "What part of your care were you least satisfied with?" women seeing obstetricians with a high frequency of medical malpractice claims offered twice as many complaints as those seeing obstetricians who had never been sued. Problems with physician-patient communication were the most commonly offered complaints.

An issue with any one survey conducted at one point in time in one state and for one specialty is its generalizability. In a follow-up study, Hickson et al. (2002) report an association between physicians' patient complaint records and their risk management records for the period January 1992–March 1998. The risk management records, which came from a large multispecialty group, included incidents with and without associated expense. No attempt was made to ascertain whether the risk management records reflected valid or invalid allegations of wrongdoing. Data came from a state other than Florida, but neither the physician group nor the state was specified.

A relatively small number of physicians generated a disproportionate share of complaints. Physicians' complaint frequency was positively correlated with risk management outcomes, ranging from opening medical malpractice files to multiple lawsuits. The authors offer practical suggestions about how management might intervene to improve patient satisfaction and hence reduce the probability of lawsuits.

Other research is consistent with this finding. Levinson et al. (1997) find that physicians without medical malpractice claims provide patients with more orienting and facilitating comments, and use more humor, than those with medical malpractice claims.

Being open and understanding with, and being accessible to, patients may well be a good defense against lawsuits *before* adverse health outcomes occur. After such outcomes occur, it is probably too late to institute many of these actions. However, in recent years, several commentators have suggested that a lawsuit may be averted if the physician apologizes for the outcome and, if appropriate, his or her role in causing it. Lawyers representing the defense and insurers caution physicians that such apologies may compromise the defense if a lawsuit is filed in spite of the apology. "I'm sorry" legislation has been proposed to protect physicians who apologize. However, if enacted, the statutes are likely to be challenged. Given this uncertainty, we feel much more confident in recommending the ex ante approach just described than apologizing after an adverse outcome.

Implications

As with "negative defensive medicine," some "positive defensive medicine" undoubtedly exists. Tests are ordered and procedures performed for which the marginal benefit falls short of marginal cost, just to improve the defense in the event that one is sued for medical malpractice. Statements that physicians order more tests because of the threat of being sued seem persuasive, but estimates of the effect size are never provided.[50] Further, physicians have a financial incentive to order tests and perform procedures. They own labs, CT scanners, and MRIs. Thus, another way of viewing such statements is that physicians use medical malpractice to justify practices that are in their financial interest.

Compared with the substantial rise in the cost of medical care that has occurred, with the exception of the Reynolds et al. (1987) estimate, even high-end estimates of the cost of defensive medicine fall very short as cost containment measures. Reform of medical malpractice, as argued in later chapters, is justified, but not to reduce the amount of positive defensive medicine.

Does the Threat of Lawsuits Deter Medical Injuries?

Medical errors remain frequent even with the threat of tort claims (Institute of Medicine 2000), in spite of the fact that tort liability has existed for years. The question posed here is whether or not the threat of tort liability deters injuries and hence improves quality of care.

The Harvard Medical Practice Study provides the best-known attempt to determine whether the threat of tort indeed deters injuries. Using data from forty-nine hospitals, the authors specified and estimated a two-equation model (Weiler, Hiatt, Newhouse, et al. 1993). One equation measured the effect of the threat of tort on the hospital's injury rate, and a second equation measured the relationship between the threat of tort and characteristics of the area in which the hospital was located that might affect the threat. Most important, the second equation contained exogenous variables that had no theoretical role in the first equation: urbanization and population density. There is no apparent reason that urbanization and population density would directly affect a hospital's injury rate. However, people may be more prone to sue in urban and densely populated areas because social ties among residents are weaker than in a small town or in a rural community. The threat of a malpractice claim was measured as the fraction of negligent injuries (as determined by the researchers' assessments of medical records at the hospital) that actually resulted in a medical malpractice claim. Dependent variables for the main equation were the fraction of hospitalizations that resulted in injuries, and the fraction of all injuries that were attributable to negligence.

Weiler and colleagues (1993, p. 132) are not as cautious about interpreting these findings as they might have been. They state:

Our econometric analysis provides some evidence, though not scientific demonstration, that the higher the number of malpractice claims, the lower the number of negligent injuries experienced by the patient population as a whole (patient population at the hospital). That result emerged from our data even though the host of constraints on the data set combined to reduce rather than enhance the likelihood that such a causal connection would manifest itself. Indeed, some might suggest that our point estimate of the impact of tort on injuries is probably understated.

And they proceed to suggest a reason. Also, Danzon (2000) infers from an insignificant coefficient in the Weiler et al. analysis and her own calculations that the threat of medical malpractice claims provides a nontrivial deterrent effect.[51]

Using the same database, Mello and Brennan (2002) report results of their reanalysis of this issue. The interested reader is urged to consult their forthright description of their investigation. They find inconsistent results, and are unable to replicate the Weiler et al. findings; in the end, they abandon their investigation.[52]

Bottom Line
There is no convincing empirical evidence to indicate that the threat of a medical malpractice claim makes health care providers more careful.

This lack of empirical support represents a serious indictment of medical malpractice as it currently exists and has existed.

Are Doctors Who Are Sued More Frequently Bad Doctors?

If it is not possible to show that the threat of a medical malpractice suit deters medical injuries, is it a least possible to show that physicians with adverse claims experience provide lower-quality care, as the term "quality" is typically understood? The best indication is that an adverse claims record in the past is a reasonable predictor of a future adverse claims experience, but physicians with adverse claims experience are not necessarily worse physicians.

Using data from a survey of 963 women who had delivered in Florida in 1987, merged with data from medical records on some of the same women,[53] Entman et al. (1994) report results of subjective and objective evaluations of the medical records of 484 of the same women.

An independent expert panel of obstetricians and pediatricians identified 166 items that conformed to expected practice in 1987. Perinatal nurses abstracted in detail all medical records according to a specific study protocol. The study team assessed compliance with defined parameters in the areas of documentation, appropriate use of ancillary tests, and events with marginal or inadequate care. Further, the reviewers decided whether the error in care was irrelevant because the outcome was good, or, if the outcome was adverse, whether the error was attributable to some underlying action or inaction.[54] At the end of the review, the team was asked, "Would you refer a member of your family to this obstetrician?"

Although the reviewers found a number of cases in which care was marginal or inadequate, in only 3 percent of cases did they conclude that quality of care was substandard. There was no relationship between prior claims experience of the obstetrician and the technical quality of the practice in 1987 as indicated by the charts on the 484 women. Furthermore, the reviewers concluded that attempting to identify physicians at risk for future clinical errors by using data on prior malpractice claims, such as the National Practitioner Data Bank, may be misjudging the likelihood that substandard care is provided by physicians with prior claims.

In another study based on the survey of the 963 women and the linked birth-death vital statistics file obtained for use in the same study, Sloan, Whetten-Goldstein, Githens, et al. (1995) examine whether birth outcomes were better in areas of Florida in which obstetricians were at higher risk of a lawsuit than in areas in the risk was lower. They considered various types of birth outcomes: fetal death, low Apgar score, death within five days of birth; infant death (death within a year of birth), and death or permanent impairment of the child at five years of age. The authors conclude that no systematic improvement in birth outcomes in response to an increased threat of medical malpractice litigation could be demonstrated.

Discussion and Conclusions

This chapter presents some bad news for both advocates and critics of the current tort system as it applies to medical injuries. For the supporters of the present system, the bad news is that evidence that the threat of tort deters medical injuries is lacking and an adverse claims record is not an indicator that a physician provides poor-quality care. While it is not true that only good doctors are sued (myth 2), being sued is not a marker of being a bad doctor either.

There is also bad news for the critics of medical malpractice as it exists today. Statements asserting that tort law accounts for much of the increase in spending on personal health care services in the U.S. (myth 5) are unfounded, as are statements that this is a major cause of barriers to such services. At most, the threat of being sued accounts for a minor part of the increase in spending. If negative defensive medicine exists, and undoubtedly it does under specific circumstances, more important access barriers are lack of health insurance and geographic inaccessibility. Some argue that the increased cost of care has led to increases in the numbers of uninsured persons in the U.S. and that exit of providers has led to geographic inaccessibility. If that is so, the magnitudes of the changes are small.

Some important theoretical work has been conducted on the effects of alternative liability regimes on physician decisions linking the threat of a lawsuit to more careful behavior on the part of potential tort-feasors.[55] Although there is some empirical support for the notion that the threat of tort induces potential tort feasors to be more careful, thereby deterring injuries in other contexts, the evidence in the context of medical malpractice provides little or no support. In principle, the system should be reformed to provide a much greater incentive for deterrence; as a practical matter, the case would be even stronger if such reform could be supported by empirical evidence.

4

Governments' Responses to Medical Malpractice Crises—and Their Effects

Motivations for Reform

Since the first medical malpractice crisis, physicians' organizations have spearheaded what is widely known as "tort reform."[1] For convenience, this terminology is used here. Ordinarily, one thinks of "reform" as an improvement. Most of the tort reforms that have been implemented to date are based on the underlying assumptions that the amount of litigation is excessive, as are payments to plaintiffs. Any statutory change that results in fewer suits and lower payments is viewed as a "success" and, conversely, as a failure when the statutory changes have no such effect. The yardsticks against which statutory changes have been measured are effects on medical malpractice premiums, the number of medical malpractice claims, and payments per paid claim. These end points reflect the narrow agenda of premium and litigation control. By contrast, a more general view of the social objective is minimization of the sum of social costs: harm from injury to victims, costs of precautions, and costs associated with the use of the legal system, which include legal costs incurred by victims, defendants, and the government in resolving disputes.

There is no consensus that tort reform has been motivated by financial gain; indeed, there is an alternative interpretation. To many physicians, medical malpractice claims are assaults on their sense of capability and distort what they see as competent clinical practice. Such claims seem counter to the concept of the physician as a professional in whom control over the meaning of competence in clinical work is vested.[2] Fielding (1990), taking a sociological perspective, argues that the medical malpractice crisis has been socially construed in economic rather than autonomy terms because traditionally economics has provided a more acceptable basis for labor unrest in the United States.[3]

In the end, whether tort reform, especially tort reform of the conventional variety, is about money, autonomy, or some other nonfinancial goal, it seems unlikely that it is fundamentally about the goals espoused by its proponents, which are said to benefit people in their roles as patients and tax and premium payers. Of course, tort reform is by no means unique in this regard. Irrespective of whether the plea benefits society more generally, private stakeholders routinely seek help from the government. In this sense, "What else is new?"

Past Policy Responses: First- and Second-Generation Reforms

Tort reforms have been classified in various ways. One method divides them into (1) traditional or first-generation reforms and (2) second-generation reforms. First-generation reforms are relatively minor modifications to the existing tort liability system as it applies to medical malpractice or, in some cases, to personal injuries more generally. The ideas underlying second-generation reforms are more recent and involve more fundamental change. Perhaps because they are more novel, but more likely because they lack strong advocates outside of the community of scholars, second-generation reforms have been enacted only rarely. Scholars are often brought in as experts by activist groups advocating a particular policy position, but as T. Baker (2005b) explains, scholars lack both the financial resources and, more important, the incentives to mount sustained efforts in terms of a particular policy position. For scholars, the incentives are to publish and to teach; public advocacy is often frowned upon.

This chapter addresses the states' responses to the three crises that have occurred since 1970. We begin by clarifying the distinction between first-generation and second-generation reforms. Using this distinction, the extent to which legislators are informed by research and the politics surrounding adoption of tort reforms is explored. Next, we discuss how state judiciaries affect the application and impact of tort reforms.

Following this, the remainder of the chapter discusses empirical evaluations of the effects of reforms and the difficulties in evaluating them, as
well as their unintended consequences.

Some first- and second-generation reforms will be discussed in far
greater detail in later chapters, as will some major insurance reforms. An
overview is provided here.

First-Generation Reforms

First-generation reforms include tort and insurance reforms (box 4.1).

Tort Reforms

The *direct* intended effects of the tort reforms may be subdivided into
those that are aimed at size of recoveries, the number of suits filed,
plaintiffs' difficulty of winning, and functioning and cost of the judicial
process. In practice, all reforms affecting size of recovery also affect the
number of suits. If there is less potential reward from suing, there will
be fewer suits. Among reforms aimed at recovery size, states have enacted
dollar limits on nonmonetary, total compensatory, or punitive damages;
permitted payments to be made to plaintiffs periodically rather than as
a lump sum; have eliminated joint and several liability; have modified
the common-law collateral source offset rule; and have restricted the use
of *ad damnum* clauses.

The rationale for periodic payments is to reduce windfalls to plaintiffs
and their families, which would occur, for example, in the event that the
injury victim died before the date anticipated at the time the verdict was
reached. Also, some have argued that juries may assign more modest
dollar amounts when the payment is made on a regular basis than as a
lump sum.[4] A suggested approach to paying damages described in chapter
5 uses the periodic payments concept.

Under the traditional common-law rule, tort awards are not reduced
by the amount of compensation the injury victim receives from sources
other than the tort claim, such as from public and private insurance. The
rationale for disregarding compensation from collateral sources is that
defendants should not benefit from the fact that the injury victim obtained
first-party insurance coverage. Also, if amounts obtained from collateral

Box 4.1
First-Generation Malpractice Reforms

Aimed at size of recoveries' difficulty (or severity)

Caps on awards

Periodic payments of damages

Collateral source offset

Joint and several liability changes

Punitive damage limits

Ad damnum clauses restricted promises

Aimed at the number of suits

Pretrial screening panels

Arbitration

Statutes of limitations

Attorney fee controls

Certificate of merit

Costs awardable

Aimed at increasing plaintiffs' difficulty (or costs) of winning

Expert witness requirements

Informed consent limits

Professional standard of care asserted

Res ipsa loquitur restrictions

Statute of frauds for medical guarantees

Aimed at functioning/cost of judicial process

Mediation

Notice of intent to sue

Precalendar conference required

Preferred scheduling

Insurance Reforms

Patient compensation funds

Joint underwriting associations

Limits on insurance cancellation

Mandates for liability coverage

Reporting requirements

Sources: Bovbjerg (1989); Kinney (1995).

---

sources are deducted from the award, potential tort-feasors will under-estimate the loss to be incurred should they commit a tort. Offsetting collateral sources would reduce the deterrent effect of tort liability. This rule has been modified as part of tort reform either to allow juries to consider payments from the other sources or to require them to do so when they decide on compensatory damages.

States have changed rules for joint and several liability so that one defendant would not be liable for the awards against other defendants. For example, under the traditional rule, a hospital defendant may be obligated to pay the amount that a defendant physician was required to pay but did not have the funds to pay. States have also restricted the use of *ad damnum* clauses.[5] Sometimes plaintiffs' attorneys have claimed huge dollar amounts when the suit is filed. Such large claims have public-ity value and may force the defendant to settle quickly.

Reforms aimed directly at suit frequency include panels and certificates of merit to screen out nonmeritorious claims, arbitration as an alterna-tive to tort, and eliminating the discovery rule. The discovery rule tolls, delays or suspends the statute of limitations for injuries that could not have been discovered with reasonable effort. The rationale is that many medical injuries are not discoverable at the time of the occurrence—for example, when a sponge is left in a patient by a surgeon.

To address the inability of some patients to file timely suits for their injuries, many states have specified that the statute of limitations does not begin until the person has at least a reasonable chance of discovering the injury. However, this has resulted in an extremely long lag between the injury occurrence and the date the claim was filed, which added to the uncertainty of pricing medical malpractice insurance.[6] Other reforms directed at suit frequency involve implementing maximum percentages on plaintiff attorneys' contingent fees, and requiring that the loser in litiga-tion pay the winning party's legal expense ("costs awardable").[7]

A third category of reforms intends to make it more difficult for plain-tiffs to prevail in court. These statutory changes include setting minimum qualifications for experts who testify at trial, setting and defining the types of misleading information that would constitute fraud, and specify-ing the requirements for consent forms. Some reform of consent forms merely outlines the information that needs to be included on written consent forms, while other reforms define the amount of information needed for appropriate disclosure of the risks and benefits of various interventions.

Another reform that makes it more challenging for plaintiffs to prevail is setting standards of care that constitute adequate medical care. Several states have enacted legislation requiring plaintiffs to prove that the standard of care was not met. Previously, leaving a surgical implement in the patient's body constituted sufficient evidence that the surgeon was negligent (*res ipsa loquitur*, which is Latin for "the thing speaks for itself"). Placing limits on the *res ipsa loquitur* doctrine made it more difficult for plaintiffs to recover for injuries; proving an implement was left in the patient's body is easier than proving the occurrence constitutes negligence.

Reforms aimed at improving the functioning and/or boosting the efficiency of the judicial process include offering mediation, requiring a notice of intent to sue, precalendar conferences, and preferred scheduling. Overall, these are relatively minor reforms.

None of the above reforms has addressed the very high administrative costs of the liability system. Also, first-generation reforms retain the same traditional legal system, including the adversarial process, and do not really constrain juries, features that physicians find problematic.[8]

Insurance Reforms

Insurance reforms aim to improve the availability of medical malpractice insurance to health care providers. The two most important of these are patient compensation funds (PCFs) and joint underwriting associations (JUAs).[9] PCFs are state-operated risk pools designed to supplement primary coverage for large losses and thereby stabilize the insurance market. JUAs are designed to be risk pools that provide coverage to providers who are unable to obtain coverage from the private market. The other insurance reforms listed in Box 4.1 are relatively minor.

Second-Generation Reforms

Second-generation reforms make more basic changes in dispute resolution (box 4.2).[10]

Box 4.2
Second-Generation Malpractice Reforms

Use of medical practice guidelines to set the standard of care
Scheduling of damages
Mandated use of alternative dispute resolution methods in lieu of tort
No-fault approaches
Limited no-fault early compensation
Neo-no-fault early compensation
Pure no-fault approaches
Enterprise liability
Private contract to implement malpractice reform

Source: Kinney (1995).

Medical practice guidelines are produced and disseminated by various medical societies and other organizations to provide guidance to physicians on best medical practice, but may also be used as a defense in litigation. The rationale for using medical practice guidelines is to provide clearer guidance to providers, and ultimately to courts, about the boundary between nonnegligent and negligent care. Production and dissemination of guidelines have the potential of improving quality of care in general, and thus have implications well beyond medical malpractice. In principle, use of guidelines should reduce defensive medicine, since all the physician has to do is follow them without feeling a need to exceed them. Use of guidelines in the context of professional liability replace the traditional approach, which has been to rely on physician expert testimony about the usual standard of care in the jurisdiction in which the case is being tried.

As of January 1, 1992, Maine began a five-year demonstration project using standards of care that were defined by guidelines for four specialties (obstetrics-gynecology, radiology, anesthesiology, and emergency medicine). Physicians choosing to participate in the demonstration project could use the guidelines as a legal or affirmative defense in a medical malpractice lawsuit. Most of the physicians in the four specialties signed up to participate. In 1993, the U.S. General Accounting Office predicted that this demonstration would be subject to litigation, which in fact it was.[11] Medical malpractice insurers were concerned at the time that if guidelines as an affirmative defense were found to be unconstitutional, they might be held liable retrospectively.

Next, scheduling damages is an alternative to damage caps.[12] Rather than establish a ceiling on awards, as described in detail in chapter 5, scheduling damages involves a more comprehensive methodology for setting such limits.

Although first-generation reforms included use of alternative dispute resolution (ADR)[13] as a substitute for tort, some proposals make this substitution a requirement. The main advantage to ADR, whether in the form of arbitration[14] or of mediation,[15] is that the process tends to be speedier than a trial. In addition, with binding arbitration, the decision reached is comparable to a jury verdict and can be overturned only if there is evidence of malfeasance in the process of reaching a particular decision.

No-fault approaches are also designed to be substitutes for tort, providing compensation without regard to fault. The no-fault concept has been widely used as a substitute for tort in auto liability and is used in workers' compensation. However, medical no-fault has been implemented in only two states, Florida and Virginia, and then on a very limited basis.[16]

An approach that had garnered some attention in the recent past is the early offer approach, which was proposed by Jeffrey O'Connell over two decades ago (O'Connell 1982). In this approach, a variant on no-fault, there is no compensation for nonmonetary loss, and attorneys' fees are lower; there is a provision for offset of collateral sources; and the defendant can offer a settlement for net economic loss. If the offer is accepted, the defendant pays the plaintiff's attorney fees, which would be on an hourly rather than a contingency basis. If the offer is accepted, the case is terminated. The defendant would presumably make an early offer if the expected loss from doing so was less than the expected loss of proceeding to trial. Thus, when a lawsuit is frivolous, an early offer would not be made. Advocates for this type of proposal argue that it would result in faster compensation, an upshot of which is lower legal expenses.[17]

Enterprise liability shifts liability from the individual health care provider to an enterprise, such as a hospital or an insurer.[18] Advocates for enterprise liability maintain that it would both improve deterrence and reduce litigation cost.[19] To the extent that errors are system errors rather than mistakes on the part of individual providers, enterprises may be more effective in quality assurance than individuals.

Finally, private contracts are offered as an alternative to the traditional tort approach. The rationale for private contracts is that tort liability determines compensation on the basis of standards of care that may differ from the standards that patients might prefer. Private contracts might set out specific circumstances in which providers might be liable, schedule damages, and specify alternative resolution mechanisms when disputes arise.[20]

The strength of private contracts is that they can reflect preferences of individuals. Individuals with higher willingness to pay for safety pay more for such care. However, individual choice opens the door to adverse selection. That is, persons who are more likely to suffer an injury because their health is more fragile may be more willing to pay for contracts offering extra precautions.[21]

Opponents of private contracting as a substitute for tort liability point out that the relationship between the patient and the provider is not one of equal power. A hospitalized patient or even an outpatient may not be well positioned to negotiate with a physician. Courts have overturned contracts reached at the point of service for this reason. But this is not when contracting would occur. Rather, contracts could be options offered to persons at the time they enroll in a health plan. A lower standard of care or a less generous schedule of damages would command a lower premium.

The Politics of Tort Reform

Adoption of First-Generation and Nonadoption of Second-Generation Reforms

By 1990, all states had adopted some form of first-generation reforms. Yet another medical malpractice crisis arose in the early 2000s. By contrast, implementation of second-generation reforms has been quite rare. Litigation delayed implementation of Maine's guideline demonstration.[22] The two states with medical no-fault were slow to enroll injured claimants.

Kinney (1995) reports that physicians and other health care providers oppose most second-generation reforms. Even though there is some support for alternative dispute resolution mechanisms, to the extent that they would streamline the dispute resolution process, she observes that these groups have not supported, or even opposed, using medical practice guidelines to establish the standard of care, especially if plaintiffs can also use the same guidelines offensively. Support for medical no-fault is also lacking.[23] Although they are supported by legal and policy scholars, there is no widespread political support for scheduling damages, enterprise liability, or for private contracting.[24]

Limited Input from the Public and from Researchers in the States' Decision-Making Process

Tort reform is essentially a state issue.[25] Numerous summaries of tort reforms and empirical evidence of their effects exist. Empirical evidence has been generally unimportant in determining legislative outcomes of the tort reform debate.

Prior research indicates that state legislators on the floor rely on consultation with committee members and experts rather than on their own reading of the data.[26] For example, Songer assesses the use of empirical research in legislative committee and floor decision-making in South Carolina, and his work is particularly pertinent because it deals with tort reform.[27] He finds that although the majority of House members on the floor had not read the report prepared for their deliberation and relied on opinions of committees for background to their votes, committee members did review the data prior to making their recommendations. Legislators are asked to vote on many issues and, especially given their part-time status, may have difficulty becoming expert in a number of substantive areas.

Often input from members of the public is lacking in legislative deliberations about tort reform. D'Arcy (1986) provides a case study of legislative decisions about tort reform in the mid-1980s in Illinois. The governor convened a task force consisting of eighteen members from the business, academic, legal, and political communities. The Trial Lawyers' Association, the Illinois Medical Society, and state malpractice insurers were not represented on the task force, but they did make a substantial contribution to the task force's fact-finding process. Although they had an opportunity to do so, no group representing the public interest appeared before the task force.

In the end, many of the task force's recommendations were enacted into law. In general, the task force proved to be a filter for various proposals, even though a few proposals supported by the medical society, but not the task force, were enacted into law. The task force process provided a mechanism for resolving disputes among stakeholders, but with little or no input from the public more generally.

Conflicts between the Legislative and Judicial Branches of State Government

While reformers have been suspicious of judges and juries, there has been little inclination among legislators to allocate more decision-making power to judges. Rather, as Rabin (1988, p. 40) notes, "The more attractive option has been a set of cutoff rules: caps on awards, a bar to joint and several liability, or the elimination of collateral source recovery . . . [but] the implications are rarely articulated in full."

The Role of the State Judiciary in Challenges to Legislatively Enacted Tort Reforms

Many of the legislatively enacted tort reforms have been challenged in state courts. Decision-making in state courts differs from decision-making in federal courts in several important ways. Much of this is due to state judges being elected for fixed terms rather than appointed for life. Further, amendments to state constitutions either by referenda or by popular initiatives are rather common.[28] This is in contrast to the U.S. Constitution, where the process of amending is arduous. Because of the difficulty in amending, the U.S. Constitution has remained relatively stable over the course of its existence.[29]

State constitutions vary considerably from the U.S. Constitution. On average, they are three times the length, average around 120 amendments per constitution, and, in the twentieth Century alone, eighteen states ratified entirely new constitutions.[30] Judicial selection, though not as important as state constitutions, plays an important role in the development of tort law. The role of the judiciary is to interpret and apply legislative and constitutional authority.[31] This gives judges considerable power to interpret laws and the constitution, as well as to fill in any gaps in between with "judge-made" law, also known as common law.[32]

Judges are often not accountable to the public for their decisions, even though judges at the state level are mostly elected.[33] This is due in part to the fact that judicial decisions receive little publicity aside from the rare case that catches the media's attention. This creates concern about judicial policymaking. In a common-law system, judicial policymaking is inevitable and frequently necessary. Nevertheless, the judiciary's power to do so has been challenged, questioned, and criticized for at least a century. As Thomas Jefferson stated in a letter to Judge Spencer Roane in September 1819, "The constitution . . . is a mere thing of wax in the hands of the judiciary, which they may twist and shape into any form they please."[34]

The state courts are split as to the constitutionality of tort reform statutes. States look to each other for guidance, but the holdings vary wildly from state to state and from reform to reform. A quick summary of a small sample of cases demonstrates the variance across the country, court, and reform. In 1996, Ohio passed a comprehensive tort reform law. The law placed limits on noneconomic and punitive damages; created statutes of repose[35] for medical claims and offsets for collateral benefits; and reformed the state's joint and several liability legislation.[36] Close to a year after the reform law came into effect, the Ohio Academy of Trial Lawyers and the AFL-CIO filed suit, challenging its constitutionality.[37] The statute was challenged on the grounds it violated provisions in the state constitution, including separation of powers, the one-subject rule, right to trial by jury, damages for wrongful death, right to remedy, equal protection, prohibition of special privileges, and prohibition of retroactive laws.[38]

The Ohio Supreme Court ruled the statute unconstitutional in toto.[39] The court addressed the other concerns raised in the challenge individually, but did not include the analysis as part of the holding. One issue the court addressed, an issue that appears in other courts as well, is that of separation of powers.[40] Because there was existing case law striking down previous provisions of the bill, the court held the enactment of the bill an intrusion on the exclusive authority of the judiciary.[41] In their opinion, the justices underscored the power struggle among the branches of government, stating that the court and the legislature had "endeavored to comport with the principle of separation of powers and respect the integrity and independence of the other, that is, until now." The court's authority even to hear such a case has been reexamined by the Ohio Supreme Court since 2001.[42]

The Missouri Supreme Court challenged the statute of limitations law in that state.[43] The statute posed a two-year statute of limitations for malpractice actions, but required minors under ten to bring their claim by the age of twelve.[44] A nineteen-year-old challenged this statute, alleging it violated the Missouri Constitution, which guarantees to every citizen "that the courts of justice shall be open to every person, certain remedy afforded for every injury to person. . . ."[45] Ultimately, the court struck down the law as violating a minor's right to access the courts. However, in a well-researched dissent, Judge Welliver lists twenty-three different state cases in which courts have found similar laws constitutional under equal protection grounds.[46] Judge Welliver further suggests that this was a case of inappropriate judicial policymaking, "reminiscent of the *Lochner* era. . . ." when state and federal courts acted like super-legislatures in striking down legislation not consistent with their own views.[47]

Contrary to what many tort reform advocates would have you believe, tort reform does not begin and end with the enactment of legislation. State courts, guided by such legislation as well as their state constitution, play an important role in the application and evolution of the law. As a result, it is often difficult to determine the status and impact of state laws. The uncertainty about whether a particular law will be found to violate the state constitution can cause a lag in the effect on medical malpractice insurance premiums. For this reason, insurers may be slow to adjust premiums in response to a cap on damages.[48] Some studies assess changes from court decisions as well as changes enacted by legislatures. Others do just the latter.

Empirical Evaluations of Effects of Tort and Insurance Reforms

Difficulties in Evaluating Reforms

A substantial number of studies have evaluated impacts of tort reforms.[49] As indicated above, the outcome measure of interest is generally some measure of claims activity, payments, or premiums. Even if these "end points" are correct, several difficulties in evaluating state-level tort reforms remain.

There are many differences in tort reform statutes. For example, in states with damage caps, limits are set at very different levels. In addition, tort reforms are often not enacted singly but in groups, making it more difficult to isolate the effects of particular laws. In spite of these limitations, evaluations of the impact of reforms are critically important. Legislation is often enacted on the basis of specific assumptions about effects, but the various participants in this "market"[50] are clever, and can succeed in circumventing the legislation's original intent. Medical malpractice review panels are a case in point. About half of the U.S. states have enacted statutes authorizing the use of such panels.[51]

The exact details of the panels vary by state, but in general there are three to seven members. One may be an attorney, a health care provider, and/or a judge. Some panels include laypersons. In general, the panels are more informal than a trial, but they do have the power to subpoena witnesses and documents, including medical records, and to hear testimony of expert witnesses, but not at the parties' expense. Arizona is one of these states. An evaluation of this program used insurance company claim files data from before and after implementation of panels.[52] Although the authors find that the panel system did not affect frequency of claims and mean payments of paid claims, there was an increase in the number of disputes in which the parties sought formal adjudication, an increase in the cost of the adjudication process, and an increase in the time within which disputes were resolved.

Functionally the panels simply added another step in the litigation process. For plaintiffs, panels are a convenient method for gathering information and determining the strength of the case for trial. They provide a new, relatively low-cost, method for determining the outcome of the suit. Other unintended consequences are possible (box 4.3). For

Box 4.3
Unintended Consequences of First-Generation Tort Reforms

Sloan and Bovbjerg (1989, pp. 16–17) listed examples of several possible unintended consequences of first-generation tort reforms. Some of these consequences have not been documented as having occurred empirically, yet they remain conceptual possibilities and demonstrate the risks of enacting statutory changes without in-depth analysis of their possible effects.

Example 1
The restriction formally imposed by the legislative change may not in fact be binding.

Legislatures may not realize, for instance, that a statutory limitation on recovery may be higher than the vast majority of recoveries actually paid in recent years. Similarly, a contingent fee limit may be above most contingent fees in the state. [The latter has occurred; see chapter 6.]

Example 2
Changes may be very slow to take effect, given the backlog of cases that can be brought under prereform law.

Example 3
Pressing down the "balloon" at one place may cause a bulge in the balloon elsewhere. For instance, limiting payment for nonmonetary loss may cause juries to be more lenient in their assessments of monetary loss. For this reason, some statutes seek to keep the juries from knowing the limits, which might work before juries hear about them generally, and claimants' lawyers adjust their tactics.

Example 4
A limitation on awards may be seen by various parties as targets or even floors rather than as ceilings. A limit on payments for nonmonetary loss (see chapter 5) could thus seem to become the right value to award in most or even all cases, including the smaller ones. Claimants' attorneys with contingent fees below the statutory limit may use the legislation to justify a fee increase; or the fee schedule may be used to facilitate price-fixing among lawyers. Reforms also may change the patterns of filings. Reductions in the statute of limitations, for instance, may speed up filings or pending cases to beat the new deadlines. Such increases in litigation, however, are likely to be short-lived.

Example 5
Proposals that decrease litigation costs to society, and thus to claimants, may encourage them to bring formerly unremunerative claims and increase the total cost to the system.

To the extent that arbitration is a low-cost alternative to litigation, for example, it may encourage claims. There is some evidence that this has occurred.

Box 4.3
(continued)

Example 6
Even if reforms generate savings in the long run, they may affect premiums much later.

Because of uncertainties, in particular whether specific changes will survive constitutional challenge and how they will be interpreted, medical malpractice insurers may be unwilling to reduce premiums until many years of claims data reassure actuaries that reforms have had their intended effects. There is some empirical evidence to support this, too.

---

example, a limit on payment of nonmonetary loss could be a target for plaintiffs more often than a binding constraint, thus raising payments. Tightening the statute of limitations could have the effect of shifting claims filing to fit the tighter limit. This would, in effect, decrease time to dispute resolution, which is advantageous to the plaintiff, who, unlike the insurer, does not collect investment returns on reserves during the time the case is pending.

Empirical Evidence on First-Generation Reforms on Claims Frequency, Payments per Paid Claim, and Premiums

There is widespread interest in the effects of first-generation tort reforms, and there are a number of excellent reviews of the literature.[53] That the impetus of the reforms was to reduce claims' frequency and severity, and premiums' effectiveness, has been evaluated in these terms. The studies have used regression analysis with reforms and other determinants of frequency, severity, and premiums as explanatory variables (table 4.1).

Among the reforms, the evidence is clearest that caps on damages reduce the frequency and severity of medical malpractice claims. The more recent evidence[54] indicates that caps reduce premiums as well. Even though premiums reflect underlying losses, they also reflect prospective investment returns and rate regulation.[55]

Evidence is uniformly negative on the effects of collateral source offsets on claims severity and claims frequency, and there is no evidence that they reduce premiums. Example 4 in Box 4.3 provides an explanation. Among the reforms aimed most directly at claims frequency, the most

Table 4.1
Study Findings on First-Generation Tort Reforms Based on Regression Analysis

Reform	Significant Decrease in Payments?		Significant Decrease in Claim Frequency?		Significant Decrease in Premiums?	
	Yes	No	Yes	No	Yes	No
Damages cap	Sloan 2 Danzon 1, 2	Zuckerman		Zuckerman	Zuckerman Thorpe	Sloan 1
Collateral source offset	Danzon 1, 2	Sloan 2 Zuckerman	Danzon 2	Zuckerman		Sloan 1 Zuckerman Thorpe
Pretrial screening panels		Danzon 1, 2 Sloan 2 Zuckerman		Danzon 1, 2 Zuckerman		
Shorter statute of limitations	Danzon 1	Sloan 2 Zuckerman	Danzon 2 Zuckerman	Danzon 1	Zuckerman	Sloan 1
Binding arbitration	Danzon 2	Sloan 2 Zuckerman		Danzon 1, 2 Zuckerman		Sloan 1 Zuckerman
Contingent fee limits		Danzon 1, 2 Sloan 2 Zuckerman		Zuckerman		Sloan 1 Zuckerman Thorpe

Key: Danzon 1 = Danzon (1984); Danzon 2 = Danzon (1986); Sloan 1 = Sloan (1985); Sloan 2 = Sloan, Mergenhagen, and Bovbjerg (1989); Thorpe = Thorpe (2004); Zuckerman = Zuckerman, Bovbjerg, and Sloan (1990). This table reproduces a table in Studdert, Mello, and Brennan (2004), with the Thorpe reference added.

analyzed are pretrial screening, binding arbitration, attorney fee limits, and, to a lesser extent, costs awardable. The evidence on binding arbitration, although mixed, is more positive than for the other reforms. For the latter, more often than not, measures of these policies have been statistically insignificant in studies of claims frequency, severity, and premiums. Effects of shorter statutes of limitation are mixed.

Effects of periodic payments of damages have not been assessed.[56] There is no evidence on effects of joint and several liability changes or on punitive damage limits, although finding much of an effect for the latter seems unlikely since punitive damages have rarely been awarded in medical malpractice cases, at least until very recently.

The other tort reforms listed in box 4.1 are much more limited in purpose and scope, and their effects have not been evaluated statistically. The insurance reforms seem to have been instrumental in restoring availability of coverage during the 1970s.[57]

Some studies have assessed dependent variables other than claim frequency and severity, and premiums. Born, Viscusi, and Carleton (1998), Barker (1992), and Thorpe (2004) find that damage caps improve insurer profitability. However, Viscusi, Zeckhauser, Born, et al. (1993) do not find a statistically significant relationship between damage caps and profitability.[58] That damage caps would increase profitability is plausible, since insurers have been reluctant to reduce premiums immediately following enactment of reforms, in particular since the reforms are subject to constitutional challenges.[59] Thus, it would not at all be surprising that a reform that decreases losses, such as damage caps, improves insurer profitability.

Using data on jury verdicts in California that were subject to the state's $250,000 limit on payments for nonmonetary loss, Studdert, Yang, and Mello (2004) document that the limit resulted in much greater (seven times greater) absolute dollar reductions in awards for persons incurring a grave injury than a minor injury. For this reason, the authors conclude that such limits are regressive.

Effects of Damage Caps on Physician Supply

The first studies on the effects of damage caps on physician supply found mixed results. Klick and Stratmann (2003) report that states that adopted caps experienced a 3 percent increase in physician supply relative to those without caps, holding other factors constant. By contrast, Matsa (2007) fails to find an effect. More recently, two studies have found that caps increase physician supply.

Encinosa and Hellinger (2005) find that damage caps increased the supply of physicians over the period 1985–2000.[60] The caps had a larger impact on physician supply in rural counties than on supply in all areas. Caps on nonmonetary loss set at or below $250,000 had more of an effect on the supply of surgeons and obstetricians-gynecologists than caps set above this dollar level, presumably because they are more likely to have been finding in the former case. While the effects of damage caps on physician supply are statistically significant at conventional levels, the magnitude of effect is to raise physician supply by about 2 to 3 percent, on average, and by up to between 5 and 6 percent for $250,000 caps in rural counties. Thus, while the effects are statistically significant, they are insufficiently large to improve patient access to care in important ways.

Kessler, Sage, and Becker (2005) use the methodology developed by Kessler and McClellan (1996) to assess the effects of "direct" and "indirect" reforms on physician supply. Recall that the direct reforms include caps on damage awards, abolition of punitive damages, no mandatory prejudgment interest, and collateral source offset reform. The indirect reforms include caps on contingent fees, mandatory periodic payments, joint and several liability reform, patient compensation fund, and statute of limitations reform. The authors measure physician supply relative to state population of physicians, physicians with less than twenty years' experience, physicians with greater than twenty years' experience, and physicians in nongroup practice. There was a separate analysis of physicians in emergency medicine, anesthesiology, radiology, and general surgery. The rationale for considering doctors separately by years of experience is that more experienced or older doctors may be more likely to retire in response to an increased threat of medical malpractice and/or higher premiums. The hassle factor may be greater for nongroup physicians than physicians practicing in large groups.

Controlling for fixed differences (differences that do not vary over time) among states, market factors and various political characteristics of the state, and implementation of the direct reforms (which include caps), physician supply increased by 2 to 3 percent, on average. The effects were greater more than three years after adopting than before this. Direct reforms had a greater effect on retirements and deterring entry into the state than on the propensity of physicians to move between states.

The two studies provide empirical support for the assertions that adopting such reforms as damage caps can increase physician supply over and above what it would be otherwise. Yet the effects, on average, are not large, and this policy should be compared with alternative methods for increasing physician supply. The implication is that damage caps alone are unlikely to be a panacea for communities with few or no physicians. And given the effect sizes, it is unlikely that the threat of lawsuits has led physicians to flee specific states.

Empirical Evidence on Second-Generation Reforms

Second-generation reforms seek more fundamental change, yet most of the reforms have not been implemented. Among those that have, the most empirical evidence exists on no-fault as a substitute for tort. When no-fault has been applied to the medical field, it has been applied in a very limited way.[61] For what it covers, no-fault has greatly reduced the overhead of administration below what it is in tort. Yet there is no indication that no-fault has substituted for tort. Tort claims frequency in areas covered by no-fault remain high.

The Institute of Medicine (2002) and the Governor's Select Task Force on Healthcare Professional Liability (2003) in Florida have recommended pilot projects of second-generation or system reforms.[62] In contrast, the overwhelming majority of states saw no reason for study prior to widespread implementation of first-generation or conventional tort reforms. And, when evaluated, most of these reforms have shown no effect, even on the goals they were implemented to achieve.

Conclusions and Implications

After three decades of experience with state tort reform and evaluations covering a period almost as long, the key finding is that only damage caps have consistently affected various outcomes of interest, including

claim frequency and severity, medical malpractice premiums, and physician supply. Profitability of insurers has also increased in states with
caps, at least in the short run. However, Studdert, Yang, and Mello
(2004) conclude from their empirical analysis that California's single
$250,000 cap is unfair in the sense that it imposes a much greater reduc-
tion in payments to plaintiffs with grave injuries than to those with minor
injuries. The authors recommend scheduled damages or maximum payments within each severity category.

Such evidence should be sufficient for private stakeholders to argue
for caps, at both the state and federal levels. However, except for the
modest impact on physician supply, caps offer nothing for patients,
health insurance premium payers, and taxpayers.

One is left with an unsatisfying feeling that there must be a better way
than caps. Perhaps some second-generation reforms can be recast in ways
that will have more popular appeal while retaining their ability to improve system performance. The following chapters address such reforms,
except for the chapter on contingent fees, which argues that limiting such
fees is a step in the wrong direction.

In discussing his finding that only caps have statistically significant
effects, Thorpe (2004) states:

> At issue is whether we should have short-term, stop-gap solutions to slow the
> growth in premiums or use the recent experience to more fundamentally evaluate
> and perhaps reform the liability system. The recent spike in medical malpractice
> insurance premiums allows us an opportunity to reexamine whether the tort
> system is achieving its goals. If it isn't, what changes in the system would improve
> the dual goals of deterrence and compensation? The results suggest that capping
> awards may improve the profitability of malpractice carriers and reduce premi-
> ums. Whether this is socially desirable or improves the goals of deterrence and
> compensation remains an open question."[63]

Finally, the discussion of second-generation reforms and the goals of
tort in general are part of a larger discussion that the United States and
perhaps some other industrialized societies should have as well. Issues
of social justice raised by a broad taxpayer-supported no-fault program
for iatrogenic injuries are pertinent to several major private and social
insurance programs as well. While addressed in response to a crisis in
medical malpractice, the efficiency and equity issues of no-fault are
common to these other programs as well.[64]

5

Ceilings on Nonmonetary and Total Losses

Compensation for Personal Injuries: The Alphabet Soup

As of 2005, more than half of the U.S. states had some form of limit on awards, mostly on nonmonetary awards, but some on total awards.[1] The attraction of such limits is that they do reduce mean payment per claim (claim "severity") by as much as 40 percent.[2] Some studies show reductions in premiums as well, but by a smaller amount than claim severity,[3] while others show no effect on premiums.[4] Yet even in states with limits on damages, premiums have risen appreciably in absolute terms.[5] Findings from research on limits on damages and other statutory changes in medical malpractice are similar to those for other types of tort claims, such as automobile liability.[6] One reason for the smaller effect on premiums is that laws limiting awards have been subject to constitutional challenges in the states, which have resulted in the laws being overturned in a minority of instances.[7] Insurers have been cautious about granting premium reductions, given the uncertainties of outcomes of legal challenges.[8]

Given that these laws have been more effective than any other type of tort reform in reducing losses from medical malpractice claims, they have substantial political support among health care providers, medical malpractice insurers, and some attorneys who represent defendants in medical malpractice litigation. The advocates for limits on awards frequently cite the success of California's 1975 medical malpractice law.[9] The major criterion for success is the relatively low growth in medical malpractice premiums since the 1975 law was enacted.[10] The most notable feature of this law was a ceiling on awards for nonmonetary loss (a cap on pain and suffering.)

Awards are meant to make the injury victim whole. This is the rationale for compensatory damages. Compensatory damages is a general category which includes payment for monetary losses, such as from medical care, lost earnings, and other services that are directly attributable to the injury. Payment for nonmonetary loss is also part of compensatory damages; however, nonmonetary loss can go under several headings, depending on the circumstances of the case, such as payment for pain and suffering, emotional distress, loss of consortium, loss of enjoyment of or a chance at life, and so on. The object of compensatory damages is to make an individual as well off as before the injury occurred. When there is permanent damage to health, this cannot be accomplished by restoring the person to his or her original health. However, assuming that people get utility out of money as well as health, money is used to compensate for the loss in health.

The rationale for payment for nonmonetary loss is that not all of the loss is monetary. To exclude payment for nonmonetary loss would reduce the potential deterrent effects of tort.[11] Injuries can be painful. They can result in loss of a lifelong partner. They can limit a person's opportunities for enjoyment of life, such as participation in nonprofessional sports.

However, theory is one thing; in practice, full compensation may be infeasible when the injury is seriously disabling with the result that loss is irreplaceable.[12] Another concern about payment for nonmonetary loss is much more widespread, namely, that there is no objective yardstick for ascertaining the extent of the nonmonetary loss even if compensation could, in principle, be made in full.

Many injuries are temporary. That is, the person was injured and after some time, the injury is self-correcting or, frequently, there is a medical or surgical intervention to correct the injury. Then payment is made to compensate for the period during which health was impaired.

Many injuries are permanent. In such cases, accuracy in payment for future monetary losses is difficult since computing such loss involves a prediction, which by its nature involves uncertainty, such as the injury victim's longevity; the level of care, which will be indicated at various points of time; the prices of such care; and the future ability of the individual to engage in remunerative activities. There is uncertainty about future rates of general inflation, and thus which discount rate to use. Computing future nonmonetary loss also involves many assumptions.

In several European countries, the process of computing future loss is simplified by having tables giving values of loss depending on such factors as the injury victim's age and degree of impairment. There is, however, a trade-off between adherence to table values, which offers simplicity and precision, and the facts of the particular case.[13]

Punitive damages are the final component of a medical malpractice award. They are intended to punish the defendant for wrongful conduct and to deter others from engaging in such behavior. They are not based on the severity of the plaintiff's injury, but rather on the culpability of the defendant's conduct and on an assessment of the amount required to get the defendant to notice the award. Thus, a large corporation may be assessed a larger punitive damage than an individual, such as a health professional, for the same injury. In contrast to product liability, punitive damages are rarely awarded in medical malpractice cases.[14] Studdert and Brennan (2000) report that punitive damages are awarded in less than 1.5 percent of medical malpractice verdicts. Nevertheless, many states have enacted laws to limit such damages in medical malpractice as well as other kinds of personal injury cases.[15]

Given that limits on awards curb losses paid by defendants and, to a lesser and more uncertain extent, medical malpractice premiums, they make good private policy. As one commentator observes, "Caps are a political success. First, they are popular and widely enacted. Second, caps in general work as intended."[16] For this reason, the American Medical Association and various other organizations representing health care providers have placed enacting caps at both federal and state levels at the top of their political agendas. There is some question, however, whether or not, at least in their present form, caps make good social or public policy.

Is There a Compelling Rationale for Paying for Nonmonetary Loss?

The Controversies
However controversial ascertaining monetary loss might be, payment for nonmonetary loss is all the more so. Not only has nonmonetary loss been

limited by many more states than has total loss, but certain proposals for reform, such as medical no-fault,[17] either severely restrict payment for such loss or eliminate it entirely.

Paying for nonmonetary loss is controversial for several reasons. Probably foremost, there is no objective standard by which to measure an injury victim's physical pain or mental anguish. Such concepts as "pain and suffering," "loss of consortium," and "loss of enjoyment of life," all elements of nonmonetary loss, are somehow unreal and cannot be quantified. That these losses are unreal is clearly contradicted by the fact that a substantial number of individuals seek medical care for these supposedly "unreal" conditions. Also, people frequently purchase prescription and over-the-counter drugs to reduce pain and discomfort. That these conditions cannot be quantified is further contradicted by the fact they *have* been quantified, and the results of such quantification have been published in refereed medical journals.[18] Specialists in the field of decision analysis have developed techniques for quantifying nonmonetary loss and are constantly refining them.

In addition to the difficulties in quantifying, some scholars have noted that there is no voluntary market for insurance for nonmonetary losses. The argument is that if there is no voluntary market for such loss, there should be no payment for such loss under tort.[19]

In a comprehensive review of the medical malpractice literature aimed at an audience of economists, Danzon (2000, p. 1373) argues:

> that consumers do not voluntarily buy coverage for non-monetary loss in any other private or social insurance program suggests that such coverage may not be worth its cost. The lack of a voluntary market for insurance for non-monetary losses may reflect severe ex post moral hazard of exaggeration of such losses, which cannot be objectively measured. Assuming that this moral hazard of loss exaggeration is at least as severe in the tort system, the evidence from private choices supports the case for limits on compensation for nonmonetary loss through the tort system.

This quotation contains three statements. The first is the observation that people do not purchase insurance for nonmonetary loss. This statement is clearly valid. The second is that such insurance may not be purchased because people would have a tendency to overstate their pain, which cannot be directly observed by others. This form of moral hazard may be a reason that a voluntary market for insurance for nonmonetary loss does not exist. This point also is not controversial. The third statement, that exaggeration of nonmonetary loss means that there should be limits on compensation for such loss from tort, is very controversial and likely to be wrong.[20] The legal process of ascertaining nonmonetary loss can be expensive. But the adversarial process of a jury trial permits examination and cross-examination of assertions of loss.

Croley and Hanson (1995, pp. 1842–1844) make a further argument for compensation for nonmonetary loss. Even if there is no private market for nonmonetary loss insurance, the Consumers Union, which purports to represent the interests of consumers, has consistently supported compensation for such loss.

Analytical techniques for quantifying such phenomena as pain and suffering have been applied in research contexts, but they are otherwise not in widespread use. Individuals' willingness to pay to avoid specific injuries, and pain and suffering from these injuries, is elicited from surveys in which respondents have nothing to gain by suggesting that they place a high value on the underlying loss. The goal of this research is to determine the average willingness of survey respondents, as a group, to pay. By contrast, in the context of insurance, if the payment were made to depend on the injury victim's depiction of his or her own pain and suffering, surely there would be an incentive to exaggerate. In litigation, experts for plaintiffs have an incentive to compute the highest possible values of damages incurred. On the other hand, experts for the defense, in criticizing the estimates of the plaintiffs' experts, have the opposite incentive. Every defendant has a right to have these counterarguments presented at trial on his or her behalf. Therefore, it is not at all clear that outlandish estimates presented on behalf of plaintiffs would prevail.

The lack of a practical, objective standard which can be applied to *individual* cases is likely to be the major reason that there is no private market for insuring against nonmonetary loss. It is easy to understand why an insurer would not offer health or disability insurance for nonmonetary loss. Any insurance company offering this kind of coverage in addition to insurance for financial loss would potentially fall prey to "adverse selection." That is, people who are particularly pain-prone would demand such coverage disproportionately. And, without a benchmark, insurers would be at the mercy of the injury victim's assertion of the extent of such loss, and such claimants would indeed have an incentive to exaggerate the loss. As explained in greater detail below, lack of an objective benchmark in the United States is also a problem for juries' estimation of nonmonetary loss.

An underlying presumption is that the law should provide the level of damages, and only those damages, which a fully informed consumer, in advance of the injury, would choose to be paid if injured. This makes the decision of the amount of nonmonetary damages to pay depend on what a sovereign consumer's preferences are.[21] People are willing to pay for additional health and safety, for example, in their cars and to forgo higher wages for greater safety in employment.[22] The willingness to pay for air bags and to forgo wages need not reflect only monetary loss associated with an injury. One reason people want air bags is that motor vehicle crashes hurt, not just because they may lead to wage loss and medical expense.

There are more practical reasons for paying for nonmonetary loss. Plaintiffs must pay a considerable part of the award—generally 33 to 40 percent—to their lawyers.[23] These fees can be paid at least in part out of the compensation for nonmonetary loss.[24] Although seemingly plausible at first glance, this argument is a weak rationale for paying nonmonetary losses. Taken to the extreme, if contingent fees were 67 percent of compensation, payment for nonmonetary loss would even be higher than it is today.[25] Plaintiffs' attorneys and consumer advocates have argued that caps on damages, with zero damages being a special case of a cap, have made it difficult for some injury victims to obtain legal representation, even when their cases are valid, because of the limited payouts.[26] Some analysts, however, have correctly noted that the extent to which caps have created a barrier to legal representation is unknown.[27]

A more convincing argument can be made on equity grounds. For example, in a well-publicized case from the authors' own university, Duke University, a Mexican teenager died after a second heart-lung transplant because, for the first transplanted organs, the blood types of the organ donor and recipient did not match.[28] Future monetary loss was relatively low since the woman had not acquired skills that would have commanded high compensation in the labor market. Yet clearly the family was indeed made worse off by the pain and the suffering of the experience and the subsequent loss of a daughter. In this type of case, paying the family more than if their daughter were a successful business executive would probably violate social norms of equity. Many citizens would plausibly feel that an executive's family should not receive considerably more compensation than this low-income family, particularly given the nature of the error.

Legal Challenges to Damage Caps

Several constitutional theories have been used in legal challenges to damage caps in litigation at the state level.[29] Limits have been challenged using the open-courts guarantee included in most state constitutions. An example of an argument employed in these challenges is that a dollar limit denies catastrophically injured patients the right to collect their full damages, and that the law creating caps contains no offsetting provision that would be of benefit to plaintiffs. A second theory is that limits violate the right to trial by jury, the premise in one state being that juries must be able to determine the appropriate level of damages, and limits are inconsistent with this right. Third, these laws have been subjected to claims of lack of equal protection. Laws that create special categories or classifications, such as distinguishing between medical malpractice and other personal injury victims, may be subject to this type of legal challenge.[30]

Due process challenges have been brought against nonmonetary damages caps. In one variant, the argument is that the standard damage cap deprives plaintiffs of the full amount of compensation without giving them an opportunity to present evidence as to why full compensation is appropriate. The separation of powers theory argues that many state constitutions vest judicial powers exclusively in the judicial system. Thus, in passing limits on damages, the legislature infringes on a judicial prerogative.

More often than not, limits on nonmonetary losses (comprising the majority of legal challenges) and on total losses have survived constitutional challenges, particularly the challenges of the former. Rather than rely on theoretical arguments or arguments about economic justice, a major and successful defense of such limits is a very practical one, namely, that they have the effect of stabilizing medical malpractice insurance premiums. In any case, payment for nonmonetary loss is most likely here to stay.

The public policy issue is less whether or not to pay it, and more about the process involved in setting damages in particular cases. Seen from this perspective, there is clearly considerable room for improvement.

In malpractice trials, large awards command a lot of public attention, but they often are not actually paid in full, given subsequent reductions of awards on appeal.[31] The complaints voiced in the public arena, however, tend to be about the magnitude of total awards, not specifically about the nonmonetary component.

Even for jury awards, the allocation between awards for monetary and nonmonetary losses is unknown. In many states, jurors are not instructed to divide the award in this way. In some states, for example, where there is a cap on nonmonetary loss, jurors are instructed to make such an allocation for purposes of complying with the statutory cap, but data have not been collected systematically, at least until recently.[32] It is often difficult, and generally impossible, to disentangle payments for each purpose from extant databases.[33] It is often possible to know the plaintiff's initial demand for payment, but not to separate payment for monetary from payment for nonmonetary loss from payments made in settlements.

Few medical malpractice claims reach the trial stage and relatively few verdicts are decided in favor of plaintiffs.[34] The vast majority of medical malpractice claims are either dropped by plaintiffs or settled. Then there is no compensation at all.

Imperfections in the Current System of Ascertaining Payment for Nonmonetary Loss

The relevant public policy issue is much less whether or not to compensate for nonmonetary loss, and more about the process involved in determining damages in particular cases. Seen from this perspective, there is clearly considerable room for improvement. Whether viewed at close range or at a distance, the current methods for determining nonmonetary loss leave much to be desired.

Even though the objective of compensatory damages is to make the injury victim "whole," the law in the U.S. gives very little guidance as to how damage awards are to be calculated. In much the same way, the process whereby such losses are computed by juries is not well understood.[35] For financial losses, there are prices and units of loss. For pain and suffering, by contrast, there are no direct measures. Values must be imputed, but the law gives no guidelines for valuation. Whereas precedent influences legal decisions, there is no role for precedent in computing compensatory loss. Each decision is independent and presumably highly individualized to fit the particular circumstances of the case.

Not surprisingly, variability in compensatory damages is the consequence—in large part by design, since circumstances of individual cases are thought to be highly variable. Not only is there variability, but there is empirical evidence that patterns of awards reflect the income, racial, and ethnic composition of the area in which cases are tried, and hence the composition of the jury,[36] as well as the type of case being tried—factors that should have no bearing on the individual plaintiff's loss. Awards for the same injury appear to be higher in medical malpractice than in automobile liability cases,[37] suggesting that juries take into account "deep pockets" of defendants in medical malpractice cases. An alternative interpretation is that auto injury victims are even more undercompensated than those with medical injuries.[38]

High payment variability—especially at the upper end of award sizes—coupled with the prospect of even higher variability over time, may be expected to have several untoward consequences. First, high awards may be precedent-setting, particularly in determining future settlement amounts.[39] Given unpredictability of the outcome of the claim, health care providers are unable to predict how their behavior will be judged if that behavior causes harm, which reduces any deterrent effect the threat of lawsuits might otherwise have.[40]

Second, once harm has occurred and a claim has been filed, the parties to the litigation are less likely to settle to the extent that their predictions of the outcome at verdict diverge.[41] Third, since insurers face greater risk, the availability of liability insurance is likely to be decreased and, when insurance is available, premiums are likely to be higher to reflect this added nondiversifiable risk.[42]

Decisions at verdict may influence terms of subsequent settlements, and the law provides no objective benchmarks for valuing nonmonetary loss. Juries are generally given broad instructions for valuing loss, such as that payment should providing "fair compensation" or "reasonable compensation," rather than providing specific criteria for valuing loss.[43] Juries do not have the benefit of knowing how loss has been determined in the past in roughly comparable situations. Such data are generally unavailable, and there is no provision for providing it even if such information were available. There is no requirement that the rationale or methods used for arriving at a specific value be justified or even explained. An appeals process exists, but appellate judges can also lack objective standards for assessing loss. Postverdict reductions in awards often occur, but most often in a settlement arrived at by the parties.[44]

Flawed Public Policy Responses

The public policy response to what is perceived as capricious and excessive awards in medical malpractice has been to impose limits on payment for nonmonetary damages (e.g., California), and in some states payment for total loss (e.g., Indiana). Not all limits on nonmonetary and total are fixed in nominal dollar terms as is California's, but most are.

Conceptually, the assumption underlying flat caps is that injury victims with large losses are relatively overcompensated, but there is no empirical evidence to support this assumption. In fact, the only systematic comparison of injury cost versus compensation in medical malpractice indicates that such injury victims are undercompensated on average.[45] Many plaintiffs receive no compensation for their injuries, either because their cases are dropped or because they lose at trial. On average, even those plaintiffs who won at trial received only 22 percent more than their monetary loss. The 22 percent was presumably for nonmonetary loss. This hardly implies that the system is out of control *on average*. Further, as explained above, imposing caps on payment for nonmonetary loss may have a disproportionate effect on low wage earners and on persons with severe injuries.[46]

In addition, it seems highly implausible that some awards are "too high" while *no* award is "too low." If juries make errors at the high end, presumably they make errors at the low end as well—for example, as a reaction to testimony by an expert for the plaintiff whom the jurors dislike.

Imposition of a cap not indexed to the rate of inflation for the economy overall or for medical inflation in the limit is both arbitrary and unfair. Considering inflation that has occurred since 1975, California's cap was effectively about $70,000 around 2005, and with inflation, its value was falling fast.[47] Pace et al. (2004) quantified the effect of not allowing the California cap to rise with increase in overall prices. Rather than reduce payments by 30 percent, which is what their empirical analysis revealed the effect of California's cap to have had, indexing the cap would have reduced payments by 21 percent (through 1999).

In a conversation the first author had with an attorney-physician who has advocated actively for flat caps, the latter argued that allowing the limits to increase with increases in the Consumer Price Index would introduce too much complexity. Yet it seems ironic that policies requiring indexing of Medicare fees for physicians are promoted by the same organizations that promote flat, unindexed caps. If an unindexed limit were the solution to an excessive number of medical malpractice claims and payments, then it could become a precedent for paying for particular medical or surgical procedures judged by a few experts to be in "excess supply." Social Security benefits are indexed annually by the Social Security Administration to account for inflation, as are damage values from tables developed for providing guidance as to levels of compensation for personal injury in some large European countries. Complexity is not an issue for such benefits.

In California, the Supreme Court upheld caps on nonmonetary damages.[48] However, in other states, damage caps have been held to violate federal equal protection and due process guarantees, and to violate various state constitutional provisions that give individuals the right to trial by jury.[49] They are especially unconstitutional given that no corresponding societal quid pro quo existed to replace the victim's right to full recovery.[50] This argument stems from a focus on the rights of individuals who were injured.[51]

From another perspective, caps in particular, and reforms in general, are meant to benefit a larger class of people, nonclaimants. By virtue of these policies, nonclaimants enjoy greater accessibility to medical care at lower fees and premiums.[52] However, as discussed in chapter 3, caps may adversely affect access to care and have a minor effect in reducing health care costs.

In sum, a flat dollar limit on damages, expressed in nominal dollars, does have the advantage of simplicity. However, it is too simple and is a bad precedent.

Better Ways to Reform Payment for Nonmonetary Loss in Medical Malpractice Registries

Lack of Guidance to Juries

Juries are asked to set damages in individual cases on a one-time basis, without any prior experience in performing this task. Nor do they have the benefit of prior experience of other juries. With exceptions of data collection efforts, which are not part of the judicial system, there are no systematic, official records of deliberations or findings to inform future jury decisions. Some institutional memory exists in trial judges' memory of prior legal decisions and in reported appellate decisions. Nevertheless, there is in general little to guide jurors in valuing loss to the plaintiff.

A few states (e.g., Florida and Texas) collect information on closed medical malpractice claims. At the federal level, the National Practitioner Data Bank collects information on all closed medical malpractice claims resulting in payment. Although useful for some purposes, such as a rough guide for monitoring quality and for research, this information is insufficient to serve as a guide for juries in ascertaining the appropriate size of an award.

For one thing, there is insufficiently detailed information on the severity of the injury and on the circumstances under which the injury occurred.[53] Moreover, for any particular case, it is not currently possible to know about the existence of similar cases and how they have been decided.[54]

Scheduling Damages

Rather than set a limit on the maximum size of an award, it would be preferable to set payment criteria for all awards, not only the large ones.[55] Scheduling damages involves such an approach. Because scheduling affects the whole distribution, not just the upper tail, it is conceptually superior to flat caps on grounds of equity of payment to claimants with very severe injuries relative to those with less severe injuries ("vertical equity"), and has been advocated by several commentators and by the Institute of Medicine.[56] The trial bar opposes this approach on grounds that it would limit the ability of plaintiffs to make a case for their special circumstances and for their attorneys to exercise skill in arguing the merits of these circumstances. Such flexibility, however, must be measured against the horizontal (equal or unequal treatment of equals in terms of injury severity) and vertical inequities of the current system.

Bovbjerg, Sloan, and Blumstein (BSB; 1989) propose three approaches worthy of consideration for reforming payment for nonpecuniary loss in medical malpractice as replacements for flat caps as well as for use in states without any limits on awards. Since they were proposed in 1989, these ideas have elicited interest in the academic community, but they have not received serious consideration by any state, probably for several reasons. First, organized medicine finds flat caps more attractive. Second, the trial bar does not wish to introduce any limitations on determinations of awards. And third, the proposals have no proactive supporters. The road from the university seminar room to the political marketplace is often not well trodden.

The first approach is an *award matrix for nonmonetary loss*. The matrix would display awards for nonmonetary loss for injuries with specific characteristics. The underlying presumption is that payment for nonmonetary loss should be based on objective factors, such as the person's age or life expectancy, severity of injury, and type of body part affected. More permanent and serious injuries are likely to have higher underlying nonmonetary loss, although the relationship between severity rank and loss may not be linear.

Existing injury severity scales may be used to classify injuries by severity levels, such as a nine-point injury severity scale in widespread use, which varies from "emotional only" to "permanent grave" injuries and death (table 5.1). The nine categories of injury severity are broad, rather objective, and mutually exclusive, thus permitting relatively little upward "creep" in category assignment by advocates of the plaintiff. Assignment to a category would be open to challenge in any event.

For temporary injuries, a younger person may recover more quickly than would an older person. However, for permanent injuries, a younger person would be expected to have to endure the nonmonetary loss for a more extended time. Thus, it would be appropriate to cross-classify by age as well as severity of injury. The values in the matrix could be based on prior awards, past research valuing life and quality of life, and/or set by a state legislature.

The approach of basing matrix values on prior awards for nonmonetary loss by past juries, adjusted by trial and appellate courts, is straight-

Table 5.1
Severity of Injury Scale

Severity of Injury	Examples
1. Emotional only	Fright, no physical damage
2. Temporary insignificant	Lacerations, contusions, minor scars, rash. No delay in recovery
3. Temporary minor	Infections, mis-set fractures, fall in hospital. Recovery delayed
4. Temporary major	Burns, surgical material left, drug side effect, brain damage. Recovery delayed
5. Permanent minor	Loss of fingers, loss of or damage to organs. Includes nondisabling injuries
6. Permanent significant	Deafness, loss of limb, loss of eye, loss of one kidney or lung
7. Permanent major	Paraplegia, blindness, loss of two limbs, brain damage
8. Permanent grave	Quadriplegia, severe brain damage, lifelong care or fatal prognosis
9. Death	

Source: National Association of Insurance Commissioners (1980).

forward in principle. In practice, states would have to set up a registry to assemble the data. The matrix would be subject to judicial review and might be modified accordingly.

There is a large literature on valuing life,[57] but it is not sufficiently specific to fill in cells of a matrix with a nine-point severity scale, several age categories, and data splits by body parts. This would require more research.[58] There is much more evidence on willingness to pay to avoid a death than for outcome measures set according to a dimension of quality of life. Values are based on inferences from market data or from surveys eliciting individuals' willingness to pay to avoid certain adverse outcomes.[59]

Also, in using estimates of value from value of life or quality of life studies, one would be making the implicit assumption that the context by which life or its quality is lost does not matter. That is, losing a life in a war, which has popular support, in a hit-and-run motor accident, or at the hands of an incompetent surgeon in the operating room have the same nonmonetary loss. Yet the context in which the injury occurred may matter. On the other hand, it may be desirable that awards are made context-free and solely on more objective factors. Values would be inflated by a price index, such as the Consumer Price Index.

Previous research has documented that (1) payments rise monotonically through the nine injury severity categories, with payments for loss of life being lower on average than for persons with grave, permanent impairments and (2) despite evidence of a plausible relationship between *mean* payments and injury severity, there is considerable variation in payments within each severity category.[60] This suggests that the legal system is taking more into account than severity per se in assessing damages. Even though paying on a nine-point scale would improve vertical equity over flat caps, merely adjusting for severity may not be an improvement over the current approach in states with flat caps, which is not to reduce payments in amounts below the statutory ceilings.

In principle, this method is simple, but it would require several steps to implement. In its defense, however, it is conceptually more appropriate than a flat cap. Payments based on an award matrix for nonmonetary loss would probably not at all resemble those based on a flat cap.

A simpler variant of the award matrix, which encompasses all awards, would be to use *flexible ranges* in lieu of caps. This system would regulate the lowest and the highest payments for nonpecuniary loss. The state would designate payments in the lowest quartile and the top deciles of payments (assuming that the data were made available through a registry or in some other way).[61] Payments for nonmonetary loss would be limited at both extremes, raised at the bottom and lowered at the top. Flexible ranges are less likely to be opposed by the trial bar since they leave some room for the application of lawyers' skill in obtaining payment for clients. However, such ranges may violate the principle of vertical equity since payments for lower and higher severity injuries may overlap.

Under a third approach, a common set of *injury scenarios* would be developed and assembled to assist juries in valuing nonmonetary loss. Juries would be given a notebook containing descriptions of particular injuries and descriptions of the pain and suffering associated with each. Dollar values would be attached to each scenario, but jurors would not be told the values. Values associated with each scenario could be set by the state legislatures, perhaps with the guidance of a study commission. Dollar amounts would be assigned to the injury after the choice of scenario was made by the jury. Jurors might be shown up to ten different scenarios from a larger number made available to the court. Juries would be told that none of the scenarios fit the case under consideration but would be asked to indicate which of the scenarios in the notebook most nearly resembles the case under consideration. Jurors might respond, for example, that pain and suffering seem less than scenario 3 but worse than scenario 5. In such a case, the midpoint of the two might be selected by the judge when setting compensation for nonmonetary loss. The judge would thus have some discretion in picking the final value. This is analogous to stating in undergraduate microeconomics that indifference curve 3 lies below indifference curve 5, and a point is selected in between the two curves.[62] There are many points between the curves, as with the scenarios.

A neutral scenario might read: "Permanent minor injury (level 5 severity). Life expectancy 25 years. Mild persistent pain, usually controllable with aspirin. Unable to engage in more than light housework."

A more colorful scenario might read: "Plaintiff Peters has completely and permanently lost the use of her right arm. Her life expectancy is 25 years, according to standard life insurance tables. Her arm throbs with pain most of the time, but the pain usually can be controlled with aspirin. She cannot do more than light housework."

The scenarios could be more detailed than this. Each scenario might be delivered to jurors by video. The scenarios might characterize actual cases tried in the state in recent years. The process of selecting cases in the notebook that are closest to those in the case being tried could be mandatory or voluntary. If voluntary, the scenarios could provide guidelines for jury deliberations. In that case, juries would be told the associated dollar values after they had identified the closest scenarios, and they would be asked to reconsider their determination of a dollar value of nonpecuniary loss arrived at independently. Even if the system were not mandatory, large discrepancies between the jury award and the scenarios' values may be subject to review on appeal.

An objection to BSB's suggestion that juries be provided information on past awards for nonmonetary loss or scheduling based on a matrix that is based on averages of past losses is that if juries have made mistakes in the past, it is inadvisable to use past decisions as guides for future ones.[63]

Geistfeld (1995) proposes an alternative method of promoting consistency of jury awards—in our list of suggestions, the fourth approach. His valuation method does not rely on past jury awards. Rather, his *jury survey approach* proposes that the jury be asked to indicate how much a reasonable person would have been willing to pay to avoid the injury in question.[64] The approach would allow the jury to consider the nuances of the case being tried, an element that scheduled damages can only approximate. The approach Geistfeld suggests is feasible to implement; it has been widely applied to study valuation in various contexts, and researchers now have considerable experience in question design (much more so than in 1995). Most frequently, the surveys are computer-administered.[65]

Geisfeld has juries asking the appropriate question—What would preventing the injury have been worth *before* the injury actually occurred? However, the valuation studies have employed hundreds of persons in the valuation task, *not* just six to twelve jurors (the usual size of juries). Having few persons valuing the loss will almost certainly lead to very imprecise estimates. One outlier response could greatly distort the estimates, but there are several possible ways to deal with this problem.[66]

Avraham (2006) is critical of all of the above approaches. He states that:

All of the proposed solutions are administratively complicated and prohibitively complicated. Who decides the schedules, matrices, scenarios, or guidelines? What criteria do they use? The more detailed the scenarios or guidelines are, the more costly it is to design them, and the less discretion the jury has. How do we know that the jury will not be overburdened with these new tasks? Even a simple matrix (conventionally used for evaluating malpractice insurance cases into which all injuries, including death, are collapsed) introduces a wide range of awards within each category. If this "simple matrix" results in such a massive variation within injury-severity type, it is clearly unhelpful, and one can reasonably expect that an even wider range of awards would result if states adopt Bovbjerg, Sloan, Blumstein's suggestion that a jury apply different scenarios to the case at hand. This problem is further complicated when it is extended to the determination of what the criteria for the judicial review of jury verdicts would be.[67]

Outcomes of any method of scheduling depend on details of how the method is actually applied. If juries are given less flexibility in applying the schedule and there are fewer categories, there will be correspondingly less variability. Flat caps on damages give no discretion to juries for awards above a given dollar value. Simplicity is gained at the expense of precision. In addition, this approach reduces variability in payment for severe injuries, but it introduces horizontal inequities since there is heterogeneity in injuries above the flat cap as well as vertical inequities, because compensation for severe injuries is disproportionately reduced.

Avraham (2006) proposes a simple approach that is sixth in our list, *basing compensation for nonmonetary loss on compensation for medical loss.* Medical loss would be multiplied by a "multiplier" to yield the award for nonmonetary loss. To illustrate, he suggests that the multiplier for medical losses of up to $100,000 could be 0.5, yielding nonmonetary damages in the range of $0 to $50,000. For losses in the $100,001–$500,000 range, the multiplier might be 0.75. And for losses of $500,001–$1,000,000 and above $1,000,000, the multipliers might be 1.0 and 1.25, respectively.

The idea clearly is simple, but it, too, has deficiencies. For example, a person who had a leg amputated would receive less compensation for pain and suffering than would a person who received several complex surgical procedures to reattach nerves in the leg and who retained use of the leg. The proposal could increase use of personal health care services, such as home care and rehabilitation services, in order to capture a higher payment for noneconomic loss. The nine-point injury severity scale shown in table 5.1 is less easily gamed.

In sum, each of the above six proposals for scheduling damages has both strengths and weaknesses, and there are undoubtedly other proposals we have not mentioned. Some form of scheduling makes sense. In deciding how best to schedule, states will need to weigh the pros and cons of the alternatives.

Better Ways to Reform Payment for Nonmonetary or Total Loss in Medical Malpractice Insurance Contracts for Future Services: Payment in the Form of Provision of Service Benefits

Some plaintiffs who seek compensation through tort have suffered permanent, serious injuries requiring lifelong care. It is such cases, rather than temporary injuries, that often lead to volatility of compensation. Currently, awards are not well synchronized with the outlays that such injury victims incur. Imprudent injury victims may squander their awards and later require public subsidies or rely on uncompensated care subsidies. Furthermore, even if awards are not excessive on average, they are likely to be either insufficient or excessive in many cases. Substantial lawyers' fees appreciably reduce any payment that plaintiffs might receive, leading to the likelihood that net compensation after fees is insufficient to cover injury cost. Grave injuries, such as quadriplegia and severe brain damage, may require substantial sums, often exceeding $100,000 per year. Even thirty annual payments of $40,000, discounted at 5 percent, have a present value of $615,000.

At present, to compensate plaintiffs for the cost of care, experts are employed to compute the sum of past cost, often including interest on such cost, and the anticipated cost of future care, often discounted to present value. Once awarded a lump sum, plaintiffs or the persons designated to manage their care have an incentive to economize on care. However, such persons may not be adequately informed about care options, and as individuals they would not typically have the bargaining power to obtain the best deals for their money.

The suggestions just described focus on determination of nonmonetary loss. There is reason for concern about the accuracy and adequacy of payment for monetary (and total) loss as well.

Even under the best of circumstances, forecasts of future economic loss will inevitably have been too high or too low ex post. Future costs of medical care and other personal care services are difficult to project. In addition, the course of disease, disability, and longevity is highly individualized and extremely difficult to predict ex ante. Life expectancy, for example, refers to the midpoint in the frequency distribution of future dates of death. There is considerable dispersion around this midpoint.

To the extent that forecasts and payments are too high, there is a potential windfall to plaintiffs. If the forecasts are too low, there is the risk that the plaintiff will not receive adequate financial support. Payment of cash at the settlement or verdict does not eliminate the financial risk that the recipient faces. In principle, the recipient could purchase private health and disability insurance with funds from the lump-sum payment. However, in practice, individual health and disability insurance policies tend to be very costly relative to group insurance policies. Also, with a preexisting condition, it may be difficult for some persons to obtain coverage, especially full coverage, at any price anywhere near actuarially fair rates. Finally, the recipient and/or his or her agents may be insufficiently prudent to plan for the future.

Periodic payments, as a "tort reform," are an annuity-like contract to provide payments on a regular basis in the future. They have two advantages over lump-sum payments. First, they deal with uncertainty about the plaintiff's longevity. Although empirical evidence is lacking, provisions for periodic payments have been enacted by state legislatures under the presumption that they will reduce overpayment to the extent that juries, in attempting to the minimize the risk of a shortfall in compensation to the plaintiff, set damages too high on average.

Periodic payments address the problem of a plaintiff being overpaid to the extent that plaintiffs die prematurely as well as the problem of the imprudent plaintiff who spends the lump sum soon after receiving it. Yet there are several potential problems not addressed by periodic payments.

First, periodic payments are often provided in nominal terms and therefore do not shield the recipient against the risk of unanticipated inflation. Second, they do not provide protection against unanticipated deterioration in health, although there may be a windfall if the person's health improves more than was anticipated. Third, to the extent that plaintiffs would want to insure against future risk, periodic payments do not take account of the high price and/or unavailability of insurance to such individuals. Fourth, if the plaintiff-injury victim receives cash rather than insurance as an in-kind benefit, and thus becomes a cash-paying "self-pay" patient, he or she is likely to be paying top dollar because of an asymmetry in negotiating power between the individual and providers. Fifth, plaintiffs and/or their agent may mismanage cash payments provided on a periodic basis. There may well be an advantage to paying injury victims in a noncash form. Sixth, particularly since the award is reduced by the amount of the lawyer's fee, it seems unlikely that the plaintiff could purchase an insurance policy that would provide financial protection against unforeseen changes in health.

As an alternative to periodic payments or a lump-sum amount, a potentially attractive reform would be for the defendants found liable to fund an *insurance contract for future services* that would provide for or pay for future services as the needs arise. In essence, rather than being paid money, the plaintiff would be guaranteed that a set of services would be provided, conditional on patient need—hence the term "service contract proposal."[68]

Under the service contract proposal, rather than award damages, juries would specify features of an insurance contract appropriate for the care of the injured person. Such features would include duration of coverage and services to be covered, typically specified in considerable detail, but would exclude services not causally connected to the injury and could provide for collateral source offsets.

Proposals from prospective contractors would specify details of services they would provide and their associated prices, which would reflect the expected cost of the contract in terms of service benefits plus a loading factor, which includes administrative costs to the insurer as well as profit.

The court would then select a contractor. Potential contractors would include academic medical centers, hospitals, and larger physician group practices, as well as HMOs and other insurers. This would be a business opportunity for providers who could specialize in particular types of injuries, such as care for the severely and permanently impaired, neurologically impaired children, or persons with cancer that becomes more advanced because of a misdiagnosis.

This alternative is more complex than the above proposals, and resolution of various details would be critical to its success. Under a service-contracting system, services to help persons cope with nonmonetary loss, such as counseling, could be part of the contract and could substitute for much or all of the payment for such loss. Since injury victims would receive more comprehensive, specialized care tailored to each individual's circumstances, including psychiatric needs, they would receive something in return for eliminating or substantially reducing compensation for non-monetary loss.

As with the other proposals, even though the proposal may seem attractive conceptually, the devil is in the practical details of implementation. First, since prices and conditions of the contract would be expected to differ, plaintiffs and defendants may not agree on the choice of contractor.

Moreover, there may be details about future care that are not specified by the court, as well as differences of opinion on where care is to be provided. Should a brain-damaged infant be housed near the family residence or in a state facility an hour or two away? Should the injury victim receive individual or group psychotherapy? At what point is care to be discontinued because the patient is considered to be terminal? In many cases, disputes would be settled informally or by private negotiation, with results being finally accepted by the court.

However, if the parties cannot agree within a prespecified time period, a court-appointed arbitrator could resolve the dispute by final-offer arbitration.[69] In this type of arbitration, each side presents its best offer. The arbitrator has his or her own idea of the appropriate settlement terms and selects the proposal which most closely resembles his or her estimate of fairness. Given that both parties know that the arbitrator will select the contract that is most "reasonable," each has an incentive to make offers toward the middle of the range of possible values. In effect, final-offer arbitration aligns the incentives of the parties. Although this approach may seem cumbersome, under the present circumstances, injury victims may be insufficiently empowered to gain resources that they will eventually need.

Another problem may arise when the parties are constantly dead-locked and/or lose trust of the insurer-provider, and the plaintiff wishes to terminate the relationship. Or the insurer may file for bankruptcy. Thus, there must be a provision for cash-out of the insurance contract. However, this is not without complicating factors as well. For example, a plaintiff who believes that he or she will use fewer services than the average plaintiff with this contract type may wish to cash out. Thus, there would have to be a financial penalty for cashing out which is part of the initial contract provisions. On the other hand, providers-insurers may wish to cash out in the event of unanticipated high rates of inflation or unanticipated regulatory (e.g., new quality of care safeguards), or technological changes (e.g., a new procedure for treating the disease). The provider-insurer may not have a formal escape clause, but it could offer an attractive settlement to encourage the plaintiff to exercise the buyout option. It is indeed possible that an unhappy provider-insurer could let service deteriorate to the point that the plaintiff voluntarily seeks a buyout on unfavorable terms. To guard against this risk, it would be important to provide safeguards in implementing the proposal. For example, the plaintiff-injury victim could be allowed to seek redress in a contempt proceeding in the court of original jurisdiction; the plaintiff could file another lawsuit; and/or complaints could be kept on file in a clearinghouse to provide a Better Business Bureau type of service to courts and future litigants.

This plan calls for a new market in insurance service-benefit contracts to cover future losses of persons who have been awarded damages by courts in personal injury cases, and specifically in medical malpractice. Since the vast majority of cases are settled, there should have been ample opportunity for this type of market to emerge by now. The next question is why such a market has not emerged, and what, more specifically, the objections to the proposal are likely to be.

We can anticipate one objection. During preparation of Blumstein, Bovbjerg, and Sloan (1991), which contained this proposal, the third author presented the proposal at the home office of a major multiline insurer. The proposal drew a skeptical response, primarily because there are no actuarial data on which to base offer prices. One possible initial source of data for projecting future losses may come from workers' compensation insurers. These insurers have the obligation to cover lifetime costs of care for certain claimants. Furthermore, the same issue arises for no-fault compensation plans, but this objection has not arisen as a major shortcoming of such plans.

Second, particularly if the market were restricted to verdicts in medical malpractice cases and there were barriers to entry from insurance companies domiciled in other states, the market may not be of a sufficient size to attract insurers willing to supply long-term service benefit contracts. Without being able to exploit scale economies, the load on the insurance policies is likely to be high. However, rather than being a structural flaw, this concern suggests that the plan not be restricted to medical malpractice cases, but to personal injury cases more generally. In addition, federal as well as state courts could implement this idea.

A third possible concern involves adverse selection. Perhaps the only plaintiffs who will consent to insurance contracts are those with private information that they will be high users of services. One way to deal with adverse selection is to make participation in the contract plan mandatory; this might encourage settlements by those who do not expect to be high users on a risk-adjusted basis. Another approach would be to implement an outlier policy so that unusually high-cost cases could be covered by a reinsurance pool.

Fourth, while service benefits may make the victim whole in pecuniary terms, the proposal does not deal with nonmonetary loss. However, there should be a gain in well-being to injury victims by not having to deal with the substantial expenditure risk in the current system. A service-contract proposal could be combined with scheduling for nonmonetary loss.

These are generally valid concerns. However, the current system masks many of the problems that the insurance contract option makes explicit, such as asymmetric negotiating power between individuals and insurer-providers, the failure for cash payments to compensate for expenditure risk, and, quite simply, the fact that after paying lawyers' fees, injured persons may not have the ability to pay for their health care.

Finally, Peter Schuck (1991, pp. 219–220) concludes that "The virtues of the [service benefit contracting] proposal are less apparent than those of damages scheduling [specifically Bovbjerg, Sloan, and Blumstein's scheduling proposals]." Schuck contends that the service benefit insurance proposal depends on a paternalistic assumption that contract rights to future services are superior to an immediate lump-sum payment because the latter might be squandered. He further argues that it is unclear why paternalism is any more justified in the case of personal injury victims deciding how to dispose of their resources than for other adults.

In fact, the proposal *is* somewhat paternalistic, and for good reason. Many families have to cope with serious, ongoing permanent injuries for years. Budgeting over the long term can be very difficult. In the case of a permanently injured child, the parents may predecease the child. The individual family is not well positioned to bargain with suppliers of care. To advocate for a paternalistic solution under these special circumstances is not at all advocating for paternalism more generally.

Private Contracting

An option that has a few strong advocates is private contracting as an alternative to tort. Private contracts might explicitly limit the circumstances under which tort liability would still apply. For example, tort liability might continue only under gross negligence. Contract provisions could also specify the method by which disputes are resolved (e.g., by arbitration), guidelines under which care is delivered that, if adhered to, would not result in payment of damages (e.g., specific guidelines or organizations promulgating guidelines, as well as schedules for paying for nonmonetary loss.

A major objection to private contracting is that patients are not as well positioned as are parties to a contract, at least relative to health care providers. In specific instances, such as in medical emergencies, this argument has even greater force.

The counterargument is that contracts can be made when patients are well, not sick. Moreover, agents for patients, such as employers, should be in a better position to deal with provider groups. Employers deal with provider groups on many matters, including fees and use of services. Danzon (2000, p. 1382) argues that if health plans can lock in patients to providers who have adopted cost-reducing contractual changes, some of which substitute for tort, there can be benefits to patients in the form of lower contributions to health insurance plans and lower wage offsets for that part saved by employers on their contributions to health plans.

Although the contracts would encompass many provisions other than scheduled damages, they could be used for scheduling. In fact, the legal environment permitting, this may be an effective mechanism for implementing scheduling and demonstrating its feasibility.

Discussion and Conclusions

In chapter 1, we described myth 4 as "medical malpractice claimants are overcompensated for their injuries." There are surely cases in which myth 4 is valid, but based on available empirical evidence, this myth is invalid on average. If there is an argument for limits on payments, it is that payments are highly variable, not that they are upward biased.

Ironically, limits on payment for nonmonetary loss and total loss may have "worked" too well. They have reduced outlays of insurers and medical malpractice premiums to a lesser extent. In accomplishing these goals, they have served the interests of defendants, and obtaining passage of such limits in states without them and at the federal level has become a political priority for these stakeholders. In the first decade of the twenty-first Century, proposals for flat caps have garnered more political support than ever, although they have insufficient support to be enacted at the federal level.

This chapter proposes specific alternatives to flat caps. The concept of scheduling damages is not at all new. For example, in a chapter titled "Visual Economics," there is a detailed description of how pensions for disability, in this case for disability on account of vision loss, should be determined.[70] Although the task of the person applying principles of visual economics was to compensate for monetary loss (i.e., loss in earnings potential), aspects of the payment scheme pertained to nonmonetary aspects as well. According to the payment schedule in 1905, loss of sight in one eye with the eye in place was to be compensated at a rate of $12 per month. However, if the eye was missing, the rate was $17 per month. The justification given was that potential employers would be willing to pay less if they saw that the eye was actually in place. While this may be considered monetary loss, from another perspective this could indeed have been a way to circumvent the statute and pay for nonmonetary loss.

Groups representing providers seek to limit outlays for medical malpractice. The above proposals could well lead to greater accuracy in determining damages and to lower risk, especially to plaintiff-injury victims, but the proposals would not automatically result in savings to insurers and health care providers. Organized medicine understandably wants policy solutions that would affect savings to its constituents. Scheduled damages are an anathema to the trial bar, as are flat caps. Both flat caps and scheduled damages limit opportunities for a skillful and industrious attorney to obtain high compensation for clients.

In contrast to these special interests, the public in general, and injury victims in particular, are not well organized politically. The public rarely gets directly involved in a medical malpractice case as a juror, as an injury victim, or as a relative of one. Thus, citizens are prone to follow the finger-pointing of the well-organized groups.

This entire agenda will not be adopted at once, and considerable compromise will be needed to adopt any of the options. The first step is recognition that the facts are not as simple as they tend to be portrayed and that existing data are insufficient to implement sound policy options. The most realistic first steps may be implementation of registries to provide the requisite data and demonstrations to test the feasibility of the proposals before full-scale implementation takes place.

Given these political impediments, then what are the next steps? It seems doubtful that insurers will implement the proposal for long-term contracts for permanently injured individuals. Yet this is potentially an excellent opportunity for a health care provider, such as an academic health center. These organizations have a wealth of talent on their faculties and staffs, and should be well positioned to manage care for permanently injured persons over the life course. This would provide teaching, research, and income opportunities for academic health centers. The advantages for teaching seem immediately apparent. For research, this would provide opportunities to study individuals over the life course as well as to study the effects of interventions of various types on the well-being of these individuals. Only some of the interventions would be medical. Others would involve special education, rehabilitation, housing, and other aspects of these individuals' lives.

Scheduled damages are part of some compensation systems, such as workers' compensation. They could be implemented as part of medical no-fault. In addition, they may possibly be part of private contracts that would provide an alternative to tort. It will be necessary to demonstrate the practical feasibility of scheduled damages before this approach has any prospect for success in a state legislature, especially given the lack of support from both sides of the political debate about tort reform.

Chapter 12 will describe feasible options for reform. Because of the political challenges in getting these proposals implemented, scheduling damages and contracts for permanently impaired injury victims should be part of the reform agenda but, with the political impediments to implementation—perhaps not at the very top.

6

Compensating Plaintiffs' Attorneys

Trial Lawyers, Contingent Fees, and Medical Malpractice Litigation: Opposing Views

The Critique

Critics of medical malpractice quickly turn to the role of the trial lawyer as a cause of the high cost of medical malpractice. In some accounts, such lawyers are seen as "ambulance chasers," arriving at the scene of an injury and readily offering their services to injury victims who, without these persuasive lawyers, would not have sued for medical malpractice. The image of greedy lawyers stirring up lawsuits is linked to payment of lawyers on a contingent fee basis because the contingent fee system presumably gives the lawyer an added incentive to pursue injury victims.[1] In medical malpractice, the injury victim may not be found literally lying on the side of the highway, but rather may be identified in some other way—or attracted by a lawyer's advertisement or other form of self-promotion. The perceived motive for the lawyer is to make a quick and big buck. There is a widespread perception in other countries that the high rates of litigation in the United States are largely attributable to the contingent fee system (box 6.1).[2]

While the victim may receive compensation from tort, whatever the victim receives is substantially reduced by the lawyer's high fee. Given the high rewards to suing, the argument goes, physicians and other potential health care defendants are sheep waiting to be fleeced. While in normal markets, entry would reduce fees to a competitive level, trial lawyers' fees are kept far above competitive levels by anti-competitive practices, typically not precisely specified by the proponents of this view.

Box 6.1
Public Opinion About Lawsuits in the United States: Unfavorable to Trial
Lawyers

> Michael Saks (1992, pp. 1162–1163) summarized results of a public
> opinion poll conducted in the mid-1980s.
>
> • By a 69–24 percent majority, people were convinced that it is too easy
> for people to sue for damages when they think they have been injured or
> wronged.
>
> • 63 percent believed that the size of most cash settlements is excessive.
>
> • A 77 percent–15 percent majority blamed the liability crisis on persons
> who think they can make a lot of money from such suits—namely, trial
> lawyers.

The near uniformity of contingent fee percentages, according to one
view[3] in the 31–33 percent range or higher, is taken as evidence of lack
of competition. They may be fixed by custom if not by collusion.[4] Some
criticisms focus on the high earnings of trial lawyers, especially on earnings as calculated (but not paid) on an hourly basis, with a rationale for
reform seeming to reflect a concern about inequities in the distribution
of earned income. But underlying concerns about inequity, even if not
expressed, are probably that the prospects of lawyers striking it rich has
led to too many medical malpractice suits being filed.[5] In light of these
allegations, states have passed limits on attorneys' contingent fees in
efforts to reduce litigation rates and payments, and perhaps to address
an imbalance in earnings from the practice of law, at least on behalf of
plaintiffs.

Another Perspective
There are sharp differences in opinions about trial lawyers and how they
are paid (box 6.2). From the perspective of perhaps a minority of citizens,
including many injury victims, contingent fees are about access to justice
through the mechanism of civil litigation or the threat of it.

Much more forceful support for the contingent fee system comes
from consumer advocates. For them, the contingent fee system for
compensating plaintiffs' attorneys in personal injury cases is a godsend

Box 6.2
Public Opinion About Lawsuits in the United States: Counterpoint

> In concluding his book on contingent fee lawyer compensation and reputation, Kritzer (2004, pp. 253–254) said, "Supporters of contingency fees describe them as the average person's 'key to the courthouse.' In contrast, critics of contingency fees see such fees as at least partly responsible for many of the evils and excesses of the American legal system (Barry and Rein 1999; Brickman 2003; Kagan 2001; O'Connell 1979) and as unjustly enriching and empowering members of the legal profession (Brickman 1989, 1996; Olson 2003). Nonetheless, from the perspective of the average citizen, contingency fees are about access to justice through the mechanism of civil litigation, or the threat of civil litigation.
>
> Does the availability of contingency fees increase the resort to litigation? It seems that the obvious answer must be Yes, of course. However, that answer is too simplistic, because one must go on to ask, "Compared to what?"

for the injury victim. Absent the contingent fee system, trial lawyers would adopt other payment approaches, such as charging by the hour.[6]

However, unlike lawyers who can diversify away the risk of losses in individual lawsuits by accepting many cases (analogous to assets in an investment portfolio), the individual injury victim has no means of diversification. He or she has only one claim. If it succeeds, the claimant may get substantial compensation. If it fails, the claimant gets nothing; and under an hourly compensation system or a loser-pay-all-legal-costs system (the English Rule), losers would be stuck with a substantial legal expense in addition to receiving no compensation. A risk-averse person may be unlikely to file a claim for which the lawyer is paid on an hourly basis because of the high risk of losing. The risk of losing when an attorney is paid hourly means being forced to pay legal expenses without the cushion of revenue from suing.

In contrast to the view that placing an upper limit on contingent fee percentages is good public policy since it limits the ability of people to file nonmeritorious claims and trial lawyers' allegedly excessive earnings, opponents of such limits see them as reducing individuals' access to needed legal services that otherwise would not be available.

More relevant to a prospective client is the expected recovery net of the fee, which is likely to vary considerably among lawyers with differing know-how and effort levels. To the plaintiff lawyer deciding to take a case, the relevant datum is the expected revenue from the case, not the fee percentage per se. If trial lawyers are doing good work obtaining compensation for deserving injury victims and make good income in the process, the income distribution suffers no harm and may even be improved. Both the claimant, who may have incurred a substantial income loss as a result of the injury, and the attorney are made financially better off.

Sloan, Githens, Clayton, et al. (1993) report that plaintiffs in medical malpractice cases who retained an attorney specializing in medical malpractice litigation obtained higher recoveries than did plaintiffs who used attorneys not specializing in this field. The specialized attorneys were plausibly much more affluent than general attorneys, but the plaintiffs who used them were much better off in the end. However, just because the recoveries were higher does not necessarily mean that specialized lawyers are more productive than others, although they may be. The higher recoveries likely reflect better case selection on their part.

Specialization is not limited to the trial bar. Specialization and skills obtained by being a repeat player are more common among attorneys for the defense in medical malpractice cases than they are among those representing plaintiffs.[7]

In contrast to much public commentary, which is often critical of contingent fees charged by attorneys, the American Bar Association's Standing Committee on Ethics and Professional Responsibility has issued a formal opinion in support of contingent fees. As long as the fee is "both appropriate and reasonable," and the client has been informed of alternative billing options, the committee considers the fee agreement to be ethical. The committee further states that it is ethical to charge a contingency fee when liability is clear and recovery is expected. Also, the lawyer is not obligated to solicit an early settlement offer when compensated on a contingent fee basis.[8]

In sum, the issue may not be so much that trial lawyers generate too many lawsuits. Rather, statutory limits on such fees, by limiting access of injury victims to compensation through tort, may result in even fewer meritorious claims being filed than in states in which such fee limits do not exist.

While this line of argumentation is helpful to opponents of limits on plaintiff attorneys' contingent fees, it also has some weaknesses. For one, among those who advocate for the existing contingent fee system on grounds that it provides broad access to legal services, there are alternatives worth considering, such as first-party insurance for legal expense, as exists for personal health services, homeowners, and automobile collision insurance.

Our View

Although all proposals have both pluses and minuses, the case for contingent fee reform, at least as implemented to date, is weak on balance. If reform is needed because the courts are overburdened, why focus on medical malpractice, which accounts for less than 1 percent of lawsuits? If the issue is too many nonmeritorious lawsuits, do limitations on contingent fees winnow out nonmeritorious lawsuits or meritorious ones as well? If the issue is an inequitable income distribution, why focus the public policy discussion on a few trial lawyers with high earnings rather than on highly paid professionals involved in other activities, such as lawyers who handle mergers and acquisitions and patent disputes, health professionals, and CEOs in general?

Statutes limiting contingent fees generally set the lowest fee percentages for the largest payment awards. This implies that the large cases disproportionately result in excess profits to plaintiffs' attorneys. At some threshold of awards, this is plausibly so, but empirical evidence on this point is lacking, including the threshold above which litigation on a contingent fee basis is "excessively" profitable.

By contrast, more recent proposals focus on limiting fees in cases that are resolved quickly, but leave fees for disputes contested over a longer time period unaffected. This implies that the cases that are quickly resolved, often for lesser amounts, are excessively profitable. Empirical evidence for this position is also lacking.

The only communality the proposals share is that they seek to limit compensation of plaintiffs' attorneys in medical malpractice litigation.

But, they leave out attorney compensation in high-profile merger and acquisition, patent, and class action suits, for example. In contrast to lawsuits against pharmaceutical and device manufacturers, which fall under the category of product liability, personal injury cases in which physicians, hospitals, or other health care providers are named as defendants do not achieve class action status.

Types of Compensation Arrangements

There are several methods of paying lawyers. There is no consensus among theoretical studies about effects of alternative methods of payment on lawyer decision-making and legal outcomes. The conclusions from the theoretical studies about effects of payment mechanism on lawyer decision-making and legal outcomes are highly dependent on the underlying assumptions made in modeling.

Kritzer (2002) classifies fee arrangements into six types:

1. Fixed fees specified in advance for routine work on tasks that are well defined and predictable

2. Time-based fees in which an hourly fee is multiplied by the number of hours worked

3. Task-based fees in which the lawyer charges fixed amounts for specific subtasks, such as writing a letter, making a telephone call, and so on (parallel to task-based physician fees)

4. Statutory, or other law-based, fee schedules based on the value of the transaction or the amount in controversy

5. Commission-based fee arrangements in which the lawyer's fee is based on some percentage of the amount recovered or the value of the matter being handled (e.g., in probate work, on the value of the estate being handled)

6. Value-based fee systems, in which the lawyer assesses the value of the work to the client and sets the fee on this basis

The most common approaches are the second, time-based compensation, and the fifth, standard contingent fee arrangements.

The Contingent Fee System

Historical Context   The contingent fee system has had a long and somewhat checkered history in the United States. Until the late 1800s, there was a common-law prohibition against contingent fees in many U.S. jurisdictions; contingency fees were considered maintenance or champerty, and were forbidden by law.[9] This formally ended in 1884 when the U.S. Supreme Court issued an opinion approving a contingent fee contract in which the lawyer was to receive 50 percent of the award.[10] Nevertheless, the adoption of contingent fees developed gradually in the common law. State courts began recognizing contingent fees and the state legislatures would take no action preventing this, resulting in the integration of contingent fees into the legal system by individual states. By the mid-1900s, most of the statutes preventing contingent fees had been repealed. However, it was not until the 1960s that contingent fees were allowed in all states; Maine was the last state to allow such fee arrangements.[11]

Advantages of Contingent Fees   There are several arguments for contingent fees. First, they offer a financing arrangement for plaintiffs who are too liquidity-constrained to pursue their cases because they lack the internal funds and/or because banks are reluctant to provide loans for a legal bill of a very uncertain size. Second, they may provide an efficient mechanism for risk sharing, especially when other financing mechanisms, such as personal insurance to cover legal expense, are unavailable.[12]

Contingent fee arrangements are not used by the defense. Unlike plaintiffs, the organizations bearing the financial risk for defendants are likely to be insurers or large-self insured enterprises such as hospitals. These organizations often have considerable ability to diversify away risk. In this sense, contingent fees level the playing field.[13] On grounds of being able to bear risk, the financial risk bearers for the defendants may have a greater self-interest in prolonging litigation than do most plaintiffs. But for various other reasons, such as reputation loss, defendants may be eager to settle.

Since attorney effort may be difficult for clients to observe, contingent fees provide a method for coping with moral hazard when attorneys bill but expend little effort.[14] Under the contingent fee system, attorneys are paid for results, not just their inputs (that is, time expended on the case). In fact, clients may achieve a larger recovery from a bifurcated (two-step schedule) rather than single fee percentage in which the attorney gets a larger fraction of the recovery if the case goes to trial.[15] Since preparing for trial generally involves substantial effort, the plaintiff's attorney may need an added incentive to be willing to make this investment.

This bifurcated approach contrasts with state-legislated fee caps which place greater limits on fees for large recoveries. The contingent fee system could encourage persons to file nonmeritorious cases since plaintiffs incur no out-of-pocket expense if their case is lost. However, the attorney lacks an incentive to accept such cases when the fee is paid only when there is success in obtaining recovery.[16]

Disadvantages of Contingent Fees   Contingent fees, as well as payment by the hour, can lead to situations in which the welfare of plaintiffs and of their attorneys may conflict.[17] Two potential problems are particularly noteworthy.

The first is for lawyers to settle cases too early. Lawyers may want to settle rather than expend extra effort to obtain a larger amount. In fact, some cases may yield (mostly modest) settlement offers with rather little effort expended by attorneys. Although plaintiffs must consent to the settlement of their claims, they often may not be able to gauge the extra gain in their recoveries to be expected from extra time expended by the lawyer on their claims.[18] In fact, attorneys are retained in large part for the expertise provided to clients. If the clients did not need the expertise, they could pursue their legal grievances without the help of attorneys.[19]

A countervailing influence is that attorneys who settle early will gain a reputation for settling early for easy cash. Not only does reputation in the community at large affect attorney demand, but so does reputation in the community of attorneys—which would affect the number of referrals an attorney receives from other attorneys. One would expect a trial lawyer who consistently settles for limited amounts to eventually receive ever smaller settlement offers. At least in some cases, plaintiffs' attorneys need to resist the temptation to settle early and hold out for higher settlements and/or litigate some cases to verdict.[20] In fact, the need for plaintiffs' attorneys to appear tough is one reason that plaintiffs lose the vast majority of cases litigated to verdict.[21] On the other hand, critics of contingent fees have argued that frivolous lawsuits can be profitable if defendants prefer to settle such cases rather than risk a trial.[22]

By contrast, payment on an hourly rate may give attorneys an incentive to prolong the case. Since lawyer compensation is not tied to the dollar amount obtained for the client, lawyers paid on an hourly basis may tend to exaggerate to their clients the chances of a large recovery at verdict. Under hourly compensation, there may be an inclination to pad bills and to allocate legal resources to cases at margins at which use of such resources is unproductive.[23] The trade-off seems to be between the financial incentive to provide a realistic appraisal of the benefits of stopping the case under the contingent fee versus an incentive to provide a realistic appraisal of continuing litigation under hourly fee payment.[24]

Do Attorneys Paid a Contingent Fee Really Earn More than Other Attorneys?

One strategy employed by advocates for contingent fee limits is to assert that lawyers paid a contingent fee have inordinately high earnings. Most often, such statements are made without reference to empirical evidence, or the evidence presented is of low quality. Differences in compensation by type of payment arrangement have often been exaggerated.

A case in point is the assertions advanced by Professor Lester Brickman in his criticism of contingent fees. He asserts that since 1960, the effective hourly rates of tort lawyers have increased 1000%–1400% in real dollars while the overall risk of nonrecovery has remained unchanged.[25] He bases this assessment partly on average jury verdicts from the years 1960 and 2001: $132,000 and $1,454,800 (in 2004 dollars), respectively. Unfortunately, Brickman relies on data from jury verdict reporters. The vast majority of medical malpractice claims are settled before verdict. He reports that changes in selection of cases that go to trial could explain the dramatic increase in payments at verdict. Further, mean jury awards may be substantially affected by a few high outlier awards. Thus, a better comparison would be based on median rather than on mean jury awards.

These fees are much larger than those reported by Kritzer (2004), which are based on data from a survey Professor Kritzer conducted in Wisconsin. Results of the survey revealed a median hourly rate of $156 and a mean of $154 (2004 dollars; Kritzer 2004, p. 187). Taking his data in combination with other data he reviewed, Kritzer concludes that a useful range to consider is $156 to $174 per hour.[26] He cautions, however, that in computing hourly rates, one should deduct expenses which would be billed separately by attorneys charging on an hourly basis. Also, many lawyers do not maintain time records for their contingent fee cases.[27] Kritzer concludes that contingency fee lawyers, on average, are paid an amount similar to defense attorneys with commensurate levels of experience.

Based on a 1988 survey of law firms, Aranson (1992) reports that compensation of partners representing plaintiffs on a contingent fee basis was 26 percent higher than for partners working for insurance defense firms. Plaintiff attorneys' mean hours of work were 12 percent lower than those of defense lawyers. Thus, on an hours-adjusted basis, contingent fee attorneys earned almost 30 percent more than those working on an hourly basis for the defense. This may be an equilibrium differential generated by the market to compensate contingent fee lawyers for assuming a risk-bearing role that lawyers paid per hour do not assume. We do not know whether a 30 percent differential represents over- or undercompensation for being risk bearers.

Daniels and Martin (2002) report results from a survey of plaintiffs' lawyers in Texas. The mean value earned in contingent fee cases was over $1 million. However, the median value was under $50,000.[28] A team of Rand Corporation researchers conducted an independent evaluation of effects of case management on dispute resolution as part of the study, in which a survey was conducted of judges, lawyers, and litigants.[29] Most relevant to an analysis of fee arrangements, the Rand authors conducted statistical analysis to determine whether or not payment on an hourly versus a contingent fee arrangement affected median days to case disposition, lawyer satisfaction with management of the case, lawyers' view that management of the case was fair, and total work hours per litigant. No statistically significant differences in responses of hourly fee and contingent fee lawyers were obtained.

A survey of 511 lawyers compensated on a contingent fee basis in Wisconsin revealed that most cases that were not accepted were declined because of lack of liability or lack of liability in combination with inadequate damages.[30] Respondents to that survey indicated that they turned away about half of the cases presented to them. This figure rose to 80–90 percent among attorneys who obtained a large share of their clients though media advertising.[31] Other studies reviewed by Kritzer[32] suggest that over half of inquiries are rejected by contingent fee attorneys. Brickman sets the figure at over two thirds.[33] Brickman concludes that as a result of this screening process, contingent fee attorneys are able to recover nearly 100 percent of their out-of-pocket advances of litigation costs, including the costs for unsuccessful cases.[34]

The same Wisconsin survey revealed that most lawyers in the study (60 percent), charged a fixed 33 percent contingent fee; however, 31 percent employed a variable fee. For variable fees, the most common pattern was a fee of 25 percent if there was no substantial trial preparation, rising to 40 percent if the case resulted in an appeal. There were sometimes reductions in fees below the rate specified in the retention agreement. Kritzer concludes that "At least in Wisconsin, the assertion by contingency fee critics that there is a uniform contingency fee is clearly false."[35] But as Brickman notes, relative to many if not most states, Wisconsin is not a litigious state; as a result, data from this state may be unrepresentative of contingent fee practices in more litigious states.[36]

Overall, the quality of the evidence on whether or not contingent fee lawyers do, in fact, earn more is not as good as we would like. At a minimum, however, the evidence suggests that claims that attorneys as a group make huge profits from contingent fees when representing individual plaintiffs *are* exaggerated. Nevertheless, while the Wisconsin survey results are probably representative of Wisconsin, there is considerable variability among states, and one should thus be careful not to generalize to the United States as a whole from evidence from a single state, even if it is "average."

State Policy and its Effects

Contingent Fee Limits and the Evolution of State Policy   Following the American Revolution, the opposition to federalism was strong, and led to the repeal of caps on attorneys' fees. Only in the mid-1970s, with the first malpractice crisis, did political support for attorney fee statutes reemerge in the legislatures of U.S. states, with some states enacting laws and subsequently repealing them. For example, since 1976, Hawaii enacted and repealed legislation regulating fee limits three times over the course of a decade before settling on a much more lenient statute requiring court approval of both parties' counsel fees.[37] Pennsylvania enacted a statute in 1975,[38] but in 1984 the Pennsylvania Supreme Court determined the statute to have been nullified by an earlier court decision.[39] Oregon enacted a limit on all contingent fees in 1975[40] and repealed it in 1987, replacing it with another statute which limits only attorney fees stemming from punitive damages.[41] Idaho enacted a cap on contingency fees in 1975 with a sunset in 1981.[42]

New Hampshire's Supreme Court ruled the state's sliding-scale contingent fee statute unconstitutional, and the legislature subsequently repealed it.[43] The Court held that the statute interfered with the freedom of contract between a single class of plaintiffs and their attorneys: "It does not regulate contingent fees generally; nor does it apply to defense counsel in medical malpractice cases, whose fees consume approximately the same percentage of the insurer premium dollar as do those of the plaintiff bar."[44] The Court recognized that there were systemic problems created by the contingent fee statute; the restrictions on contingent fees unfairly burdened the malpractice plaintiffs and their attorneys. By regulating only attorney fees in the medical malpractice arena, it made these types of cases unappealing to the plaintiff bar.[45] In its place, the legislature enacted a more lenient statute that requires court review of fees over $200,000.

In 1980, Florida enacted a statute, repealed five years later, allowing courts to award a reasonable attorney fee to the prevailing party in medical malpractice cases.[46] Attempting to curb rising costs associated with a crisis in medical malpractice, the Florida legislature proposed an amendment to the state constitution, filed with the secretary of state on

September 8, 2003. The amendment, titled "Claimant's right to fair compensation," became effective after approval by voters in November 2004.[47] Under the new amendment, when a contingent fee is involved, a claimant in a medical malpractice case is entitled to 70 percent of the first $250,000 recovered, and 90 percent of all damages in excess of $250,000 recovered.[48] This statute has simply reversed the wording of a contingent fee limit—30 percent of the first $250,000, and 10 percent of all the excess.

Florida's approach to containing contingent fees was soon sidestepped by plaintiffs' attorneys. To avoid the limit, clients were asked to sign waivers allowing their lawyers to take a higher fee. In 2006, the Florida Supreme Court decided that any constitutional right can be waived, and thus, the use of waivers was acceptable.[49]

In sum, states have been involved in limiting attorney fees for over three decades. This legislation has largely arisen as a response to the medical malpractice insurance crises. This implies that stakeholders representing health care providers have been particularly active and effective in assuring passage of statutes to limit attorney fees in litigation that affects them most directly.

The Current Situation   Existing rules governing fees generally treat contingent fees as more worthy of regulation than other payment methods—for example, the requirement that the terms of contingent fee arrangements be in writing.[50] The underlying assumption appears to be that the state needs to provide more protection for clients when the lawyer is paid on a contingency fee basis.[51]

Three types of regulations are currently used to limit attorney fees: sliding scale,[52] court review,[53] and maximum percentage.[54] Less than half of the states use one of these restrictions, but almost all of the states that do use restrictions have had their statutes in place since the mid-1980s or earlier.

The sliding-scale limitation is employed by ten of the twenty-three states with fee limits. The formulas limiting fees specify that contingent fee percentages decrease as the award increases, implicitly assuming that absent government intervention, lawyer compensation under contingent fee arrangements is relatively excessive for large awards. Nevertheless, the formulas do not account for especially large jury verdicts. Thus, past some threshold, the assumption appears to be that compensation does not become more excessive.

To address this issue, eight states have enacted a process of court review of attorney fees, which approves what is deemed to be a reasonable fee.[55] In states where judicial review is not mandatory, the right must be affirmatively invoked; however, it is questionable whether a typical plaintiff would contest a fee after months or possibly years of litigation. As enacted, fee-capping statutes are not likely to be binding. Most states with these statutes cap fees at the standard contingency fee of one third of the recovery, but one state allows up to 50 percent of the award to go to attorneys' fees, a percentage that is well above the usual contingency fee agreement.

As mentioned before, in Florida not only did limits recently win legislative approval, but they were voted upon by the electorate in 2004 as well. The voters in Florida presumably believed the arguments of the advocates for these tort reforms. Finally, as with Florida's no-fault program for neurologically impaired infants,[56] lawyers are able to pursue their financial incentive to sidestep the intent of the reform.

Empirical Evidence of Contingent Fee Regulation

An early study by Danzon and Lillard (1983) estimates the effect of restricting contingent fees on settlement rates. They find fee restrictions were associated with a 1.5 percentage point increase in the settlement rate. Studies by Sloan (1985) and Danzon (1986) find no effect of attorney fee regulation on medical malpractice premiums, claims frequency, or mean payment per paid claim.

More recently Helland and Tabarrok (2003) used two databases, one cross-sectional[57] and the other time-varying,[58] to investigate contingent fee statutes. Their study aimed to find the effects of contingency fee statutes, both those requiring judicial review and those imposing limits, on the probability that a case is dropped, as well as the time to case resolution. The underlying theory is that measures that make contingent fee payment less attractive to attorneys will lead to greater attorney reliance on pay by the hour. The probability that a case was dropped is taken as an indicator of the legal quality of the case. Whether or not a lawyer was willing to accept a case on a contingent fee basis is interpreted as a signal of whether the lawyer thinks the case is meritorious. In contrast, payment on an hourly basis provides an incentive for lawyers to take cases, irrespective of their legal merit. Further, lawyers paid on an hourly basis have a greater incentive to delay case resolution.

Results from both databases indicate that the probability of a case being dropped increased following imposition of statutory constraints on contingent fees; the time to resolution also increased. The authors conclude that "Limits on contingency fees were supposed to prevent people with poor information from paying too much for legal representation. The results of this study cast doubt on whether this goal was achieved. Our results indicate that, as in other areas, restrictions on the freedom to contract have unintended consequences."[59]

The fact that dropping of cases increases following enactment of contingent fee limits may not have been anticipated by proponents of statutory fee limits. But the result makes perfect sense. Once an attorney receives the bad news about the prospects of winning a case, possibly as a result of exchange of documents during the discovery process or from depositions, the lawyer compensated on a contingent fee basis has an incentive to recommend that the case be discontinued.[60] Under an hourly fee arrangement, lawyers do not have this incentive. Overall, limits on contingent fees charged by attorneys appear to have none of the effects sought by the proponents of these statutes—namely on the cost of medical malpractice insurance to physicians—most likely because the limits were not binding constraints on such fees.

Fee-Shifting Rules: The Loser Pays All Attorneys' Fees

Historical Background
In the United States, the common-law rule, and the usual practice, is that each side assumes its own attorneys' fees irrespective of the outcome of the legal dispute. However, the United States has some experience with fee shifting wherein the loser is responsible for all litigation cost, also known as the English Rule.[61] As a new colony, the United States followed the English Rule of fee shifting. The English Rule was in practice until

1789, when Congress enacted legislation authorizing federal courts to follow state law concerning fee awards.[62] Despite this legislation, the use of the English Rule by the states continued until the U.S. Supreme Court specifically addressed fee shifting in a 1796 opinion. This case involved an award of attorneys' fees which were challenged; the Supreme Court ultimately struck the award of attorneys' fees. Because there were no federal statutes on the issue during the period 1800–1853, and all the statutes that allowed the recovery of attorneys' fees had expired by 1800, federal courts used state statutes on attorneys' fees. As a result, the English Rule was frequently applied. An 1830 decision by the Supreme Court,[63] despite precedent and relevant statutory authority, held that the law did not limit the power to award attorney fees; this power was in the Court's discretion.[64] Subsequently, Congress enacted the 1853 fee bill that prevents collection of attorneys' fees from a losing party. The rule that developed from the bill was named the American Rule. This new rule called for each litigant to pay its own attorneys' fees, regardless of the success of the parties.

Exceptions to the Use of the American Rule in the United States

The most comprehensive fee-shifting statute in the United States is in the state of Alaska. This state has had a fee-shifting statute since the mid-1800s, before Alaska even became a territory of the United States.[65] Alaska's legislative and judicial development partly explains its continued use of the English rule. After the United States purchased Alaska in 1867, seventeen years passed before Congress gave Alaska instructions for a civil government. In 1884, Congress declared Alaska to be a civil and judicial district, and the general laws of Oregon would apply. Oregon's statutes allowed one-way fee shifting for the plaintiff, including witness fees, court fees, deposition expenses, and costs relating to the preparation of documents used as evidence at trial. This law was in effect until 1900, when Congress passed a code of civil procedure for Alaska. This new code had a provision for attorneys' fees similar to the Oregon statute. In 1949, Congress amended the statute designating the civil procedure code so that the Federal Rules of Civil Procedure would apply to the U.S. District Court in Alaska. However, as Congress had not repealed the statute granting jurisdiction over attorneys' fees to Alaska, and the Federal Rules were silent on the matter, Alaska kept the fee-shifting practice.

Alaska's rules evolved over the next several years to establish a more reasonable fee schedule and grant courts the discretion to award fees when cases fell outside the parameters of the fee schedule. After 1959, when Alaska became a state, the former territorial laws and court rules were codified in the newly created Alaska code. Rule 82, which still applies, was adopted into the Alaska Rules of Civil Procedure.[66] This rule set forth schedules for trial courts to award attorney fees to the prevailing party. Over the next several decades, the rules were repealed, rewritten, and amended, and the Alaskan Supreme Court has heard many challenges to Rule 82. A Supreme Court subcommittee has evaluated the rule twice; on both occasions, the Court has chosen to leave the rule in effect. Substantial revisions were made the last time Rule 82 was reviewed (1992).

Rule 82 gives fixed percentages of actual reasonable attorneys' fees based on length, degree of difficulty, bad conduct, attorney conduct, and a few other considerations. The prevailing party always receives attorney fees as long as a motion is filed within ten days from the date shown on the certificate of distribution on the judgment.[67] However, the parties can agree to waive the fee requirement. Attorneys in Alaska have said that the motion practice for Rule 82 is routine, and simply another part of the litigation process.[68]

Empirical Evidence on Effects of Switching from the American Rule to the English Rule

There is some empirical research on the effects of changing to the English Rule. This rule should reduce claiming since it places a presumably risk-averse plaintiff under substantial financial risk. Hughes and Snyder[69] investigate the effects of changing to the English Rule, using data on Florida closed medical malpractice claims. They find claims were more likely to be dropped under the English Rule, suggesting that weak claims are less likely to be pursued. Those claims that were pursued were more likely to be litigated. In general, they found that the English Rule encouraged plaintiffs with strong cases to pursue their claims but discouraged those with weak cases from doing so.[70] Interestingly, the Florida Medical Association, which had favored the English Rule initially, sought its repeal because, in practice, plaintiffs often did not have the funds to pay the winner.[71]

Alaska's experience with the English Rule has been evaluated by Di Pietro and Carns.[72] A deficiency with that study is that there was no control group, although some comparisons were made.

The study reaches three conclusions. First, the English Rule discourages some middle-class persons from suing. Second, it discourages pursuit of cases of questionable merit on both plaintiff and defense sides. Third, it encourages litigation in strong cases that would otherwise settle. While wealthy persons presumably can afford to pay the winner's fees, collection from the poor is infeasible, so the English Rule would have no effect in such cases.

The authors also report general satisfaction with the rule among attorneys in Alaska. However, in the vast majority of cases, the amounts of fees assessed the losing party were small (well under $10,000) and, interviews of knowledgeable persons in the state suggested that the English Rule did not affect plaintiff claiming.

There is a 12 percent difference between Alaska's civil court filings and those for states without fee shifting. In 1992, the national median number of court filings was 6,610 per 100,000 population, compared with Alaska's 5,793 per 100,000, a difference of 810 lawsuits per 100,000 persons.[73] In one sense, a 12 percent differene is meaningful. Yet, we do not know anything about what types of cases were reduced (e.g., whether or not cases involving low-income injury victims were disproportionately affected).

Overall, although the English Rule has the potential to benefit premium payers, it places injury victims at such a substantial disadvantage that unless it is implemented as part of a reform package which gives some important benefits to victims, it has virtually no chance of passage except on a very limited scale. And if it is enacted, the Florida experience is likely to be repeated. On balance, fee shifting seems worse than the disease it is trying to cure.

Another Type of Reform of the Contingent Fee System: Early Offers

An additional approach is to limit the fees in cases in which the plaintiff accepts an early offer from the defendant(s). Jeffrey O'Connell and Patrick Bryan[74] develop and advocate such a proposal they label "early offers." Under this plan, the defendant has up to 120 days after the filing of a suit to offer a no-fault-like periodic payment of a claimant's net economic loss.[75] In later variants of the proposal, the period is shortened to sixty days.

Acceptance of the offer forecloses the plaintiff's right to pursue a separate tort claim for noneconomic losses. The plan specifies that an early offer will compensate the plaintiff for all costs, including medical and rehabilitation expenses and wage losses not covered by collateral sources. The plan also encourages defendants to apologize for errors, something that does not currently occur because such statements may be used against the defendant in court.

In its 2004 version the plan required that contingent fees not be charged against settlement offers made prior to plaintiff's retention of counsel. If the offer is accepted by the plaintiff, the attorney's fees are limited to hourly rate charges and are capped at 10 percent for the first $100,000 of the offer and at 5 percent for any amounts in excess. There is a provision requiring notices of claim submitted by plaintiff's counsel to include basic, routinely discoverable information designed to assist defendants in evaluating plaintiff's claim, and conversely for defendants to provide such information to plaintiffs. When plaintiffs reject defendants' early offers, contingent fees may be applied against net recoveries only in excess of these offers. Finally, if no offer is made within sixty days, the early offer plan does not affect the attorney's contingent fee.[76]

Early offers have several potential advantages. The plan seeks to cut time elapsed from the filing of a suit to the time it is resolved. By accepting an early offer, the plaintiff can benefit from speedy compensation at the cost of being foreclosed from suing in tort for nonmonetary loss. Defendants save time and the aggravation of a lengthy legal process, and third-party insurers save legal expense and payments for nonmonetary loss as well as the unpredictability of some claims. The early offer includes the plaintiff's attorney fees, based on a reasonable hourly rate, which is substantially less than the customary range of contingent fees described above. Some medical malpractice plaintiffs state that learning what happened is a major motivation for suing,[77] and thus plaintiffs may be better off from receiving both an explanation and an apology. At the same time, by not permitting contingent fees during settlement offers made prior to plaintiff's retention of counsel, the possibility of offers soon after providers discover an error may be increased. The provision, which disallows contingent fees on the early offer if the offer is rejected, is meant to dissuade attorneys from convincing their clients to reject early offers.

The plan is ostensibly designed to help the injury victims who are said to be victimized by trial lawyers under the contingent fee system. That the plan increases the well-being of injury victims is debatable. The basic argument for the plan is that it would cut losses, in terms of both legal expense and compensation, although there would be benefits in terms of speed of claim resolution and the lower amount of the early offer taken by the attorneys' fees.

The plan is likely to make it harder for people to obtain legal representation even if they have valid grievances. Proponents of the plan speak of the windfall trial lawyers currently enjoy. However, evidence of client dissatisfaction is at best ambiguous; if clients truly are disappointed with their attorney and fee levels, they do have recourse to appeal; the judge can overturn or reduce the fee. Further, a survey of medical malpractice claimants in Florida revealed that the vast majority of claimants, whether or not they received compensation, were satisfied with the system.[78] This evidence is from one state and only for medical malpractice claims involving birth injuries and injuries in emergency rooms. Thus, generalizability is an issue. But evidence based on systematically collected data suggests that clients are generally satisfied with the dispute resolution process.

The notion of widespread windfalls assumes that the cost incurred by lawyers in making initial evaluation of the legal merits of a claim is negligible. This may be true in some cases, but definitely not in others. Advocates for the proposal can argue that defendants are precluded under the current contingent fee system from making early offers of settlement because this would signal a weakness in their case and would certainly be rejected. If no early offer is made, defendants are in the same position as before.

Litigation cost currently absorbs a very high share of the medical malpractice premium dollar. Thus, any plan that would reduce such cost would, other factors being equal, reduce the overhead of receiving compensation. This is a plus. Another argument advanced by advocates of early offers is that it will clear the court dockets by encouraging early settlements. In turn, this would reduce the "excessive" costs of the current tort system.[79] However, it is not clear that the court dockets are clogged with personal injury claims, and certainly not with medical malpractice claims, which constitute only a very small proportion of total personal injury claims.

In the end, this proposal leaves us with more questions than answers. What should be done about poorer victims who incur insubstantial monetary loss when injured? What about victims with early offers that do not adequately compensate their damages, but whose case would not survive the higher burden of proof required for trial?

Replacing the Contingent Fee System: Legal Expense Insurance

Overview
A more promising alternative to the current contingent fee system may be legal expense insurance. If people have insurance coverage for legal expenses, a large part of the rationale for the contingent fee system would no longer apply. People would have access to legal representation without having to grant the plaintiff's attorney a large share of any recovery. On the other hand, the experience with other forms of first-party insurance has not been that good. For one, health insurance distorts individuals' incentives to use medical care wisely.

Legal Expense Insurance in Europe
Legal expense insurance has been used for decades in Europe.[80] Thus, the experiences in these countries provide a basis for evaluating the shortcomings and strengths of prepaid legal service plans. Currently in Europe there are four types of legal expense insurance (LEI): after the event (ATE); before the event (BTE); stand-alone; and add-on policies.

While it seems that ATE would save a claimant the expense of insurance without losing the benefits, insurers offer ATE only if the claimant's chance of success is high.

In England, most policyholders use BTE, with a small but growing segment of the market using ATE. Most of the policies in England are add-on policies; toward the end of the 1990s, the Association of British Insurers was aware of only one personal stand-alone product on the U.K. market.[81] By contrast, in Germany, stand-alone BTE policies are the dominant form. These policies allow their holders to mix and match the areas of law they prefer to have covered, based on their needs.[82] England also has commercial policies, a form of insurance that does not exist in Germany. These policies are sold on a stand-alone basis and account for one third of the LEI market's gross premiums.[83]

About 42 percent of households in Germany are covered by legal expense insurance.[84] Such insurance constitutes only a small share of the total insurance market; in Germany, where legal expense insurance is prevalent, it accounts for only 6 percent of insurance premiums, compared with 46 percent for auto.[85] Nevertheless, German LEI provides coverage for 3.6 million cases annually and over €1.5 billion in lawyers' fees, making up a quarter of all the fees earned by German lawyers.[86]

Mandatory use of fee schedules for attorneys' fees is only one element of public regulation. Germany and Switzerland require that LEI be offered only by specialized insurance companies. As of 1986, there were thirty-two such companies in Germany and twelve in Switzerland. Europe as a whole, not including Scandinavia, had a total of ninety-five specialty companies; and, over 600 other insurance companies provided some form of LEI.[87] In Germany, in-house lawyers are not allowed, ceding private attorneys control over all private causes of action. Also, Germany does not allow contingent and conditional fees; any fee that is outcome-determined is not permitted.

Proponents of LEI argue that a well-developed LEI market removes pressure for government funding of programs such as legal aid or other organizations that focus their efforts on indigent clients. In Germany, about eight times as much was spent on LEI as all the federal German states combined spent on legal aid. Since such insurance covers tort litigation, access to legal representation may be enhanced in this sense.

However, less than half of German households have legal expense insurance. This could mean that the other half can afford legal assistance at their own cost, or it could mean that a vast majority of German citizens do not have access to the legal system. Of the small amount spent on legal aid by the government in Germany, 80 percent is spent on family law cases, an area not covered by legal expense insurance. By contrast, in England and Wales, where LEI is relatively new and not as heavily relied upon, governments spent twenty-eight times as much per capita on legal aid than the population spent on LEI premiums.[88]

Legal expense insurance has achieved widespread acceptance in Europe. Such insurance has the advantage of providing risk protection against high legal losses without resorting to contingent fees. However, there are important differences between the United States and Europe, especially in acceptance of government regulation and in particular in government's role in setting fees. Some of the issues that have plagued health insurance, discussed above, may also plague its legal counterpart. However, the technological change that underlies much of the growth of personal health spending is not present in the legal context.

Legal Expense Insurance in the United States

Prepaid legal service plans (LSPs) have had a challenging beginning in the United States. At the beginning of the twentieth Century, both the American Bar Association and many state bar associations had strict ethical rules which prohibited a lawyer's involvement with group legal services, parallel to the objections against prepaid medical service plans by the medical establishment.[89] However, this opposition did not totally preclude entry of some group legal service plans. In 1930, the Brotherhood of Railroad Trainmen established one of the very first group legal service plans.[90] Its activities gave rise to a series of cases which ended in 1964 with *Brotherhood of Railroad Trainmen v. Virginia ex rel. Virginia State Bar*.[91] In this case, the U.S. Supreme Court found that Virginia statutes prohibiting group legal services were a violation of the First and Fourteenth Amendments. One year prior to this decision, the Supreme Court held that the National Association for the Advancement of Colored People (NAACP) had a constitutionally protected right of political association, which gave its attorneys the right to bring civil rights suits on behalf of the members, setting the precedent for group legal service plans.[92]

Nevertheless, criticisms from the legal community continued after the U.S. Supreme Court decisions. The concerns centered on one main issue—conflict of interest.[93] The conflict of interest is twofold, encompassing both confidentiality issues and interference with independent professional judgment. Both of these issues stem from the involvement of a third party, the legal service organization. Confidentiality issues are raised because legal service organizations want to know the extent of clients' issues and to be involved in deciding what the course of action should be. Concern about independent judgment arises because, with insurer involvement, attorneys may not act in the best interests of their clients. These concerns were addressed by a series of revisions to the Code of Professional Responsibility, American Bar Association opinions, and local bar opinions. Since 1983, the ABA has officially encouraged development of legal service plans.

Interestingly, the same confidentiality and conflict of interest issues have arisen in the context of health insurance in general and in managed care in particular. These issues provide much of the reason for the managed care backlash. Without some sort of insurer intervention, however, moral hazard becomes a major problem in contexts of legal and health insurance. The same issues arise on the defense side. Third-party insurance covers litigation expense as well as payments to claimants. The interest of the insurer and the defendant may often be in conflict.

Contemporary LSPs function much like preferred provider organizations (PPOs). Monthly premiums are paid and plan benefits limit out-of-pocket expense, particularly if the covered person uses a lawyer in the network.[94] Legal service plans can be barebones or comprehensive in their coverage.

Legal insurance does not provide adequate coverage for most personal injury cases. For medical malpractice actions, few, if any, legal service plans cover the amount of preparation and trial time required for litigating a claim. Some more comprehensive plans cover this type of litigation, but even those put a cap on the amount of time spent on the case—past this limit, the plaintiff is responsible for the charges, albeit at a discounted fee.

Differences Between Legal Expense Insurance in Europe and in the United States

There are several important differences between the European legal expense insurance and the legal service plans in the United States. These differences affect the functionality and accessibility of group legal services in the United States. First, LSPs do not insure against monetary loss; rather, they allocate a preset number of lawyer's hours to the insured. Even though risk is curbed by limits on the number of hours, attorney fees in the United States vary markedly, which complicates LSPs' risk calculations. Public regulation of fees in Europe simplifies this aspect of the risk calculation.[95] LSPs typically fund the expenses of litigation only for a defendant. An ordinary plan allows a member to have a limited amount of funding for consultation with an attorney, usually over the phone, and basic legal services, such as will drafting. Nevertheless, even though the most comprehensive plans limit and/or exclude coverage, most comprehensive plans are structured so that a typical middle-class family is likely to be covered for 80–90 percent of personal legal services they may need to use.[96] In general, there is no requirement that a specific event occur (such as a claim filed against the insured) for the policy to take effect. Members may take advantage of routine services and consultation immediately, in contrast to LEI plans.

Perhaps the most important difference between LSPs and LEIs, and the largest obstacle to their growth, is the fact that LSPs are usually set up as an employee benefit trust or as a union benefit.[97] Given the growth of the cost of other fringe benefits, expanding reimbursements to cover still another type of benefit has been highly problematic. In contrast, LEIs are directly financed by households.

Is Legal Insurance a Desirable Alternative to the Contingent Fee System?

First-party legal insurance coupled with payment of plaintiff attorneys could indeed be an alternative to contingent fees. If it is provided on a group basis, adverse selection could be largely avoided. But employers are likely to resist a mandate that they provide such coverage. Individually purchased legal insurance would be potentially subject to adverse selection.

The other major problem plaguing insurances of all types is moral hazard. With nearly complete or complete insurance, insured individuals would use legal services at greater rates. To combat this, insurers would need to impose limits on utilization of such services or otherwise impose some type of active case management. This would in turn result in conflict of interest issues discussed above; moreover, the limits may be too restrictive to allow lawyers to actively pursue a complex medical malpractice claim.

It matters from which point one starts. If the United States had started with European-style LEI in the modern era, it would be relatively easy to continue along this path. Yet contingent fees are so entrenched in the U.S. culture, especially in the realm of personal injury, that changing course at this stage would be hard to do.

Discussion and Conclusions

Some who would reform the contingent fee system fall into the same trap as previous reformers. They presume to know how the system works, but that presumption is based largely on a single case or even atypical cases that capture media and public attention. Not surprisingly, the direct beneficiaries of proposed changes in methods of compensating lawyers rush to support the statutory changes that they like. We agree with Herbert Kritzer,[98] who concludes, "I do not presume that there are never situations in which lawyers take advantage of clients to obtain fees that raise equity and ethical issues. However, abuses of this type are confined neither to lawyers working on a contingency fee basis[99] nor to members of the legal profession." And Haltom and McCann note:

A public image that includes financial self-interest hardly separates tort lawyers from other business persons, stock traders, and almost any powerful figure in American society. . . . In short, the public assessment is contradictory; lawyers are respected and distrusted for the same aggressive client representation.[100]

This is not an excuse for overlooking injustices and inefficiencies when they occur. However, to the extent that principal/agent problems are rife when consumers deal with professionals, this is worthy of a more general examination than a limited focus on personal injury attorneys and attorneys who represent claimants in medical malpractice cases in particular.

For those who would see imposing limits on attorney compensation as a method for reducing the high cost of medical malpractice, empirical evidence has provided no support for the claim that limits in fact lead to savings. The evidence suggests that application of the English Rule could accomplish this goal, but Florida's experience with the English Rule is instructive.

The system currently in place in the United States is a blend of the English and American rules. It provides access to the courts to people who must rely on contingent fees, and it also allows parties who desire fee shifting a statutory basis for asking the court for attorneys' fees, especially in cases where there is abuse of the legal system. With over 1,200 statutes (to date) allowing fee shifting in this country, the American Rule in effect allows fee shifting. There is a strong argument that virtually all of the plaintiffs and defendants we want to protect qualify for one exception or another. Those who do not qualify for an exception are those whom most people think of as typical litigants; they have a potentially legitimate problem or issue, and they do not abuse the system in order to obtain compensation. These are not the persons who should be deterred from filing. What the proponents of the English Rule should be arguing for is more frequent or expanded use of existing exceptions.

In the United States, the people—through their elected officials—decide which cases will permit fee shifting, not the courts. Furthermore, the English Rule is applied in an entirely different legal context in England. In that country, judges, not juries, hear personal injury cases. Changing this factor alone would satisfy those who claim there are "outrageous jury verdicts." But, Americans see jury trials in civil cases as their right.

As in England, when the defendant in the United States is an organization rather than an individual, the defendant tends to have considerably greater resources and knowledge than the plaintiff. The defendant has the resources to delay settlement and force a case to trial.—Under the English Rule and combined with the high rate of success at verdict for the defense in medical malpractice disputes, the result for an unsuccessful plaintiff would be crushing attorney fees.

In practice, most legal disputes in both the United States and England are settled before trial. However, faced with the possibility of paying the attorney fees of an opponent, many potential victims with legitimate claims will never bring their claims; it is too large a risk for a plaintiff with anything but a "sure-thing" case.

In regards to first-party insurance for legal expense, the concept is intriguing, but is unlikely to be implemented as a substitute for contingent fees in the United States. As with no-fault, discussed in chapter 11, historical context can be critical to the success of a change. While legal expense insurance has been successful in Europe, it faces special challenges in the United States. In particular, coping with moral hazard and adverse selection would lead to many controls that both lawyers and individual policyholders are likely to resist. Many of the issues facing health insurance would likely be repeated, including how to provide financial support for claims filed by persons without legal insurance. Another issue that arises is the various cost containment issues when personal out-of-pocket expense falls far short of total expense.

In the end, it seems that the current system for paying attorneys may be as good as any of the other alternatives. As the saying goes, "If it ain't broke, don't fix it." If there are to be changes in medical malpractice law, it is best to look elsewhere.

Nevertheless, one aspect that could be "broke" is the lack of a competitive market for plaintiffs' attorney services. However, rather than implement regulatory interventions, or such proposals as early offers, which would at best address part of the issue of lack of competition in the market for attorneys' services, a better course would be for antitrust authorities to investigate whether or not there are impediments to price competition in this sector. Such an investigation should not be limited to contingent fee arrangements, but should investigate price fixing in hourly fee arrangements and referral agreements as well.

7

Juries and Health Courts

Introduction and Overview

Several articles on juries start "The American jury is on trial" or an equivalent statement.[1] While this statement applies much more generally than only to medical malpractice, one criticism of juries is that they are ill-equipped to decide complicated issues of causation and duty of care. Not only is it said that juries lack expertise to deal with the technical issues in many medical malpractice cases, but in participating in a single trial, individual jurors lack the experience that they would accumulate by participating in many trials involving medical malpractice. Jurors' ability to process the technical information presented at trial is certainly not helped by the lawyers and attorneys representing both sides who cannot agree on the applicable scientific principles themselves.[2] Even if they are not limited in technical expertise and experience, jurors are often said to be sympathetic to plaintiffs. Their interpretation of the facts in this light[3] may cause them to view litigation as a vehicle for redistributing wealth from wealthier defendants to less affluent plaintiffs. Some have also alleged race and gender bias.[4]

In the United States, tort cases proceed through several stages. Most simply, the stages are determination of liability, compensation (especially nonmonetary compensation), and punitive damages. The first stage is the trial stage, where the plaintiff must show proof of injury and proof that defendant's negligence was the cause in fact of the injury. After successful completion of this stage, the trial moves to the compensatory stage, in which the court decides the amount of compensation necessary to make the plaintiff whole. In a third stage, the court may ask whether punitive damages are warranted, that is, whether or not the defendant's conduct was sufficiently malicious, reckless, or careless to warrant an additional penalty designed to deter future behavior of the sort presented at the trial, and if it is, the appropriate amount of punitive damages.[5]

Criticism of juries is not new. Ever since juries or jurylike organizations have existed—in ancient Rome, in eighteenth-century England, and in the early twentieth-century United States, they have been attacked for their incompetence.[6] American juries have been the subject of criticism at all three stages. Jury sympathy for the plaintiff may spill over into sympathy in setting compensatory and punitive damages.

Much of the literature focuses on punitive damages in product liability cases, where such damages are fairly common, especially in the high-profile, highly publicized cases. Punitive damages are now very uncommon in medical malpractice.[7] However, they may become more common in the future, especially if caps on nonmonetary compensatory loss become binding constraints on payment to medical malpractice claimants.

"Runaway Juries"

One often hears about "runaway juries." Quotations, such as the following, from the front page of the *Wall Street Journal*, are common:

"The real sickness is people who sue at the drop of the hat, judgments are going up and up and up, and people getting rich out of this are the plaintiffs' attorneys," says David Golden of the National Association of Independent Insurers, a trade group. The American Medical Association says Florida, Nevada, New York, and Pennsylvania and eight other states face a "crisis" because the "legal system produces multimillion-dollar jury awards on a regular basis."[8]

The media provide a biased sample of jury verdicts. A disproportionate number of extremely high verdicts are discussed by the media.[9] Although high verdicts receive a substantial amount of publicity, many high awards at verdict are subsequently reduced, either by the judge, on appeal, or by a postverdict settlement.[10] These reductions are much less likely to be highly publicized. A study by the Rand Corporation finds that about 70 percent of amounts awarded at verdict are actually paid. For punitive damages, slightly less than 60 percent of the award is paid.[11]

Although concerned not with medical malpractice but tobacco litigation, John Grisham's fictional account summarizes what many believe to be nonfiction.[12] (Parenthetically, some of the major plaintiffs' attorneys in tobacco litigation specialized in medical malpractice litigation before becoming involved in lawsuits against tobacco companies.)

In medical malpractice cases, the defendant is typically a physician, not a tobacco manufacturer. The alleged plot does not typically involve a particular juror, but rather jurors more generally, who may be well-intentioned, but whose decision-making is allegedly not governed by medical knowledge or legal principles, but rather by sympathy for the injury victim.

Compared to the large number of anecdotes, there are a small number of in-depth empirical studies of juror behavior, most of which do not specifically deal with medical malpractice. The empirical evidence is mixed, suggesting some support for perhaps a partial runaway jury.

Empirical Evidence on Juror Behavior in Determination of Liability

The Percentage of Cases Won by Plaintiffs at Trial Is Low
A review of thirteen studies of verdicts in medical malpractice cases revealed that the median plaintiff win rate for the studies taken as a group was 29.6 percent.[13] In a recent review of civil trials disposed of in state courts in the seventy-five largest counties in the United States in 2001, the plaintiff win rate in medical malpractice cases was nearly 27 percent.[14] These low win rates do not eliminate the possibility of jury bias in favor of plaintiffs, but they tend to place an upper bound on such bias.

Nontechnical Nature of Many Medical Malpractice Disputes
While the conventional wisdom is that medical malpractice claims involve much technical material beyond the comprehension of juries, many medical malpractice disputes are in fact not technical. Vidmar presents brief summaries of the issues in a sample of verdicts from North Carolina in the mid-1980s in which the verdict favored the plaintiff.[15] These issues included surgery on the wrong foot, permanent paralysis and brain

damage following drug overdose administered to the patient after heart surgery, and a patient receiving ten times the prescribed dosage of chemotherapy, which resulted in nerve damage, paralysis, organ damage, and loss of sexual function.

One can also find examples in which technical details are central to the legal dispute, such as *West v. Johnson & Johnson*,[16] a medical product liability, not a medical malpractice, case. The medical issue was whether Johnson and Johnson's tampon was a defective product. Sugarman uses this case to argue that jurors selected at least in part for their ignorance about the topic are asked to decide extremely difficult scientific issues.[17] He would presumably have the same opinion of choice of jurors in complex medical malpractice litigation involving scientific issues.

Empirical Evidence on Myth 3: Dispute Resolution Is a Lottery

The above thinking about limitations of jurors leads to the inference that outcomes of litigation are often random. There is a body of empirical evidence, however, that leads to the opposite conclusion: that outcomes are *not* random. Even so, this does not imply that juries never make mistakes.

Taragin et al. compare outcomes of claims, whether or not the dispute ended with payment to the claimant, with assessments of physicians employed by an insurance company, the New Jersey Medical Inter-Insurance Exchange.[18] The physicians were asked to review the medical records and provide a neutral evaluation of whether or not they believed that the named defendants in specific cases were negligent. The raters' decisions were confidential and could not be presented as evidence at trial.

Most claims were "defensible," meaning that the raters found no negligence. The vast majority of defensible claims were resolved before discovery. Of those defensible claims that reached the trial stage, the vast majority resulted in no payment for the plaintiff. By contrast, among indefensible cases that reached trial, of those that did not settle, virtually all resulted in payment. About half of these cases resulted in payment when the case was decided on appeal.

In sum, there is substantial consistency between assessments of physicians working for the insurer and outcomes of the claims, both those settled prior to verdict and those decided at verdict and on appeal. Moreover, judgments for the plaintiff and the severity of the plaintiff's injury were unrelated, contradicting the view that jurors are unduly sympathetic to plaintiffs who sustain serious injuries. The authors' conclusion is that "unjustified payments are probably uncommon."[19]

Farber and White report similar results. Their data consisted of medical malpractice claims filed against a single hospital, which the authors did not identify.[20] As in the Taragin et al. study (1992), physicians assessed case-specific quality of care. Overall, the authors find strong evidence that care quality affects the outcomes of medical malpractice disputes. The hospital's expected liability for damages was twenty-five times higher when negligence occurred than when "good care" had been rendered. The data covered all claims against the hospital, not just jury verdicts.

Sloan, Githens, Clayton, et al. compare independent physicians' assessments with outcomes from medical malpractice disputes.[21] In 1986 and 1987, the authors surveyed 187 plaintiffs in Florida who had filed medical malpractice claims stemming from permanent birth-related injuries or injuries in a hospital emergency room. The survey obtained information on the respondents' clinical histories prior to the injury that led to the claim, events that led the plaintiff to sue, information on utilization of personal health services and other data used to estimate past and future monetary loss for each injury, and plaintiff satisfaction with the legal process. In addition, permission was obtained to give the authors access to the respondents' hospital records.

Medical evaluations of liability were conducted by a panel of physicians. The ratings were systematically and significantly related to the outcomes of the cases. Among cases dropped by plaintiffs without payment, the physician raters were three times more likely to have found no liability than to have found the defendant to be liable. Among cases settled with payment, the ratio of not liable and liable cases was reversed. For cases decided at verdict, the liability ratings were related to the trial outcome. When the plaintiff lost at trial, the independent raters were more likely to have found no liability, and the converse was true for those cases won by plaintiffs. The relationship between the raters' findings and the case outcomes was not perfect. However, case outcomes were systematically related to the independent findings of the raters. In a large number of cases, the raters indicated that they lacked the information from the medical records and interviews needed to determine defendant liability. If the authors had attempted to force an answer and not allow for uncertainty about liability, there would have been more discrepancies between ratings of liability and case outcomes.

A fourth and more recent study provides the most conclusive evidence on myth 3. Studdert, Mello, Gawande, et al. report results of assessments of a random sample of 1,452 medical malpractice claims extracted from the files of five liability insurers to determine whether or not an injury occurred, and if it had, whether or not the result was due to medical error.[22] Unlike the previous studies, the five companies were located in all regions of the United States. The authors focused on four clinical areas: obstetrics, surgery, missed or delayed diagnosis, and medication. The physician reviewers were trained in one-day sessions at each study site. Reviews lasted 1.6 hours per file on average; each file was handled by one reviewer.

Reviewers scored severity of injury on a widely used index ranging from emotional injuries to death.[23] If no injury was apparent from the record, the assessment of the file was terminated. This occurred in 3 percent of claims. More important, the physicians recorded their judgments of whether or not an error occurred. This scale ranged from little or no evidence that an adverse outcome resulted from one or more errors (scored 1 out of 6) to virtually certain evidence that an error had occurred. The full scale is shown in figure 7.1, which is reproduced from the study. Claims receiving a score of 4 or more (with 4 being "more than 50–50 chance of error") were classified as claims involving medical error. Claims with scores of 3 ("close call, but <50–50 chance of error") were classified as not involving error. Physician reviewers were *not* blinded as to whether or not payment was actually made in the case.[24]

As in the three other studies, there was a clear pattern of physician assessor agreement with the actual outcome of the claim (figure 7.1). For those claims for which there was "little or no evidence" of medical error, payment was made in only 19 percent of claims. By contrast, when the evidence of error was "virtually certain," payment was made in 84 percent of claims. The claims for which error was ambiguous fell between the two extremes in terms of the percent of claims paid, with the percent

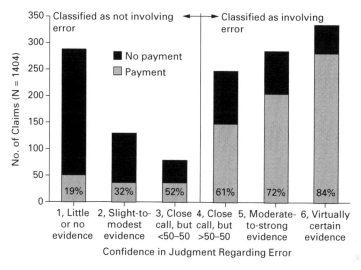

Figure 7.1
Relationship Between Physician Rate Confidence in Judgment Regarding Error
and the Probability That Payment Was Made to Claimant. Source: Studdert,
Mello, Gawande, et al. (2006).

paid increasingly monotonically with the degree of certainty that an error
had been committed.

Interestingly, the authors drew a line between "close call, but <50–50"
and "close call, but >50–50." Thus, a case for which the evidence was
49–51 was considered not to have involved an error, while a case for
which the evidence was 51–49 was considered a case in which an error
had occurred. The evidence clearly suggests that the probability that any
payment was made is systematically related to whether or not an error
had occurred, but the system is not perfect. Of course, there was only
one physician reviewer per case, and such reviewers may make mistakes
from time to time.

The article indicates that claims not involving errors accounted for 13
to 16 percent of the system's total monetary cost. However one views
this percentage (substantial or small), and whether or not a case involves
an error, depends substantially on where in figure 7.1 one draws the line
between error and no error. This is a fundamental point to keep in mind
in assessing the accuracy of dispute resolution in medical malpractice.

In most claims rated for this study, physician reviewers were somewhat uncertain as to whether or not a medical error had been committed. Unfortunately, the study conclusions do not stress or even mention that the estimates of error are subject to a very high degree of uncertainty.

In particular, results from the Harvard Medical Practice study suggest the opposite conclusion, namely, that most medical malpractice claims are "invalid".[25] At first glance, this view seems to support myth 3 and contradict the evidence from the four studies just described. Even if a review of an entire file revealed that there is "little or no evidence of error," this may not have been obvious at the time the claim was filed. As more evidence is accumulated, many claims are dropped without payment.[26] Filing a claim gives the claimant the option of pursuing a claim to trial. The Sloan, Githens, Clayton, et al. study surveyed plaintiffs many years after the injury occurred. Assessments were based on survey evidence in addition to medical records. Also, the ratio of invalid to valid claims strongly depends on whether or not the study allows for an "uncertain about liability" category. Just as in a trial, there will be disagreements among the experts about liability. It is not appropriate to treat the views of raters as an ironclad "gold standard."

Empirical Evidence Suggesting That Jurors Make Errors in Evaluating Liability
All of the four studies just described focus on comparisons between case outcomes and physician assessments of liability. There is a substantial body of literature, not specific to medical malpractice, focusing on juries' decision-making processes.

Literature from cognitive and social psychology documents various biases that apply to individuals of all types, including jurors and judges. People tend to underestimate the frequency of low frequency and to overestimate that of higher frequency.[27] People find an anchor or reference event for assessing probabilities, termed the availability heuristic.[28] That is, the probability of the event in question is compared to some other event. Well-publicized hazards tend to be assigned a higher risk than less publicized ones, especially in the case of phenomena that were previously unfamiliar, such as terrorist attacks or SARS.[29]

Some research, as well as anecdotes, suggests that jurors are suscepti-ble to relying on such legally irrelevant factors as the physical character-istics of litigants, the presence and content of pretrial publicity, and inadmissible evidence.[30] Since there are no minimum educational require-ments for individuals to serve on juries, and persons with high demands on their time may be more likely to try to avoid jury duty, many jurors have low levels of educational attainment.[31]

Much of this research is based on evidence from mock juries,[32] that is, individuals organized into fake juries in order to research how groups of individuals make various assessments of the types that juries often make. Results of research based on data obtained from mock juries criti-cally depend on how well the questions are phrased.[33]

There is some empirical evidence that jurors have difficulty making such benefit versus cost trade-offs. That is, jurors are swayed by the cost associated with an iatrogenic injury while ignoring the benefits that could have been anticipated at the time clinical decisions were made that caused the injury.[34]

Viscusi compares assessments of ninety-four judges from all parts of the United States versus those of jurors.[35] Compared to the jurors, judges tended to be better educated, had more exposure to risky decisions in their roles as judges, and had experience with conditions under which judicial errors are overturned on appeal. Furthermore, the judges were better able to assess objective probabilities of risk, although they, like the citizens, tended to underestimate large and overestimate small prob-abilities of risk. The judges were more likely than the jurors to reach decisions based on a benefit versus cost calculus. They were less likely to confuse ex ante and ex post risks than were the jurors. While such comparisons are interesting, they are not very surprising, and, as dis-cussed more fully below, we are unclear what the implications of the findings really are.

In sum, the myth that jury verdicts are random on liability is rejected by the empirical evidence. However, viewed from another perspective, there is no perfect consistency with the judgments of independent expert raters either. In some cases, perhaps the raters may have been in error because, for example, they lacked some of the information presented to juries. In many other cases, the raters may have been right. This is truly a situation of "cup half empty" versus "cup half full."

Rather than focus on deficiencies of juries, since the American jury is here to stay, it seems advisable to focus on how legal procedures can be improved. Courts are currently provided insufficient guidance about (1) recent scientific findings and the weight given to those findings by independent experts, and (2) the thinking that led to prior judicial decisions about liability.

Empirical Evidence on Juror Behavior: Determination of Compensatory Damages

Do Jurors Make Major Errors in Assessing Damages?

There is also a body of empirical evidence on jury assessments of compensatory damages. Some studies have focused on the accuracy of assessments of nonmonetary loss. Other research has compared total compensation with monetary loss. Payment for nonmonetary loss is derived as the difference between total compensation and monetary loss. Rather than focus on outcomes and make indirect inferences about juror behavior, some research examines juror behavior directly.

Vidmar and Rice compare assessments of nonmonetary loss between persons waiting to serve on juries and twenty-one arbitrators for various personal injury, contract, and labor disputes. They find that the assessments of the laypersons and arbitrators were positively correlated and that the laypersons did not assign higher values to such loss than did the arbitrators.[36] Another study found no difference in "pain and suffering" awards when the defendant was an individual, two individuals, or a hospital or corporation. This casts doubt on the "deep pockets" hypothesis.[37]

Some other studies are more critical of juries. Optimal deterrence requires that punishments increase when the probability of detection decreases. In research using mock jurors, there was no difference in recommended penalties depending on the probability of detection they were asked to assume.[38] In theory, there should be a negative relationship between the probability of detection and the size of the award. For example, if the number of highway patrols per highway mile is reduced, the fines for speeding should be increased. Sunstein, Schkade, and Kahneman report that even law students trained in deterrence theory rejected making judicial decisions on the basis of such economic thinking about damage awards.[39] This suggests that the problem does not apply only to jurors but also to those trained in the law.

Experience seems to help. Judges seem more likely to think in terms of the risk-cost trade-offs inherent in the concept of optimal deterrence than do jurors.[40] This has led some experts to conclude that a shift from jury to judge determination of damages might be worthwhile.[41]

Vidmar criticizes this line of research, arguing that the personal injury scenarios presented to the subjects were too short to allow them to make an informed judgment.[42] The longest of the scenarios presented to the subjects contained fourteen sentences, much less information than would be conveyed in a trial.

There is evidence from some studies of individual decision-making that individuals have difficulty making the kinds of decisions about damages that juries are asked to make. Yet even if assessments of plaintiff loss are inaccurate by some standard yet to be defined, they are not upward biased on average.

Empirical Evidence on Myth 4: Medical Malpractice Claimants Are Overcompensated for their Losses

The survey of the 187 plaintiffs in Florida obtained information on the cost of injuries.[43] Using these survey data as well as information from other primary and secondary sources, the authors performed an independent analysis of monetary loss in each of the 187 cases for both past and future loss. These estimates were then compared with the compensation the plaintiffs ultimately received.

The costs resulting from major injuries were considerable. Twenty-six percent of the plaintiffs received no compensation. On average, including those cases for which no compensation was received, compensation amounted to about half of *monetary* loss. Even including compensation for nonmonetary as well as monetary loss, compensation fell far short of injury cost. In cases in which the plaintiff won at trial, compensation exceeded monetary loss by 22 percent on average—hardly an indication of a "runaway jury." Some or all of the 22 percent was probably payment for nonmonetary loss.

The authors report a systematic relationship between injury cost and compensation, although variations in injury cost explained only part of the variation in compensation. A sensitivity analysis did not reverse the findings; the analysis adjusted for lawyers' fees, compensation from collateral sources, and favorable tax treatment of funds received from tort. None of the plaintiffs received punitive damages.

The authors conclude that the empirical evidence does not suggest that compensation is excessive *on average*. This does not eliminate the possibility that compensation was excessive in selected cases. Further, the results do not support imposition of caps on damages.

Some reforms, such as those proposed in Chapter 5, may have merit because payment for nonmonetary loss is inconsistent among cases; moreover, juries are given little or no guidance regarding the criteria to be used for setting such compensation.

Determination of Punitive Damages

Why is the Subject of Punitive Damages a Public Policy Concern?

Polinsky and Shavell begin with the statement "One of the most controversial features of the American legal system is the imposition of punitive damages."[44] Punitive damages are designed to fulfill the social functions of punishment, deterrence of injuries, and general deterrence of the defendant's conduct that violates social mores.[45] For punitive damages to be awarded, the plaintiff must show that the defendant intentionally harmed the plaintiff, or recklessly harmed the plaintiff by actions or inactions undertaken with knowledge that harm would occur, or with gross deviation from ordinary standards of care. Awards for punitive damages are often highly publicized, but are rare in medical malpractice cases.[46]

The sheer size of the dollar awards in some cases has raised concerns.[47] Other concerns are the substantial variability of awards for punitive damages and discrepant punishments by different juries for essentially the same act, reflecting in part the vague instructions to juries for assessing the appropriate level of damages, leaving it to individual juries to develop their own criteria. The situation in civil law, particularly in regard to punitive damages, stands in sharp contrast to criminal law, where sentencing guidelines have become far more common.[48]

One dispute in the academic literature stems from results of comparisons of patterns of awards for punitive damages between juries and judges. In Hersch and Viscusi's (2004) sample of jury and bench verdicts, juries, which decided 95 percent of cases, were more likely to award punitive damages than were judges, and award levels of punitive damages were higher. They found little relationship between compensatory and punitive awards, a finding in contrast to earlier studies by Eisenberg, Goerdt, et al. (2002), Eisenberg, La Fountain, et al. (1997), and Karpoff and Lott (1999), who found that the size of punitive damage awards is positively related to the size of compensatory awards. Hersch and Viscusi's (2004) analysis shows that study findings are quite sensitive to the explanatory variables included in the analysis. The unstated implication of Hersch and Viscusi's analysis is that relying on juries to set punitive damages is bad public policy.

Comparisons between the performance of judges and of juries raise some more fundamental questions. First, when opinions differ, are the opinions of the judges always the correct ones? Here it is useful to examine other empirical evidence on the performance of judges. Tabarrok and Helland investigate why trial awards differ among U.S. states.[49] The key hypothesis is that elected judges will be particularly sensitive to the state of residence of plaintiffs and defendants. Plaintiffs almost always live in the state in which the trial takes place. By contrast, for many personal injury cases, not including medical malpractice, the defendant's headquarters is out of state. In medical malpractice, defendants tend to be in state.

The authors present evidence from one state (Florida) that at least 80 percent of campaign contributions to judges in that state were made by lawyers. Contributions from trial lawyers could lead to bias in favor of granting high awards to plaintiffs. Tabarrok and Helland find that the expected total award was about $240,000 higher in states with elected judges when the defendant was out of state.[50] Thus, judges, too, can be biased.

It is not surprising that decisions of judges and juries sometimes differ. If we were to limit the voting population to persons with a graduate degree and/or household incomes over $200,000, election outcomes would probably differ appreciably. However, such restrictions hearken back to the literacy tests enacted by states under Jim Crow.

The Bottom Line: Rationale for Reform of Courts

The American jury is under attack from a much broader group of stakeholders than physicians, hospitals, and medical malpractice insurers. It is also true of some criticisms of awards for compensatory damages and of attorneys' fees, the subjects of the previous two chapters.

Two criticisms of the existing system seem more fundamentally applicable to the legal system and to resolution of medical malpractice disputes in particular. The system's outcomes may be inequitable in both horizontal (equal treatment of equals) and vertical (equal treatment according to harm done) dimensions. That is, while the current system is highly individualized to the circumstances of a particular case, individualization can go too far, especially if decision-makers are subject to substantial errors in judgment and even biases. Random outcomes may also weaken any deterrent signal that a judicial outcome may otherwise have. Greater consistency in decisions seems like a worthwhile goal, providing a possible rationale for health courts as well as for scheduling damages (discussed in Chapter 5). Juries currently receive little guidance about past judicial decisions, and their rationale, to inform their deliberations. Scientific information is presented anew. Such replays in the courtroom seem inefficient at best.

Health Courts

Rationale for Health Courts
Proponents of health courts contend that these special courts would offer several potential benefits: reducing medical malpractice insurance premiums; increasing access for all who have been injured; and encouraging patient safety measures.[51] In addition to providing victims with consistent, fast, and relatively easily obtained compensation when this is war-

ranted, health courts are also intended to reduce cost by streamlining the process, maintaining consistent medical standards, and capping or scheduling damages.

Several factors have led to proposals for specialized health courts. For instance, there is a general distrust of juries, especially by groups likely to be adversely affected by their decisions. In addition, there are concerns about the inadequacies of juries to decide technical matters common in medical malpractice litigation, and the inexperience of judges in the mainstream judiciary in medical matters. Nevertheless, the concept of specialized courts is not new. There are specialized courts for family matters, juveniles, taxes, bankruptcy, admiralty, mental health, drug, and even the homeless.

Administrative approaches are another alternative to the status quo. In this chapter, we limit the discussion to health courts. (Administrative approaches are discussed in detail in chapter 11.)

Health Court Proposals

Alternative specialty courts for medical malpractice are receiving a great deal of public attention in the first decade of the twenty-first century. The Common Good and the Public Policy Institute are driving the campaign in both public and private spheres, garnering support along the way from health policy scholars, physicians, attorneys, leaders of universities and medical schools, and directors and heads of consumer organizations, among many others.[52] A decade and a half earlier, the American Medical Association (AMA) introduced a proposal utilizing a specialized administrative health court system in 1988.[53] The Public Policy Institute and the Common Good's proposals share essentially the same features as the AMA proposal, albeit with a simplified design.[54] However, unlike the current health court proposal, the AMA proposal received little publicity or support.

Health courts eliminate jury trials for medical malpractice actions and establish damage schedules with caps on nonmonetary damages. Although they differ in some details, the major proposals for alternative courts for medical malpractice legal disputes all are fundamentally the same. Juries are removed and decision-making power is placed with a special judiciary that has scientific training. In addition, to preserve the neutrality of expert opinions, experts are selected and compensated by the court, not the parties. Also, decisions about standards of care are made as a matter of law by the judge. Compensation schedules are set by an independent body, and reviewed periodically to account for inflation and changing costs specific to medical malpractice injuries.

The process is designed to be accessible and fast for claimants. Physicians are required to inform the patient immediately after an adverse event. Then, to initiate a claim, an injured patient must only complete a simple claim form and send it to a review board. These forms would be available throughout the state, and could be completed without legal assistance. An initial review board would then evaluate the circumstances under which the injury occurred.

After the review board receives the initial complaint, it would obtain information from medical records and interviews with patients, health care providers, and others with primary knowledge. Similar to some variants of a medical no-fault, cases arising from avoidable events or clearly due to negligence or malpractice would receive immediate payment from the health care provider according to the schedule of damages.[55] Cases that clearly do not constitute medical malpractice or are too minor to merit an award would be dismissed with a limited right to appeal to the health court.[56] If it is not clear how the injury occurred, the claim would be sent to the health court for a full trial. If, in the plaintiff's opinion, the judge fails to apply the law correctly, plaintiffs would have the right to appeal the decision to a dedicated court of medical appeals.

Full-time judges are a major feature of the health court proposals. The judge would deal only with malpractice cases, entirely replacing the function of a jury. In one proposal (Common Good's), specialized judges would shape legal standards for medical malpractice, creating a body of science-based common law that health care providers could rely on when making treatment decisions.

In theory, a body of science-based common law seems valid and useful, but raises issues of its own. In the context of health courts, standards for medical practice would develop under state law. Yet, without federal regulation each state would be free to develop medical standards by way of the common law, allowing the possibility of variable legal and medical practice standards. Another proposal (the Public Policy Institute's) suggests creating legislation that would allow the U.S. government to regulate health courts under the power of the interstate commerce clause.[57]

Health courts face several implementation barriers, including challenges to the constitutionality of scheduled damages, the limited right to appeal, removal of juries, the questionable skill of appointed judges, and access to the system. In the past, tort reform statutes have been overturned on grounds of unconstitutionality. Opponents of such courts have argued that health courts would not survive judicial scrutiny. Proponents, however, have countered that the U.S. Supreme Court has not extended the Seventh Amendment right to a jury trial to state courts.[58] While many states have granted this right in their own constitutions, advocates for health courts have suggested that the U.S. government could easily overcome this barrier at the state level by enacting federal legislation preempting existing state guarantees.

To the extent that access to the courts is improved, medical malpractice payments and premiums could conceivably increase, not decrease. Since currently so few adverse medical events actually result in claims,[59] increased payments and premiums may be in the public interest. But this is not the type of outcome that proponents of health courts are likely to have in mind. This was the experience with state statutes facilitating alternative dispute resolution in medical malpractice, which presumably increased claimant access by lowering the cost of dispute resolution.[60] Even if many larger awards were eliminated, partly due to fewer findings for plaintiffs and partly due to scheduling of damages, these savings may be offset not only by additional claims, but also by the additional cost of the public subsidies for a new kind of court.

The Experience of Other Specialty Courts

The concept of specialty courts has been implemented in other contexts. While there are differences as well as similarities, specialty courts provide insight into the challenges of creating a separate system for health courts. Two specialty courts with long histories are bankruptcy and tax courts— the first American bankruptcy court emerged in 1841, and tax courts began in 1924.[61] Unlike proposed health courts, they are both federal administrative courts. More recently, drug courts were created in 1989 in Dade County, Florida, with positive reception; since then, virtually every state has implemented a drug court.[62] Mental health courts began in 1997 in Broward County, Florida. Their development was accelerated by subsequent federal legislation.[63]

The current trend toward specialization of courts has been well accepted, but not without some controversy. Both these courts were developed in order to provide defendants an opportunity to receive financial assistance for their recovery in lieu of fines and jail time. However, these courts often require a guilty plea before an alternative judgment is issued. In some cases, only those who plead guilty have access to the drug or mental health court; those entering a not-guilty plea must remain in the general court system.

Because entry into the system does not require a guilty plea, unified family courts may offer a better paradigm. A unified family court is a system in which family cases, both criminal and civil, are tried in one separate family court. Juvenile and family courts had parallel developments.[64] The theory on which both courts were established is that state intervention can prevent social problems (e.g., juvenile delinquency) if courts are able to deal with the source: neglectful and abusive families.[65]

These issues created a drive to develop an alternative court system. For family courts, this meant centralizing resources, unifying jurisdiction of all domestic relations cases, training judges, and resolving a family's legal problems in as few court appearances as necessary. Three national organizations worked together to draft the Standard Family Court Act,[66] with the stated purpose "to protect and safeguard family life in general and family units in particular by affording to family members all possible help in resolving their justiciable problems and conflicts . . . in a single court, with one specially qualified staff under one leadership . . . with one set of family records, all in one place under the direction of one or more specially qualified judges."[67] This model is sometimes referred to as "one judge, one family."

When the Standard Family Court Act became law in 1959, several states fashioned family courts completely separate from the general docket. The family court concept was received positively; over the next few decades many more states would enact their own statewide family court systems, some with exclusive jurisdiction and others permissive. Some states expanded their existing juvenile courts to include family issues.[68]

Mental health courts, which work with prosecutors' offices, are a much more recent development than family courts. Mental health courts are designed to offer the mentally ill an opportunity to avoid extensive prison time, provided they adhere to treatment protocols established by the courts on a case-specific basis. Defendants must plead guilty and submit to a detailed psychiatric evaluation before becoming subject to the mental health court's jurisdiction. Maintaining contact with mental health providers and adhering to medication protocols are monitored by the mental health court.[69]

Specialized courts offer many advantages over general courts. First, duplication in judicial attention has been wasteful and ineffective. One advantage of family courts is that they retain jurisdiction over defendants, promoting continuity of supervision and accountability.[70]

Second, specialized courts are particularly appropriate when coordination between the judiciary and various other public and private organizations is likely to be productive. Such coordination takes place over time. In the context of medical malpractice, a specialized court would be able to monitor the service benefits described in Chapter 5.

Third, forum shopping or judge shopping is a common occurrence among litigants.[71] This problem is by no means limited to family law; medical malpractice suits are also subject to this problem, perhaps even more so. With giving just one court jurisdiction, and assigning the case to just one judge, forum shopping is prevented. However, state law determines medical malpractice and family law statutes, so it is likely that when parties are in different states, some forum shopping will still occur. Nevertheless, single jurisdiction family courts help reduce forum shopping by limiting the number of available forums. Unifying the authority of a court to hear certain types of cases eases the caseload from the general court. With at least 25 percent of civil filings being family cases, it eases the burden considerably.[72]

Fourth, specialized courts such as family courts have the potential to save money in the long run. Initially, however, as would be the case for health courts as well, a unified family court system is an expensive venture requiring much investment for its start-up.[73]

Despite the start-up costs, recent studies show that family courts have realized some long-term savings through judicial efficiency, economy, competency, quality of adjudication, and coordination among judicial officers, police, and treatment personnel.[74] Unified family courts also save money for the state due to the need for fewer justices.[75] Moreover, if the court functions so as to resolve cases more quickly, nonmonetary costs from a lengthy and drawn-out process will be saved immediately. In addition, and perhaps more important, children are spared multiple trips to the witness stand, and families will receive the aid they need quickly and have the support services to obtain it. Fast compensation and reliable support services are goals of health courts as well.

Domitrovich documents savings of about 20 percent in New Jersey.[76] Speedier resolution of disputes can reduce the nonmonetary cost, as well as legal cost, of medical malpractice litigation; however, the overall savings to the system would be minimal, given that so few cases ever reach the trial stage. Ironically, savings in per-case litigation costs could lead to more litigation. Trial lawyers may be more willing to accept cases on a contingent fee basis if their litigation cost is reduced. If there is a case for health courts based on the family court experience, the case should be advanced on another basis than reduced litigation cost.

Critics, and those interested in reforming existing unified family court systems, point out that many courts fail to fulfill their purpose. To begin with, in order to avoid judicial burnout,[77] many jurisdictions require that judges rotate through the court system as often as every eighteen months.[78] Aside from preventing judges from developing expertise, rotating judges may cause families to see more than one judge, defeating the fundamental purpose of family courts. Even judges who do not rotate through the system may have short terms on the bench; judicial appointments can range from nine months to a lifetime.[79]

Another potential problem is hiring and retaining skilled justices. Family and juvenile courts have a reputation as the training ground for new justices before they move to a general court.[80] Lower pay and fewer opportunities for career advancement compound the problem. The negative effect of the short terms and high turnover of judges is exacerbated by the fact that unified family courts have wide jurisdiction over several areas of law, both civil and criminal.[81] Medical malpractice cases are sometimes high profile. This disadvantage may not apply to health courts.

Although instructive, the experience of other specialty courts is not entirely comparable. Bankruptcy and tax courts are federal administrative courts, and their jurisdiction is fundamentally different from that of proposed health courts. Federal courts are governed by federal rules of procedure and federal substantive law, which has produced a large body of case law followed by all federal bankruptcy and tax courts. Without federal intervention, states have jurisdiction over medical malpractice claims and may create legislation as they choose.

Health courts would be created by state legislation, and there would be considerable variation among states. In contrast, bankruptcy courts have original and exclusive jurisdiction over bankruptcy cases. This means states are prohibited from enacting bankruptcy laws or asserting control of the field.[82]

Tax courts provide experience in one aspect that can instruct the development of health courts: unrepresented litigants. In tax court, 43 percent of litigants are pro se.[83] Taxpayers often have cursory knowledge of the Tax Court Rules, the Internal Revenue Code, and the Federal Rules of Evidence, whereas their adversary, a government agent, is well versed in the rules, procedures, and techniques needed for trial. As a result, the majority of cases result in verdicts for the government.[84] Without contingent fees, many malpractice litigants in health court would be faced with two options: represent themselves or not file a claim.

As mentioned before, these plaintiffs may find it difficult to obtain representation with scheduled damages and a 20 percent cap on attorneys' fees. These factors indicate there may be many pro se litigants. This is especially true if the process is as easily initiated, as health court proposals suggest: by filling out a readily available user-friendly form. As in tax court, health court plaintiffs would have only a cursory knowledge of procedural rules and of tort law and its vast and ever-changing precedent. Defendants, on the other hand, would have resources to hire skilled counsel with expertise in procedural rules and the nuances of the substantive law. As with tax courts, there is a clear risk that health courts could develop a defendant bias.

The Bottom Line

It is unrealistic to expect health courts to solve all, or even most, of the problems with the existing system, as the advocates of such courts would have it. However, with the more recent success of and demand for specialty courts in other areas of the law, this may be an idea worth pursuing.[85]

Health courts have some potential benefits. Probably the major advantage is the courts' ability to coordinate with other agencies. For example, rather than pay a lump sum to a family with a birth-injured child, care can be monitored and coordinated over time.

Another positive feature is the possibility of broadening the standard for individual negligence. Much like no-fault systems,[86] this would have the effect of increasing the number of injury victims compensated, allowing clearly avoidable mistakes to be compensated in the first hearing, without a trial, thereby reducing the burden on the court system and the time it takes for injury victims to be compensated. Increasing the number of compensated injuries and holding more adverse events as liable would also create an incentive for health care providers to adopt patient safety measures, but only if coupled with provisions requiring experience rating of medical malpractice insurance premiums.

Currently, the mean time it takes to resolve a malpractice case is over two years, with many of the more complex cases taking much longer to resolve.[87] For a patient needing compensation to pay health care and other immediate expenses, this delay can be extremely burdensome. By eliminating the need for trial for cases in which adverse events are clearly avoidable, a greater number of patients would receive compensation more nearly synchronized with the time it is most needed.

Very few cases in state courts currently involve medical malpractice. Thus, judges cannot be expected to be highly knowledgeable about the technical issues in these cases, making it more difficult, for example, to know when inaccurate scientific information is being introduced by an expert. By specializing in these cases, judges could become more generally knowledgeable about medical issues.

Health courts also have some important weaknesses. For one, there is concern about specialty courts becoming "ghettoized." In addition, it may be hard to find high-quality candidates for judicial positions who are sufficiently neutral. Underlying biases may be a reason that judges are currently appointed or elected. A judge with strong views on medical malpractice may be elected or appointed for this reason. Consequently, plaintiffs may prevail too frequently or not frequently enough. Additionally, if appointment of experts is in the judge's discretion, it is not entirely clear that the experts chosen will be neutral. Allowing the parties to use their own experts would assure that all viewpoints are heard and are on the record.

To deal with the appointment process and its consequences, a state could establish a special board whose sole responsibility is appointing judges to health courts. Terms on the board could be rotating and of sufficient length that a governor would not be able to appoint most of the board members even if he or she serves two consecutive terms.

Another concern is that health courts would be overwhelmed by the influx of cases. This has happened in other specialty courts; family court dockets have been steadily increasing, and the burden is borne by the individual justice.[88] Over time, malpractice cases' frequency is likely to decrease but, at least initially, health court judges may be as overwhelmed as family court judges are.

Opponents have raised the question of whether the development of law in a specialty court reflects the development of other principles of law in the general court system. They argue that an area of law can become isolated from the development of law. Generally, the development of law influences courts in their decisions across specialties. Standards for admitting evidence or expert testimony and the application of constitutional rights have evolved over time, as have most other areas of law, affecting development across subject matter. Bankruptcy and tax courts have been accused of ignoring those developments and creating an entirely distinct body of law. The common-law system functions on precedent. It is important for specialty courts to be involved in incorporating and building on the precedents of other courts.

Perhaps the most common criticism is the removal of juries. The Seventh Amendment to the U.S. Constitution guarantees a citizen's right to a jury trial in civil cases.[89] Channeling a medical malpractice plaintiff to a health court is not necessarily denial of the right to trial by jury. It depends on how such courts would operate in practice. Undoubtedly, if they are instituted, health court constitutional challenges would eventually be considered by the U.S. Supreme Court.

In the end, even considering all the benefits of a specialty court, there are limits to what specialty courts can accomplish. A family law expert from the District of Columbia Bar Association acknowledged, "Reforming the court will not solve the underlying societal problems that lead to the abuse and neglect of our city's children. . . . A judge can only do so much."[90] Though he was discussing family courts in particular, his words are entirely relevant to all specialty courts. Health courts are by no means a panacea, as is sometimes asserted.

Conclusion

This chapter has both discussed performance of the existing system, as in our refutation of myths 3 and 4, and assessed the advantages and disadvantages of specialized health courts. Along the way, we have presented evidence on specialized courts in other contexts, with a view toward whether and how the lessons learned from these other experiences apply to proposals for health courts.

The criticisms of jurors raise much larger issues currently plaguing the social sciences which have broad implications for public policy. Although the critics of juries focus on the limitations of individuals in these settings, many others have questioned the ability of individuals to make fully informed rational choices in many other contexts. Perhaps because of the "wisdom of crowds" (albeit small ones, six to twelve persons), collective decision-making of juries may be much better than individual decision-making in family units. The studies that are critical of juries do not compare decision-making in this context with other decisions people routinely make.

Should health courts be adopted? This chapter has presented some pros and cons of health courts. The most attractive feature is the potential for the court to monitor payment and care of injury victims over time and to facilitate coordination among agencies as family and mental health courts do. Health courts are worth considering, but only if the problems raised by them are viewed through a framework in which alternative methods for addressing the same set of issues are considered. For example, states might consider different approaches for presenting scientific evidence to courts. Perhaps the public sector should fund research that summarizes the empirical evidence on specific scientific controversies that arise in medical malpractice cases. Nontechnical summaries could be provided to juries.

Another possibility is using the standard of review set out in *Daubert*[91] to disqualify incompetent witnesses whose testimony might mislead jurors. Still another possibility is the use of expert juries. Viewed in the context of a number of other realistic alternatives, health courts are indeed well worth considering.

8

Patient Safety and Medical Malpractice

Patient safety has moved to the top of the health policy agenda in recent years. Widespread interest in the topic can be traced to the publication of an Institute of Medicine (IOM) report in 2000, titled *To Err Is Human*. But no matter how competently they are done, reports tend to gain widespread public attention only when their release occurs in an environment receptive to the findings. Concern about patient safety plausibly was building under the surface, and release of the IOM's report, with its very comprehensive review of the literature and specific recommendations, provided an important catalyst for galvanizing the public's and policymakers' attention on this important public policy issue.

The concepts of patient safety and medical malpractice are closely linked, at least in theory. Whether this is true in practice is quite another matter. As discussed in chapter 3, the weight of the empirical evidence is that the threat of being sued does not deter injuries. Yet deterrence is at the top of nearly any list of what imposing tort liability should achieve. But in defense of tort—admittedly a somewhat lame defense—all empirical studies have assessed deterrence under varying degrees of a threat of tort liability. No study has compared patient safety in a world in which the threat of tort liability was totally absent with rates of patient safety as tort liability operates currently. Perhaps such a comparison would have revealed that the entire removal of the threat of tort increases rates of medical errors.

Patient safety is related to medical malpractice in that an important purpose of imposing tort liability on health care providers is to provide a negative incentive or a "stick" to induce provision of socially optimal levels of precaution. Ideally, there would also be positive incentives for providers or "carrots" to engage in activities that result in preventing the occurrence of diseases and adverse health outcomes.

During the first decade of the twenty-first century, increased public interest in medical malpractice arose at the same time as increased interest in patient safety—probably a coincidence. Many advocates for public safety desired to keep the two issues separate, apparently out of a concern that becoming muddled in medical malpractice issues would blunt the patient safety movement's momentum. Patient safety and medical malpractice are in fact inextricably related, a situation that is clearly understandable for political reasons.

Some experts and policymakers not only allege that there is no relationship between patient safety and medical malpractice, but they go a step further in arguing that medical malpractice is actually *counterproductive* in assuring patient safety and patient welfare more generally.

The Alleged Patient Safety-Medical Malpractice Mismatch

Arguments for a Mismatch
There are several arguments for a mismatch.

One argument is that medical malpractice is forcing health care providers out of practice, thus decreasing patient access to care. This is negative defensive medicine.[1] Putting aside whether or not the threat of lawsuits and rising premiums have affected career choices, in a sense, if medical malpractice is doing its job, it should be encouraging some exits from practice.

Ideally, the tort system should identify and remove physicians who consistently commit errors or are negligent, and upon their removal, more qualified physicians would fill the vacancies. This applies to the provision of services as well; when care is below standard, the office, unit, or hospital providing it should be closed. For example, a hospital in upstate New York voluntarily closed a cardiac surgery unit due to a 17.6 percent mortality rate, which was nearly four times the state average.[2] Before reopening the unit, the hospital took several measures to ensure an increase in patient safety. It implemented a quality assurance program, created a full-time service chief, increased nursing staff, and created weekly teaching conferences. In less than ten years, the hospital had reduced the cardiac surgery mortality rate to 1.77 percent.[3] This story provides an interesting example, but perhaps not an ending that generalizes.

A study conducted in the 1980s revealed that the distribution of medical malpractice payments in Florida is highly skewed, with a few physicians accounting for much of the loss, even after accounting for factors such as specialty.[4] The same study indicated that physicians with adverse claims experience were *less* likely than others to subsequently quit practice or move to another state. And although physicians with very adverse claims histories were more likely to have complaints against them filed with the state's licensing board, the rate of actual sanctions was very low. A physician's adverse claims history does not necessarily imply poor quality of care but, at a minimum, it would seem appropriate to examine his or her practices. At least in Florida, neither the threat of tort liability nor the licensure process seems to have been effective.

Some tort reformers are concerned that engaging in unnecessarily heightened patient safety will put physicians at an even greater risk of a lawsuit. There is an argument that defensive medicine is self-reinforcing; the more physicians provide aggressive treatment for low-risk conditions or order unnecessary tests, the higher the probability that those practices will become the legal standard of care.

Some critics of tort liability as it applies to medical care have gone a step further, maintaining that the threat of medical malpractice suits not only does not improve patient safety, but it may even *cause* provision of care to be less safe than it would be in its absence. The critics assert that the threat of litigation has a chilling effect on discussions among providers about adverse outcomes. In addition, some critics argue that doctors fear the possibility that their private discussions could be discoverable by a plaintiff's attorney during the course of litigation.[5] It is unknown to what extent this fear actually exists; there has been neither systematic documentation demonstrating that liability forces physicians into silence nor studies linking malpractice exposure with frequency of error reporting.[6] Tort liability is relevant to the topic of patient safety; some would argue that the primary goal of imposing tort liability is to deter injuries.

If "to err is human," not wanting to admit to errors is also human. Even if there were no threat of tort, it seems unlikely that providers would generally be willing to make their errors known to others for various psychological, if not professional and business, reasons.

The avoidance of error reporting in the absence of tort can be seen with the Veterans Administration (VA) system. At VA hospitals, physicians are protected from liability through the Federal Tort Claims Act; patients are precluded from bringing suit against individual providers.[7] But even without the threat of lawsuits, public regulation was necessary to require disclosure of errors. Until a disclosure policy was implemented in the 1990s, the VA system was "significantly under-reporting patient safety incidents."[8] The experience of the VA indicates that the embarrassment and shame from the publication of medical errors is what prevents disclosure, not necessarily the fear of litigation itself.

Markets and Market Failure

Quality differs in markets for an almost endless list of goods and services. Some individuals are willing to pay more for a higher-quality good or service; such higher quality is supplied if the additional number consumers are willing to pay for such extra quality exceeds the marginal cost of providing the extra quality. Higher quality may reflect a combination of better materials used to manufacture the product, more investment in product design to achieve a more attractive product, and more resources devoted to looking for product defects during the course of production. In addition, higher quality includes a greater redundancy of inputs in the production process, greater product selection, more consumer assistance in product selection, faster delivery, and more lenient product exchange and return policy.

Societies have decided that for most products, quality provision and quality assurance should not be left to markets alone, and governments have intervened for various reasons. Governments do not, however, regulate the quality of T-shirts or picture frames.

The key rationale for government intervention in regulating quality is asymmetric information between buyers and sellers of the product. Sometimes, although full information is available to decision-makers in the market, it is argued that these decision-makers form irrational decisions and thus require the benefit of public regulation to constrain or channel choices.[9]

Markets may fail when some parties to a transaction provide misleading or false information to the other parties or fail to mention facts that these other parties may regard as pertinent to making a specific choice. Consumers of medical care may not be well-positioned to evaluate characteristics of alternative products, and certainly are not as well-positioned as the seller of the product, giving rise to asymmetric information. For such goods, an element of trust on the part of the purchaser is required. Such goods are called "credence goods."[10]

At least some types of medical care (e.g., emergency room visits, complex surgery, and some kinds of hospital stays) are logically credence goods. Since consumption of credence goods is inherently based on trust, it seems unlikely that we would observe advertisements for B-quality hospital care in the way that we observe advertisements for Motel 6. Hospitals might claim that their care is of the highest quality, but they would be reluctant to assert that their care is A-quality and their competitor across the street offers B-quality care. These claims are sometimes made in direct-to-consumer advertisements of pharmaceutical products, but such ads are still comparatively rare (and could be the subject of a lawsuit on the basis of false advertising, unless such claims are supportable by strong empirical evidence).

The localized nature of hospital and physician services has limited the amount of rating by national organizations and publications that evaluate nationally (and internationally) marketed products, such as automobiles. One can compare fuel consumption, speed, agility, and other characteristics under controlled conditions. Frequency of repair is compared, although different automobiles are often driven differently.[11] Minivans seem unlikely to be run in drag races as often as are some sports cars, or if drag races are unseemly, around mountain curves, as in the television advertisements for some cars. Yet owners of sports cars may be more concerned about oil changes than are owners of minivans.

Because quality comparisons are commonplace, automobile manufacturers need to consider marginal cost versus marginal return of increased investments in quality, lest they market their products at uncompetitive prices and lose market share.[12] The Big Three automobile producers in the United States have learned this lesson the hard way by losing substantial market share. This has driven them to improve the quality of their products markedly in recent years. For automobiles, market forces provide a strong incentive for manufacturers to make cost-quality trade-offs.[13]

In the health care sector, there is nowhere near the same market for products of varying quality as in most sectors. Quality varies, but the relationship between product quality and price appears to be weaker than for many goods and services. The localized nature of these markets is only one reason for the difference. Other reasons include the cottage industry nature of the sector,[14] the complexity of the products, and the important role of professional norms.

Frequency of repair in the context of automobiles has its counterpart in adverse health outcomes that result from the receipt of medical care. Yet while we are often willing to overlook differences in consumer behavior when comparing frequency of automobile repair (e.g., fast driving, poor maintenance), health care providers warn that comparisons of rates of adverse outcomes may be misleading in the context of medical care because patients differ in severity of illness in ways that are not measured. Thus, for example, if hospitals are to be compared on the basis of patient outcomes and some hospitals accept relatively sicker patients for treatment, and the comparisons fail to account for these differences, the reported differences in patient outcomes will be misleading (i.e., overstated). As a consequence, hospitals will seek patients who will make them look good, and severely ill patients may be denied access. Car dealers, in contrast to doctors and hospitals, would be foolish to query potential customers about their driving records and habits. However, this type of screening may well occur in the context of medical care, especially when health outcomes are publicized without adjusting the outcomes for differences in patient mix.

To the extent that patients (or even their doctors) are unable to judge the quality of care of particular hospitals and doctors, health care providers have had comparatively little to gain financially from reducing rates of adverse outcomes. Of course, there may be nonfinancial reasons to be concerned about quality (e.g., ethics, professional norms), but the financial incentive to improve quality seems to be less than it should be. Health care executives often seem to view various investments in quality as costly and unprofitable, which is consistent with the view that the necessary financial incentives are lacking at present. Also, many hospitals are still operated as freestanding, independent organizations, and physicians' practices are generally much smaller than hospitals. The high fixed cost of investments in quality can be an important impediment to undertaking such investments. Thus, absent market incentives, the role of assuring quality is necessarily a function of public regulation and civil litigation.

Adverse Events and Negligent Injuries

How the Estimates of Adverse Outcomes Have Been Generated

Since the mid-1970s, as noted in Chapter 1, there have been three major studies of the epidemiology of medical injuries among patients hospitalized in the United States: studies conducted in California and New York, and a follow-up to the New York study in Utah and Colorado.

In preparing its estimates of iatrogenic injury in U.S. hospitals for *To Err Is Human*, the IOM used a group of experts to extrapolate the data from these studies to the entire U.S. population. The IOM used its public relations department to widely disseminate the report among members of the public, bypassing the medical profession.[15] *Err* was written to present a message that everyone could understand (Box 8.1).

The message is indeed powerful. One can quibble with the estimates and not agree with all of the report's conclusions, but at the same time not disagree with the basic message that medical errors are an important public health concern.

The Quality of the Estimates

The estimates of deaths per annum in hospitals due to medical errors are indeed "softer" than the IOM's message implies. For one thing, medical accidents, unlike motor vehicle and workplace accidents, are not discrete

Box 8.1
Press Release for *To Err Is Human*

> Experts estimate that as many as 98,000 people die in any year from medical errors that occur in hospitals. That's more than die from motor vehicle accidents, breast cancer, or AIDS—three causes that receive far more public attention. Indeed, more people die annually from medication errors than from workplace injuries. Add the financial cost to the human tragedy, and medical error easily rises to the top ranks of urgent, widespread public problems.
>
> *To Err is Human* breaks the silence that has surrounded medical errors and their consequences—but not by pointing fingers at caring health care professionals who make honest mistakes. Instead the book sets forth a national agenda—with state and local implications—for reducing medical errors and improving patient safety through the design of a safer health care system. http://www.nap.edu/catalog/9728.html#description (accessed July 3, 2006).

events. Many persons enter the hospital in a frail condition and hence are particularly vulnerable to medical errors. But even if the error had not occurred, many persons admitted to a hospital do not have a lengthy life expectancy. For this reason, years of life lost would be a much more precise characterization of the harm attributable to errors.

Negative outcomes do occur, and with an appropriate level of informed consent, patients know or should know about these before agreeing to undergo or to forgo a procedure. To determine whether an error has occurred, it is necessary to parse the adverse event into a part that reflects an error (and hence substandard care) and a part that presents an unfortunate mishap that at the same time reflects an appropriate level of care.

For each medical record, physician reviewers graded the confidence that an adverse event occurred on a scale from 0 to 6.[16] If the confidence level exceeded 1, a judgment was made whether or not there was negligence. Then, further notation was made as to the confidence level in this judgment. There were two physician reviewers for each record, and reviews were conducted independently. When there was disagreement between the reviews, this was noted by a medical records analyst and resolved through an independent review by a supervisory physician.

No subspecialists in various fields served as medical record reviewers. Thus, a general surgeon might have reviewed an adverse outcome resulting from the care of an ophthalmologist, for example. This was an "implicit review," meaning that it was up to the physician to make an assessment of negligence without following explicit criteria. Especially considering that these reviews were conducted at a time when quality of care assessment was in its infancy, it would have been a practical impossibility to develop explicit criteria for negligence for each type of adverse outcome and specialty.

Courts, by contrast, have to consider only one case at a time. The reviewers had to rely on what is written in a medical record. Courts, on the other hand, have much more than a medical record on which to base judgments. What is or is not recorded (or altered) in a medical record may be a subject for consideration in a legal dispute.

Holding these medical assessments as the "gold standard" of levels of quality of care and negligence would be to give them too much credit. Yet what the study team accomplished was indeed very pathbreaking, particularly at the time. Furthermore, such studies require substantial resources and patience in order to conduct them at the standard at which these studies were conducted.

In many cases, the underlying technology encountered in a particular medical record review may not have been very complex, and determining whether an adverse outcome occurred, and if that adverse event was attributable to negligence, would not have been very difficult. The most common adverse event in the New York study involved drug complications (19 percent), followed by wound infections (14 percent). Neither may have required appreciable technical and specialized skills to analyze.

For other alleged errors, expertise that is more specialized is likely required. Errors in management were identified for 58 percent of adverse events, with nearly half of these attributed to negligence. Failure to diagnose was also common, as were adverse events in the emergency room.[17]

A determination of whether or not there was negligence assumes that the appropriate care standard has been defined. Sometimes there is a consensus about an appropriate care standard, but often it is lacking, as attested to by the substantial geographic variation in patterns of care that have been widely documented. Moreover, care standards often change as technologies improve.

The reviewers could not have known about outcomes that became evident months or even years after the hospitalization evaluated in the study occurred. At the time of discharge from the hospital, there would have been no adverse outcome. Many major injuries (e.g., birth injuries) are latent for years; the fact that an injury had occurred becomes evident only then.

Even though there are often several defendants in a tort case, liability is generally attributed to individuals, not to organizations. But rather than attribute most medical errors to individuals, the IOM report emphasizes the role of errors by medical *systems*. Because it focused on systemic changes, *Err* states that it did not deal with tort liability or tort reform, and deliberately excluded discussions of tort or medical malpractice. By avoiding the legal aspect of medical error, the authors wanted to focus the reform movement on patient safety—not on the resulting lawsuits.[18] Likely an additional unstated reason for this absence is the contentious nature of tort as a public policy issue. Focusing on system issues would avoid some of the conflict inherent in discussions of tort.[19]

Err's Recommendations and the Follow-up to *Err*: The Experience of the First Five Years Post *Err*

The Recommendations
The report contains four basic recommendations for improving patient safety. First, *Err* encourages creating a national focus on patient safety, including establishing a Center for Patient Safety. Second, a national mandatory reporting system would focus on serious adverse events attributable to error. Implementation of voluntary reporting is also encouraged for errors causing minimal or no patient harm. Information from the reporting system would be publicly available. Such reporting would supplement an existing system for reporting medication errors.[20] Third, *Err* recommends raising performance standards and quality of care expectations for health professionals, to be accomplished in part

through direct public and private regulatory mechanisms, such as licensing, certification, accreditation, and minimum performance levels for providers and their employees. *Err* recommends that federal regulatory agencies (e.g., the U.S. Food and Drug Administration) should increase their performance standards.[21]

Fourth, *Err* recommends that safety measures be implemented at all care sites, including systematic collection of data on injuries and implementing systems for hospitals to track their own performance over time. Health care providers are encouraged to implement redundancy or backup systems, continuous training to deal with unexpected events, and improved communication among staff. Various process measures to offset human frailties are also encouraged, such as designing jobs for safety (e.g., higher staffing ratios or fewer work hours), avoiding reliance on memory and vigilance (e.g., use of checklists, protocols, automation of procedures), employing constraints in the work process (e.g., a computer in the pharmacy that requires entry of allergy medicines before the prescription is filled), simplifying key processes (e.g., reducing the number of handoffs or limiting choice of drugs in the pharmacy), and standardizing the work process (e.g., standard order forms, prescribing conventions, and placement of supplies).

The First Five Years Post *Err*

The above recommendations all seem sensible at first glance, but they raise the question of why it is taking health care providers so long to implement them. Safeguards listed with the fourth recommendation are widespread in other industries, such as in the airline and nuclear power industries. Various forms of private and public regulation of health care providers have been implemented, some mechanisms for almost a century, including hospital peer review by medical staffs, certification, accreditation, and licensure. An argument advanced by proponents of a pluralistic health care financing system in the United States is that it would assure the public, or at least some of the public access to high-quality care, assuming that this level of safety, and the additional cost of implementing it, would be demanded and paid for by well-informed consumers.

Finally, though it is not discussed in *Err*, there is little in the recommendations that would imply that the existence of tort liability prevents medical errors. Providers oppose reporting of errors on grounds that such reports might be used against the provider in litigation. But there are other reasons for opposing such reporting, such as simply looking bad to outsiders. Firms in the other industries do not admit to their errors largely for business reasons.

Given the publicity following publication of *Err*, administrators in private and public sectors, and legislators at both state and national levels, came under substantial pressure to address and implement safety initiatives. The pressure was amplified by the report's ambitious objective of a 50 percent reduction in errors within the five years following publication.

Hospitals subsequently adopted measures to reduce and prevent adverse events; for many this included creating a new budget dedicated to patient safety or increasing an existing patient safety budget.[22] Nevertheless, a major barrier hindering development of hospital patient safety programs is lack of adequate funding. In large part, delays reflect a lack of strong financial incentives for hospitals to implement patient safety programs.

There is no way to tell whether there was a 50 percent reduction in errors within five years of *Err*'s release. Administrative data collected for other purposes are the only potential (albeit highly imperfect) data source.[23]

Broad social goals are specified relatively easily. The devil lies in the details of actual implementation and in measurement. The best one could hope for from this recommendation is that individual health care organizations would decide that error reduction is a high priority and institute programs and measurement systems to accomplish this objective.

Despite the lack of funding, several specific patient safety measures recommended in *Err* have been implemented on a limited scale, including (1) reduced work hours for medical residents,[24] (2) error reporting systems, and (3) U.S. Food and Drug Administration (FDA)-required bar coding.

Error reporting has received a substantial amount of attention. The value of consistent, honest error reporting per se is not to be disputed, particularly as a first step in error reduction. And the threat of tort may be *one* of the factors inhibiting honest and accurate reporting.

Error reporting is a necessary but not a sufficient condition for improving patient safety. For one thing, compiling of error reports does little other than create an illusion of open communication and disclosure. Error reports must be reviewed and acted upon in order to have any value. Standing on their own, they report single adverse events, frequently offering no clear remedies.

Particular types of errors are common to many institutions. In this sense, error determination is a public good.[25] It should be unnecessary for each and every organization to experience each particular type of error before anything is done about it.[26] If a representative number of hospitals were to accurately report the sources of errors, this should suffice for learning about sources of errors in hospitals. But currently, each hospital has an incentive to wait for the other hospital to do the reporting (even if the identities of the reporting hospitals were confidential). For this reason, there is a case for public intervention since private markets will not supply this information in adequate amounts unless they are paid or are required to do this by a government authority.

State legislatures have increasingly become involved in patient safety policy. When legislatures have been involved in requiring or encouraging error reporting, adverse events have been defined quite narrowly, effectively limiting reports to events resulting in death.

However, this captures only a fraction of adverse events. Using such limited data, hospitals have been unable to identify patterns of error. Also, inclusion of near misses in addition to actual errors would be useful information to have, even if such errors were released only to hospitals.[27]

A more fundamental challenge to the success of error reporting is actually obtaining the reports. Several states had enacted statutes creating reporting systems, but rather than expect hospitals to use their own funds for this purpose, the decision was made by the legislatures that public funding is appropriate; however, states faced funding problems of their own during the years immediately following release of *Err*.[28]

Some states have had reporting systems since the early 1970s.[29] But in these states, underreporting has been a chronic problem. New York's reporting system, implemented in 1985, receives 20,000 reports annually. California has had an error reporting system since 1972, but as of the late 1990s, the state received fewer than 4,500 reports annually, despite the fact that it has almost twice the population of New York.[30]

The third important innovation since *Err,* with much promise for improving patient safety, is the adoption of *bar coding.* Drug errors are common, and many arise from predictable mistakes (e.g., unintelligible written orders, pulling the wrong medication for a patient, or neglecting to consider the patient's history when prescribing).[31]

In 2004, after several proposed rules, comments, and revisions, the U.S. Food and Drug Administration released a bar code regulation. The regulation required that standardized bar codes be used on prescription drugs, blood products, vaccines, and over-the-counter drugs under medical orders in hospitals.[32]

However, the regulation has a major deficiency; the FDA lacks the statutory authority to regulate hospitals. Thus, in the end, it is the hospital's decision to acquire scanning equipment. Presumably, if and when use of bar codes becomes the community standard, hospitals that choose not to purchase scanning equipment will be at increased risk of tort liability.[33]

One study of VA hospitals reports a 24 percent decrease in drug-related errors soon after implementation of its national bar-coding system in 1999.[34] But despite the success of the VA, diffusion of bar coding in U.S. hospitals has been slow. By the mid-2000s, only about 5 percent of hospitals in the United States had implemented such systems, mainly because of their high cost.[35] Also, the reduction in adverse events from use of bar coding may be low.[36]

The Leapfrog Group estimated 567,000 serious medical errors would be avoided per year with the use of *computerized physician order-entry* (CPOE) systems.[37] But five years post *Err,* only 5 to 9 percent of U.S. hospitals had implemented CPOE.[38] The slow rate of diffusion reflects the considerable expense of acquiring equipment and software and then making a system operational.[39] Some hospitals chose to allocate their entire patient safety budget to CPOE, leaving inadequate funding for addressing other safety efforts.[40] Although implementation cost is high, the potential for subsequent cost savings appears to be substantial.[41]

Even though the purpose of CPOE is to reduce errors, it has led to new errors being made.[42] Technical aspects of the system can make use difficult; multiple screens appear, sometimes without the patient's name, causing confusion as to which patient is to receive the order; and the actual input of the order can be tricky.[43]

One source of error in hospital settings potentially made worse by CPOEs is the lack of coordination of care of hospitalized patients.[44] Patients inevitably are seen by multiple physicians, some of whom are unfamiliar with the patient. With CPOE, each physician inputs instructions, which may result in contradictory treatment plans; reconciliation by machine is difficult.

Why Is There Underreporting of Errors?

Underreporting in mandatory reporting systems has several potential causes. However, much has been both said and written suggesting that the major factor is the threat of tort. Legal discovery of error reports is thought to prevent full disclosure by many providers.[45] But a study of nineteen states with mandatory reporting systems[46] reveals several reasons for underreporting other than a fear of increased liability, including lack of effective internal systems within hospitals to identify incidents; insufficient resources to implement reporting; unclear definitions or requirements for what must be reported; lack of enforcement of mandatory reporting by the state; and a perceived lack of benefit from reporting to the facilities themselves.

The Health Care Quality Improvement Act of 1986 (HCQIA) provides limited protection in support of disclosure and error procedures. While it grants immunity for peer review groups, it does not extend this immunity to the documents they produce.[47]

State laws offer slightly more defense from discovery. As of 2003, every state except New Jersey had statutory protections for discovery of records and deliberations of peer review committees.[48] These statutes vary widely among states; as a result, protection from discovery may be unreliable. Several statutes protect only the documents generated by the peer review committee, while others protect all the information provided to peer review committees. For example, Texas protects all materials and information, including, but not limited to, root cause analyses, annual hospital reports, action plans, and departmental summaries.[49] Nevertheless, even with statutory protections, information may be discoverable for other purposes, such as allegations of negligent supervision or credentialing.

Kesselheim et al. (2006) assess several existing and emerging physician clinical performance assessment (PCPA) initiatives in light of legal rules governing the types of information that can be used as evidence in civil litigation. Their basic conclusion is that evidence from such initiatives cannot be introduced in court, but the conclusion is somewhat guarded.[50]

For reporting to be effective, the reporting process needs to be clear and easily done. Lack of enforcement of reporting requirements and/or lack of effective use of the information provided reduces the incentives for facilities to report errors. Some states offer money incentives, in the form of grants, to entice hospitals to comply.

Even when the confidentiality of individual reports is protected, hospitals often worry that release of error-reporting data will lead to loss of reputation for hospitals with high reported error rates.[51] If they are successful in increasing their rates of error-reporting, when the state subsequently releases a summary of error-reporting data from all the hospitals in the state, it will appear that they are a dangerous hospital because of the high number of error reports.

Addressing this concern, a few states have created patient safety organizations (PSOs) to serve as a safe harbor for error reporting.[52] As independent nongovernmental organizations,[53] they can give medical professionals a vehicle for reporting errors without the threat of repercussions. Recently enacted federal legislation extends this protection by safeguarding information that is voluntarily reported to these organizations, thereby providing hospitals and providers with a reliable system for confidential reporting of adverse medical events.[54]

The U.S. Patient Safety and Quality Improvement Act of 2005 protects providers' communications with a PSO, creating a $10,000 civil penalty for each illegal disclosure and preventing accrediting bodies from taking action against a provider's good-faith involvement in the PSO.[55] This law prevents any information confidentially given to a PSO from being used against medical professionals and other administrators in malpractice suits. However, the mandatory reporting laws of the states are recognized and respected by the Act, meaning providers would be required to file using the state-mandated procedure. This significantly narrows the broad protection offered by the Patient Safety and Quality Improvement Act.

Regardless of whether or not there is accurate reporting, the process of reporting to an external body is likely to be ineffective unless states implement a system that provides timely feedback to providers and hospitals. If a response is prompt, it conveys the message that error reporting is valued and, more important, useful. Releasing safety reports to the public can also create incentives for hospitals to change their policies, or, it can create a disincentive for reporting of errors. To prevent the latter, New York released facility-specific reports only for facilities with very low reporting rates, in order to encourage reporting.[56]

Implications

To Err Is Human has had an important effect in calling attention to patient safety issues. The focus of these efforts has been on hospitals because many patient safety systems involve large initial investments. Due to the large fixed costs, mid-sized and large hospitals may be more efficient in implementing patient safety systems than smaller hospitals and most physicians' practices. Thus, not surprisingly, the majority of adopters have been hospitals.

The record post *Err* demonstrates practical pitfalls in implementing systems and approaches to reduce error rates. Although policies have emphasized public disclosure, what is really needed are incentives to change the internal mind-set of health care organizations about patient safety, assuming that higher levels of patient safety are indeed a public objective worth the extra cost of achieving this goal. It seems unlikely that public regulation alone can achieve this objective. Medical malpractice cannot bear the total burden of ensuring much higher levels of patient safety.

Quality Assurance Mechanisms, Government Oversight, and Regulation

Why Other Regulatory Mechanisms May Fail

Medical malpractice is only one of several quality assurance mechanisms. The trial bar has argued, with considerable justification, that there would be no role for tort liability if the other quality assurance mechanisms functioned well.[57] However, absent effective private mechanisms and government intervention, tort liability with contingent fees gives injury victims, irrespective of their financial status, a way to address grievances and, hopefully, prevent injuries for someone else. Based on the resolution of the legal dispute, a warning is issued about the consequences of failure to exercise due care. This is a contentious issue with lawyers for the defense.

Since there has been criticism of medical malpractice, why might the other quality assurance mechanisms fail as well? There are several reasons.

First, public bureaucracies may be beholden to special interests or simply unresponsive, given the internal incentives of staff or understaffing. More generally, the capture theory of public regulation implies that regulation is often used to protect existing sellers from entry rather than to pursue the stated goals of regulation.[58] Second, given the complexity of medical care, it is difficult for public agencies or private credentialing organizations to oversee all aspects of care that may potentially affect quality. Third, imposing *and* enforcing minimum standards runs the risk of denying care to persons in areas where care is generally inaccessible. For example, applying minimum volume standards to hospitals in rural areas might often result in particular types of care being geographically inaccessible to residents of such areas. Finally, individual health care providers lack an incentive to honestly disclose indicators of quality, in large part because their competitors may not be as truthful and thus gain a competitive advantage. This is an important rationale for public disclosure requirements.

Other Regulatory Mechanisms: Licensure, Certification, Peer Review, Credentialing, Report Cards, and Disclosure Statutes

The oldest quality safeguard is *licensure* by state governments. Licensing of health professionals varies by state because the system is based on individual licensing boards for each profession in each state. Licensure is at best a weak safeguard of quality. Unless a physician moves to another state, licensure is a once-and-for-all process.[59] Loss of license is rare and is in response to very major lapses and major misconduct. Sloan, Mergenhagen, Burfield, et al. find that even physicians with very high and persistent medical malpractice rates were investigated by the licensing board only very rarely.[60] The definition of what constitutes a complaint and how it is handled differs according to individual licensing board standards.

However, as Ameringer documents in his excellent historical account of the licensure process, state licensure boards have changed, largely in response to political pressures to serve the public interest.[61] Medical malpractice in the United States predates medical licensure and state medical boards.

Certification, on the other hand, speaks to a physician's educational credentials and practical training, and imposes some requirements for continuing medical education, but continued certification is not linked to direct measures of physician performance. Physicians may be certified through twenty-four different specialty boards. Not all of these boards require recertification, and those that do, typically require it only every seven to ten years.[62]

Peer review in ambulatory settings occurs informally. By contrast, hospitals have a formal structure for peer review. One rationale for hospital peer review by medical staff, albeit a comparatively modern one, is that some internal mechanism for quality monitoring is needed if hospitals are really to compete. However, there are risks to such peer review. In particular, medical staff peer reviewers are likely to be competitors with the physicians they review. Banning a physician in part or in full may allow peer reviewers to improve their own competitive position.[63] Physicians denied hospital privileges have often sought legal remedies on grounds that the medical staff's decision was anticompetitive. Also, to what extent peer reviewers monitor medical errors is unknown.

As discussed above, peer review statutes offer some protection to documents, but the protection varies by state, and information can still be discovered in some civil actions, such as when there are allegations of negligent supervision or credentialing. At both the state and the federal levels there are statutory protections by way of privilege, confidentiality provisions, and limited immunity for the participants and the work product of the peer review committees.[64] In sum, statutes provide only limited protection.

Credentialing is another quasi-regulatory mechanism aimed at quality assurance.[65] Hospitals must be accredited by JCAHO or undergo regulatory review in order to participate in Medicare, and with 40 percent of revenue from Medicare payments, hospitals have great incentive to comply with JCAHO standards.[66]

Although JCAHO and other credentialing organizations, including the U.S. Centers for Medicare and Medicaid Services, have made and continue to make important strides in quality of care assessment, importantly moving a reliance on structure and process of care indicators to evidence-based quality of care indicators and health outcome-based indicators, much work remains to be done.

Bradley et al., studying data for 2002–2003 from 962 hospitals participating in the National Registry of Myocardial Infarction, find that although process of care measures[67] are positively correlated (if a hospital uses one, it is more likely to use the others), all of the publicly reported process measures for acute myocardial infarction (AMI)[68] explain only 6 percent of the variation among hospitals in the thirty-day mortality rate for AMI. Clearly, doing just a few things right is not going to make that much difference in outcomes.

Specialty societies can play an important role in promoting patient safety. Most prominently, anesthesiologists, faced with high mortality rates associated with procedures they perform and high insurance premiums reflecting high claims frequency, took action. They studied the frequency of claims, identified the errors, and implemented corrective measures.[69] The American Society of Anesthesiologists created mandated patient monitoring standards, redesigned procedures and equipment to decrease the severity and frequency of errors, shortened residents' hours, set practice guidelines, standardized the operation of machines, and created safety devices for the machines These actions reduced the mortality rate from 1/10,000–20,000 to 1/200,000 in around a decade.[70]

Mandatory error reporting has been a popular safety initiative.[71] The reports of adverse outcomes can be used by state regulatory agencies to identify where errors are occurring. If reporting systems provide timely and complete information to regulators, this should, at least in principle, improve the agencies' role as monitors. However, reporting alone does not alter the incentives such public agencies face. If these agencies are not motivated to take action, reporting will not make this more likely. The other rationale for mandatory reporting is to inform the public about variations in quality of care so that more informed consumers can make better health care consumption choices.[72]

At first glance, mandatory reporting would seem to enhance efficiency of consumer decision-making. But there are at least two concerns. First, health care providers worry that reporting adverse outcomes will stimulate medical malpractice suits. These worries appear unfounded. Marchev reports that public officials in states with mandatory reporting did not find a pattern of increased medical malpractice litigation following implementation of mandatory reporting, a situation possibly attributable to the concurrent enactment of data protection statutes.[73]

Another barrier to informed consumer choice is that most states that released incident-specific information did so only upon request.[74] Requests were made after the incident occurred, implying that incident-specific reporting cannot do much to inform consumers prospectively (i.e., in advance of their health care decisions).

There is an additional concern relating to a consumer's ability to make informed decisions even if detailed facility-specific information is provided prospectively. The information revealed by observing an adverse outcome critically depends on the risk of adverse outcome the patient had before the procedure. There is plausibly considerable heterogeneity in such risk. As noted at the beginning of this chapter, if adverse outcomes are reported but there is no adequate adjustment for patient risk ex ante, providers will have an incentive to select healthier, low-risk patients for treatment in order to improve their report records.

Dranove et al., focusing on cardiac surgery report cards in New York and Pennsylvania, find evidence that patients more likely to survive surgery tend to be selected as a consequence of public disclosure of facility-specific mortality rates following coronary artery bypass surgery—just as the critics of public disclosure fear.[75] By contrast, Jin and Leslie, who study the effect of introducing hygiene quality grade cards in Los Angeles in 1998, find that grade cards caused restaurant health inspection scores to increase, consumer demand to become sensitive to changes in restaurants' hygiene quality, and the number of foodborne illness hospitalizations to decrease.[76]

A reason for the difference in findings is plausibly that restaurants have much more difficulty gauging the risk of patrons' getting food-borne illnesses when they enter the restaurant. A cardiac surgeon is in a much better position in advance of surgery to gauge the risk of an adverse outcome for a patient with heart disease than is a restaurant to know, at the time a patron is seated, whether he or she is most likely to get sick.

As discussed earlier, a major problem with mandatory reporting systems is underreporting. A major, often overlooked, aspect of underreporting is that adverse events that occur after discharge are usually not reported. To capture adverse events that are delayed or occur after discharge, the revision of the American Association for Accreditation of Ambulatory Facilities standards requires any deaths within thirty days after a surgical procedure at an accredited facility be reported.[77] Care provided in ambulatory settings is by law subject to regulatory scrutiny, and states are including outpatient facilities in their mandatory reporting laws.[78] If inpatient facilities are covered, ambulatory facilities should be covered as well.

Implications

Each quality assurance mechanism is deficient in some respect. None will do the job of assuring patient safety by itself. What is also lacking in health care is a market for quality. For too long, health care providers have insisted to the public that "we are all good." One reason that medical malpractice is so widely despised among many health professionals is that lawsuits seem to contradict this assertion. However, for tort law to promote patient safety, some fundamental changes are needed.

Restructuring Tort Law to Improve Patient Safety

Changes in Tort Law and Medical Malpractice Insurance Needed

Tort law does not seem to have had a major role in improving patient safety, and some would say that tort law/medical malpractice are a contradiction in terms, plausibly for several reasons.[79] Two major changes are needed to give tort law and medical malpractice insurance a positive role in promoting patient safety. First, it seems unlikely that the scale in many practice settings is sufficient to implement suggested patient safety methods. Perhaps large physician groups can take advantage of scale economies, but most physicians do not practice in large groups. Second, there needs to be a financial penalty for making errors. Currently, the main deterrent effect of malpractice suits for an insured provider is the time and aggravation involved. By contrast, in other areas—motor vehicle liability,[80] workers' compensation,[81] unemployment insurance,[82] and, in a more minor area, dram shop liability[83]—premiums rise following a paid claim. There is considerable empirical evidence from these other areas that when decision-makers are exposed to higher premiums following paid claims, care levels increase.

Role of Enterprise Liability

Enterprise liability[84] first gained prominence as a medical malpractice reform in the 1990s. Under this approach, the focus on medical malpractice litigation would be shifted from individual health care providers, most frequently physicians, to health care organizations under whose auspices care is delivered. The two major candidates for enterprise liability are hospitals and health plans, the latter being the proposed enterprise under the Clinton health plan.

Enterprise liability has several attractive features. It reduces the number of defendants, which potentially reduces the time for dispute resolution and litigation cost. A single defendant focuses the responsibility for quality of care and simplifies settlement negotiations.[85]

Probably the most important advantage is that enterprise liability potentially allows integration of patient safety activities with medical malpractice insurance, implementing systems-based loss control mechanisms and quality assurance programs not feasible for a smaller organization. By combining the function of preventing injuries with that of insuring loss if and when in fact injuries do occur, the way to injury prevention is combined with the willingness to do so (an adaptation of an old cliché). The question of whether hospitals or health plans should be this organization has been debated, but, given the managed care backlash of the late 1990s, the prospects for health plan-based enterprise liability are very slim.[86]

As for hospitals, their size, resources, and status as continual defendants places their systems in an excellent position for liability.[87] Shifting liability to a hospital or hospital system would also create deterrence and provide incentives to implement systemwide safety measures. Hospitals are already structured to take precautions including monitoring of medical staff; but hospital enterprise liability would create a greater financial incentive for peer review at the hospital level and for overseeing care levels of the members of its medical staff. It is likely that hospitals would become more cautious in recruiting their medical staff members than they are currently.

While enterprise liability provides a vehicle for creating incentives to introduce patient safety measures from the party that is in the best position to introduce them, there is a widespread concern among practicing physicians about a loss of professional autonomy. While these concerns are understandable from the perspective of individual physicians, patient safety is incompatible with autonomy of the individual professional. How can a hospital promote patient safety if each physician member of the medical staff practices totally independently?

Experience Rating

Arguably the largest obstacle to producing and implementing safety measures is the lack of financial incentives. Neither market forces nor the threat of tort liability seems to provide sufficient incentives. An important reason that tort liability has not been effective in promoting patient safety is that medical malpractice insurance shields potential defendants from the financial burdens of being sued. Such insurance tends to be complete;[88] that is, there are no deductibles or coinsurance, and, at least for physicians, liability limits of coverage are rarely exceeded.

To reduce the effect of such insurance further, experience rating of premiums is rare for medical malpractice insurance.[89]

Thus, in general, physicians with relatively adverse medical malpractice records pay the same premiums as others.[90] For hospitals, however, the situation is different. Most hospitals self-insure, at least for primary liability coverage.[91] For this reason, they bear much of the financial risk of being sued.

There are several reasons for the lack of experience rating of medical malpractice premiums. The most plausible one has already been stated: that the data on losses at the level of the individual physician practice tend to be insufficiently numerous for insurers to develop sufficiently accurate premiums. In the context of motor vehicle liability, accidents and violations are sufficiently common to allow insurers to develop fairly reliable premiums at the level of the household. By contrast, medical malpractice claims are rare. In a given year, few physicians are sued. And equally important, in contrast to motor vehicle claims, medical malpractice claims often take many years to resolve. Experience rating should be based on paid claims, not on claims that are filed and subsequently dropped by claimants or lost by claimants at verdict.

Research clearly shows that, actuarially, physicians within a specialty should be charged appreciably different premiums. Studies have analyzed claims frequency as a Poisson process.[92] Based on the within-specialty heterogeneity, the studies obtain very different expected claims rates for physicians within specialties, suggesting that observed differences in claims rates reflect more than a random process as well as systematic physician-specific differences in the propensity to be sued.

Simulations conducted by Sloan and Hassan indicate that most hospitals have a sufficient number of medical staff members for experience rating at the hospital level to be feasible.[93] Even small hospitals, given a sufficient record of past claims (five or six years), could be an experience-rating unit. In general, experience rating is based on differences in expected claims frequency. Sloan and Hassan find that considering differences among physicians in claims severity as well as frequency suggests that physicians with adverse claims frequency and severity should (on an actuarial basis) be paying surcharges of 400 to 500 percent. Malpractice insurers would resist imposing such surcharges based on the survey evidence presented above.

Experience rating at the level of the hospital allows hospitals to combine financial incentives, including surcharges on medical staff, with adverse claims experience, but given medical staff organization, it should be possible to use other methods of deterring injuries as well.

Discussion and Conclusions

There is now a widespread consensus that patient safety in health care is not what it should be. This conclusion is admittedly somewhat impressionistic, and is not based on rigorous analysis of the benefits versus the costs of higher levels of patient safety. Even the estimates of deaths attributable to errors in hospitals are questionable. Whatever the optimal level of patient safety is, imposing tort liability is at best part of the solution.

This point is made in a very effective way by the authors of *Freakonomics* (see box 8.2). They describe the steps administrators took at Cedars-Sinai to improve hand-washing compliance. Certainly there must be an easier way than tort to encourage health professionals to wash their hands. And it is a bit difficult to hold tort responsible for the current low rate of compliance with hand hygiene regimens.

Market forces potentially play an important role, as do internal structures such as peer review by a hospital's medical staff, private credentialing, and public regulation. It is inappropriate to blame tort for all of or even most of the quality of care problems currently facing the U.S. health care system. When tort is blamed, the effect seems to be to justify the status quo. It seems unlikely that absent the threat of tort, physicians would become like idealized Stakhanovite workers[94] of the Soviet Union of the 1930s—selfless and industrious individuals interested solely in serving the public good and freely admitting errors, without being motivated by individual financial incentives. True Stakhanovites did not exist in practice, at least not in more than trivial numbers. Likewise, it seems unlikely that absent the threat of tort, physicians and other health workers would admit to their errors in large numbers. If there is

Box 8.2
"Freakonomics" and Patient Safety

The notion of washing hands between patients has been around for about a century and a half. Yet as Dubner and Levitt (2006), the authors of "Freakonomics," indicate, the practice has been difficult to enforce. There was a problem with inadequate rates of hand washing at Ceders-Sinai Hospital, a highly respected institution. The hospital decided that it needed to devise an incentive that would increase compliance without alienating doctors on its medical staff. At first, administrators reminded doctors about washing, using e-mail messages, posters, and faxes. This approach did not seem to work. Then they started a Hand Hygiene Safety Posse that went around the hospital offering a $10 Starbucks card when they found a physician washing up. Nurse observers reported that following implementation of this incentive, compliance with the hand-washing regimen increased to about 80 percent from 60 percent.

The hospital's leadership was not satisfied with this improvement since the chief accrediting body required a compliance rate of 90 percent. Thus, at a meeting of the Chief of Staff Advisory Committee, which consisted of about twenty persons, mostly physicians, the hospital's epidemiologist cultured each of the committee members' hands. The photographic images were disgusting. One photograph was made into a screen saver that appeared on every computer at the hospital. Following this, hand hygiene compliance rose to nearly 100 percent (Dubner and Levitt 2006).

no one around to notice an error, why admit it? Individual incentives for physicians should be aligned with the organizations with which they work.

Increased premiums may themselves facilitate bringing physicians under the hospital's insurance umbrella. Mello, Kelly, Studdert, et al. report that following sharp increases in premiums in Pennsylvania, West Virginia, and Florida in 2002, some hospitals were directly employing physicians in high-premium specialties.[95] Other hospitals were arranging for physicians to obtain medical malpractice insurance through the hospital's insurer and making alternative arrangements for physicians on their medical staff to find coverage and to subsidize their premiums.

9

Medical Malpractice Insurance and Insurance Regulation

Why Study Medical Malpractice Insurance and Insurance Regulation?

At first glance, insurance and its regulation seems to be a very unexciting topic, one best left to the specialists. However, sudden decreases in availability and sharp increases in the price of medical malpractice insurance are the immediate precipitators of each crisis. A frequent response to sharp price increases is to blame the companies whose product prices have increased. Witness, for example, accusations that multinational oil companies are gouging consumers following oil price shocks. Responding to widespread criticism, the companies attribute the price increases to factors beyond their control and, at the same time, offer advice to consumers as voters and to political officials that imposing price controls and/or withdrawing tax advantages will adversely affect the companies' access to capital, and hence adversely affect industry capacity in the long run.

As with medical malpractice, there have been spells when oil products were simply not available, especially during the 1970s. Oil supply disruptions loom on the horizon, mainly due to geopolitical events. Although they were never implemented, the federal government has had plans to ration scarce oil products—most notably during the Carter administration and previously during World War II.

There are parallels between oil/gasoline and medical malpractice insurance, but there are also important differences. As with oil, there have been allegations that insurers in general, and medical malpractice insurers in particular, gouge consumers, especially following sharp premium increases. More than oil, insurance has been subject to a considerable amount of regulation. Unlike oil, which in many high-income countries, including the United States, has remained in private hands, with for-profit being the only ownership form, public and quasi-public provision has sometimes been substituted for private provision of medical malpractice insurance. Even more commonly, alternative private organizational forms have substituted for the for-profit form.

Insurance regulation seeks to prevent insurer bankruptcies, which can cause a disruption in the flow of funds to insured individuals and organizations that have incurred losses and to counter exploitation of market power by insurers, which absent a countervailing force might result in premiums set above the level needed to attract capital to insurers. To a far greater extent than with oil, one potential source of market power in some insurance markets is a lack of consumer information about what is being purchased and about financial and nonfinancial characteristics of sellers of insurance in a given market. However, lack of consumer information is less of a policy issue for medical malpractice than for some other lines of insurance, such as motor vehicle, homeowners, and life insurance.

There are three important interrelated questions. First, how well do markets for medical malpractice insurance function? Second, to the extent that there is a case for government intervention in these markets, how effective have such interventions been? Third, what types of policy changes, if any, are indicated?

Important Features of Medical Malpractice Insurance and the Regulatory Environment

Since medical malpractice insurance is almost always complete—no cost-sharing is imposed on insured physicians when they incur medical malpractice losses,[1] and experience rating of premiums is relatively rare[2]—physicians are largely protected from the financial consequences of lawsuits. By contrast, hospitals often are self-insured for much of medical malpractice loss, and they purchase reinsurance for protection against very large losses; such reinsurance tends to be highly experiencerated. Insurers of physicians rather than physicians themselves purchase reinsurance.[3] Thus, in contrast to physicians, hospitals do bear the monetary costs of medical malpractice lawsuits.

Medical malpractice insurance is a form of property-casualty insurance. Property insurance is first-party insurance. Casualty insurance is third-party insurance. It covers the obligation that an insured individual, business, or other organization incurs by negligently causing personal injury to, and/or property loss by, another person. The most common type of property-casualty insurance is fault-based automobile liability. In comparison, medical malpractice insurance is a very small line of casualty insurance.

Firms providing medical malpractice insurance may be organized in several alternative forms. Some diversity in ownership form is seen among property-casualty insurers more generally. As in other lines of insurance, some firms are organized as stock companies, mutuals, reciprocals, and direct underwriters (e.g., Lloyd's associations).[4] Ownership forms other than the conventional stock form are much more common for medical malpractice insurance. Authorizing new organizational forms of insurance was a major part of the insurance reform movement of the 1970s.

Although the provision of insurance is fundamentally a private activity in the United States, there is also a long history of both federal and state governments serving as insurers.[5] The federal government has taken on the largest obligations, such as covering losses from natural disasters and insolvent banks; state governments provide workers' compensation coverage, hail insurance, unemployment insurance, and coverage plans for uninsured motorists, to name a few. All states have insurance departments that regulate insurers within their jurisdictions and have regulated insurance market for decades (box 9.1), though policies and practices differ substantially among states.[6]

Insurance regulation is overwhelmingly the responsibility of state government; generally insurers must be state-licensed to conduct business. In spite of the challenges posed by state regulation, insurers often operate on a regional or a larger scale. By contrast, until quite recently, many medical malpractice insurers limited their sales to the states in which they were domiciled, especially those companies originally sponsored by state medical societies, which until recently operated in a single state.

Box 9.1
Insurance Market Interventions by State Governments

• Regulation of solvency, premiums, policy forms, underwriting practices

• Creation of new forms of private insurance, such as mutual and reciprocal companies, as an alternative to conventional stock insurers

• Authorization of pooling arrangements, such as joint underwriting associations, to provide coverage to potential purchasers that otherwise would have difficulty in obtaining insurance, and guaranty funds which cover losses incurred by policyholders in the event of insurer inability to pay (bankruptcy)

• State patient compensation programs, which provide state-issued medical malpractice insurance above specified dollar thresholds or for persons who have experienced particular types of medical injuries

• State-funded indemnity coverage for individuals who are in an employment relationship with the state

Two factors contributing to a state-specific orientation are (1) state regulation and (2) legal liability is most often subject to state law interpreted by state courts. The same factors pertain to other lines of casualty insurance; these other lines tend to have multistate insurers as dominant sellers. But in these markets, industry interest groups in the states have not generally organized their own insurance companies.

Most medical malpractice coverage is sold on an individual basis, not to large groups or larger incorporated business entities. Relatively few physicians are covered by the hospitals in which they practice, although hospitals are an entity that naturally groups individual physicians together.[7]

Rationale for Insurance Regulation

Regulation is an important feature of insurance markets of all types. Four major justifications are (1) to prevent bankruptcies by maintaining insurers' solvency; (2) to keep premiums at nearly actuarially fair rates by preventing insurers from exercising market power; (3) to assure availability of coverage by implementing laws and regulations to assure availability; and (4) to supply information to insurance purchasers to improve the performance of insurance markets and assure fair play.

Historically, the main roles of insurance regulation were to assure solvency of insurers in advance of insurer bankruptcy and to mitigate losses of policyholders in the event that bankruptcies occur. The purpose of insurance is to mitigate a policyholder's financial risk; thus, if and when an insurer goes bankrupt, in the end the insured party has not really been relieved of any risk. Additionally, individual purchasers may have insufficient information, combined with too much complexity for consumers of insurance to know which insurers are less likely to become insolvent.[8] Toward this end, regulators monitor whether premiums are adequate to cover expected loss, with a reasonable load to cover the cost of administering the plan, and whether or not insurers are taking unreasonable financial risks with their investments. Ex ante (before bankruptcy occurs), government oversight involves seeing that premiums are adequate to cover anticipated losses and expenses, and that the asset mix is not too risky. Another task of regulators is to restructure insurers for which insolvency seems imminent. Ex post mitigation of loss includes government requirements that insurers contribute to a risk pool or guaranty fund, which compensates policyholders who otherwise would not receive payment for losses they incur due to insurer bankruptcy.

Regulation of premiums is intended to prevent insurers from exercising market power in setting premiums. Governments monitor whether premiums are too high, as well as too low, which is part of solvency regulation, in order to assure the public access to insurance at quasi-competitive rates. Excessive prices in the market may result from lack of consumer knowledge and high consumer search costs, which limit competition.[9] In addition, competition may theoretically be diminished because it is difficult for insurers to determine consumers' risk level, creating an informational advantage to existing insurers and a barrier to entry.[10]

When insurance price spikes occur, governments are asked to act in various ways to reduce prices or limit further rises in prices. On the other hand, insurers facing competitive threats or attempting to increase their market shares may actually set premiums too low relative to expected losses.[11] Setting prices too low may lead to insurer bankruptcies or, more commonly, insurers' exit from those lines of insurance in which high losses are being incurred. There is an analogy to the fairy tale "Goldilocks and the Three Bears": "This porridge is too hot. This porridge is too cold. This porridge is just right." In the long run, it seems likely that the porridge—that is, insurance premiums—are just right. However, in the shorter run, the porridge may either be too hot or too cold—excessive prices when too hot, and inadequate prices when too cold. Both potentially lead to disruptions in medical care markets.

But can public regulation lead to getting insurance prices right, that is, set at levels that would prevail in competitive insurance markets? Since governmental oversight of price is a complex process and subject to differing opinions, this fairy tale does not necessarily have a happy ending, even though, as seen in the next section, medical malpractice insurance premiums appear to have been adequate but not excessive during the late 1970s and 1980s. To our knowledge, no one has accessed adequacy of premiums more recently.

Another goal of insurance regulation is to assure that insurance is readily available to potential purchasers. Some types of insurance are seen as essential to socially valuable undertakings, including the delivery of medical care. For this reason, state legislatures have sought to keep medical malpractice insurance available by, for example, permitting sale of insurance by companies other than those organized as for-profit companies with stockholders as the owners—"stock" companies.

In a competitive insurance market, some potential policyholders may be excluded as bad risks. It may be in the public interest that such risks be covered. Such concerns have arisen in automobile insurance as well as medical malpractice insurance. In the former, being able to drive may be essential to maintaining employment, and availability of liability insurance is directly linked to being able to drive in states with compulsory liability insurance laws. In the latter, a physician may be high risk, not because he or she is a bad physician, but rather because he or she delivers services that may result in medical malpractice suits. Joint underwriting associations, described below, are one mechanism states have used to assure availability of coverage.

A final rationale for insurance regulation is information provision and fair play. This rationale is relatively unimportant for medical malpractice insurance. Information provision and review of policy forms are more important when the customer is not highly educated and/or an infrequent purchaser of coverage. The motive of fair play sometimes leads to requirements that insurers sell insurance to high-risk customers at premiums below the actuarial value of the loss. This has occurred in automobile insurance most prominently,[12] which has been combined with withdrawal restrictions forcing insurers to remain in an unprofitable market for longer than they would voluntarily choose to do.[13] Governments do not require that medical malpractice insurers cross-subsidize high-risk insured health care providers, but medical malpractice insurers do this voluntarily.

Are Medical Malpractice Premiums Adequate or Excessive?

Sloan, Bovbjerg, and Githens (1991) use two alternative analytic approaches to assess adequacy of medical malpractice premiums during the late 1970s and 1980s, one based on a discounted cash flow framework and the other based on the capital asset pricing model (CAPM). A discussion of the technical details of their analysis would take us too far afield. They report that during 1978–1979, medical malpractice premiums yielded returns in excess of those that would prevail in a competitive insurance market. But they do not make much of this finding, since policy concern is raised only by persistent excess returns rather than temporary ones. By 1982, premiums were adequately priced. The authors conclude that during the period they study, premiums were on average neither too high nor too low. A problem in conducting this type of analysis is that it can be done only years after the insurance for a specific policy year was sold. Thus, as this book is written, it is too soon to evaluate adequacy of premiums after the late 1990s.

The good news that premiums are adequate does not necessarily imply that government regulation of insurance is superfluous. What is observed are premiums after interventions of state insurance departments, not without it.

Alternatives to Government Regulation of Insurers

Alternatives to direct government regulation of insurers are (1) implementation of statutory changes that permit changes in ownership form and (2) direct public provision of insurance. If the insurer is operated under an organizational form other than for-profit (e.g., the insurance company is owned by policyholders), then the insurer's incentive to exploit policyholders by extracting maximum profit from them is plausibility reduced. A stock insurer may be likely to exit a market as soon as selling policies in that market is unprofitable. Insurers organized under the alternative forms may be less prone to exit since the owners, the residual claimants, pursue objectives other than obtaining maximum profit. For example, the "bosses" of a physician-sponsored medical malpractice insurer may have a special interest in seeing that the insurer remains in business in the state.

Also, some aspects of insurance may defy private contracting, justifying a larger role for public insurers that do not have maximizing profit as an organizational goal.[14] For example, the quality of the legal defense supplied to the physician policyholder by the insurer may be difficult to specify contractually. A company owned by those insured by the company may see that a defense is conducted more closely in accord with the wishes of insured defendants. A for-profit insurer may calculate whether settling the case is more profitable, but the defendant may want to continue the case as a matter of principle. Insurers organized on another basis may not be able to continue the case without limits, but they may be more sympathetic to views of the persons they insure.

Public insurers would not ordinarily completely avoid the principal-agent (the insured individual being the principal and the insurer, the agent) problems of stock companies. Direct public provision of insurance of large claims has been motivated by reasoning that absent government participation in the market, the volatility of both the frequency and the size of these claims has increased the cost of capital to medical malpractice insurers and has led to both premium increases and insurer exits.

An insuring organization not subject to state regulation is the risk retention group. Groups of physicians, such as anesthesiologists, jointly purchase coverage from an existing insurer. To promote availability of coverage, the U.S. Congress passed the Risk Retention Act in 1981 (amended in 1986), which exempts such groups from state regulation.[15]

Differences Between Medical Malpractice and Other Forms of Property-Casualty Insurance

Distinctive Features of the Medical Malpractice Insurance Market

The most common loss covered by property-casualty insurance is fault-based motor vehicle liability. Motor vehicle liability insurance pays many claims per insured individual (claims frequency), but low amounts per paid claim (claims severity). High claims frequency means that insurers receive frequent signals, not only about their policyholders' behavior but also about how judges and juries determine liability and award damages. This in turn allows insurers to classify insured individuals according to their risk of incurring a loss. Medical liability insurance, by contrast, is a low frequency/high severity line of coverage, making it more difficult to classify individual physicians according to the probability that claims will be filed against them in the future, one reason for the lack of experience rating of medical malpractice insurance premiums.

In motor vehicle liability, the delay from the date of an accident to the date a claim is paid is often short. By contrast, medical liability claims often take many years to be resolved. As a result, using data on a relatively few claims, a medical malpractice insurer must estimate the likelihood that a jury far in the future will hold the defendant liable, and the amount that jury would award in damages. It is generally not possible to compute an accurate estimate of expected future loss on an individual physician basis.

In most states there is a compulsory minimum amount of motor vehicle liability insurance a driver must have to make it more likely that injurers will be able to compensate those they injure.[16] Without insurance, many individual drivers are "judgment proof" after being involved in a major traffic accident (i.e., they have insufficient assets to compensate the injury victim for his or her loss). Unlike motor vehicle insurance, states, with some exceptions (e.g., Pennsylvania and Kansas), generally do not require health care providers to purchase minimum amounts of medical malpractice insurance coverage. However, hospitals and physician groups may make affiliation conditional on a physician's purchase of adequate coverage. Because physicians tend to have substantial personal assets, few are willing to risk their career earnings on the outcome of a single claim by "going bare" (i.e., forgoing insurance). Instead, physicians faced with rapidly rising insurance costs may leave practice, change their scope of practice in order to reduce premiums, or move to another state where premiums are lower.

Although there are periodic complaints about automobile liability and insurance, such as delays in payment, high legal fees, and the ambiguity of fault, there is widespread acceptance of the overall litigation and insurance system by drivers and voters. By contrast, medical malpractice has very few defenders in the physician or health provider community. Physicians reject, almost universally, the premise that tort liability serves a useful role in medicine.

Types of Medical Malpractice Insurers

The market for malpractice insurance consists of three broad categories of insurers. First are traditional "multiple-line" insurance companies, such as the St. Paul Group of Companies, which historically was the largest stock insurer selling medical liability coverage. It stopped writing new policies in 2000.

A second group consists of physician-sponsored, "single-line" medical malpractice insurance companies, many of which were chartered during the "crisis of availability" in the 1970s. The common organizational forms are mutuals and reciprocals. The growth of these organizational forms is an institutional response to the crisis in availability of medical malpractice insurance in the 1970s. Under the mutual form, the roles of policyholder and owner are merged. The policyholders supply capital to the insurance company. Policyholders (in this context, mainly physicians) are given a say in company financial decisions during the time their policies are in force. The mutual form aligns the incentives of owners and policyholders since they are the same, but one potentially important control mechanism present in the stock form is absent: buyout of inefficient organizations. Nevertheless, lack of buyout potential and less flexibility to leave the medical malpractice line of business is an advantage in terms of greater stability of insurance supply.

Reciprocals resemble mutuals, but with two differences. First, a reciprocal is unincorporated and owns no capital. By contrast, a mutual is incorporated with a stated capital and surplus. Second, the policyholders appoint an individual or corporation as an "attorney in fact" to manage the organization with an advisory committee to provide some oversight of management. In a mutual, the board of directors has responsibility for management oversight. In some reciprocals, policyholders can control managers by exercising their option to withdraw their contribution to surplus, or policyholders as a group can legally force dissolution of the association. Originally chartered in one state, some physician-sponsored insurance companies have entered markets in other states, sometimes using a low-price strategy to gain market share, as was described in chapter 2.

Self-insured organizations such as large hospitals assume their own risk and set aside appropriate reserves, typically reinsuring large losses above a high deductible. A large hospital might also use a captive insurer, a wholly owned subsidiary that keeps formal insurance accounts but is usually chartered abroad, and therefore exempt from domestic insurance regulation. Risk retention groups are analogous to a buyers' cooperative. Limited-purpose insurers that operate under federal rather than state law, they generally represent members of a single physician specialty or hospitals in a particular geographic region that decide to share risk.

Private surplus line insurers offer insurance to high-risk individuals as in other lines of insurance, most notably automobile insurance. These companies insure only a very small number of physicians. Alongside lower underwriting standards are higher insurance premiums.

In addition, there are alternative forms of coverage, such as joint underwriting associations (JUAs), self-insurance vehicles, captive insurance companies, and risk retention groups, in which individuals, trade organizations, or existing insurers reduce their exposure by creating and operating their own insurance company. In general, these alternative insurers emphasize providing stable coverage rather than maximizing profits; they structure their finances so that they are less likely to exit due to adverse market conditions.

JUAs are cooperative ventures of existing insurers that are mandated by states to supply insurance to individuals who, in principle, are unable to obtain insurance from other sources. JUAs are a response to a social objective of promoting access to medical care by assuring that physicians have access to medical malpractice insurance.[17] In automobile casualty insurance, assigned risk plans are much more common than JUAs. Assigned risk plans provide a method for placing high risk insured individuals with specific private insurers, often at less than an actuarially fair rate (i.e., premiums are too low in relationship to the losses that the insurers can expect persons assigned to them to generate).

Lack of Experience Rating
Experience rating is rare in the medical malpractice line of insurance, not in terms of the number of insurers who engage in some form of experience rating but rather in terms of the number of physicians adversely affected by this practice. A national survey of insurers conducted by Schwartz and Mendelson[18] reports that 90.3 percent of companies employed surcharges in 1985. However, only 1.6 percent of insured physicians were subjected to surcharges and another 0.9 percent faced other sanctions, such as restrictions on the scope of their practices or requirements for further training and supervision. A survey of fourteen medical malpractice insurers conducted in 1987–1988 revealed that only one of the fourteen insurers had never implemented an experience rating program of any type. At the time of the survey, less than 1 percent of physician enrollees paid more than standard premiums because of adverse claims experience.[19]

Due to a lack of experience rating, doctors with favorable and unfavorable loss experience pay similar malpractice premiums. Preserving a connection between tort liability and quality of care is a major goal of the medical malpractice system.[20]

The widespread view among physicians that determining liability is a haphazard process has been a barrier to setting premiums according to individual physicians' claims histories.[21] Low claims frequency makes it even harder to experience-rate premiums, even though claims against a few physicians account for a major part of overall losses to malpractice carriers.[22] This perpetuates a vicious cycle in which lack of acceptance of a constructive role for tort in advancing medical quality is an impediment to meaningful structural reform of the malpractice system. Governments have intervened to promote use of experience rating, but the results have been mixed at best.[23]

Is the way out of this dilemma to reintroduce experience rating? Generally the unit for rating is the insured individual, but there are alternative experience rating units ranging from medical groups to a hospital and/or its medical staff. When insured individuals are rated as part of a larger organization, the group must allocate premiums by individual or decide to cross-subsidize the premiums of some of its members. How the organization allocates its premium expense among the group members is the organization's private concern.

Sloan and Hassan seek to answer the question of whether the hospital/hospital's medical staff is sufficiently large to be experience rated.[24] The alternative being considered here is whether or not a hospital's and/or its medical staff's total experience contains a sufficient amount of information to provide reliable evidence for purposes of experience rating. In their simulations, they use data on medical staffs by hospital size from the American Hospital Association and from Florida medical malpractice closed claims. The closed claims were aggregated to the level of individual physician. Then physicians were randomly selected to "staff" hospitals of particular sizes and medical staff composition by specialty.

To gauge whether or not experience rating at the level of the hospital would be feasible and practical, Sloan and Hassan computed the level of initial capitalization that would be consistent with a specific bankruptcy risk. More specifically, while taking the timing of premium income versus payment for loss into account, the authors computed the probability that losses would fall short of premium income. The problem was to set the hospital/hospital medical staff premium in total, allowing the organization to figure out how premiums would actually be financed. The hospital could decide to have each physician share equally (say by specialty) in the premium obligation, but impose other carrots/sticks to avoid losses due to claims. That is, the task of monitoring is shifted from the level of the insurer, where the task is not performed well, to the hospital/hospital medical staff, where monitoring costs are likely to be much lower. Further, it is the hospital's legal obligation to monitor, an obligation typically delegated at least in part to the hospital's medical staff. Hospitals could improve their loss experiences by implementing more effective peer review, improving systems which promote patient safety, and being more selective about the physicians they retain or admit to their medical staff.

Without discussing the details of the findings here, the message is a positive one. The specific question the study addresses is how much the group would need to hold in reserves to achieve a given level of insolvency risk. A lower insolvency risk requires higher levels of reserves. Initially, each physician member of the hospital's medical staff covered under the plan would be required to make a contribution to reserves. When the levels of required reserves is higher, the per-physician contribution would also be higher.

Setting the probability that a plan would have insufficient funds to cover losses over a six-year period at 2.5 percent (or 0.4 to 0.5 percent per annum), the initial contribution per physician on the staff of a hospital with fewer than 100 beds would be 4.2 times the annual premium. The ratio of initial capitalization to annual premiums was lower than this for larger hospitals. If the bankruptcy probability percentage of 2.5 percent over six years is thought to be too high, a lower percentage could be employed. As a consequence, the initial capitalization would be correspondingly higher. A 0.4–0.5 percent per year insolvency rate does not seem inordinately high, however, especially since contracts with individual physicians could include a provision for ex post assessments which would be required only very rarely.

Government-Sponsored Risk Pooling Arrangements

Government-sponsored risk-pooling arrangements address the solvency, availability, and fair play objectives of government intervention in the context of medical malpractice insurance.

Joint underwriting associations (JUAs) and guaranty funds are publicly created entities that provide insurance as a last resort. In this role, state governments facilitate transactions within the private insurance sector that alter risk pools in order to serve the public objectives of assuring availability of coverage and protecting consumers against insurer insolvency. Without state action, it seems unlikely that insurers would coordinate their activities in order to establish high-risk pools. These pools would likely be unprofitable.

Joint Underwriting Associations

In response to the medical malpractice insurance crisis of the mid-1970s, many states authorized the formation of JUAs. At the time, legislators saw a need to fill the gap in coverage that arose when private insurers withdrew from the market.[25] Unlike mutual insurers with ties to medical societies, which also were created in many states in the 1970s, JUAs and patient compensation funds, described below and in the next chapter, are public organizations. Under typical legislation establishing JUAs, all companies writing liability insurance of any kind are required to participate. JUAs are often conceived as temporary measures, but some of those established in the 1970s remain active.[26] Moreover, there have been proposals to form JUAs for medical malpractice as recently as 2002.[27]

JUAs are designed to be "insurers of last resort," that is, to cover providers who are unable to obtain insurance from other sources. The Kansas JUA provides an example. As already noted, having medical malpractice insurance coverage is mandatory in Kansas. The Kansas statute imposing this requirement also implemented an availability plan for backup basic coverage and an excess coverage plan. These plans are supported by the Health Care Stabilization Fund, which is financed by a surcharge on providers.[28] The basic coverage sets premiums in excess of those charged by private insurers and is available only to providers able to demonstrate that they cannot obtain private coverage.

If the JUA's premium income is insufficient to cover losses and administrative expense, each member company is assessed a pro rata share of the shortfall. In competitive insurance markets, owners of companies demand a reasonable rate of return on the capital they supply. The only way to earn this return is for companies that subsidize the JUA (either all malpractice insurers or all property-casualty insurers) to increase

premiums to their policyholders. As a result, obtaining medical malpractice insurance becomes more expensive relative to JUA coverage, leading
more physicians to substitute JUA-obtained coverage for private coverage. When state governments form a JUA, they facilitate transactions
among private insurers in forming risk pools. Some JUAs established
in the 1970s remain active even though they were often conceived as
temporary fixes.[29]

Rather than serving the intended purpose of providing medical malpractice insurance coverage to health care providers who cannot obtain
it from the private market, JUAs have become a main source of coverage
in a few states, such as South Carolina. Pooling arrangements therefore
may crowd out private medical malpractice insurance, as occurred in
some states with JUAs in the 1980s.[30] At that time, JUAs dominated
the market in Massachusetts and Rhode Island, which like other New
England states, lacked physician-sponsored medical malpractice insurers.[31] Moreover, both JUAs were in substantial financial trouble,[32] in
large part because the political process by which they set premiums
underestimated the actuarial value of their loss exposure.

During the crisis in Pennsylvania, which was at its worst during
2001–2004, hospitals and physicians increasingly relied on coverage
through the state's JUA and other alternative coverage sources such as
risk retention groups. In 2002, it was estimated that Pennsylvania's JUA
had 1,700 physician policies in force, up from 351 in 2001.[33] Between
1999 and 2002, the number of health care providers in this state who
obtained coverage through the JUA increased by a factor of more than
7.[34] In 2002, 12 percent of hospitals in Pennsylvania had their primary
coverage through the Pennsylvania Joint Underwriting Association.[35] In
Florida, there was also a substantial increase in the number of physicians
enrolled in the state's JUA, but the JUA in that state covered only a small
fraction of physicians in the state.[36]

Although JUAs can provide coverage when private insurance does not,
they also have deficiencies. Some weaknesses are common to all JUAs,
while others are unique to particular states.

Providing coverage through a JUA may conflict with deterring medical
injuries. Although some physicians who experience difficulty in obtaining coverage may have clean records, particularly during a generalized

insurance crisis, others lack access to private coverage because of a history of repeated claims. When physicians with many past claims are able to obtain coverage at standard rates, subsidized by physicians with better track records, they lack an incentive to improve (or leave practice). In addition, there is rarely any mention of loss prevention in the literature on JUAs. The major focus is on insuring physicians, not on developing programs to reduce the probability of claims.[37]

Some states have recognized that pricing should reflect underlying risk, and offer premiums matching the insured's expected loss. For example, Pennsylvania's JUA now includes a provision for premium surcharges based on prior claims and claim expense, or based on regulatory actions suggesting poor provider quality have been taken by licensing boards, hospitals, Medicare or Medicaid, the federal Drug Enforcement Administration, or Pennsylvania's controlled substance act.[38] This is clearly a step in the right direction.

However, underpricing has occurred in well-publicized cases. Not only does pricing JUA coverage lower than that available in the private market make it a more attractive option, theoretically, it also may increase the prices that the private market must charge for coverage. Each company linked to the JUA is assessed a pro rata share of the deficit if the JUA's administrative expenses and losses exceed its premium income. Since owners of member companies who subsidize the JUA must provide a reasonable rate of return on their capital, pro rata assessments force increases in premiums for policyholders of private companies. This makes the JUA's premiums even more appealing, resulting in health care providers dropping private coverage in exchange for JUA coverage.

Overpricing is also a risk for some JUAs due to the pressure from private insurers to assure that the JUAs do not compete with them. Like underpricing, this is to be avoided, lest providers not buy JUA coverage in situations in which using it would be socially optimal.

State Guaranty Funds

Another form of government-organized risk-pooling are state guaranty funds, which, like JUAs, are institutional arrangements not unique to medical malpractice insurance. In addition to directly promoting insurer solvency, insurance regulation protects policyholders' ability to collect on future claims by mandating guaranty funds. Between 1969 and 1981, all states enacted laws to establish guaranty funds.[39] Guaranty funds provide a mechanism for assessing surviving insurers after the fact for losses incurred by insolvent insurers.

Almost all states guarantee that valid property-casualty claims will be paid, if necessary, by these state-overseen funds. When an insurer is in receivership and management cannot meet its obligations to policyholders, the receiver can draw against the state's guaranty fund.[40] A guaranty fund raises money to cover these payments by assessing property-casualty insurers who do business in the state. Except for the New York fund, they are all post-insolvency assessment funds. Members are assessed a fixed percentage of premium volume to pay claims that exceed the assets of the insolvent insurer.[41] Thus, guaranty funds are mechanisms for taxing all property-liability policyholders to cover losses of a particular firm in a particular line, such as a seller of medical liability insurance.

Guaranty funds offer physicians and other health care providers who purchase medical liability insurance the ultimate in protection from insurer insolvency. A physician whose insurer goes bankrupt before indemnifying an injury victim does not risk his or her personal assets. As with JUAs, however, consumers of other types of liability insurance may be required to subsidize the losses of physicians (of course, the opposite may occur as well if auto liability insurers fail). These redistributional effects are real, but are not transparent to consumers of health care or to citizens as voters.

There is a frequent trade-off in insurance between risk protection and efficiency. Guaranty funds offer protection against loss, but at a cost. Because the state guaranty fund will honor claims against a health care provider if the provider's primary carrier becomes insolvent, providers who have a choice among primary insurers may not consider financial strength an important attribute.[42] This in turn creates an incentive for insurers to engage in risky underwriting and investment practices.[43] This effect is exacerbated by the fact that guaranty fund assessments are not based on the riskiness of an insurer's business strategy,[44] but it seems unlikely that this would apply to a small line such as medical liability insurance.

While it is the function of insurance to repay policyholders after a loss is incurred, the government insurance pooling arrangements can shield policyholders from avoidable as well as unavoidable losses. This occurs when guaranty funds pay claims incurred by insurers who became insolvent because they assumed excessive business risk, or when JUAs insure health care providers at less than actuarially fair premiums. Admittedly, there may be situations in which charging actuarially fair malpractice premiums conflicts with assuring that medical care is available in an area underserved by physicians. But it is preferable to isolate these specific situations and provide explicit subsidies, rather than to redistribute resources sub rosa to the group of providers and insurers that seem to be at highest risk of business failure.

Evaluation of Government Risk Pooling Arrangements

Aside from descriptive information about program operations, very little is known about the performance of JUAs and guaranty funds. Lessons have been learned and used to improve public programs over time.[45] To states considering implementing or changing their programs to tackle medical malpractice, the experiences of other states that have programs in place are potentially quite valuable. Nonetheless, states appear to run their programs in isolation. As a result, so little know-how is shared that some of the same mistakes happen again and again.

The conventional wisdom that the private sector is more efficient does not seem to apply, as these programs have succeeded in achieving a low administrative cost. An inherent risk of public provision is that it will crowd out private coverage, yet with some exceptions, nothing indicates this has occurred on a wide scale.

The lack of data collection and formal program evaluation makes it impossible to know, for example, whether JUAs have made medical malpractice insurance more available to health care providers or, alternatively, whether they have crowded out private insurance coverage. Despite the fact that patient safety is a general concern, nothing is known about actions JUAs have taken to improve patient safety, an especially important consideration since these pooling arrangements often enroll substandard risks. It is not known how frequently guaranty funds have been used in the medical malpractice insurance field, or what the effect is of the existence of such funds on insurer efforts to manage their losses.

There is no empirical evidence on the performance of state guaranty funds. Even less is known about guaranty funds than about JUAs, either in other lines of property-casualty insurance or in the context of medical malpractice insurance.

One concern is that guaranty funds may not reduce insurance cycles, but instead exacerbate them. State guaranty funds may intensify a capacity shortage because the crisis phase of the insurance cycle is coupled with large numbers of insolvencies.[46] Just as insurers are leaving the market, industry capacity is further reduced when net worth decreases as a result of assessing funds from the remaining insurers. While some consumers are protected from their insurer's insolvency, guaranty funds may cause premium levels to increase across the industry. Prefunding the system, as in New York, could avoid the possibility of such problems.[47]

Regulation of Medical Malpractice Insurance

Critique of Public Regulation

Public regulation has long been a feature of many industries. There has been a trend toward deregulation in several sectors, but generally to a lesser extent in insurance. The major goals of regulating medical malpractice insurance were described above. Although these are praiseworthy, they may come at a cost. Free entry and exit is the hallmark of competitive markets.

While there is a concern about losses incurred by policyholders in the event of insurer insolvency, solvency regulation may offer protection to otherwise inefficient firms and confer the ability to exercise market power on those firms that are protected. Rate regulation may reduce the exercise of market power. Yet to the extent that rates are too low, the supply of the product may be reduced below socially optimal levels.

Assuring availability of coverage has the benefit of potentially preserving the public's access to medical care. But attaining this goal may conflict with injury deterrence and result in cross-subsidies from insured parties which exercise care to those which do not. The fear of losing insurance at standard rates may be an incentive to some potential injurers to take precautions. This incentive becomes weaker if insured parties are guaranteed coverage, particularly at less than actuarially fair premiums, even if they do not exercise care. Information provision is less relevant in the medical malpractice field than for other lines of insurance. Fair play, however, is likely to be equivalent to advocating cross-subsidization of premiums.

Lacking specific evidence that private markets are not accomplishing social objectives (market failure), the presumption of many economists is that societal well-being is best served by leaving markets alone. If there is some evidence of such market failure, then this may provide a rationale for public intervention with one major caveat, namely, that government intervention actually improves social welfare even in the presence of market failure absent such intervention.

Some prominent scholars, many of whom are economists, have been critical of the view that regulation serves the public interest.[48] They argue that there is a market for regulatory controls just as there are markets for other goods and services. In the context of regulation, the suppliers are government agencies and legislators. Public regulation is demanded by special interests. Thus, for examples, farmers demand government controls, such as limits on farm production, since such restrictions result in higher product prices. In return, being made subject to these restrictions, the regulated groups make financial contributions and vote for the suppliers.

The general electorate tends to be indifferent or even not knowledgeable about particular regulations because it is most often not directly affected or is affected in ways that are quite subtle. Since being actively involved in the political process is costly, most people are not interested in most issues most of the time. Lack of widespread public interest facilitates capture by the industry being regulated. Conversely, when the public becomes more involved, capture by private interests becomes more difficult to achieve.[49]

These generalizations may fit any particular industry in very general terms, though each industry is somewhat idiosyncratic. The most in-depth study of regulation of insurance is a book by Kenneth Meier.[50]

Professor Meier emphasizes the heterogeneity of circumstances under which regulation takes place, even within the insurance industry. A number of lines of insurance, such as motor vehicle and homeowners insurance, are important to a large number of persons. Other lines of insurance, including medical malpractice insurance, are far less relevant to the general public. Bureaucracies tend to have greater influence on public policies when policies are complex and not particularly salient to the public.

Salience is important because it may be difficult to arouse legislative interest on the basis of financial contributions and personal influence (lobbying) alone. To elicit the public's (and hence legislators') interest, the issue must be made salient. For example, to motivate state legislators to introduce tort reform legislation, the insurance industry has needed to raise saliency enough to place the issue on the legislative agenda. Salience has been increased by issuing news releases and other forms of publicity warning the public and government officials about the "crisis" and its consequences. The industry has tried to simplify the issue to increase public participation. In dealing with the medical malpractice crisis, the interests of insurers and health care providers are aligned. The task is to get the public to assist in pressuring for statutory change.

Empirical Evidence on Effects of Regulation: Studies of Other Lines of Insurance

The above general points about insurance regulation are largely theoretical or sometimes impressionistic. There is a body of empirical research which assesses the actual impacts of regulation—showing, for example, that even though regulation reduces premiums, it may also increase the market shares of JUAs and other assigned-risk plans.[51]

The most detailed analysis of solvency regulation in the property-casuality insurance industry is Munch and Smallwood.[52] The authors find that minimum capital requirements (maximum premium-to-surplus ratio) reduce the number of insurer insolvencies. This was accomplished solely by blocking entry of small, relatively risky insurers. While erecting entry barriers has the benefit of reducing insolvencies, it also has three adverse effects. For one, some insurance purchasers may be willing to tolerate some additional insolvency risk in trade for a lower premium.[53]

Empirical Evidence on Effects of Regulation: Studies of Medical Malpractice Insurance

Sloan, Bovbjerg, and Githens report results of a survey they conducted of fourteen medical malpractice insurers in 1987–1988.[54] Part of the survey dealt with regulation. Based on these findings, they concluded that for most companies in most years, regulation has not been a major influence on entry of insurers and, with some important exceptions, on pricing of medical malpractice insurance. The national commercial insurers responding to the survey expressed far more concern about the regulatory climate than did physician insurers. The one instance of an insurer leaving the state (among the fourteen respondents) involved a national insurer.

Born, Viscusi, and Baker examine the long-run effects of major tort reforms on insurers' losses, using a sample of individual firms writing medical malpractice insurance during 1984–2003.[55] One of the legal variables included in their analysis is prior approval rate regulation, which identified states with the most stringent form of rate regulation, but such regulation has no statistically significant effect on losses. An earlier study by Viscusi and Born analyzed variations in the loss ratio for medical malpractice insurers.[56] The authors found premium regulation had no effect on this ratio, defined as losses attributable to premiums written in a policy year to the value of premiums earned in that year. Viscusi and Born's analysis of medical malpractice insurer losses, premiums, and loss ratios revealed no effect of prior approval regulation on these dependent variables.[57] By contrast, they reported that certain tort reforms did improve insurer profitability.

Between 1984 and 1991, about 1 percent of all insurance companies in the United States failed. This represented thirty-seven firms. The insolvency rate had more than doubled the rate for years before this. Increasing frequency of failure was only part of the problem. There was increased severity associated with the insurer failures as well.[58] Comparable statistics are not available for medical malpractice insurance.

The PHICO Bankruptcy: Business Failure in Spite of Solvency Regulation

A well-publicized failure occurred in the early 2000s in spite of state insurance departments' efforts to oversee financial performance of insurers writing coverage in their states. The failure involved the Pennsylvania Hospital Insurance Company (PHICO).

In an attempt to provide affordable insurance, the Pennsylvania State Hospital Association created PHICO in 1976. The company enjoyed success, partly due to its conservative management, and paid claims up until the time of its liquidation in 2002. During 1995, a quiescent period for insurance, with the appointment of a new chairman to the company's insurance board, PHICO changed its priorities. Instead of continuing its focus on consistently affordable insurance, the company decided to break into the national market.

PHICO was able to obtain licenses to sell insurance in all fifty states, the District of Columbia, Puerto Rico, and the U.S. Virgin Islands. As a result of this expansion, premium payments from physicians rose from $10.7 million to $130.5 million.[59] This dramatic growth was not surprising; premiums were set below market value. PHICO used this as its selling point; a 1997 advertisement boasted that premiums would be a 25 to 35 percent savings for policyholders.[60] PHICO's methods worked. In five years the premium income rose from $94.7 million to $181.5 million.[61] By 2000, PHICO had become the seventh largest medical malpractice insurer in the country.[62]

The excessively low premiums set by PHICO in the mid-1990s allowed the company's growth to be substantial, but the growth was extremely unstable. Insurance regulations are determined by the states, so each state has unique requirements for operation. In order to be profitable, companies must consider the state regulations, local markets, and competitors before expanding.

Low premiums coupled with inadequate forethought and planning led to financial distress. For premiums collected in 2001, PHICO paid, on average, $1.40 for every dollar of premium it received.[63]

In its lawsuit against PHICO, the Pennsylvania Department of Insurance offered a different opinion as to the company's problems. It alleged that mismanagement was an important factor: "The company aggressively under-priced the competition even in markets in which the company had no previous experience. The strategy of offering low prices in highly competitive and unfamiliar markets was fraught with risk."[64]

Many questions remain as to how this could have happened to a stable company with a nearly thirty-year history. It was not due to a lack of insurance regulations; PHICO did business in all fifty states, all of which had insurance regulations in place and requirements for licensure. Some accuse the Pennsylvania Insurance Department of failing to adequately monitor PHICO's business practices and not taking steps to correct the rapidly deteriorating situation. In response to this heavy criticism, the Insurance Department claimed it was impossible for it to monitor the company's financial status because PHICO had filed misleading reports.[65] Unsurprisingly, questions have been raised as to the appropriateness of existing regulations.[66] There were also some political allegations. State regulators who were also insurance executives and legislators who also worked in the insurance industry drafted regulations.[67]

Regardless of blame, regulations may not have been the problem, as the Pennsylvania Insurance Department argued—even though lack of adequate oversight may have been. In 1999, PHICO's outside auditor, Price Waterhouse Coopers, advised the company that it was facing massive losses and its reserves needed to be increased by $130 million.[68]

PHICO took no action; in 2000, accounts were renewed with no meaningful adjustment to the underwriting terms or price.[69] Instead, the leaders of PHICO attempted to resolve the problem in a different way, restricting the power of those in charge of the reserves. In May 2000, the authority of the claims department was restricted, preventing it from being able to set reserves. In addition, PHICO imposed an arbitrary incurred loss budget, which prevented the claims department from increasing the reserves.

Many knowledgeable observers were surprised by the extent to which PHICO was underreserved. When state regulators placed PHICO into rehabilitation under Pennsylvania's insurance law, its financial statement showed a meager $6.8 million surplus. After liquidation, it became apparent that PHICO's reserves had not just been dwindling, they had been nonexistent. Regulators estimated the firm was underreserved and insolvent by at least $250 million.

The impact of PHICO's collapse has been far-reaching; 38,000 doctors and nearly 900 hospitals across the country were forced to find alternative liability insurance, usually at much higher rates.[70] Pennsylvania, where PHICO was one of the major malpractice insurers, was hit especially hard by its downfall. Other insurance companies, their shareholders, and claimants also felt the loss; PHICO left behind 16,600 pending claims.[71] Hospital systems also faced huge losses.

PHICO's insolvency, along with several other insurance companies leaving the market, has created debate over the underlying causes of the insurance failures.[72] Some argue a bad economy and poor business decisions by company executives are to blame for the failure of so many insurance companies during 1995–2005.

Could this have been prevented by stricter state regulations and closer monitoring of business activities? The evidence suggests that insurance regulation had nothing to do with either causing *or* preventing the company's failure, the latter being the primary function of state insurance regulation. Failure to prevent the company's bankruptcy amounts to a major criticism of the regulatory process, at least in this case. Whatever the role of regulation, some insurance companies have fared much better, at least to date. NORCAL Mutual Insurance Company is an example of such companies.

NORCAL: A Physician-Sponsored Insurer with an Outcome Different from PHICO's

Like PHICO, NORCAL was born out of the 1970s' medical malpractice crisis. It, too, was started by a group of medical professionals in an attempt to provide consistent, reasonable malpractice premiums. NORCAL was started, owned and controlled by its member insureds. The company initially was associated with Casualty Insurance Company Service, Inc., but in only three years NORCAL was independent.

NORCAL, unlike PHICO, slowly expanded its business over the course of twenty years. Between 1983 and 1990, the company focused its efforts on doing business statewide. When the company was ready to expand nationally, NORCAL slowly acquired other insurance companies.[73] Its conservative approach was successful; it has received an A rating from A.M. Best Co., a body which grades the performance of insurance companies, for twenty-one years in a row. On its Web site, NORCAL attributes its continued success to conservative business principles: "Our strong financial position is a result of our commitment to financial stability and reliance on long-held principles of underwriting to the standard of care, making conservative investments and pricing our coverage responsibly." In addition to sound business decisions, NORCAL, and several tort reform advocates, maintain that the 1975 California statute placing a $250,000 cap on attorney's fees and pain and suffering damages allowed the company to charge low premiums.[74] NORCAL has been able to keep the rate increase gradual and proportional, which it attributes to decreased liabilities.

However, others point to Proposition 103, passed in 1988, which grants the state insurance commissioner as well as outside parties the power to challenge proposed rate hikes.[75]

Regulation May Adversely Affect Solvency: The Case of Savings and Loan Banking

The Federal Deposit Insurance Corporation (FDIC) has provided insurance coverage for consumer deposits in private banks. While instituted to protect depositors against bank insolvency, a possible adverse effect of the deposit insurance system is that it may provide a moral hazard for excessive risk taking.[76] Moral hazard arises when consumers become much less cautious about the business practices of the banks in which they have deposits if they have insurance in the event of bank failure. The loss of market pressure to be prudent may correspond with less financial scrutiny by public regulators of bank activities.

Richard Grossman compares risk-taking of insured and uninsured savings and loan banks during the 1930s, finding an interaction between regulation, insured savings, and risk-taking of banks.[77] Those banks that operated under relatively permissive regulatory regimes and whose deposits were insured were more likely to undertake risky lending activities than were other banks. Rather than focus on the interaction between regulation and deposit insurance, Michael Keeley, studying a much more recent period, hypothesizes that moral hazard would be worse under conditions of market competition among banks than under a regulatory regime in which competition was restrained.[78] Increased competition may have reduced banks' incentives to act prudently with regard to risk taking since the value of a bank charter fell due to comparatively free entry of banks under deregulation which occurred in the early 1980s in the United States. He finds that banks with more market power hold more capital relative to assets on a market-value basis and have a lower default risk (reflected in lower risk premiums on large, uninsured certificates of deposit). Having more capital lowers bankruptcy risk. The lower rate on CDs demanded by investors is plausibly because investors required a lower return since they perceived the banks' bankruptcy risk to be lower.

Using data from Kansas on individual banks from a period before the FDIC was established (1910–1928), Wheelock and Wilson study determinants of bank failures. Membership in the voluntary state deposit insurance system increased the probability of bank failure.[79] Richard Cebula measures bank failure rates directly, finding that bank failure rates rise as the fraction of deposits covered by federal deposit insurance rises, which is direct evidence of moral hazard.[80] He also reports that bank failure rates declined with increases in the capital-to-asset ratio and with increased competition among banks. Thus, at least under certain circumstances, there is some reason to be concerned about the effect of public insurance coverage on firms' incentive to be cautious.

Conclusion

To answer the first of three questions posed in this chapter's introduction—Is the market for medical malpractice insurance broken?—we conclude that the market has been fixed so often that it is difficult to contemplate a market for medical malpractice insurance absent government intervention. Empirical evidence from the late 1970s and the 1980s indicates that on average, medical malpractice insurance premiums have been adequate, not excessive; but, as acknowledged above, the correctness of these premiums is measured in the presence, not the absence, of state regulation.

The answer to the second question is more straightforward. In principle, regulation is necessary to address unique potential problems for insurance consumers, such as access to coverage, financial insolvency among insurers, the complexity of insurance contracts, timely payment of claims, and affordability of premiums, among other issues. In practice, the record of insurance regulation is mixed. While regulation probably has not caused more than minor harm, it is not clear that society has been very well served by it either. Insolvencies occur in spite of regulation. The PHICO bankruptcy is a case in point.

Risk-pooling programs meant to help accomplish the goals of regulation often have unintended side effects. More empirical evidence is needed on guaranty funds, yet we can already see the potential problems with crowding out private insurance in the case of JUAs. New programs incorporating catastrophe bonds, puts, and options are potential methods to spread risk among investors willing to supply capital on more favorable terms.

Hospital self-insured medical malpractice insurance programs and reinsurance are currently not subject to insurance regulation. To answer the third question, in light of the evidence, we are reluctant to recommend additional regulation. Publicly provided reinsurance may be worth considering if some of the past mistakes described more fully in the next chapter can be avoided.

10

Reinsurance

Why Reinsurance Is Important

As we indicated in chapter 2, shocks to both availability and premiums are one precipitating cause of insurance cycles. Reinsurance is as vitally important to primary medical malpractice insurers, especially small, single-line insurers, as it is to self-insured hospital medical malpractice insurance programs. Private reinsurance is not generally subject to state or federal regulation. However, some states have implemented public reinsurance programs, which, if important prior mistakes can be avoided, provide a promising approach for adding stability to medical malpractice insurance markets.

Reinsurance 101

In the medical malpractice market, physicians and hospitals are the customers. Primary insurers sell coverage to nearly all physicians, and in turn purchase *reinsurance*. Purchasing reinsurance helps a primary insurer to reduce its exposure to losses in the aggregate above a certain dollar threshold of loss or to very high-cost claims. Primary insurers or self-insured entities, such as hospitals, seek to mitigate the risk from large claims in this way because such claims can drain insurer reserves or threaten financial solvency.[1]

Reinsurance is important for single-line medical malpractice insurers. Some claims may be nearly as large as the surplus (equity) of these firms. Without reinsurance, some smaller insurers may not be able to pay a costly claim, or may go bankrupt.

Rather than buying primary insurance, many hospitals, especially larger ones, self-insure for much of their anticipated medical malpractice loss. When hospitals self-insure, they frequently purchase *excess insurance*, which is essentially reinsurance for hospitals. Excess insurance is typically obtained from the same reinsurance companies that primary insurers use. Several "layers" of reinsurance (or of excess insurance, in the case of self-insuring hospitals) may often be purchased with a package of coverage assembled by a broker. With a self-funded layer, the hospital is still at risk for claims falling in that dollar range. Excess insurers sometimes insist on this layer, known as a "risk corridor," to help mitigate moral hazard on the part of hospitals. Larger facilities and health systems rely on brokers to assemble a group of excess insurers for a desired range involving several layers of excess coverage. In these complicated arrangements, two or more carriers are often jointly responsible for any given layer and coverage is made more affordable, if necessary, by raising the attachment points or reducing the upper limits of coverage. An attachment point reflects a corridor between primary coverage and the dollar amount at which reinsurance begins to cover the loss.

Reinsurance companies face bankruptcy risks of their own. Reinsurers located in the United States are subject to the solvency regulation in their domiciliary state.[2] However, many if not most private companies reinsuring medical liability are located outside of the United States, and thus are not subject to regulation by U.S. governmental entities. In property-casualty insurance generally, foreign companies issue two-thirds of the reinsurance obtained by parties in the United States.[3]

The most troubling difficulty for reinsurers/excess insurers with losses at the "long tail" or high end of the claims distribution is not financial insolvency, but the fact that large claims are rare. Large claims are volatile in both their amounts and their frequency, making the frequency of the very few large claims, especially large paid claims, difficult to predict. Since large claims are so infrequent, private reinsurers may have difficulty ascertaining when a true shift in the rate of these claims or in their size has occurred, as opposed to variation due to random noise. Additionally, from the time an injury occurs to the time a claim is filed is often years, and the time span from filing to the date when the claim is closed can be several more years.[4] This slow resolution is in sharp contrast to insurance lines such as automobile liability and health insurance. Since events such as judicial decisions, high jury verdicts, or new laws can intervene during this long resolution process, the high uncertainty associated with premium setting is multiplied.

As a result, after a few large payouts, private-sector reinsurers may be quick either to refuse to underwrite coverage or to substantially raise premiums to reflect a (correctly or incorrectly) perceived increase in risk. Volatility in the high-loss end of the claims distribution leads to volatility in the private supply of reinsurance/excess insurance. This volatility may then exacerbate the insurance cycle and cascade into volatility in the availability and price of primary medical malpractice insurance as self-insured entities and primary insurers pass on premium increases to their customers.[5] High premiums or unavailability of coverage may also occur when insurers have difficulty estimating the ex ante probability of a loss occurring.[6]

Changes in premiums are justified when the underlying distribution of losses changes, but not justified in response to a one-time occurrence, unless the latter signals a longer-term change in the distribution of losses. Distinguishing between one-time shocks and more permanent changes can admittedly be a very difficult task.

Three important aspects of reinsurance/excess coverage that reinsurers make decisions about are (1) whether or not to cover; (2) what price to charge for coverage; and (3) which attachment point to set for coverage.

Attachment points have two purposes. First, if there is no corridor between primary coverage and reinsurance, the incentive the primary insurer has for loss mitigation may be reduced. Claims near the point at which reinsurance applies may not be fought aggressively unless there is a corridor at which the insured entity is at risk. In particular, primary insurers may have less reason to exercise caution when the upside risk is limited by the presence of reinsurance.[7] Second, having a corridor reduces the number of reinsurance claims, thereby reducing a reinsurer's administrative expense.[8]

In late 2003 and early 2004, the first author and colleagues at Duke University conducted a survey of reinsurers. This was at a time when the most recent insurance crisis was at its height. Even during this crisis (but not at the onset of the crisis, when availability problems may be at their worst), the reinsurers surveyed either wrote or would have considered writing hospital excess coverage in all states, but sometimes only at high attachment points. Rather than refuse to write coverage, they quoted premiums at a very high level in locations when insurers did not want the business.

Research Findings on Private Reinsurance

Most of what is known about reinsurance comes from industry sources— just speaking with people in the industry. Very little scholarly research has been conducted on the topic, perhaps because it is such a specialized subject, and data needed for research are largely in private hands, not available to researchers.

Primary Insurer Decisions to Reinsure: Theory and Empirical Evidence

Hoerger, Sloan, and Hassan studied determinants of the decision to reinsure property-casuality insurance in general and medical malpractice insurance in particular.[9] Their study considers primary medical malpractice demand for reinsurance, not hospital demand for excess insurance.[10] In their theoretical framework, the motive for reinsuring is to avoid bankruptcy. Bankruptcy is costly to insurers, although such costs may be reduced by the existence of guaranty funds, which were described in chapter 9. When a bankruptcy occurs, policyholders receive the remaining assets less the administrative cost of distributing the assets.[11] The authors use their model to assess how the insurer's surplus, size, and volatility of losses affect the amount of reinsurance the primary insurer purchases.

Their empirical analysis reveals that insurers facing higher loss volatility, lower surplus-to-premium ratios (a measure of the amount of equity the firm has relative to the premiums written in a year, with higher ratios indicating more funds available for distribution in the event of an unexpectedly high level of payouts), and smaller primary insurers demand more reinsurance. These results imply that that if primary insurers observe that volatility of their losses has increased and experience a depletion of their net assets, as would occur if they had to pay claims that were much larger than anticipated, they will demand more reinsurance in subsequent years. In this sense, adverse experience in a year or two will generate higher demand for reinsurance, which causes reinsurers to bump up against their capacity constraints.[12] For this reason, crises may be exacerbated and extended. Further, it is expected that smaller single-line medical malpractice insurers will demand more reinsurance.

At the level of the market (as opposed to the individual firm in a market), increased volatility and some large losses occurring to more than one company are likely to increase the price of reinsurance. An increased price should in turn decrease the demand for reinsurance and/ or could cause some insurers to exit the line of insurance which experienced the increase in volatility. If a series of large paid claims leads reinsurers to believe that further large payouts have become more likely, this will increase the price of reinsurance as well. Thus, while a change in payments on large claims will shift the demand curve for reinsurance to the right, the resulting price increase (i.e., movement along the demand curve) will tend to have the opposite effect.

Reinsurance premiums have become very high in recent years. Reinsurance premium information is highly confidential; in private conversations with purchasers of reinsurance, the first author has been impressed with how high excess insurance premiums charged to hospitals have become. Not only are premiums high relative to anticipated losses, but they seem high relative to the *maximum* loss that the insured entity could incur.

This raises a question as to why any organization, such as a hospital, would demand such insurance. Our speculation is that payment of one or two large claims could adversely affect the hospital's financial performance in a year. Hospital administrators are loathe to report adverse financial results to their boards. Thus, they would rather essentially prepay their losses in return for a steady cash flow than fully self-insure the risk of incurring a catastrophic expense and experience added volatility in cash flows reflecting volatility in payments for medical malpractice claims. Primary medical malpractice insurers may be motivated to purchase expensive reinsurance for much the same reason.

Why Is the Price of Reinsurance So High?

Hoerger et al.'s analysis does not include a measure of the price of reinsurance. This type of information is very closely held by both purchasers and suppliers of reinsurance for competitive reasons. More recently, Froot reports data on reinsurance quantities and prices for a broad group of catastrophe reinsurance purchases across the insurance industry.[13] He finds that between 1989 and 1998, the observational period of his study, the ratio of reinsurance premiums to expected loss ranged from a maximum of over 7 (in 1994) to a minimum of slightly under 2 (in 1989). Thus, reinsurance premiums were far greater than losses that might be anticipated, the latter being a rough benchmark for fair value. He concludes that "Fair pricing does not prevail in the markets for reinsurance claims, and . . . premiums are a multiple of expected losses."[14] He concedes that his measure of expected loss may be downward biased. But such a bias would not explain the substantial variation in the premium/expected loss ratio between 1989 and 1998.

Does Froot's result imply that reinsurers are charging excessively high premiums? Not necessarily. Some markup over anticipated loss would occur even in a competitive reinsurance market, since there is plausibly a loading factor attributable to marketing, claims processing, and legal costs which such companies incur. More fundamentally, in view of the high volatility of large claims *and* positive correlations among large claims (e.g., among jury verdicts),[15] some risk premium (premium set in excess of anticipated loss plus the loading) is certainly justified. One reason there is no easy answer to this question is lack of data. There are no publicly available data on premiums, losses of private reinsurers (in contrast to primary insurers),[16] or costs included in the loading; the data available to Froot are an exception, and are for only one company.

Froot considers possible explanations for the high price of reinsurance as measured by the ratio of premiums to losses, and the reasons for cycles in the ratio of premiums to losses and in the quantity of reinsurance supplied that have been observed. The first explanation relates to the high cost of equity capital, particularly for reinsuring the most highly catastrophic risks. Depletion of equity capital by a large shock (e.g., a series of hurricanes or large verdicts adverse to insurers) is likely to result in a major capital shortage, with the result that premiums for reinsurance are raised appreciably above the expected loss of such coverage. Froot presents some empirical evidence on reinsurance during the year following Hurricane Andrew which is consistent with this view. Such shocks to capital are more likely to happen when the risks are from earthquakes or hurricanes than from verdicts, but shocks to capital from natural disasters, by affecting reinsurer equity, could have an impact on reinsurance premiums in the medical malpractice insurance markets. Individual verdicts may be correlated, but not to the extent that losses of individual insureds from earthquakes or hurricanes in the same geographic area are correlated.[17]

The second explanation relates to the exercise of market power by reinsurers. This would lead to increases in price accompanied by decreases in the quantity of reinsurance. Although there has been some consolidation in the industry, suggesting that each of the remaining participants in the market may consequently possess more market power, Froot notes that there was considerable entry into traditional reinsurance in the 1990s. The 1990s were not crisis years, but sellers could have been poised for entry when and if prices of reinsurance rose. Contestability (i.e., potential entry by new firms) in the face of increased prices would limit exercise of market power by existing reinsurers. Moreover, there appear to be no important barriers to entry in the reinsurance business. In fact, some companies operate in highly unregulated environments, such as the Caribbean.

Froot's third explanation is that the corporate form of reinsurance may be inefficient. In particular, it may be costly to give discretion to managers, who may pursue objectives other than firm value maximization. Shareholders seem to demand high returns from their investments in companies that supply reinsurance, perhaps reflecting such "agency" costs as managers not pursuing the interests of the principals) (the stockholders) but pursuing their personal financial interests. A high cost of equity capital to reinsurers would plausibly be reflected in a higher price of their product.

Kunreuther, Pauly, and Russell also suggest that suppliers of equity capital may believe that the high losses they experienced are not random and may reflect reinsurer mismanagement.[18] Although this is a possibility, neither Froot nor anyone else has provided empirical evidence to support this agency cost hypothesis. Thus, it should be viewed as speculative.

The fourth explanation is that reinsurance contracts are illiquid financial instruments, and investors demand high returns for this reason. In an alternative, brokerage costs and servicing expenses are high. Froot rejects such factors ("frictional costs of reinsurance") as determinants of observed price and output patterns.

Fifth, high prices of reinsurance may reflect the presence of moral hazard and adverse selection. Moral hazard arises in this context since it is costly for reinsurers to monitor underwriting and loss prevention activities of primary insurers.[19] Reinsurance agreements often contain a provision that reinsurers will charge more following a claim, coupled with a requirement that the reinsurance purchaser[20] will continue to buy reinsurance following the claim. This type of clause might be used to limit both moral hazard and adverse selection. To the extent that there is repayment in the form of higher reinsurance premiums following payment of claims, this might explain cycles in the ratio of premiums to expected loss for particular years. Even if the reinsurance purchaser attempts to switch reinsurers, questions about past claims experience are likely to be asked. Also, high deductibles, or equivalently the corridor discussed above, and coinsurance in virtually all of these contracts limit both adverse selection and moral hazard, the latter being the incentive for insured parties to use the covered benefit because it is covered.

Since experience rating is not common in medical malpractice insurance, adverse selection can be a problem for voluntary insurance markets if premiums do not precisely match risk. That is, those with relatively high risk will view coverage as particularly attractive since they can purchase insurance for the same premium as those at lower risk of loss. Adverse selection is likely when experience rating is not used and high-loss physicians or hospitals are able to purchase coverage at average rates. However, premiums of private reinsurers/excess insurers are highly experience rated and therefore avoid this problem.

Sixth, ex-post financing of catastrophes, such as by the U.S. government in the event of major hurricanes, would reduce demand for private reinsurance. However, decreased demand for private reinsurance as a consequence of "crowding out" by public coverage would explain low quantities of private reinsurance but not high prices. Prices would be decreased by public provision.[21] There was no trend in the percentage of medical malpractice premiums ceded [premiums collected by primary medical malpractice insurers, but transfused to a reinsurer, which in turn bears the risk of poss] during 1991–2002. It remained about 15–16 percent.[22]

The above explanations may account for high prices of reinsurance. However, they do much less well in explaining cyclical variation in price and availability. Among the latter explanations, the strongest and most compelling one for cycles may be shocks to equity resulting from natural disasters which could adversely affect the cost of capital to these firms and their capacity to sell reinsurance. Such explanations as exercise of market power would seem to operate equally at all phases of the cycle if this is an important factor at all.

Is There a Strong Case for Government Intervention in This Market?

Reinsurance and Insurance Cycles
Strains on the private reinsurance market appear to be partially responsible for the recent malpractice insurance crisis.[23] Medical malpractice is, however, only one line in the global market for reinsurance and excess insurance. The early 2000s' "hardening" (decreased supply, increased premiums) of the markets for reinsurance globally was experienced by the market more generally and was not specific to medical malpractice. Since data from the years following 2000 show increases in premiums globally, across lines of insurance, and reductions in reinsurer capacity, a strong argument exists that the most recent crisis was the result of an external shock to reinsurance reserves from nonmedical catastrophes, such as the events of September 11, 2001.[24]

As was discussed in Chapter 2, the phenomenon of the insurance or underwriting cycle is an important characteristic of insurance markets.

The return to the crisis phase of the cycle can be explained not only by inadequate premiums, but also by external shocks to capacity resulting in forecast errors,[25] such as natural disasters or terrorism, naïve loss forecasting by insurers, demand shocks from changes in actuarial calculations,[26] regulatory lags, or public policies. While trends in judicial decisions or in the propensity toward litigation may cause shocks that are correlated within a country, correlations across countries for these reasons seem unlikely.

Market Failure in the Reinsurance Market?

The question of whether the market for reinsurance and excess insurance is "failing" or is "broken" in some fundamental way is a complicated one to answer definitively. If a market failure could be conclusively demonstrated (that is, circumstances in which markets do not produce economically efficient outcomes), then there would be a rationale for government intervention in the market.

Market failure could also reflect a deviation from the competitive norm. Exercise of market power would lead to a higher price and lower quantity of reinsurance than would prevail under conditions of perfect competition. As noted in chapter 9, when purchasers lack information, this might be a source of sellers' market power. In the market for reinsurance, however, purchasers (e.g., primary insurers), are sophisticated more often than not, and, as noted above, there appear to be no important barriers to entry. However, sound empirical evidence is lacking.[27] In a market economy, absent a specific demonstration that a private market is unable to achieve social objectives, the tendency is to leave activities to the workings of private markets.

While at least at first glance the case for government provision of reinsurance in medical malpractice insurance markets appears to be quite weak, there may be a justification after all. Withdrawal of care can be an important public concern. Having continuous medical malpractice coverage at "affordable rates" may be a prerequisite, at least in some cases, for maintaining patient access to affordable care. Increases in the risk of large claims lead to higher premiums for reinsurance for primary insurers and self-insured hospitals, causing them to raise premiums for medical malpractice insurance for physicians.[28] If physicians do not have the ability to raise their fees, they may stop practicing altogether or cease providing services perceived as high risk. If this is indeed happening, it is an undesirable outcome and a failure of the market to provide for the social objective.

Public Intervention in Reinsurance Markets

Public intervention offers some other potential benefits. In particular, governments may achieve a redistribution which will not occur with complete reliance on the private sector. For example, government provision of reinsurance gives higher-risk individuals greater access to coverage at "affordable" rates than would occur without government involvement. Cross-subsidization may be seen by some as unfair, but in some cases it may achieve an important public purpose, such as keeping an emergency room open in an area where low-income families live.[29]

Moreover, governments can diversify risks over the entire population and spread past losses to future generations of taxpayers. This is a form of cross-time diversification that the private market cannot achieve. Also, the government can constrain adverse selection by enforcement of insurance purchase (mandatory coverage).[30]

While there are benefits, there are also some arguments against government intervention. First, a link between rising premiums and withdrawal of care has not been demonstrated empirically. This is not to say that this *never* occurs, but rather that it is not a sufficiently frequent occurrence to explain why people do not get care. Second, there is concern that government provision will supplant (crowd out) private provision. Third, as explained below, government intervention in reinsurance markets has a mixed record—sometimes good and other times not so good.

Fourth, publicly supplied insurance does not change the underlying long-run risk; it merely changes the identity of the risk bearers.[31] Also, as in other markets, the risk of insolvency should be reflected in the price of premiums. Policyholders desiring inexpensive insurance can choose to bear the associated risk of insolvency. But, in reality, consumers are not in a position to judge an insurer's underlying insolvency risk ex ante.

The Experience of Patient Compensation Funds: Public Provision of Reinsurance for Medical Malpractice Losses

Background

Patient compensation funds (PCFs) were initially created during the crisis of 1975–1976 as components of comprehensive malpractice reform legislation. Their goal was to assure availability of medical malpractice insurance by paying for large losses incurred in a few cases. As discussed above, it is difficult for medical liability insurers to achieve adequate diversification against the adverse financial consequences of the most severe cases. In fact, for some single-line carriers,[32] a single very large claim could result in insolvency. The rich experience of the states that have implemented PCFs can provide guidance on (1) the utility of the concept in general and (2) mistakes to avoid if and when a PCF is implemented.

PCFs are often packaged with tort reforms, including limits on payment for nonmonetary or total loss, limits on attorney contingent fees, modification of the collateral source rule, and other statutory changes that fall under the general rubric of "tort reform." Not surprisingly, the risk assumed by PCFs is sensitive to the effects of these provisions, especially damage caps that place a ceiling on an excess insurer's dollar exposure per claim.

As of early 2003, eleven states had established PCFs: Florida (1975), Indiana (1975), Kansas (1976), Louisiana (1975), Nebraska (1976), New Mexico (1978), New York (1986), Pennsylvania (1975, 2002), South Carolina (1976), Wisconsin (1975), and Wyoming (1977). Florida's program closed in 1983, having underpriced coverage,[33] but was still paying claims as of April 2003. Pennsylvania passed legislation in 2002 that schedules a phaseout of its program by 2009. Ohio considered implementing a PCF, but the Ohio Medical Malpractice Commission ultimately recommended that no further action be taken. Wyoming's program was never implemented.

PCFs are created by state law and organized as either a state agency or a trust fund (table 10.1). PCF operations are monitored by the state's Department of Insurance or by a special Board of Governors. Administration—actuarial reviews, claims processing, defense of claims, asset management, and so on—is performed by a dedicated staff and/or by outside organizations retained by the PCF.

Participation may be mandatory—all health care providers fitting the statutory definition must obtain excess coverage through the PCF—or voluntary, with providers enrolling at their option. Eligibility for PCF coverage is triggered at levels that range from $100,000 to $1,000,000 per occurrence. Some PCFs offer unlimited excess coverage, but most cover only an incremental layer of $500,000–$1,000,000 per occurrence.

The programs typically are funded from premium income and investment returns, not from state subsidies, a notable exception being New York State. Providers pay premiums to the state PCF as well as to private primary insurers. Accordingly, PCFs may improve insurance availability but nevertheless be expensive for policyholders. Assessments are generally structured as a fraction of the premium paid for primary coverage, and may be paid separately to the PCF or collected and passed along by the primary insurer. PCF assessments are not experience rated except to the extent that prior experience is reflected in the insured's primary insurance premiums. PCFs do vary premium contributions by specialty, either mirroring physicians' primary insurance classification (as in Pennsylvania) or establishing a few specialty-based risk classes (e.g., four in Wisconsin). Some PCFs act like insurers and maintain reserves on unpaid claims. Others are financed on a pay-as-you-go basis, assessing premiums as funds are expended. Like JUAs, moreover, PCFs often have the authority to assess insured physicians retroactively to cover unanticipated losses.[34]

The first author and Duke University colleagues surveyed nine PCFs in late 2003 and early 2004. The survey revealed that the two major motivations for forming PCFs were to provide (1) physicians and hospitals with affordable and reliable coverage by reducing volatility in losses from large claims, and (2) adequate compensation for injured patients. Medical organizations were interested in the first objective, and the trial bar was interested in the second. In addition to the survey, the authors obtained other information available on these PCFs, including financial data. No organizational representative surveyed could give direct evidence of improvements in availability or affordability due to the state's

Table 10.1
Summary of Major PCF Provisions

State	Enabling Legislation	Financial Structure	Participation	Eligibility
FL	Fla. Stat. §766.105	nongovernmental trust fund	physicians voluntary, hospitals mandatory	phys./hosp.
IN	Burns Ind. Code Ann. §34-18-6- and 34-18-7	separate trust account	voluntary	phys./hosp.
KS	K.S.A. §40-3401–3419	state treasury trust	mandatory	phys./hosp.
LA	La. R.S. §40:1299.41–49	separate escrow fund	voluntary	phys./hosp.
NE	R.R.S. Neb. §44-2801–2855	separate trust account	voluntary	physicians
NM	N.M. Stat. Ann. §41-5-1–29	state treasury trust	voluntary	phys./hosp.
NY	N.Y. C.L.S. Ins. §5502	excess liability pool	voluntary	physicians, dentists with hospital privileges

Required Primary Coverage	Coverage Limits	Funding Approach	Reserves Authorized?
$250K/claim, $500K/ occurrence (1990 levels adjusted for CPI)	Phys: $1M/$3M or $2M/4M Hosp: $2.5M/claim	annual, semiannual, or quarterly assessments paid to fund	yes, but maximum collection of $17.5M per year
Phys: $250K/ $750K Hosp: $250K/ $5M or $7.5M	$1.0M per occurrence	Decided using actuarial principles; collected by primary insurer	yes
$200K/$600K	purchaser's options: of $100K/$300K, $300K/$900K, or $800K/$2.4M	decided using actuarial principles; collected by primary insurer	yes
$100K/ $300K	$500K + future medical expenses primary coverage	decided using actuarial principles; collected by primary insurer	Yes, but surcharge must be reduced if fund exceeds $15 million
Phys: 200K/ $600K Hosp: $200K/$M	$1.05M per occurrence	Assessments as percentage of underlying premiums through insurer	$4.5M maximum
$200K/ $600K	unlimited medical + $600K noneconomic	decided using actuarial principles, collected by primary insurer	yes
$1M/$3M	$1M per occurrence	state general fund	not applicable

Table 10.1
(continued)

State	Enabling Legislation	Financial Structure	Participation	Eligibility
NC*	N.C. Gen. Stat. §58-47-1–50	trust fund	voluntary	physicians
OR**	ORS §752.005–055	trust fund	voluntary	physicians
PA	40 P.S. §1303.101–910 P.L 154, no. 13	state treasury fund	mandatory	phys., hosp., health care practitioners
SC	S.C. Code Ann. §38-79	state treasury fund	voluntary	phys./hosp.
WI	Wis. Stat. §655.27	not specified	mandatory with exceptions	phys./hosp.
WY**	Wyo. Stat. §26-33-101, 105	trust fund	voluntary	physicians

* Repealed.
** Fund never enacted.
Notes: In 2004, Alabama was considering creating a patient compensation fund for nursing homes as part of a larger bill that would cap damages at $250,000.

Nevada Governor Kenny Guinn stated his support for a patient compensation fund as part of a larger medical malpractice overhaul in a policy briefing in *Roll Call* "The Health of Our Nation Policy," *Roll Call* (July 2003).

Required Primary Coverage	Coverage Limits	Funding Approach	Reserves Authorized?
$100,000/yr.	$2M/yr	assessments determined by board, paid to fund	yes
$200,000/yr.	unstated	assessments determined by board, paid to fund	undetermined: fund must be set up by executive branch
phys.: $500K/$1.5M Hosp.: $500K/$2.5M	$500K/$1.5M	based on primary premium collected by insurer	no
$200K/$600K	unlimited medical + $600K noneconomic	Annual member fees and default assessments to fund	yes
$1M/$3M	unlimited	assessments determined by board billed to health care providers	no
$50K/occurrence	$1M in excess coverage	decided using actuarial principles, collected by primary insurer	$4M maximum

West Virginia's House of Representatives has passed H.B. 2122, a plan which, among other things, would create a patient injury compensation study board to design and implement a patient compensation fund.

Source: Based on "Preliminary Report on the Feasibility of an Ohio Patients Compensation Fund," produced for the Ohio Department of Insurance by Robert J. Walling, of Pinnacle Actuarial Resources. Thanks to Justin Sadowsky of Columbia Law School for updating this table.

PCF. However, respondents did indicate that PCFs reduced the volatility of losses experienced by insurers. Since all the PCFs, with the exception of Pennsylvania's, are handling the largest losses, this claim is almost certainly valid.

Respondents to this survey also stated that PCFs have increased the attractiveness of their states to primary insurers by limiting their exposure to high losses, even in states without caps on nonmonetary or total loss. However, no direct empirical evidence exists to verify that this has been a factor in actually attracting primary insurers. Brokers and private reinsurers/excess insurers, as competitors of public insurers, were not nearly as enthusiastic about PCFs as were respondents from the PCFs.

Performance of PCFs—Do They Reduce Total Payments for Medical Malpractice Claims?

Trends in claims frequency, from data filed with the National Practitioner Data Bank (NPDB), are strikingly similar for states with PCFs and those without such programs. During 1995–2002, PCF states had systematically higher claims frequency. There were sizable differences in recent trends in losses paid by PCFs among the five PCF states for which trends could be measured between 1998 and 2002.[35] Unfortunately, it is not possible to calculate total losses incurred or mean total severity of loss by private and public insurers in PCF states because PCF payments are not included in NPDB data. Furthermore, it is difficult to attribute the trends solely to the presence of a PCF, as other factors may have been responsible.

Most states with PCFs do not have damage caps, but do have an upper limit on PCF coverage. Thus, even with PCF coverage, health care providers remain at risk for very high claims if they do not or cannot purchase insurance from a private reinsurance/excess insurer. With some notable exceptions (e.g., Pennsylvania, which covers a middle layer of losses), it has been uncommon for juries to exceed the PCF layer of coverage in their awards.[36]

The frequency with which private reinsurance is purchased in PCF states is not known. PCFs understandably limit demand for private insurance coverage for very large losses. According to a survey of reinsurers and brokers conducted by the first author and colleagues at Duke University in 2004, reinsurers base the availability and price of excess coverage across locations on several factors: "good PCFs"; cultural factors (for example, less sophisticated law firms, more educated juries, less litigious environments); and whether or not hospitals are seen as assets to the community or as adversaries.

But the most important determinants of premiums are exposure in terms of size and scope of services provided, and claims experience over a long time period (e.g., a decade). The importance of high awards in driving premiums for excess coverage cannot be overstated, and likely is a main factor in insurers' decisions to differentiate based on geography.

Structural Features of PCFs

There are four main differences between private liability insurers and state PCFs: (1) public sponsorship, which ensures availability of coverage when commercial insurers find other lines of insurance or locations more attractive; (2) mandatory participation in some states, though generally with a choice of private insurer; (3) lack of regulatory oversight in some states to assure adequacy of rates; and (4) pay-as-you-go financing in some states. Depending on how the program is structured, PCFs either promote or discourage entry of private insurers.

Public Sponsorship
State governments operate PCFs. Public sponsorship has an important advantage: assuring availability of coverage. Like joint underwriting associations (JUAs) and unlike private insurers, PCFs do not withdraw from the market during crisis periods. Demand for private reinsurance by primary medical malpractice insurers is directly related to the volatility of loss.[37]

However, financing generally comes entirely from premiums paid by physicians and hospitals as well as investment income. Neither state general funds nor revenue from a dedicated tax source are typically used to support PCFs. In addition, PCFs do not reduce medical liability exposure, unless they undertake specific loss prevention actions. Rather, they transfer costs to a different funding mechanism.[38]

Primary malpractice insurers that purchase private reinsurance have an incentive to defend claims—even those that clearly exceed the primary policy limits—because current losses are likely to be reflected in future reinsurance premiums. This incentive is attenuated when a PCF is involved, particularly if the PCF has the power to assess insured providers directly for losses in excess of those initially projected.

Mandatory Participation

Voluntary insurance markets are vulnerable to adverse selection if premiums do not precisely match risk. As previously noted, medical malpractice insurance is not usually experience rated. Compulsory participation in a PCF can avoid adverse selection, which is otherwise likely to occur if high-loss physicians or hospitals are able to obtain coverage at average rates. However, requiring low-risk participants to subsidize high-risk participants may be viewed as unfair.

Lack of Regulatory Oversight

Many arguments for regulatory oversight of insurers are thought not to apply to PCFs. Because PCFs are public organizations, they plausibly lack an incentive to exploit their dominant market position by charging monopoly-level premiums. Nor are they driven by the profit motive to engage in risky financial decisions that may lead to insolvency. PCF assets may also be managed by a well-staffed, politically accountable unit of state government that has responsibility for several state agencies. On the other hand, problems do arise in practice. Because of budgetary constraints, for example, the PCF may not be well staffed, and civil service rules may limit its ability to compete with the private sector for personnel.

Financing in Advance or Pay-as-You-Go Financing

PCFs may collect funds adequate to pay all losses and associated expenses from claims occurring during the current policy year whenever those amounts are actually spent, *or* they may be funded on a pay-as-you-go basis. Under the latter approach, the PCF limits its assessments to amounts anticipated to be spent on claims and expenses in the following year. This approach has practical appeal, particularly in an unpredictable, "long-tail" line such as medical liability insurance, and helps solve short-term crises in availability of excess coverage without imposing the immediate pain of high premium assessments. In the first few years of a PCF's life span, losses tend to be low because most claims have not yet been resolved, allowing assessments to be low as well. Later, however, losses mount, and PCFs often must raise premiums sharply, incurring the wrath of premium payers and precipitating political pressures for reform.

Structural Weaknesses of PCFs

PCFs also have several structural weaknesses, although there is substantial heterogeneity among plans.

Continued Provider Vulnerability
Because most statutes have not established upper limits on liability, health care providers remain vulnerable to very high dollar claims.[39]

Reduced Incentives for Loss Prevention
The existence of a PCF may reduce incentives for loss prevention: improving patient safety, reducing the probability that a claim is filed, and managing claims to reduce the amount of indemnity, legal fees, and other expenses incurred by defendants.

PCFs do not surcharge primary insurers based on their loss experience. By contrast, private reinsurers set premiums on an experience-rated basis. A primary insurer with a poor loss history is likely to be at a disadvantage in the market for reinsurance, and this will likely translate into higher premiums for its customers. A parallel argument applies to hospitals. If hospitals can obtain excess insurance that is not experience rated, they have a reduced incentive to be conscious about patient safety and avoid large claims.

Voluntary PCFs and Adverse Selection
In some states, participation in the PCF is voluntary. A provider therefore can avoid a full assessment by not renewing after the PCF becomes expensive. Providers who are at low risk for future claims will drop out

of the PCF at that point, leaving only high-risk providers enrolled. This is a classic adverse selection problem.[40] Unless the PCF is subsidized from another source, it will eventually face chronic deficits or charge such high assessments to its few remaining customers that it collapses.

Loss-Reserving Practices

PCFs differ according to whether they reserve for anticipated losses or operate on a pay-as-you-go basis. Essential to a PCF's long-term viability is the method of financing the program. Several funding mechanisms exist, including reserving for anticipated losses by making actuarial projections, and pay-as-you-go financing.[41]

Setting premiums based on anticipated future payments from claims filed in a particular policy year is the standard financing approach in the private insurance sector.[42] Such a system is known as loss-reserving and involves educated guesses of losses, with premiums being set on the basis of predictions of an actuary. Lack of enthusiasm on the part of health care providers for increased premiums based on less than certain projections is reasonable. Nonetheless, loss-reserving has become the time-tested, traditional approach for private insurers.[43]

Loss-reserving also eliminates the main problems with pay-as-you-go financing, which are intergenerational transfers and inevitably increasing funding requirements. Initially several state PCFs employed pay-as-you-go financing, which assesses providers based on the currently incurred PCF losses. Intergenerational transfers are created under this system because current providers can be charged premiums based on claims that might have originated many years in the past. Health care providers who leave or retire enjoy protection from the PCF despite not being fully assessed for their coverage. Since trends in the cost of living are dwarfed by increases in malpractice losses, under pay-as-you-go financing, premiums unavoidably increase and providers entering practice are among the financial losers. These speculations have not been proven, and empirical evidence is still needed to demonstrate that these intergenerational transfers are truly causing older providers to retire early or to move, and are deterring younger providers from entering the state.[44]

Pay-as-you-go financing is a common practice among social insurance programs, such as Social Security and Medicare. In the Social Security program, for example, premium taxes from currently employed persons and their employers pay for benefits of retired workers. The implicit contract is that although younger persons subsidize the benefits of older persons, younger persons' benefits will in turn be subsidized by others when they become age-eligible.

Even though most states with PCFs do establish loss reserves, when actuarial evaluations are performed, the recommendations are not always followed.[45] This problem is not limited to the public sector. A survey of private primary malpractice insurers revealed much the same picture; insurers said that they had overridden their actuaries' recommendation at least once in the previous five years.[46] Reasons may differ between the two groups, with private insurers more worried about losing market share and PCFs responding to political rather than competitive pressures.

Since it seems prudent for insurers to loss-reserve, why would legislatures in some states have eschewed the practice? One reason, suggested by Hofflander and Nye (1985), is that it simplifies administration. Instead of having to compute reserves and invest those funds prudently, the PCF assumes that providers are aware of the liability that is accruing and hold reserves of their own. Reserves held by public agencies are also vulnerable to exploitation for unrelated purposes.[47]

The most important explanation, however, is politics. Failure to reserve attracts political support for a PCF because excess coverage seems inexpensive in the fund's initial years. Payment obligations are delayed so that many of the elected officials in office during the beginning years are likely to have moved on by the time liabilities must be financed. At first, losses are low because resolution is slow for losses that have already occurred and claims are infrequent. Without having to pay the full bill, pay-as-you-go financing gives the appearance of fixing a crisis. However, over time, losses mount, another round of medical malpractice reform is called for, and PCFs often have to raise premiums.

Proponents of pay-as-you-go financing argue that such a system may help insulate providers from nonmeritorious claims since it does not base assessments on a provider's claims history. However, this holds true only if juries often make mistakes in their determinations of damages and in their findings of liability.[48]

Since health care providers would remain at risk if the state PCF is vulnerable to an eventual insolvency, the arguments for loss-reserving over pay-as-you-go financing appear much more convincing. When the unfunded liability from past policy years eventually becomes due and payable, it is easy to label the malpractice system "out of control" instead of confronting the design flaws in the PCF.[49]

Pay-as-you-go financing for medical malpractice coverage has a certain rough justice. If juries frequently make errors in their findings of liability and determinations of damages, a pay-as-you go system that guarantees insurability and does not base assessments on a provider's claims history helps insulate providers from nonmeritorious claims.

However, the countervailing arguments are stronger, and apply equally to public agencies and private insurers. First, the objective of insurance is to protect policyholders against loss. If there is substantial insolvency risk, health care providers remain vulnerable.[50] Second, insurers have a comparative advantage in loss-reserving. Unlike actuaries, health care providers do not possess the requisite data or expertise to make such projections.

Third, pay-as-you-go financing inevitably leads to intergenerational transfers. The pool of health care providers in practice at a particular time may differ substantially from the pool that existed at the time the losses were incurred. If current premiums rise to cover past losses, this could discourage entry by new providers and encourage exit of existing ones. In a pay-as-you-go system, providers who retire or leave the state are subsidized by those who remain or enter. The former realized the benefits of excess coverage through the PCF while they were in practice in the state, but were not assessed a full premium for such coverage. Conversely, providers who enter practice in a PCF's later years or are still many years from retirement are the financial losers. As with Social Security, one could justify this cross-subsidy in terms of a social contract between "young" and "old" providers. Because the secular trend in malpractice losses far exceeds changes in the cost of living, however, the old receive a substantial net subsidy. The desire to avoid these obligations arguably deters younger providers from entering practice in the state, and induces older providers to retire early or move to states without PCF assessments.

To Subsidize or Not to Subsidize from Sources Other than Provider Premiums

Rather than employing a PCF to provide reinsurance directly, New York subsidizes such coverage, and is the only state to do this. The assumption and justification are that medical care is a merit want. A merit want is a good that society deems should be available to all, and its allocation should not be subject to normal market forces.[51]

Reinsurance excess coverage is a vital input in the production of affordable medical care, and so it is considered necessary to subsidize it in order to assure accessibility. In addition, the intergenerational inequities of the pay-as-you-go approach are avoided. Such subsidies might increase the demand for coverage and result in an increase in total premiums (prior to the subsidy) if implemented in a less regulated environment than New York.

Lessons Learned from the PCF Experiences

Funding Is Often Through Implicit Taxation

If a goal of government interventions is to subsidize high-cost insurance, and if injury victims are to be protected from loss, then revenue for the subsidy must come from somewhere else.

Unfortunately, a recurrent theme is that the taxes are implicit. Rather than raise revenue explicitly, it is often easier to shift the burden to unsuspecting groups, such as random classes of insurance policyholders. Covering the shortfalls in medical liability insurance with automobile liability insurance revenues, as in Pennsylvania, seems inequitable. If assuring the availability of medical care is a societal priority, the tax base should be as broad as possible, and taxpayers should understand the tax rates they pay.

Another implicit transfer occurs under the PCFs set up on a pay-as-you-go rather than a fully reserved basis. Here, health care providers do not pay the full freight of their losses at the time they are incurred. The bills come due in the end, which often coincides with the time the country reawakens to a new medical malpractice crisis.

Confusion about the Role of Public Insurers

In reading unpublished correspondence from public insurers, we are struck by the lack of consensus about whether or not they truly are insurers. Often when assessments of programs are conducted, the reviewers remark that the agency lacks sufficient actuarial capacity. This theme is closely related to others stated previously: enactment of programs during crises when actuarial capacity seems a minor detail, and the availability of implicit taxes which seem to make standard loss-reserving practices unnecessary.

Like private insurers, public insurers collect premiums and bear risk. In a long-tail line, such as medical liability, public insurers, like their private counterparts, face actuarial uncertainty. That the insurer is public does not change the fact that expected loss differs among policyholders. The rationale for experience rating and risk classification, loss-reserving, and prudence in investing reserves therefore applies equally to public and private insurers. The main difference is one of mission. A public agency's decision to supply insurance should be less responsive to immediate rates of return, although even public insurers' deficits eventually require an offsetting revenue source.

Programs' Lack of External Oversight

These programs frequently operate for years without public oversight. Often there is no written evidence that an organization has ever been formally evaluated.[52] Lack of oversight should be the exception rather than (almost) the rule. Sound public policy requires that program evaluations be scheduled when public programs are implemented. Prompt evaluation may identify problems in their early stages and facilitate midcourse corrections. Evaluation also provides an opportunity to discuss program goals, assess whether goals are being met, and determine whether there still is a public need for the program. Program oversight should be independent but geared to the mission of the agency.

Relevant Experiences from Other Contexts

There are parallels between losses from medical liability and losses from catastrophes such as terrorism, earthquakes, hurricanes, and floods. The record of government intervention in providing catastrophic coverage, like that of PCFs, is mixed. Again there are important implementation issues.

Federal Emergency Management Agency (FEMA)

In 1968 the Housing and Urban Development Act created the National Flood Insurance Program (NFIP), to be controlled by the newly formed Federal Insurance and Mitigation Administration (FIMA), a subagency of FEMA.[53] The NFIP was designed to provide subsidized flood insurance to property owners unable to find affordable private insurance.[54] Unlike almost all PCFs, except New York, a broad general tax revenue base supports FEMA, not payments from parties at risk of incurring losses from natural disasters or assessments from insurance companies.

Shortly after the program began, subsidized rates of insurance were not creating incentives for communities to join the NFIP or to individually purchase flood insurance. In response, Congress created the Flood Disaster Protection Act of 1973, which required federally regulated lenders to make flood insurance a condition of granting or continuing a loan.[55] Over the course of years and repeated devastation from natural disasters, the NFIP grew; as of 2003, there were 4.5 million flood policies in place, a huge increase from the 95,000 such policies in the early 1970s.[56]

FEMA did not have the ability to price this insurance and reinsurance more accurately than the market—in fact, quite the opposite; the same high-risk properties have been covered repeatedly at premiums below expected loss.[57] By late 2005, FEMA had depleted its reserves and was unable to continue reinsuring. Shortly thereafter, FEMA ordered private insurers to stop paying on private claims.[58] This left many policyholders without payment or recourse. As of 2005, policyholders had filed close to 225,000 flood claims from hurricanes Katrina, Rita, and Wilma; of these claims, FEMA has paid only 15 percent of the $23 billion in losses resulting from these three hurricanes.[59]

State-Sponsored Programs

States have intervened to provide coverage to otherwise uninsurable owners. Florida created the Florida Windstorm Underwriting Association (FWUA) in 1970 to provide hurricane and windstorm coverage to property owners who could not obtain it from private insurance companies.[60] In 2002, the legislature combined the residential property and casualty underwriting association with the FWUA, forming Citizens Property Insurance Corporation (Citizens).[61] As with NFIP, Florida has inadequate reserves from charging rates that are too low in comparison to the risk. As a result of these unusually low rates, Citizens is undercutting the private market.[62]

Implications for Public Intervention in Markets for Medical Malpractice Reinsurance

The record of FEMA presented above predates Hurricane Katrina and the problems for FEMA that followed, only some of which related to insurance of catastrophes. However, the earlier failure to assess and contain program costs, although partly attributable to FEMA, may also speak to the desirability of expanding the public sector's role as a provider of reinsurance. FWUA's underreserving and crowding out of private coverage should likewise be a warning that some oversight of operations is essential.

Conclusions and Recommendations

Is the Private Market for Reinsurance and Excess Insurance Broken and in Need of Repair?

Private reinsurance/excess insurance plays a vital role in provision of medical malpractice insurance, yet it is often expensive, and the markets are volatile. Although some volatility is inevitable, for personal investors the advice is to take actions that reduce volatility. Insurance cycles exact some cost, and volatility in reinsurance and excess insurance markets contributes to cycles in medical malpractice insurance premiums and availability. The fact that much of the reinsurance is not subject to federal or state regulation is at most a secondary concern.

Are PCFs Worth Having?

A case can be made for government involvement in providing insurance for high-cost claims. First, a public agency can provide reinsurance at a lower price and, just as important, the volatility of pricing is reduced. Thus, having a PCF may help avert at least some crises. PCFs are appealing because their decisions to supply coverage are not guided by prospective rates of return, so they can keep excess coverage available. Public funding does not eliminate the risk but shifts the burden of risk bearing; however, such shifts may be in accord with social preferences. The public status of PCFs implies that they are willing to supply coverage under circumstances that are unattractive to private, profit-seeking insurers, but does not alter their function as risk bearers.

But most important, the shortcomings of existing PCFs, such as Pennsylvania's, derive not from the concept but from how it was implemented. If a PCF funds liabilities according to actuarial principles, implements some form of experience rating, provides corridors to mitigate moral hazard, and/or requires participation (is mandatory), PCFs can play a constructive role. Although this discussion has focused on deficiencies, there are examples of well-run public insurers. And there is evidence that some of the errors of the past are being corrected.

In particular, pay-as-you-go financing offers short-term political advantages, but exacts a much higher price in the long run. The fact that prudent loss-reserving and accurate premium assessments may create a larger fund which subsequently becomes a political target for spending unrelated to medical liability seems a small price to pay for stability and solvency.

Finally, other instruments for dealing with high-end losses are being implemented. Hedge instruments are a financial mechanism to transfer tail risk to investors. They include catastrophe bonds, catastrophe options, and catastrophe puts.[63] Insurers have recently begun to use these instruments to protect themselves against large losses. Such losses should be more easily absorbed in a multitrillion-dollar global capital market as opposed to limiting them to a single property-casualty insurance industry, as in the case of reinsurance.

Designing and Implementing an Effective Patient Compensation Fund

If implemented, a PCF should have the following characteristics. There should be a high dollar threshold for coverage and, unlike current practice, the dollar threshold should be indexed to reflect changes in price levels. Since medical losses reflect the cost of medical care in part, the price index should be a blend of the medical and the all-items Consumer Price Index. The threshold would initially be set not to exceed the top 1 percent of the claims distribution.[64] Except when dictated by state statute in the form of a dollar limit on payment for nonmonetary or total loss, there should be no upper limit on coverage. This would eliminate the motive of insurers or self-insured organizations to obtain higher layers of coverage from private sources.[65]

The program would use standard loss-reserving principles, not pay-as-you-ago financing. Premiums would be paid by all health care providers who purchase medical malpractice insurance or self-insure for such loss. An independent committee of actuaries would oversee the process of calculating actuarial value of the losses and setting premiums. The premiums at baseline would reflect factors that are predictive of high loss claims, including specialty and types of procedures performed to the extent that the procedure mix affects expected loss. As done by private reinsurers, subsequent premiums would reflect the policyholder's loss experience. This would be more effectively done if the experience rating unit is a large physician group or a hospital rather than an individual physician.

The states serve as independent laboratories for specific innovations. It is therefore particularly important that states considering public insurance programs learn from the experiences of others. Unfortunately, while the diversity of the U.S. federal system is a strength, states seldom avail themselves of knowledge gained in other states, and therefore tend to reinvent the wheel.

Some public insurers also could benefit from structured technical assistance, which could be financed in part by the agencies receiving it. Research would be facilitated by data clearinghouses, which exist in other fields but not for medical liability or liability insurance more generally. It is important to develop criteria for gauging program success which are acceptable to the various stakeholders. Such criteria should reflect goals in addition to cost containment.

11

No-Fault for Medical Injuries

Rationale for No-Fault

Under a tort system, compensation is based on a case-by-case determination of fault. No-fault programs for iatrogenic injuries would provide compensation for injuries caused by medical care without regard to fault of the medical provider. Such programs involve more than merely discarding a critical element of tort—the negligence rule. Claims are adjudicated by a special administrative agency rather than by courts, and the benefits may be scheduled or computed on an individual basis, but these is little or no payment for pain and suffering. No-fault seeks to address deficiencies in tort, as the critique from Australia illustrates (box 11.1)

Proponents of no-fault cite three sources of savings.[1] First, benefits are generally only for monetary loss with collateral source offsets.[2] Second, eliminating fault should reduce litigation cost. Third, when experience rating is combined with no-fault, there should be added deterrence of injuries. The first advantage can be obtained under tort. Although there is a strong conceptual argument for experience rating, not all no-fault plans are experience rated. Furthermore, a no-fault program can be financed by a broad-based tax on medical providers, insurance companies, or general revenues.[3] Financing by a broad tax would largely eliminate deterrence, since losses attributed to physicians and hospitals would be picked up by taxpayers without defendants incurring a financial penalty. However, this option may be viewed as more socially equitable, and having a broad tax base may ultimately be the only way to have a

Box 11.1
Arguments Against Common-Law Negligence Action as a Basis for Compensating Transport Accident Victims

---

• the failure of the common-law negligence action to provide compensation for a substantial proportion of transport accident victims;

• the failure of the fault principle to fulfil [*sic*] its stated aims and the practical difficulties in its application;

• the deficiencies of assessing damages on a once-and-for-all basis;

• the difficulties and inconsistencies which arise in assessing damages for noneconomic loss;

• the adverse effects of the common-law negligence action on the rehabilitation of many transport accident victims;

• the delays and consequent hardship experienced by many transport accident victims in obtaining common-law damages;

• the burden on the court system, and the drain on judicial resources, caused by deciding claims arising out of transport accidents;

• the substantial legal and administrative costs associated with common-law negligence actions; and

• the increasing cost to the community of a compensation system relying heavily on the common-law negligence action.

Source: New South Wales Law Reform Commission (1984), pp. 46–47.

---

broad no-fault program for iatrogenic injuries. As for the second reason, eliminating negligence does not eliminate the possibility of litigating over injury cause under no-fault.

Although there may be a saving in administrative cost and from not paying for nonmonetary loss, one would indeed expect that compensating a much larger number of injuries would increase the cost relative to tort. Yet, advocates for no-fault alternatives contend that a major positive attribute of no-fault is the reduction in expense involved in payments to lawyers, dispute resolution, and reduced time in resolving claims. Rather than lawyers from both sides spending years litigating a dispute and incurring great expense on vigorously determining negligence, a no-fault system saves the legal expense and sets up predetermined awards for certain injuries, resulting in injury victims being compensated much quicker. Other possible advantages cited include more expert claims resolution, more effective deterrence through more systematic case identification, and greater fairness and predictability than under tort.[4]

No-Fault Programs for Iatrogenic Injuries

One set of no-fault proposals would pay for all iatrogenic injuries from a general revenue source rather than premiums paid by health professionals. Claims adjudication would be done by an administrative agency rather than by courts. Payment for nonmonetary loss would be eliminated or capped at a low level. There would be collateral source offset for monetary loss. Under a proposal advanced by Weiler, Hiatt, Newhouse, and colleagues,[5] medical malpractice claims in the United States would be resolved under a no-fault system. A surcharge assessed to patients for each day spent in the hospital would provide revenue for the no-fault fund. A professional panel that would also determine monetary losses would review the appropriate threshold for medical injury and eligibility.

Weiler et al. argue that their no-fault plan would be no more costly, or could be made no more costly, than medical malpractice is currently, even though more injury victims would be compensated, and compensated much more speedily.[6] The lower overhead expense and speedier compensation records of no-fault systems in Sweden and New Zealand, and of workers' compensation in the United States, are taken as evidence that such a program could be financed at little or no additional cost over what is now spent on tort. Some recent published empirical evidence buttresses the argument that no-fault would be no more expensive than tort.[7] While these programs have indeed achieved some successes, we question whether or not their experiences are relevant to the United States context. Further, the experiences with the no-fault programs in Florida and Virginia raise issues of their own. A more modest proposal would shift the locus of liability from the individual physician to an enterprise such as a hospital or health plan.

U.S. Experience with Medical No-Fault

Even though policy discussions of no-fault in the United States often refer to the experience in foreign countries, there is rich experience with no-fault in the United States as well. No-fault has been implemented for birth-related injuries in two states. A national no-fault program for adverse outcomes attributable to vaccines has been in effect for two decades. A number of states have no-fault programs for motor vehicle accidents. And for nearly a century, states have had workers' compensation programs for injuries occurring in the workplace.

State Programs for Neurologically Impaired Infants

In response to the medical malpractice crisis of the mid-1980s, Florida and Virginia implemented no-fault programs for severely neurologically impaired infants. The first no-fault program in the United States was Virginia's Birth-Related Injury Fund (BIF) in 1988. Shortly thereafter, Florida enacted legislation establishing the Neurological Injury Compensation Association (NICA) in 1989. The primary initial goal of both programs was achieving savings in medical malpractice insurance payments for birth-related injuries and improved patient access to obstetrical care.

Obstetricians faced higher and more rapidly increasing insurance premiums through the 1980s. Because of the high premiums, legislators were told that access to care was threatened, either from obstetrician-gynecologists leaving the state for states in which premiums were lower or from such physicians dropping the practice of obstetrics, focusing instead on gynecology, for which medical malpractice insurance premiums were considerably lower. Improving compensation for injury victims and speedier claims resolution were secondary objectives.

Both programs were established as, and continue to be, true no-fault programs. Fault is not a criterion for payment. To be eligible for payment, the infant or child must satisfy quite narrow eligibility criteria and the provider must have been a participant in the no-fault program at the time of the delivery. The clinical criteria for eligibility for coverage are so narrow that most birth-injured children are ineligible. Of the two programs, BIF has the stricter eligibility criteria. Benefits are not scheduled, but are set by the agencies operating the no-fault programs on a case-specific basis. Payments are paid at the time the expense is incurred. Eligible expenses to be covered are medical, custodial, rehabilitative, and educational; there are also payments for special vehicles and modifications to homes necessary for care of the child. Physician participation in these programs is voluntary in both states, and Florida makes hospital participation mandatory.

Other similarities between BIF and NICA include operation by independent public agencies, lower assessments by the programs for nonparticipating physicians, and the exclusion of tort for injuries covered under the programs. Clinical criteria for injury-victim eligibility are designed to match those cases that ordinarily result in high payments in tort. Both programs substantially eliminate payment for nonmonetary loss, and lawyers' fees are much lower under no-fault than under tort.

These two no-fault programs are government-run. This is in contrast to motor vehicle no-fault and workers' compensation, for which the states set the framework, but private organizations operate the programs. Since NICA and BIF enroll so few injury victims, it seems unlikely that private for-profit firms would have been interested in operating programs at such a small scale. Realistically, there could have only been one private insurer per state.

Designers of both BIF and NICA intended that no-fault would totally replace tort for eligible cases. Applying to these programs for compensation is voluntary. Neither program has actively sought out applicants in case finding. Case finding is the act of finding individuals for medical treatment. Since the programs rely on a narrow premium base, case finding would be disastrous to their finances.

No-fault programs should be evaluated by examining performance in assuring availability of reasonably priced liability coverage, improved injury deterrence, efficiency in administration and management of loss, and in correctly identifying and compensating injury victims and responding to their needs.

Compensating Injuries

The primary goal of the no-fault *concept* is compensation of a broad range of injuries.[8] In evaluating this facet of the Florida and Virginia no-fault programs, we need to review the context in which the programs were enacted. In Virginia, advocates for BIF at the time the program was enacted were the Medical Society of Virginia, the Virginia Hospital Association, the Virginia Hospital and Healthcare Association, the Virginia Society of Obstetricians and Gynecologists, and the Virginia Insurance Reciprocal.[9] These stakeholders would not be likely to have had patient compensation as their primary goal. Understandably, they principally represent the private interests of their memberships.

The narrow criteria for eligibility meant that the no-fault assessments on physicians and hospitals were low. In Virginia, the first payment to a claimant did not occur until five years after the establishment of BIF. In BIF's first fifteen years (1987–2002), only seventy-two claimants received payment.[10] This may seem like a windfall to providers at first glance, but narrow eligibility criteria were likely to mean that there would not have been much of a reduction in medical malpractice insurance losses and premiums.

Only "permanently and substantially mentally and physically" impaired infants weighting at least 2,500 grams at birth are eligible for compensation under NICA. Hence, the experience in Florida has been similar to Virginia's. Until 2003, 161 claimants had been awarded compensation, fewer than twelve paid claims per year.[11]

The number of paid claims was low relative to the pool of injuries that might have been compensated.[12] The vast majority of no-fault claims paid in Florida were to families in which the child had been diagnosed with cerebral palsy, although the statute does not restrict eligibility to those infants.[13] In Florida, about 2 percent of children with cerebral palsy has been compensated by no-fault; about the same percentage has been compensated in Virginia. In both states, injuries attributable to "genetic" or "congenital" abnormalities are excluded. Injuries caused by "maternal substance abuse" are excluded in Virginia. Among those families surveyed by Sloan et al. who received compensation from NICA, the vast majority indicated that they were satisfied with most aspects of the medical no-fault program.[14]

Three possible reasons have been given for the paucity of claims paid by NICA.[15] First, the incidence of birth-related injuries may have decreased sharply during the 1990s, which the authors consider unlikely.

Second, there may have been a change in claiming behavior after NICA was introduced. This may have been due to publication of research suggesting that the link between obstetrical mismanagement and cerebral palsy was more tenuous than previously thought.[16] This the authors do not dismiss as a possibility. The findings could have chilled interest among both plaintiffs' attorneys and otherwise eligible claimants. However, if the research findings had such an influence on claiming, it would have affected tort much more directly than no-fault claims. If anything, this factor would make no-fault claims more, not less, numerous. Third, claims for a wide range of birth-related injuries, including some apparently compensable under NICA, may simply persist in the tort system. This seems like the most likely explanation for the paucity of claims paid by NICA. Sloan, Whetten-Goldstein, Entman, et al. report that one third of all families with severely birth-injured children who responded to their survey in Florida and filed tort claims had never applied to NICA.[17]

Failure to Give Notice and the Persistence of Tort

NICA and BIF administrators had strong incentives to limit caseloads in order to avoid raising premiums to physicians and hospitals. Neither physicians nor hospitals had any reason to publicize the programs to their patients before labor-delivery, since they would not have wanted to place undue stress on the possibility of medical injury during a prenatal visit or to encourage tort claims from those deemed ineligible for no-fault after labor-delivery. Many patients learned the details of the program and their physician's participation only after the injury occurred.[18]

Trial lawyers in Florida, facing much lower compensation under NICA than under tort, seized the opportunity to use this "failure to give notice" as a way to steer their obstetrical cases back into the tort system. Any bar to suing that no-fault may have erected was not airtight because of judicial decisions favorable to the trial bar. Plaintiffs' attorneys drove a wedge through the cracks to avoid this limitation on suing. As Studdert, Fritz, and Brennan conclude, "The restrictiveness of NICA compensation criteria partly explains the persistence of tort. More precisely, the mutually reinforcing effect of a contingent approach to jurisdiction and narrow compensation criteria appears to have provided a ready foothold for the tort system to assume an ongoing role in the compensation of birth-related injuries."[19] Studdert et al. suggest that

To maintain exclusivity in the absence of a comprehensive shift to no-fault, it may be necessary to define a scheme's boundaries according to compensation criteria that wholly encompass subgroups of medical injury. For example, the scheme might be designed to cover a complete class of injury (e.g., obstetrics or surgical), whether or not every claim for injuries in that class satisfies the compensation criteria. Alternatively, jurisdiction might simply be defined according to whether the injury in question was suffered at the hands of a participating provider or within the walls of a participating institution.[20]

The authors concede, however, that public support for no-fault may dissolve if the design leaves a large number of injured patients ineligible for compensation in any forum.

But using broad eligibility criteria to avoid these boundary disputes can result in a very expensive public program that is not politically viable. However, narrow criteria for eligibility inevitably lead to disputes about claimant's entitlement to benefits when their claims fall at the boundaries of the definition of eligibility. There are many approaches available to motivated lawyers for steering claims to tort. Thus, with narrow eligibility criteria, it is very unlikely that no-fault compensation can be a practical substitute for tort.

One advantage of BIF's and NICA's small size has been the ability to individualize the management of benefits more closely. The programs have been careful in managing expenditures, securing favorable prices from vendors, and questioning the benefits of unconventional therapies.[21] A larger, national no-fault program would have to implement more formal rules and procedures to reach a similar level of performance in this regard.

Administrative Efficiency

The legislative committee in charge of assessing BIF determined that a lack of actuarial data projecting lifetime expenses for those covered, resulted in underestimates of the cost of care.[22]

Since there are dollar limits on medical malpractice awards in Virginia, total compensation per infant/child covered under the no-fault program may be higher than under tort.[23] Under BIF, injury victims receive no payment for lost wages or nonmonetary loss, and payment is reduced by an amount equal to any collateral sources, such as health insurance.

Compared to the tort system, overhead has been quite low in both states' no-fault programs.[24] Of total BIF disbursements in 2001, administrative, financial service, and legal costs totaled 9 percent.[25] Interview and program data indicate very conservative fiscal administration of both the Florida and Virginia programs.[26]

This high level of administrative efficiency may have come at a certain cost to injury victims seeking legal assistance with their no-fault program claims. If attorney compensation is too low, it becomes difficult for worthy victims to find representation. The Florida and Virginia programs pay a "reasonable" hourly rate rather than contingency fees. This hourly rate may not have been sufficient to attract enough lawyers to obtain no-fault compensation for all potentially eligible victims. There are circumstances under which a contingency fee system may be economically efficient.[27]

During BIF's initial years, assessments of physician participants were reduced because the program appeared to be overfunded.[28] Virginia's State Corporation Commission later found that BIF had an unfunded liability of $88 million. The fund manager and the program staff had failed to share financial information which would have allowed for proper financial oversight.[29] The commission decided to conduct future reviews on an annual basis.[30]

Assuring Coverage and Reasonable Rates

Initially after implementation of no-fault in both states, mean medical malpractice insurance premiums paid by obstetrician-gynecologists decreased; this decrease exceeded the amounts individual physicians paid in no-fault program assessments.[31] The cause of the lower rates, according to a legislative committee reviewing BIF, was fewer malpractice claims against obstetricians and hospitals.[32]

In 2003, obstetricians still faced very high premiums years after the implementation of NICA. The Florida Governor's Select Task Force on Healthcare Professional Liability Insurance indicated that obstetrician-gynecologists in areas such as Jacksonville would be operating without insurance, retiring early, or becoming college faculty members in order to obtain sovereign immunity.[33]

In Virginia, the Joint Legislative Audit and Review Commission found reason for concern in the lower percentage of participation in BIF among rural obstetricians.[34] Barriers to access to care tend to be worse in rural areas because most physicians locate in urban areas. Since assessments are not based on the number of deliveries the physician performs, rural practices may have been paying much more in no-fault assessments per delivery. Additionally, costs of tort and levels of premiums are not as much of a problem in rural areas since juries in such areas tend to be less generous to plaintiffs. A narrowing of the gap between the costs of tort and no-fault in rural areas creates a strong reason for assessments to be based on the number of deliveries performed. While BIF does seem to have had a favorable impact on premiums paid by physicians, it seems to have had little effect on the availability of obstetricians.[35]

The experience with no-fault programs in Virginia and Florida serves as both fascinating and important testing grounds for medical no-fault in the United States, not because of their conceptual innovations but rather for what they say about practical implementation of no-fault, particularly in the U.S. context. The experience is not devastating to the no-fault concept, but it is rather sobering.

The programs have been successful in providing individualized compensation to families quicker and with less administrative cost than the tort system. This is no small feat. But NICA did not succeed in averting a new malpractice crisis in Florida for obstetricians after 2000. Some of the programs' weaknesses may be attributed to their hasty formulation in response to the malpractice crisis of the mid-1980s, but haste is sometimes needed to achieve program implementation.

The experiences of these programs do not support the notion that a more general medical no-fault program would be less expensive than tort. Operating on such small scales,[36] use of informal procedures, and a small staff are possible. However, if the programs were expanded to cover a less narrow set of injuries, administrative cost per accepted case would surely increase because more formal administrative procedures would be needed. If they were expanded to cover less seriously injured children, no-fault program savings from not paying nonmonetary loss would be far lower than for the more serious injuries that these programs currently cover.

The assertion that no-fault would reduce tort claims frequency for those injuries covered is not supported by the Florida experience, although there is some support for this in Virginia.[37] One could interpret this as a positive outcome to the extent that some injuries were compensated that otherwise would not have been. Still, the result is inconsistent with an important advantage asserted by proponents of no-fault. The programs did not become substitutes for tort, in part because the definitions of covered injuries were so narrow and lawyers had strong financial incentives to find avenues to steer no-fault claims back to tort. A desire for retribution may have also kept some cases in the tort system. In Florida, no-fault claimants were much less likely than tort claimants to be motivated by a desire for retribution.[38]

The political context in which the no-fault programs were adopted was not conducive to adoption of a broad-based program advocated by leading academic supporters. The focus was overwhelmingly on medical malpractice cost containment, not on the unmet needs of injury victims. These programs consequently were developed to rely on a narrow funding source.[39] For an expanded no-fault program to support many more claims, a much broader funding base would be required, including use of general tax revenues rather than an exclusive reliance on funds from physicians and hospitals.

Even if administrative savings from tort were large enough to fund a broad no-fault program, there is an inherent conflict between physicians' and hospitals' understandable goals of saving money on premiums and the financial needs of a no-fault program with broad eligibility standards. Would physicians and hospitals really be willing to contribute their savings to a program that serves broad societal purposes? A strong argument can be advanced that it is not their sole responsibility to do this.

The National Vaccine Injury Compensation Program

The National Childhood Vaccine Injury Act of 1986 became effective in October 1988. It established the National Vaccine Injury Compensation

Program (VICP) as a no-fault alternative for resolving vaccine injury claims. VICP was enacted when the nations's vaccine supply was at risk; existing manufacturers were threatening to stop selling childhood vaccines unless the rapidly increasing liability threat was brought under control. The VICP is the largest medical no-fault program, and the only such national program in the United States

VICP's primary initial goals were to alleviate the vaccine supply problems resulting from tort claims and to compensate injuries associated with routinely administered childhood vaccines.[40] By most accounts, VICP has succeeded, but the thimerosal issue looms on the horizon.

The U.S. Department of Health and Human Services (DHHS), the U.S. Court of Federal Claims, and the U.S. Department of Justice (DOJ) jointly administer the VICP. All vaccines recommended by the Centers for Disease Control and Prevention for routine administration to children are covered under the program.[41] Since 2004, some vaccines administered to adults have also been covered.

The process begins with an individual claiming injury or death from a vaccine filing a petition with the U.S. Court of Federal Claims. At that point a physician at the Division of Vaccine Injury Compensation of the DHHS reviews the petition and makes a recommendation to the DOJ. An attorney represents the DHHS at the DOJ hearing before a "special master," who makes a decision on whether to compensate and, in a separate hearing, on the amount of the award. This decision can be appealed to the Court of Federal Claims and then to the Federal Circuit Court of Appeals.[42]

A claimant qualifies for compensation by (1) demonstrating that the injured person received a vaccine listed on the Vaccine Injury Table and that the first symptom of the injury/condition on the table occurred within the period listed in the table; *or* (2) proving that the vaccine *caused* the condition; *or* (3) by proving the vaccine aggravated a condition existing before the vaccine was administered.[43] The table lists specific injuries and the time frames in which they must occur for a claimant to qualify for payment. While the Vaccine Injury Table allows a statutory "presumption of causation," and even though the injury is listed in the table, if the court finds that the injury was unrelated to the vaccine, compensation is not paid. Claims for table injuries are more likely to be compensated; yet most claims filed are for off-table injuries.[44] If a claim is found to be ineligible for compensation, the claimant may take the case to tort. However, if the claimant accepts payment from VICP, he or she is barred from the tort system. As of June 2006, 11,830 claims had been filed with VICP. Of these, 1,985 were compensated, 4,340 were dismissed, and the rest were pending.[45]

The number of lawsuits for just three vaccines (diphtheria, tetanus toxoids, and pertussis) reached a peak of about 250 in 1986, then fell dramatically after VICP was implemented.[46] After about 2000, however, concerns about liability as a barrier to vaccine research and development (R&D) and to entry into the United States market began to reappear, as did concerns over the thimerasol issue.[47]

VICP, coupled with other policies, may have increased incentives for vaccine innovation.[48] However, tort liability may still inhibit vaccine R&D if vaccine manufacturers do not think they would gain coverage under VICP.[49]

The issue of attorney fees has been a controversial one for the VICP.[50] Attorneys with successful claims earn slightly more, but attorneys' fees and expenses are paid regardless of the outcome. An absolute ceiling of $30,000 is set for legal expenses; the "special master" has the authority to adjust the lawyer's billing if it is deemed unreasonable. Contingent fees are not permitted.

A large number of injury victims have been compensated, although many have also been rejected, and therefore have been free to obtain compensation from tort. Unfortunately, there are no data to indicate how often rejection of a claim by VICP was followed by a lawsuit.

The effect of VICP on injury deterrence and patient safety is difficult to gauge. Despite the vaccines' being administered to such large percentages of the population, vaccine-related injuries and deaths are extremely rare.[51] It is difficult to know what safety precautions might exist in the absence of the no-fault program.

Since attorney compensation and client awards are potentially large in the tort system and almost always limited in a no-fault program, there are incentives to find loopholes to steer cases from no-fault to tort. Ambiguity in the VICP regarding whether or not vaccine preservatives fall under the VICP has been used by lawyers as a vehicle for bringing cases involving vaccines containing thimerosal to tort. Thimerosal has not been explicitly covered under VICP.

Thimerosal is a mercury-containing preservative once widely used in vaccines, and still used in some vaccines and other pharmaceuticals. Of the 10,886 cases filed with VICP between 1988 and 2004, 4,335 were thimerosal/autism-related.[52]

Thimerosal/autism claims have continued even though the Institute of Medicine concluded there is no connection between thimerosal and autism.[53] The results of the IOM report were hotly contested by proponents of the thimerosalautism link.

A major victory for plaintiffs came in March 2006 when a federal appeals court allowed a thimerosal suit against three manufactures to proceed in federal court (W. Davis 2006).[54] The thimerosal issue serves to highlight one of several border issues that complicate the administration of no-fault programs. A trade-off exists between ensuring compensation of all appropriate injuries and reducing the risk of compensating injuries that are not causally related to the vaccines, and as a result bankrupting the fund or causing it to be no less expensive than the tort system.

The VICP created the Table of Injuries to streamline the compensation process so that certain known side effects and injuries could serve as a "presumption of causation" rather than needing to be independently evaluated as to whether each claim of a similar type was caused by the vaccine. When VICP was established, the U.S. Congress acknowledged that the Table of Injuries would result in a presumption of causation favoring the families, and that this would likely result in some children being compensated who were not actually injured by a vaccine.[55]

The table represents not only a "line in the sand" regarding what is to be compensated and what is not, but also the edge of what is known in the scientific literature. Thus, claims that are off-table represent claims either entirely illegitimate (not causally related to the vaccines) or outside the bounds of what the scientific literature can speak to in terms of causation.

The table was changed four times between 1998 and 2004.[56] One concern is the speed with which legitimate adverse events are recognized and added to the table. Another issue, which seems likely to remain no matter how often the table is updated, is the difficulty in proving whether or not the vaccine caused a condition not in the table. Still another is the addition of adverse events to the list which are later found to have no connection to vaccines. By 2004, this had occurred for four conditions once listed on the table.

There are issues of causation in general and in specific individual cases. Much of the debate on thimerosal has centered on such issues. Often medical and scientific experts have been asked to testify, yet much of their testimony has been rejected or given little consideration by the special masters who decide these cases.[57] Weight has been given to Institute of Medicine reports, broader legal notions of causation, and a "preponderance of evidence" standard rather than more limiting legal criteria.[58]

Similarly, in the context of two birth-injury no-fault programs in Florida and Virginia, the connection between mode of obstetrical delivery and the probability of subsequently developing cerebral palsy has been debated.[59] The crux of the issue relating to the feasibility of medical no-fault is that vaccine no-fault has worked because of lenient rules for establishing causation. To the extent that these rules become less lenient, it will become easier to circumvent no-fault and steer cases back to tort.[60]

It is certainly daunting to imagine an expanded system implemented in conjunction with a broader medical no-fault program. Institute of Medicine reviews are required every two years to evaluate whether changes to the Vaccine Injury Table are necessary in light of recent scientific literature and adverse events.[61] Attempting similar monitoring, reviews, and updates across the entire spectrum of medical injuries would represent a formidable challenge. The challenge for proponents of a broad medical no-fault program is in the details of designing better ways to collect, verify, and use safety and injury information.

Conclusion

All three no-fault programs demonstrate difficulties in the design decisions and implementation intricacies of how broad or how narrow to make the eligibility and causation requirements. Issues of which injuries to include and compensate, and whether and when to compensate off-table injuries, are difficult and are bound to be a source of conflict. If the no-fault program is structured to include many injuries, policymakers risk bankrupting the program, especially if issues akin to the thimerosal issue arise. If the design is narrow, as in Florida and Virginia, then it is easy for lawyers to chip away at the program and bring cases back to tort. How to determine causation and the issue of how to go about updating the list of injuries to be compensated have been especially difficult for all three medical no-fault programs. For the obstetrical programs, the link between oxygen deprivation and cerebral palsy is the pertinent example.[62] In VICP, even though no thimerosal/autism cases had been compensated as of early 2006, the number of thimerosal claims filed and discovery documents to be processed was financially burdensome.

U.S. Experience with Other Types of No-Fault: Workers' Compensation

Policy discussions of medical no-fault frequently cite workers' compensation as a success story that demonstrates the feasibility of a medical no-fault program in very practical terms. However, beyond broad statements praising workers' compensation, these discussions lack in-depth analysis of how workers' compensation programs in the United States actually operate and specific lessons to be learned from these experiences.

Adoption of Workers' Compensation by the States

Workers' compensation represents one of the major tort reforms of the twentieth century in the United States It shifted liability for workplace accidents from a negligence standard to a form of shared strict liability.[63] Under strict liability, payments are made to injury victims without demonstration of negligence, but with evidence that a particular action (use of a particular product) or inaction (failure to provide an adequate warning) caused the injury in question.

Adoption of workers' compensation served the self-interests of various politically influential stakeholders—employees, to the extent that expected postaccident benefits rose substantially following the switch from tort to workers' compensation;[64] unions—the greater presence of unionized manufacturing industries increased speed of adoption;[65] private insurers—when states kept a role for private insurers in workers' compensation;[66] manufacturers, especially large ones, since they had borne the brunt of tort liability, which was increasing prior to adoption of workers' compensation;[67] and state bureaucracies—because the size of bureaucracies increased in response to a need for administrative oversight of the programs.[68]

The Scope of Workers' Compensation Benefits

Workers' compensation covers both injuries resulting from an accident occurring in the workplace and chronic diseases thought to have been caused by having been in the work setting. For many chronic diseases, there is the task of deciding whether a claim is in or out of the system. Smith argues that workers' compensation creates incentives for workers to report hard-to-diagnose off-the-job injuries as having occurred on the job.[69] Ruser reports that policies enhancing the attractiveness of receiving workers' compensation benefits relative to work increased the ratio of carpel tunnel syndrome cases to cuts and fractures, the latter being comparatively easy to diagnose and attribute to specific events.[70] A decrease in the waiting period for benefits increased the number of back sprain cases relative to those involving fractures.

Probability of Applying for Worker's Compensation Benefits

A criticism of the no-fault programs for neurologically impaired infants is that most families who would be eligible for benefits do not apply. Parallel to this, Biddle et al. estimate that most workers with work-related illnesses do not file for benefits even though workers' compensation has broad eligibility standards for compensation.[71] Leigh and Robbins estimate that in 1999, most of the costs of occupational disease were not covered by workers' compensation.[72]

Experience Rating

Premium setting in workers' compensation involves three factors. First, manual rates are established by formulas set by a rating bureau based on the company's industry and its occupational mix. Second, for companies of sufficient size, premiums are experience rated. Experience rating is designed to measure whether or not an employer is better or worse than the average risk as reflected in the manual rates. Experience rating is typically based on actual loss patterns of the employer over the past three years. Those with better-than-average loss experience are awarded a credit; those with poorer experience than average receive a debit rating.[73] Third, larger companies may be permitted to self-insure at least a part of loss. This automatically exposes these enterprises to experience rating.

One advantage of being self-insured or insured with experience rating relates to the incentive to take precautions. When workers are covered by workers' compensation, they tend to be less careful.[74] But offsetting the disincentive that workers' compensation provides for workers to be careful, employers may have a greater incentive to promote workplace safety when covered by workers' compensation, especially in states with high compensation benefit levels. Moore and Viscusi conclude that employers' incentives for safety monitoring under workers' compensation dominate any disincentive workers' compensation may provide for employees to be less careful in their workplaces.[75]

The Record of Rising Costs and Reform of Workers' Compensation

As problems with the workers' compensation program have emerged, states have implemented various fixes. For example, in California, the workers' compensation system has been revised and reformed repeatedly since the passage of the Boynton Act in 1913. Legislators have grappled with issues of inflation, benefit increases, fraudulent injury claims, and fluctuations in the economy.

In April 2004 Governor Arnold Schwarzenegger of California signed the latest reform attempt, SB 899, into law. It remains to be seen how this latest attempt will fare in a system that has grown increasingly complex and expensive over the years.[76] Schwarzenegger made reform of workers' compensation a major issue during his campaign and during the initial part of his administration, as box 11.2 illustrates.

Implications for Medical No-Fault

Prior to its enactment in the states, various stakeholders supported implementing workers' compensation. In contrast, supportive constitu-

Box 11.2
Statement by Governor Schwarzenegger Following Enactment of Workers' Compensation Reform in California, 2004

> Governor Arnold Schwarzenegger made the following statement upon signing workers' compensation reform legislation (SB 899, Poochigian):
> "Today I delivered on my promise to create real workers' compensation reform. This bill completes a process that brought together Republicans and Democrats, business and labor, and all the affected parties to produce billions of dollars in savings, protect workers, and root out fraud and waste in the system. No longer will workers' compensation be the poison of our economy. Our message to the rest of the country and the world is that California is open for business. We are making our state once again a powerful, job-creating machine." (Office of the Governor for the State of California 2004)

encies for medical no-fault are lacking. Scholars support medical no-fault, though they hardly constitute a major voting bloc. Other potential supporters are health care providers, but their main goal is curbing the cost of medical malpractice insurance. Patients as a group are not well organized, as was true of unions in the case of worker's compensation.

Boundary disputes as to what to cover have been important in workers' compensation. There is evidence that experience rating is important for worker safety, although not all evidence points in this direction. Workers' compensation costs have risen, California being a case in point. The workers' compensation experience should serve as a warning that cost containment may be difficult to achieve under medical no-fault.

U.S. Experience with Other Types of No-Fault: Motor Vehicle No-Fault

Claims involving motor vehicle accidents are among the most common tort claims.[77] In Australia; Quebec, Saskatchewan, and Manitoba in Canada; Israel; New Zealand; Sweden; and many states in the United States, first-party liability has replaced third-party liability insurance for motor vehicle accidents.[78] That is, rather than hold the injurer liable; each party purchases his or her own insurance, much like standard motor vehicle collision insurance, which is first-party insurance. The rationale for motor vehicle no-fault is that determination of negligence is a reason for the high cost of dispute resolution under tort and delays in compensating injury victims. But eliminating the negligence standard may reduce the incentive drivers have to be cautious, unless no-fault premiums are experience rated (as are third-party motor vehicle insurance premiums), which is a general concern about no-fault insurance.

The effect on deterrence of the change from third-party to first-party liability depends on (1) the fraction of claims barred from tort and (2) the sensitivity of first-party insurance premiums to the driver's precaution level. Since a primary purpose of no-fault is to eliminate costly inquiries into fault, it seems unlikely that no-fault premiums would be highly experience rated. In the United States, *some* states with no-fault for motor vehicle accidents do permit premium surcharges based on insured individuals' driving records.[79]

Empirical research on the effects on deterrence of switching from third-party to first-party coverage has yielded mixed results. In the earliest and probably most widely cited study, Landes found that implementation of no-fault in U.S. states increased rates of motor vehicle fatalities, but Kochanowski and Young and Lund and Zador reported no effect on fatalities.[80] Sloan, Reilly, and Schenzler's analyses obtained mixed results on fatalities and binge drinking.[81] Using data from New Zealand, Brown did not find an increase in the amount of driving (which would occur because the financial consequences of having an accident were somewhat reduced by no-fault coverage) or in the accident rate following implementation of no-fault in 1974.[82]

More recent research using U.S. data concludes that switching to no-fault increases motor vehicle fatalities.[83] But this is contradicted by Loughran, who reports no statistically significant relationship between no-fault and fatal accidents and other measures of driver care.[84] Among research studies conducted in other countries, Gaudry, using data from Quebec, finds an increase in the number of accidents and accident victims after implementation of no-fault, a result confirmed by Devlin.[85] More recently, Lemstra and Olszynski, using a case-control methodology, find that conversion from tort to no-fault coverage resulted in a five-year reduction in total injury claims per 100,000 residents in Saskatchewan and a five-year reduction in Manitoba. This was as compared to British

Columbia, which retained tort, and Quebec, which retained no-fault, during the observational period.[86]

In sum, even after two decades of empirical research on the question of whether or not converting from a tort to a no-fault system leads to higher or lower injury rates, this issue is not settled. The implication for medical no-fault is that a switch to a nonexperience-rated no-fault plan may well decrease patient safety. While the lesson that premiums should be experience rated seems straightforward, this is not an easy matter under a no-fault system in which premiums come from individuals.

Experiences with Medical No-Fault in Other Countries

Overview

No-fault programs in Australia, New Zealand, Canada, and Sweden differ appreciably from the two or three medical no-fault programs adopted to date in the United States, especially in their relative breadth of coverage and distribution of compensation.[87] The plans in these countries do restrict eligibility for coverage to iatrogenic injuries rather than to acute and chronic medical conditions. However, these no-fault programs include a wider range of benefits (e.g., such as special education services) than first-party health and disability insurances typically do.

Sweden

The No Fault Patient Insurance Scheme (NFPI) was implemented in 1975.[88] The program provides three separate remedies for injury victims, each functioning independently. First, individuals may file a complaint with the Independent Patients' Advisory Committee; which receives around 25,000 complaints annually.[89] The committee does not have any binding power, but it facilitates interactions between patients and physicians or nurses. Second, individuals may file a grievance with the Health and Medical Care Liability Board, asking that medical staff receive a reprimand. The board receives around 3,000 letters per year. The last option is financial compensation. The no-fault program, known as Patient Compensation Insurance (PCI), receives approximately 9,000 claims per year, accounting for just 0.16 percent of health care expenditures. This compares favorably with U.S. medical malpractice insurance premiums, which amount from 1 to 2 percent of total health care expenditures.[90]

The low cost is partly attributable to its limited coverage. Only a small subset of injuries is eligible for compensation; during its first two decades of existence, 40 percent of around 100,000 complaints resulted in some compensation.[91] The system is funded by levies on Swedish county councils that provide medical care.[92]

To avoid compensating every iatrogenic injury, Sweden has implemented program requirements to narrow the pool of eligibles. The fundamental requirement is that an injury must have been avoidable, although the patient need not identify individuals who failed in their duty.[93] In addition, the injury must be accompanied by at least a ten-day hospital stay, the use of thirty days of sick time, or death.[94] Deductibles are applied to the recovery amount; also, the claimant must establish a causal relationship between the injury and the health care services received, based on a preponderance of probability.[95]

Subsequent reforms have created additional exclusions to compensability. For instance, individuals may not recover on grounds of lack of informed consent or for treatment administered during emergency situations.[96] Wound infections resulting from the patient's own bacteria are excluded, substantially reducing the claimant pool.[97] During the first three years of the program, 22 percent of compensated injuries were for infections that developed during the first three years of the program.[98] During the program's infancy in the mid-1970s, approximately 75 percent of claims received payment; this number fell to 18 percent during 1986–1991.[99] More recent estimates place compensation rates at close to 50 percent of all claims, suggesting a reduction in barriers to payment.[100] But 42 percent are rejected outright.[101]

If a claimant desires to contest rejection of his or her claim or the amount of compensation, he or she retains a limited right to appeal. Appeals are considered by the Patient Injury Board,[102] which reviews the claim's compensability and also the amount of compensation. The board's decision is advisory, but the final outcome coincides with the panel's decision in about 90 percent of cases.[103] If a claimant is dissatisfied with the board's decision, he or she may continue the appeal process and take the case to a binding court of arbitration, but on matters of process only; substantive matters may not be reviewed.[104] Costs from appeals to the court of arbitration must be borne by claimants.[105] Contingent fees are illegal; attorneys are paid on an hourly basis.[106] With the cost imposed on claimants and a success rate of about 20 percent, on average the arbitration board reviews only thirty-three cases annually.[107]

A major difference between the experience with medical no-fault in the United States and in Sweden is the amount of physician involvement. In 1997, Sweden passed a reform requiring every health care provider to purchase no-fault insurance.[108] If a provider has not purchased such insurance, the patient receives payment nonetheless, as all insurers are jointly and severally liable for compensating injuries attributable to uninsured providers.[109] Additionally, the physician responsible for treatment is "obliged to inform the patient" if damage has occurred, and to "assist the patient in applying for compensation."[110] This ethically imposed duty explains why compensation forms are readily available in all clinics and hospitals and why physicians are actively involved in 60–80 percent of claims.[111] By contrast, in Florida's NICA program, for example, there is generally no provider involvement with the claim, and the program has not been aggressively advertised in order to avoid NICA's being deluged with claims.

The administrative overhead of the PCI program is substantially lower (18 percent) compared to the administrative costs of the U.S. tort system (50 percent or higher), but comparing these figures directly is misleading. The PCI does not have the tort costs for investigation, feedback, and management, and Sweden also has social insurance programs.[112]

PCI's low overhead reflects several factors. First, the speed of claims resolution lowers overhead expenses; from the time of filing a claim to its final determination is about six months.[113] The claims process is done with little attorney involvement, saving a significant amount in legal fees.[114] In addition, successful claims are paid using a fixed benefits schedule, eliminating the cost of setting damages on an individualized basis.

To compare the expense of no-fault against tort in the United States, Studdert and Brennan use data from Utah and Colorado, assuming (counterfactually) that the two states had no-fault programs based on the Swedish model.[115] They estimate that Utah would have a $10–15 million increase, and Colorado a $25–35 million increase, in expense. Although no-fault would be more expensive, far more claimants would be compensated than under tort. Studdert and Brennan estimate that administrative cost under a no-fault plan would be appreciably lower than under tort.

Their estimates of spending under a Swedish-style no-fault plan may be overly optimistic. For one thing, depending on how the program is structured, rates of claiming could be far greater than Studdert and Brennan predict. Further, Danzon has raised serious questions as to whether the United States, with its very different tort and health care institutions, could ever implement a program similar to the PCI and obtain similar results.[116] Even though individuals in Sweden have access to both tort and no-fault, the Swedish tort system is much less favorable to plaintiffs than in the case in the United States. The burden of proof is roughly a 75–85 percent threshold probability of negligence, and expert testimony is difficult to secure. Also, contingent fees are illegal, and payments under tort in Sweden are subject to full collateral source offset.[117]

Given the higher returns to pursuing a tort claim in the United States. than in Sweden, remaining in tort would often be more attractive to claimants and their attorneys in the United States. Substituting no-fault for tort would be a much greater challenge in the United States than in Sweden.

Another difference relates to level of physician involvement in Sweden versus that in the United States. At least until it was clear that medical no-fault would withstand constitutional challenges, it seems unlikely that physicians in the United States. would readily inform their patients when an error occurred.

New Zealand

Established in 1972, New Zealand's original no-fault program was broad and inclusive. Justice Owen Woodhouse, who spearheaded the development of the system, held that the basic principle of no-fault should be collective responsibility, acting as a form of social insurance.[118] Since its inception in 1972, the Accident Compensation Corporation (ACC) has administered New Zealand's no-fault program.[119] Initially, all accidental personal injuries were covered, including medical malpractice, which was labeled "medical misadventure." However, total expenditures from the program rose rapidly.

Originally, funding came from levies on employers, motor vehicle owners, and subsidies from the government, with funds from each source placed in a separate fund. The funding changed dramatically over the course of three decades and several reforms; a pay-as-you-go financing structure was established, a new levy for registered health professionals was created, and seven separate funds administered by the ACC were established. Also, the government retained the power to require risk-rated premiums for health professionals.[120] Administrative cost, however, was only 10 percent of total expense.[121] Even so, the overall costs of New Zealand's no-fault program have proven to be burdensome. Cost per claim has risen considerably.[122]

In response to rising costs, there was a major reform in 1992 which substantially restricted the scope of covered injuries, shortened the time within which claims could be brought, and eliminated lump sum payments for pain and suffering.[123] As in Sweden, the New Zealand program now required a fourteen-day hospital stay or twenty-eight sick days as a requirement for eligibility.[124] The newly restricted definition of medical misadventure introduced an element of fault, limiting claims to injuries resulting from medical error or mishap, and thus removing the problem of having to distinguish between injuries resulting from medical care and unavoidable or inevitable injuries.[125] The introduction of fault in the 1990s was not a surprise; courts had used fault in their analyses of medical misadventure throughout the 1980s, and a substantial body of case law had developed.[126]

In 2002, the no-fault system was reformed again with the Injury, Prevention, Rehabilitation, and Compensation Act of 2001. With this act, the ACC was restored as the sole administrator of accident compensation schemes, and efforts were refocused to emphasize restoration.[127] The most recent reform occurred in 2005, when New Zealand modified its no-fault program in order to establish firm boundaries and definitions for eligibility. The new system eliminated the element of fault from the eligibility criteria, returning New Zealand to a true no-fault system.[128]

In addition to monetary compensation, claimants in New Zealand have the option of pursuing nonmonetary remedies. In 1994, the New Zealand Parliament created legislation establishing the Health and Disability Commission (HDC).[129] The HDC is also responsible for handling disciplinary complaints.[130] However, the most common form of nonmonetary relief sought from the HDC is not disciplinary action; rather, it is a request for corrective measures to address the cause of harm.[131]

Error reporting in New Zealand is a regular part of the medical culture; acknowledgment of injuries in patient records is extremely high.[132] Truthful, consistent error reporting provides opportunities to evaluate quality of care problems, a sharp contrast with the United States, where such reporting is rare. Also, in contrast to tort in the United States and like Sweden, compensation is delivered quickly; the ACC is required to provide notice of its decision within nine months.[133] Patients are offered different forms of accountability—much like Sweden's system. Since many claimants desire only an explanation, accountability, apology, assurance of a system change, or intervention, the HDC allows patients to initiate patient safety measures through their complaints.

Despite these positive results, a recent survey of physicians in New Zealand demonstrated that many physicians do not believe the ACC and the HDC are achieving their stated goals.[134] Nearly 40 percent did not think most complaints were warranted, and another 33 percent did not believe complainants were normal people.[135] In addition, the complaint and disciplinary system is nicknamed "death by 1000 arrows" by some (Figure 11.1) due to its complexity.[136] Some view this complexity as standing in the way of New Zealand's no-fault programs' accessibility, efficiency, and effectiveness. Also, New Zealand's no-fault system may lack incentives to improve patient safety, given its broad funding base and lack of experience rating.

Implications for Medical No-Fault in the United States

The United States is far more litigious than the other countries that have implemented no-fault programs.[137] It seems likely that a substantial amount of litigation would develop in the United States at the boundaries of no-fault coverage, with lawyers for claimants arguing that injuries were not covered by the no-fault program, thus making the claimants

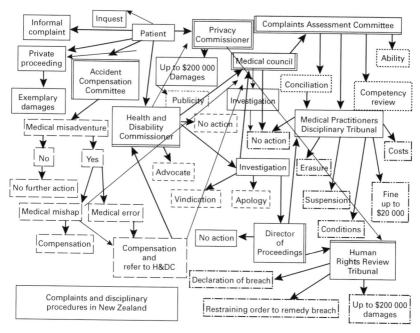

Figure 11.1
Death by 1000 Arrows: The Multiple Pathways of the Current Complaint System in New Zealand Source: Cunningham (2004).

eligible for payment under tort. Also, Sweden and New Zealand have much different health systems from that in the United States. Health care services are publicly financed and lower cost in the other countries than in the United States, in which half of such services are privately financed. These factors tend to make no-fault in the other countries more affordable.

Consistent error reporting and physician involvement are essential to the success of a no-fault program. Even though some advocates for a medical no-fault program in the United States assert that under no-fault, health care providers would willingly admit their errors, this seems highly questionable in the U.S. context. In New Zealand, by contrast, the culture seems more conducive to error reporting. Finally, while the United States has had a tumultuous relationship with its tort system, the concept of civil action is deeply ingrained in U.S. history and culture.

Many citizens believe that civil actions for negligence are a fundamental right that should not be withdrawn.[138] While supporters of the medical no-fault concept in the United States often cite positive experiences of no-fault in other countries as evidence that such programs work, others are much more doubtful. Danzon argues that rather than providing a prototype for other countries to adopt, the original New Zealand no-fault program demonstrates pitfalls to avoid.[139] We agree with her assessment.

Finally, a continuing theme is the lower administrative cost and speedier payment under no-fault. This positive attribute is sufficiently universal to be accepted as an important benefit of no-fault compensation programs.

Is There a Role for No-Fault in the U.S. Context?

This chapter has described the pros and cons of no-fault programs. No-fault programs have some important advantages. Injury victims are compensated who would otherwise not be compensated, and compensation is made at a much lower administrative cost and much more quickly, on average, than by tort.

In the United States, we have never had a real national discussion about the merits of providing coverage for persons who are injured during the course of receiving or, in some cases, not receiving medical care as opposed to other groups, such as those who do not have any health insurance coverage. If a serious public discussion were to occur, it seems unlikely that covering those persons with iatrogenic injuries would receive top priority.

Instead of a broad medical no-fault program, advocates of medical no-fault in the public arena (as opposed to discussion among academic experts) have had another focus: to reduce payments to medical malpractice claimants and associated legal expenses. This priority has led to adoption of a very few programs with narrowly defined eligibility criteria, which although generally efficient in terms of administrative cost and speed of payment, serve the compensation objective in only a limited way. Further, although there are savings in time and expense of litigation, other problems have emerged. For one, although negligence is not an issue with no-fault, causation issues are. The most striking example is over causation in the thimerosal/autism debate. Having a no-fault program for vaccines has not stopped vaccine manufacturers from asserting that they do not invest in vaccine research and development to the extent that they otherwise would because of the looming threat of tort. The birth-injury no-fault programs in Florida and Virginia have relied on premium income from hospitals and physicians. This narrow funding base, obtained from virtually the only strong advocates of medical no-fault in these states, has inevitably led to pressure on program administrators to keep the programs small. If redistribution of income from "someone" to families with birth-injured children is indeed an important social objective, it seems odd that the "someone" should be hospitals and physicians. General tax revenue would seem to be a more logical and just alternative.

The practical reason that hospitals and physicians are taxed is simply that these no-fault programs were adopted to relieve hospitals and physicians from lawsuits and high premiums. Thus, it was felt that these groups should be willing to be taxed. However, these no-fault programs have not consistently reduced the cost of medical malpractice to providers and manufacturers. Certainly, if the goal is lawsuit and premium relief, there are more effective approaches, including adoption of flat caps on nonmonetary or total loss, a solution we argue is inequitable.

The notion that a broad no-fault program financed from general tax revenue, such as by the personal income tax, would be adopted in the United States seems to us to be pure fantasy. The debate over universal health insurance has occurred over many decades without progress being made. More limited public programs that cover certain demographic and income groups appear to have higher priority; Medicaid and SCHIP programs have been adopted. The political context of the other countries with medical no-fault programs is different from that of the United States; one indicator is that they have universal health insurance.

If this type of no-fault program is unrealistic, are there alternatives? One possibility is a mandatory no-fault program financed by an excise tax on payments to hospitals and physicians for the services they provide.

Presumably at least some portion of this tax would be shifted forward to health insurance premium payers. Essentially this would be a tied sale with hospital and physicians' services bundled together. This seems close to an unfunded mandate which would require health insurers to provide no-fault insurance with health insurance coverage. If history is any guide, health insurers would almost certainly oppose this unfunded mandate. However, a program financed by an excise tax/unfunded mandate has a much higher probability of adoption than does one funded from general tax revenue.

Still another possibility is a voluntary no-fault program based at hospitals. Both hospitals and their medical staffs would decide whether to offer such coverage, and patients would decide whether or not to accept the offer of no-fault coverage at the hospital or remain in tort. Such a program would include specific injuries resulting from care within the walls of the hospital, whether inpatient or ambulatory care. The hospital would be the experience rating unit. Thus, hospitals with effective patient safety programs would be able to offer such coverage at a lower cost. Having a no-fault program could be a feature that would make the hospital attractive to consumers. Details of how the program is financed would be left to the hospital. The state Department of Insurance would oversee the program as it currently does for other forms of insurance. Disputes, including those about injury causation, would be resolved by a mechanism specified in an agreement signed by the patient.

There are admittedly complex issues to be resolved even for such a voluntary program. One of the major issues is the method of enrolling patients into the program. Signing a document giving up tort rights in return for no-fault coverage at the time care is received is likely not to be viewed favorably by courts. But it should be possible to enroll patients in advance. One occasion would be at the time employees enroll in a health insurance plan with their employers. Hospitals in the area could present documents describing their no-fault insurance programs, including any payments required of enrollees and methods of resolving disputes. Also, when hospitalized, patients could sign up for the program for future stays.

Such a program remains voluntary for both providers and patients. Trying to develop universally applicable rules as to which injuries are avoidable and which are not, updating these rules with changes in technology and in knowledge as to whether the injuries are avoidable or not, as well as resolving thorny issues of causation, is best left on a decentralized basis. Government should facilitate production and dissemination of relevant information and provide general program oversight, but not get involved in detailed rulemaking, as is inevitable under a mandatory program.

12

Reforms: What Can Be Done

The empirical evidence and discussion of relevant health care institutions in this book thus far has provided a foundation for proposals for achievable reforms to be discussed in this chapter. Proposals for reform start with a premise that something is broken and requires fixing. Medical malpractice in the United States is broken, but generally not for the reasons stated by advocates of tort reform.

One constant has been the rhetoric of tort reform. The preface to a January 1975 symposium issue on medical malpractice began with this statement:

The term "medical malpractice" has been an increasingly frightening one to patients, doctors, and insurers as well. In recent months, the spectre of physician strikes, astronomical damage awards, soaring liability insurance premiums, and allegations of poor-quality medical care have stirred debate in state legislatures, in the Congress, in the press, and in scholarly journals. The medical malpractice crisis is real, and the problems which created the crisis remain with us."[1]

Except perhaps for the "spectre of physician strikes," using some white-out for the date, this statement could have been published in January 2005. The many tort reforms since the 1970s have not altered the tenor of the public policy discussion. Caps on damages have "worked" to reduce payments by medical malpractice insurers and create premiums below what they otherwise would have been (Chapters 4 and 5),[2] but caps have not altered the incentives of the participants in this market (Chapter 1). Furthermore, if there is a benefit to caps, it is mainly in redistributing income from injury victims and their attorneys to health care providers rather than in improving efficiency in allocation of resources. If there were overclaiming, one could say that by reducing

access to legal representation, caps are efficiency enhancing. But, if anything, the empirical evidence supports underclaiming and undercompensation on average (chapters 1 and 5).

It seems unlikely that any savings in medical malpractice insurance
premiums would accrue to patients as taxpayers and health insurance
premium payers (chapter 3). Organized medicine plausibly supports caps
first and foremost primarily in response to pressures from its
constituency for financial relief.

The title of this chapter is "achievable reforms." Starting with the crisis
of the mid-1970s, as the above quotation indicates, scholars, other
experts, and some policy analysts have proposed broad reforms of
the current system. Broad examples include proposals to substitute
no-fault for medical injuries for tort (chapter 11), abolition of the jury
for medical malpractice disputes as part of a plan for special health
courts (chapter 7), substitution of alternative dispute resolution (ADR)
mechanisms for traditional methods of dispute resolution used in tort,
enterprise liability, using insurers or hospitals as the enterprise, substitution of private contracts for tort,[3] limits on plaintiff attorneys' fees
(chapter 6), and scheduled damages, especially for nonmonetary loss
(chapter 5).

Many, and probably most, of these reforms are not achievable. As
Baker contends, "No-fault compensation for medical injuries turns out
to be an idea that lots of people like in theory, but almost no one likes
in practice."[4] Abolition of the jury for medical malpractice seems warranted on grounds that there are cognitive limitations of individuals in
general and lack of experience in their role as jurors in particular. But
juries provide a potential check on abuse of power by medical providers,
and hence eliminating juries in medical malpractice cases will understandably encounter some opposition. By lowering litigation cost to
plaintiffs, statutes enacted to encourage alternative dispute resolution
(ADR), which involves mediation and/or arbitration, appears to have
increased medical malpractice payments.[5]

Private contracts seem attractive in principle, but the concern is that
patients are not well-positioned to be effective negotiating partners in
the contracting process. Although, as discussed below, enterprise liability
has attractive features, it has been disregarded, and even opposed, by

organized medicine.[6] Similarly, while scheduled damages have attractive features and support from the academic community,[7] they are vehemently opposed by the trial bar. Limits on plaintiff attorneys' fees in medical malpractice cases enjoy some political support from organized medicine. These proposals focus on high incomes of plaintiff attorneys and not on attorneys for the defense, physicians with high incomes, and CEOs.

Ironically, but understandably from the vantage point of promoting one's self-interest, the same medical organizations oppose limits on physicians' fees. And while medical organizations are major opponents of the status quo in medical malpractice, several members of this community have supported imposing tort liability on managed care organizations.

Indeed, a problem common to many of these mainly "second-generation" reform proposals (chapter 4) is that they lack a strong political constituency. At the state level, there are strong political constituencies for damage caps. The U.S. Congress has not even enacted traditional "first-generation" (not to speak of second-generation) reforms.[8] Trial lawyers and consumer advocate groups have more political clout in the U.S. Congress than in many state legislatures. Whatever deficiencies the second-generation proposals may have, the real reason for no action on fundamental reform is that it lacks a sufficiently influential political constituency.

The prudent course involves identification of the major deficiencies of the existing system *and* incremental reform. Admittedly, incremental reform is far from anyone's conception of the ideal, but the real choice is between no change and incremental change.

What's Good and What's Bad with the Existing System?

Positive Aspects
The current system has a few positive attributes. First, being able to sue in combination with the contingent fee method for compensating plaintiffs' attorneys gives patients who are unsatisfied with outcomes a mechanism for addressing their grievances that may not be possible through other channels. The regulatory apparatus is sometimes controlled or

substantially influenced by health care providers or for bureaucratic reasons may be unresponsive to patients' complaints. As Mechanic argued over three decades ago, "One of the remaining sources of power for the patient is his ability to threaten or initiate malpractice litigation when he feels that his interests have been abused. Although patients rarely do so, the remote threat may to some extent control the bounds of physician behavior."[9] Second, the American jury, in spite of possible limitations, gives ordinary citizens a role in this dispute resolution system. Regulatory agencies may not be equally sensitive to consumer interests. Third, if one views secular trends in medical malpractice payments and premiums, as opposed to very large increases in premiums at the onset of "hard markets," the increases in payments and premiums are rather modest, only slightly higher than the changes in prices in general.

Negative Aspects

The current system has serious deficiencies, although they are not the same as those typically depicted in the popular, trade, and medical professional press and in testimony before state legislatures and the U.S. Congress by various stakeholders. First, unlike other fields of personal injury tort, there is no empirical evidence that the threat of medical malpractice lawsuits deters injuries (chapter 3). Particularly since injury deterrence is typically listed as the first goal of tort liability, this is a very serious deficiency. Nearly complete insurance coverage for medical malpractice liability, the lack of experience rating, and the low enforcement rate (low claims frequency relative to negligent adverse events) account for part of the failure of tort to deter. Tort liability focuses on mistakes of individual providers, but errors frequently reflect simultaneous omissions or misjudgments on the part of several individuals. Backup systems for correcting errors when they occur are often lacking.

When asked, almost all physicians in the United States maintain that they practice defensively on account of the threat of being sued. To the extent that this is so—and there is limited empirical evidence to support the view that there is some defensive medicine—it would seem not that physician decisions are affected by tort, but that the signal from tort is insufficiently precise or even wrong.[10]

Several studies have attempted to measure the cost of defensive medicine (chapter 3). To the extent that it can be accurately measured, the effect of the threat of lawsuits on cost appears to be modest, especially when placed in context of the appreciable increase in real expenditures on personal health care that has occurred in the United States since the mid-1960s, when Medicare and Medicaid programs were first implemented. Defensive medicine is at best a second-tier driver of increased real expenditures.

Perhaps just as serious, or even more serious, is the health care provider community in the United States' almost total rejection of the view that medical malpractice has a constructive role to play in health care delivery. Providers generally see no link between medical malpractice litigation and provision of high-quality care. Some public policy discussions of iatrogenic errors, such as those by the Institute of Medicine (chapter 8), have explicitly excluded considerations of medical malpractice. Including medical malpractice in public discussions of patient safety has been seen as muddling the analysis and, more important, risks provoking opposition from the provider community, thus impeding introduction of both high-tech and low-tech approaches to improving patient safety.

Much commentary in both assessments of medical malpractice and patient safety see medical malpractice as part of the problem rather than part of the solution. The problem is said to be that the threat of medical malpractice litigation leads to excessive secrecy about specific medical errors, both out of fear that discussion of medical errors will lead to more lawsuits and that the discussion could be introduced by plaintiffs at trial as evidence of defendant liability. These concerns probably have some validity.

Yet it seems unlikely that insulating providers from threats of liability will lead to widespread disclosure of errors. Nor can the threat of lawsuits be the only reason that health care organizations do not adopt patient safety measures, such as systems to prevent errors in drug delivery in hospitals. Even under no-fault, disclosing errors would lead to an increased number of compensated cases. As long as health care providers are asked to fund medical no-fault insurance programs, one cannot expect providers to be eager to disclose their mistakes. Even absent a financial disincentive to disclose, it is not human nature to want to be known for one's "bloopers," even if the bloopers are disclosed only to colleagues and coworkers, and not to the public. Public disclosure only increases embarrassment.

At present, the business case for investments in patient safety leaves much to be desired. Health care product markets do not demand high levels of patient safety, or at most are only beginning to do so. And if providers were to incur the additional cost of error-reducing innovations, they would receive little financial incentive in terms of reduced medical malpractice insurance premiums. In sum, if quality of care falls short of socially optimal levels, there is little financial incentive to raise it to optimal levels.

Litigation is an extremely inefficient system for compensating injury victims. Various forms of first-party insurance are much more efficient in distributing compensation to persons who have incurred a loss due to personal illness or injury.

Thus, in sum, on most lists of the goals of tort, medical malpractice does badly on the first two objectives—injury deterrence or improved patient safety, and compensation of persons with iatrogenic injuries. Its strongest, and most important, features lie in the category of giving injury victims a day in court and making injurers accountable to ordinary citizens who serve as jurors.

Creating Financial Incentives for Preventing Injuries

The highest priority is to focus on providing financial incentives for preventing injuries, not on preventing all injuries but rather those injuries for which the cost of prevention does not exceed cost. The literature on prevention of medical injuries, admittedly not as rigorous as it might be, suggests that many opportunities for injury prevention exist.[11] Furthermore, the evidence is for *average* benefits and costs, and there is likely to be substantial variation about these averages. Even if private incentives were aligned to encourage adoption of injury-prevention innovations that are often socially desirable, there will be situations in which adoption is not appropriate. For example, it may not be appropriate for all hospitals (e.g., for small hospitals) to adopt computerized physician order entry systems. The case for adoption should be made on a project-specific basis.

Enterprise Insurance for Hospitals and Their Medical Staffs: A Promising Achievable Reform

Historical Context

Before the 1970s, medical malpractice insurance was provided by commercial property-casualty insurance companies. In the mid-1970s, in response to a lack of availability of medical malpractice insurers, states enacted statutes permitting physician-sponsored, single-line medical malpractice insurers.[12] This solved a short-run problem of availability of coverage, at least until the third crisis.

Both the commercial and the physician-sponsored companies have not been as active as they should have been in loss prevention and certainly in injury prevention. Also, insurers may be inherently inefficient in injury and loss prevention; they are not located where services are being delivered and are not part of the delivery process.[13]

Also, given the lack of experienced-rated premiums, physicians also have not had a meaningful financial incentive to allocate resources to injury prevention. The lack of experience rating undermines tort's objective of corrective justice since individual defendants do not suffer the financial consequences of any injustice they may have committed.[14]

Definition and Rationale

Baker coined the term "enterprise insurance."[15] Physicians who work or render services to patients in hospitals or other health care organizations would obtain their medical malpractice insurance through such an organization. He argues that enterprise insurance avoids some of the shortcomings of enterprise liability from which the term "enterprise insurance" was derived.

Hospitals and health plans have not welcomed the concept of enterprise liability; to these organizations, assuming greater liability seems to be an added burden. Nor has organized medicine been enthusiastic about ceding such liability to these health care organizations, plausibly because organized medicine and its membership worry about loss of professional control over medical decisions. An additional unstated reason is a concern about the loss of financial independence.

In the variant of *enterprise liability* that seems most sensible, medical staff would be insured for medical malpractice by the hospital for all care delivered within the walls of the hospital. Physicians would generally continue to purchase medical malpractice insurance to cover claims arising from care delivered in their offices.[16]

There is a strong case for the enterprise to be the hospital. Most of the medical malpractice losses arise from care delivered in hospitals.[17] Large hospitals, including those affiliated with academic health centers, provide medical malpractice insurance now.[18] An example is the Duke University Health System, which provides such insurance to hospitals in its system and to physician faculty members (box 12.1). If Duke were to extend coverage to other physicians who practice at its community hospitals, it would be necessary to change its insurance company's charter. Hospitals could form their own insurance companies for the purpose of providing liability coverage for services provided within their walls, or they could partner with an established insurance company as a joint venture.

Being part of an insuring group has its advantages and disadvantages. The efficiencies inherent in combining patient safety measures and insurance, including premium-setting, are definite pluses. There is a potential to save on premium dollars. Further, since the insurer is much better able to "poke inside" the clinical organization, it may be less likely to raise premiums dramatically, given a change in loss experience, since it has a better sense of what is going on. The minus side, however, is that physicians often prefer to maintain their independence. Even though participating in an enterprise insurance plan need not result in loss of independence, some physicians may regard this as a slippery slope.

A survey of hospitals conducted by the Hospital Association of Pennsylvania found that as of 2001–2002, 41 percent of responding hospitals had noncommercial primary layer insurance, presumably including self-insurance, insurance through a captive or risk retention group, leaving only 38 percent commercially insured. Among teaching hospitals and relatively large hospitals in the state, the leading form of self-insurance was the single-parent captive insurer.

Box 12.1
Enterprise Insurance at an Academic Health Center: Duke University Health System

The Duke University Health System (DUHS), headquartered in Durham, North Carolina, consists of three hospitals, the Duke University Hospital, and two community hospitals, as well as clinics throughout central North Carolina and southern Virginia, ambulatory care centers, wellness centers, home care specialists, and a hospice. As of 2006, DUHS had nearly 17,000 full-time employees. Its professional liability program is administered by a captive insurance company, Durham Casualty Company, Ltd., domiciled in Bermuda. The program covers DUHS hospitals and faculty physicians, house staff, and other physicians who are members of the Private Diagnostic Clinic (PDC). The PDC is not part of the DUHS, but for the purpose of provision of medical malpractice insurance, all PDC-affiliated physicians are covered. Duke University Hospital has a closed medical staff, with staff membership limited to Duke faculty. Almost 1,000 physicians who are not faculty members have admitting privileges at one of the DUHS community hospitals. These physicians are not covered by the plan. Duke self-insures but purchases reinsurance coverage for its larger losses.

The plan offers several advantages. First, even though there is no experience rating of individual physicians, the cost of medical malpractice insurance, as determined on an actuarial basis, is deducted from physician billings. During periods of relatively adverse loss experience, such deductions are great. Physicians experience variations in deductions. Variations in loss attributable to physicians are not totally borne by hospitals or DUHS more generally. Second, DUHS has an active patient safety program. There are efficiencies in combining incident identification and prevention, claims management and settlement authority, physician credentialing with indemnification of liability and associated financial incentives which cannot be realized when liability insurance is purchased from a nonaffiliated organization. Third, potentially lower premiums and lower volatility should be an advantage. Fourth, while many physicians desire to own their own facilities, enterprise insurance could provide a mechanism for attracting physicians to hospitals.

Also, hospitals and other large health organizations, such as large medical group practices, are in a better position to prevent and manage their losses than are individual physicians and small medical groups. Simulations performed by Sloan and Hassan (1990) provide empirical support for the notion that large and even medium-sized hospitals have medical staffs of sufficient size to support this risk-bearing role.[19] That study assumed no injury and loss prevention program would be implemented. With such programs, the case for enterprise insurance is much stronger.

Two other factors also support enterprise insurance and having hospitals as the enterprise. With the hospital as the insuring enterprise, hospital medical staff would have added incentives to be selective about the quality of physicians they admit to and retain on their medical staffs. And medical staffs have a much more direct incentive to support adoption of patient safety measures in order to reduce medical malpractice losses at the hospital, especially if medical staff are placed at some risk for losses above a threshold value. It would be up to individual hospitals to negotiate cost-sharing incentives with their medical staffs.

An issue is whether or not regulatory oversight would be needed, and if so, the form it should take. Insurance regulation is almost entirely a state responsibility. U.S. law delegates the regulation of the business of insurance, and every person engaged therein, to the laws of the several states. Congress is forbidden from enacting legislation that will invalidate, impair, or supersede any law of a state relating to insurance.[20] This has resulted in heterogeneity among states in insurance law and regulation. However, there is federal law partially superseding this for certain forms of insurance, preventing state legislatures from regulating risk retention groups unless the group has been chartered in that state.[21]

Possible Objections to Enterprise Insurance

Baker lists several possible objections to enterprise insurance.[22] Such insurance may

interfere with the health care market, create a windfall for physicians with hospital practices, force hospitals to bear too much of the cost of medical liability, reduce the autonomy of physicians and other practitioners, lead to an increase in medical malpractice claiming, and present insurmountable administrative complications.

That such insurance would interfere with the health care market and present insurmountable administrative complications could be said for virtually any change. Existing insurers would not welcome the change because enterprise insurance will probably mean that these insurers will lose business. A rebuttal to the "insurmountable administrative complications" is that such insurance has already existed for years, albeit on a limited basis. Shares of premium expense borne by the hospitals and individual physician members would depend on market factors and would vary among hospitals with enterprise insurance.

Autonomy of physicians and other practitioners often conflicts with the goal of improving patient safety, which requires a team approach. Physicians must be actively involved in implementing measures to reduce medical errors, particularly since they play a lead role in the provision of care in hospitals. But some loss of individual physician autonomy is inevitable if meaningful changes in patient safety are to be realized. Major improvements require that physicians and other hospital per-sonnel function as a team.

If enterprise insurance substantially improves loss and injury preven-tion, it is not inevitable that there would be an increase in medical mal-practice claims. There is substantial underclaiming now. In contrast to enterprise liability, individual physicians would be named in medical malpractice suits as they are now. It is not obvious that a hospital would be viewed by jurors as having deep pockets any more than a large insurer would.

The most serious objection is a more general one and not in Baker's list. If the concept of enterprise insurance is so attractive, why is it not more common now?

There are several answers. First, in the United States, in contrast to other high-income countries, hospital medical staffs have been largely independent of hospitals.[23] Although some physicians are employed by hospitals, the vast majority practice in hospitals with the only formal relationships being membership on the hospital's medical staff and on some committees. Physicians have resisted being under the control of hospitals, both for financial reasons and out of concern for possible loss of professional autonomy. As technology has become more sophisti-cated, this independence is becoming more and more realistic.[24] Since about 1995, physicians have increasingly joined physician-hospital organizations for purposes of negotiating contracts with health insurers, ostensibly because such joint negotiations raise physicians' market power. Yet any proposal from the outside that would cede control of medical decision-making to hospitals is likely to be resisted by many physicians. The key will be to have active physician involvement in hospital-based enterprise insurance with a meaningful financial incentive for individual physicians to prevent lawsuits.

Second, there are substantial differences among hospitals in their sophistication about risk management and medical malpractice. In part, this is a function of hospital and medical staff size. Indeed, smaller hospitals may be of an insufficient size to operate a medical malpractice insurance plan on their own.[25] Such hospitals might join regional compacts, which in turn form a risk retention group.

Third, in many years, premiums charged by medical malpractice insurers are below fair value. In such cases, hospitals and others have a financial incentive to purchase insurance coverage rather than to self-insure.

Finally, accountability incentives are not likely to provide sufficient motivation for hospitals to create systems management of medical injuries.[26] Hospitals and physicians have many nonliability objectives and concerns. Implementation of enterprise insurance alone may not lead to optimal levels of patient safety in hospitals. Yet the converse does not follow. Just because enterprise insurance is not likely to be the silver bullet does not imply that it is a BB gun (i.e., it cannot have an important role in promoting patient safety).

Captive Insurers and Risk Retention Groups

There is a major trend in the United States to use of captives, such as the Durham Casualty Company (see box 12.1).[27] Captives provide an organization for performing traditional functions of insurers, such as computing loss reserves and investing premium income from the time it is received until loss payments are made. There are also tax advantages to captives, as well as regulatory advantages if the captives are domiciled offshore.[28]

A captive insurance company is an insurance company which is owned by the entity it insures.[29] Captive insurance involves the insured creating a subsidiary or sister corporation (the captive), which acts as a funding vehicle for the insured, assuming some or all of the owner's financial liability for medical malpractice.[30] Typically captives are incorporated offshore, and as a result they face fewer regulations, such as lower capitalization requirements and, as mentioned before, tax advantages.[31] As of 1995, 70 percent of captives worldwide were formed offshore. There has been a recent trend to decrease regulations for formation of onshore captives, but state laws and regulations remain demanding, much more so than the laws of offshore domiciles. Regardless of where they were formed, most captives are subject to state insurance regulation, but for some tax-exempt organizations, insurance code regulatory violations may be avoided.[32]

Risk retention groups are an option for small hospitals, physicians not affiliated with large medical groups, hospitals offering enterprise insurance, or hospitals that decide that forming their own insurance program is inadvisable. The Risk Retention Act was initially enacted as the Product Liability Risk Retention Act of 1981.[33] In 1986, during the liability crisis of the mid-1980s, the law was amended to apply to all other liability coverage, including medical malpractice.[34] The act, as amended, authorizes "risk retention groups" to pool similar risks for self-insurance and risk "purchasing groups" to be formed to purchase coverage on a group basis. These organizations must be chartered in only one state. In other states, such entities are freed of most insurance regulation and do not receive the protection of state guaranty funds.[35]

There is a danger, however, that large risk retention groups would vitiate the important advantage of enterprise liability: the integration of delivery, injury prevention, and insurance functions. Thus, when the hospital is of sufficient size to support an enterprise insurance plan, this is preferable to a risk retention group.

Established Forms of Liability Applicable to Hospitals: Stepping-stones to Enterprise Liability?

Until the most recent medical malpractice crisis, medical malpractice was largely viewed as a problem for physicians. Hospitals and nursing homes were rarely mentioned as victims of tort. However, a large number of medical malpractice claims originate from care provided in hospital settings, and the physician specialties paying the highest medical malpractice premiums all deliver a substantial amount of their care in hospitals.[36] Moreover, the vast majority of claims involving alleged wrongdoing on the part of physicians for care provided in hospitals name members of medical staffs of hospitals as defendants, not physicians who are employees of the hospital.

The doctrine of *respondeat superior* has been applied to staff model health maintenance organizations, forcing them to bear legal responsibility for their employed physicians.[37] *Respondeat superior* is a legal doctrine which makes employers liable for the actions of their employees during the course of their employment, and allows plaintiffs to hold otherwise unrelated parties vicariously liable. However, in most U.S. hospitals, in contrast to those in the vast majority of other countries, physicians typically are not employed by the hospital, but serve on an independent contractor basis. This has made it difficult to use the doctrine of *respondeat superior*, as it requires an employer/employee relationship; direct employment by the hospital is needed.

In the absence of an employee/employer relationship, an alternative theory of liability is ostensible, or apparent, agency.[38] Ostensible agency is based on the principle that an agent (the physician) acting for the principal (the hospital) may cause a third party (the patient) to reasonably believe the principal has employed the agent. Ostensible agency is a cause of action that courts have recognized in place of *respondeat superior*, but in the process they have also raised the standard of proof for plaintiffs, requiring them to prove both an apparent agency relationship, and a reliance on that relationship.[39] Factors that courts consider in determining reliance on an agency relationship include, but are not limited to, the fact the hospital supplied the facilities, equipment, and medical personnel, and also set policies and procedures for the hospital. Perhaps more important, the court considers whether or not the patient looked to the institution, not the individual physician, for care and had a practical opportunity to choose other physicians.[40]

Corporate liability is another cause of action that courts have used to hold hospitals liable for the actions of their providers in the absence of an agency relationship. Corporate liability extends the scope of a hospital's potential liability. Under this doctrine, a hospital may be directly liable for medical errors on the part of physicians selected by and under contract with the hospital, a common practice for physicians in a few specialties (e.g., emergency room medicine, anesthesiology, pathology, and radiology). They can also be held directly liable for medical errors of physicians who have been reviewed by the medical staff for privileges and selected by the patient for treatment.[41]

The transition from the days of the charitable immunity doctrine, which protected most hospitals from liability for actions undertaken by medical staff, to agency and corporate liability has been gradual, with the effect that only since about 2000 has hospital medical malpractice been widely considered to be a major issue.[42]

Under corporate liability the hospital is directly liable for the negligent acts of its medical personnel, even those working on a contract basis. Thus, a plaintiff can sue the hospital directly, omitting the need to prove the existence of an agency relationship.[43] Unlike enterprise liability, to be discussed next, corporate liability does not consolidate the causes of action; a plaintiff may sue the hospital in addition to individual health care providers. It is also necessary for the plaintiff to prove the physician's malpractice as a prerequisite to a valid claim against the hospital.

One of the most important elements the plaintiff needs to prove in order for a claim to be successful under a corporate liability theory is that the hospital breached one of its duties.[44] The court in *Thompson v. Nason*[45] explains the hospital's duties in its opinion. Labeled the "Thompson duties," they are "to use reasonable care in the maintenance of safe and adequate facilities and equipment; to select and retain only competent physicians;[46] to oversee all persons who practice medicine within its walls as to patient care; and to formulate, adopt, and enforce adequate rules and policies to ensure quality care for the patients."[47]

Although the breach of one of these four duties is essential to the case, absent obvious negligence, the prima facie case against the hospital is made up of three parts. First, there must be a breach of duty; second, there must be actual or constructive notice of the defects or procedures that created the harm; and the final element is proving that the hospital's conduct was a substantial factor in causing the harm.[48] Many states have adopted corporate liability through case law, and these duties have also been codified by the Joint Commission on the Accreditation of Healthcare Organizations (JCAHO), as well as state legislators and hospitals.[49] However, without specific legislation, it is unlikely that liability will progress past corporate liability, forgoing the benefits of consolidated claims.

Enterprise Liability for Hospitals: An Attractive Reform That Faces Political Obstacles

Definition and Rationale

Under enterprise liability, the hospital would be the named defendant in lawsuits brought by plaintiffs who allege they were injured as a consequence of care received while they were being treated at the hospital. Separate suits against individual physicians would not be filed. This is in contrast to enterprise insurance, where the enterprise would be the insurer of physician defendants, but would be named in lawsuits only under the doctrine of vicarious liability just described. In this important sense, enterprise liability is a larger change from the status quo than is enterprise insurance.

The concept of enterprise liability for hospitals is at least three decades old. In 1975, Myron Steves, then a partner in an excess and surplus lines insurance agency in Houston, Texas, proposed "shifting liability exposure and the cost of insuring it from individual practitioners to institutional providers for incidents occurring within institutional settings."[50] He further proposed that exposure to nonhospital risk be insured separately on an individual basis. He advocated that hospitals self-insure for medical malpractice expense coupled with aggregate excess insurance (reinsurance) for high losses.

In addition to the advantages of enterprise insurance discussed above, Steves argued that once it is exposed to medical malpractice lawsuits for care delivered within its walls, the hospital would have an incentive to develop databases for medical injuries as well as claims. Hospitals are well positioned to assemble such data, certainly compared to physician practices (except for large medical groups). Steves also proponed that if a case goes to trial, there is an advantage to defendants in presenting a common defense. With 25 percent of malpractice suits involving more than one defendant, a common defense would consolidate many of the costs associated with filing, litigating, and defending a suit.[51] There would be fewer attorneys involved, lower court costs, and a lesser amount of related legal expenses. In addition, with only one defendant, the need for adversarial litigation tactics would be decreased because the defendants do not have competing interests; thus negotiation and settlement time are reduced.

Left unsaid in general discussions of enterprise liability is specifically how the burden of hospital premiums would be shared. It would be advisable that physicians bear some part of the premium burden to provide some incentive to avoid claims. Hospitals could implement their own systems of surcharging physicians with many medical malpractice claims. Of course, hospitals, or medical staffs operating on their behalf, would retain the option of removing physicians with adverse claims experience or those who do not comply with hospital patient safety regimens from their medical staffs. In fact, they would have a greater incentive than they do currently to monitor physician performance and to remove physicians with adverse claims experience.

Comparison with Enterprise Insurance

Enterprise insurance does not change the cause of action against physicians and hospitals, nor does it change the named defendants. Enterprise insurance merely shifts the identity of the insurer from commercial insurance to an insurer linked to the enterprise. Because enterprise insurance does not alter the nature or function of a malpractice case, it remains in the best interest of each defendant to assert a defense that would exonerate him- or herself, regardless of fellow defendants. Theories of defense from the various defendants can be contradictory, and proceedings between the parties, such as settlement negotiations, are adversarial. In some cases, individual defendants settle, leaving the hospital to litigate the claim.[52]

With enterprise liability, claims against various physicians and other providers are consolidated into one cause of action against the hospital. This shifts liability from physicians to the hospital, making the hospital responsible for defending its choices and also the quality of its providers, among other things. The hospital also would be responsible for the negligence and errors of its physicians. Actions can be brought for negligent hiring (not properly reviewing providers' credentials), breach of duty to provide adequate health care,[53] and failure to maintain facilities. This is by no means an exhaustive list. Regardless of what theory the case is brought under, the defense will be common to both hospital and provider, as the hospital has a vested financial interest in vindicating itself and its providers.

The Clinton Administration's Attempt to Incorporate Enterprise Liability in its Health Reform Program

To date, the only federal legislation regarding enterprise liability was contained in the Health Security Act of 1993, a major proposal of the Clinton administration's first term. The Clinton plan proposed imposing enterprise liability on health plans, thereby transferring liability from physicians to the health plan.

Having health plans assume physician liability is deficient for several reasons. First and foremost, the typical physician contracts with a number of health plans. Multiplicity of plans has deterred widespread use of plan-specific practice guidelines. Further, there has been substantial entry, exit, and mergers of health plans. This provides an unstable anchor for a long-tail line such as medical malpractice insurance.

Particularly following the revolt against managed care in the 1990s, it seems highly unlikely that anyone would advocate that liability be transferred to such plans. Physicians were never enthusiastic about this aspect of the Clinton proposal, which promoted managed care more generally. Both patients and providers were uncomfortable with the notion of "corporate healing."[54]

Objections to Enterprise Liability

Even with the hospital designated as the enterprise, various groups have expressed concerns about enterprise liability. A major concern is that by removing an individual physician's liability, the incentive for deterrence would be lost.[55] But if this objection is at all sincere, there is little empirical evidence that the threat of tort liability—as it exists today—deters injuries.

With hospital enterprise liability, the deterrent would be internalized to the hospital. These organizations could impose a combination of financial and nonfinancial incentives for individual physicians to prevent injuries, coupled with increased surveillance measures. Also, the hospital and physicians at the hospital collectively would have an incentive to promote patient safety since the enterprise's premiums would depend on future anticipated losses from medical malpractice claims.

A second objection is that enterprise liability would create a deep pocket which would increase claims frequency, primarily because tort claimants would be more successful in obtaining higher compensation from supposedly rich and faceless institutions, many of which have headquarters in a distant city, than from individual physicians practicing in their own communities.[56] But some insurers presumably have deep pockets as well.

Third, enterprise liability may restrict patient choice of provider. Physicians may have to limit their admissions to the one hospital at which they receive medical malpractice health insurance coverage. Physicians frequently have privileges at more than one hospital. This potential concern can be largely remedied by limiting physician coverage to care delivered within the walls of the facility under the hospital's policy. Thus, if a physician practiced at three hospitals, he or she would be covered under three hospital policies. In addition, the physician would need to obtain medical malpractice insurance for care delivered in the office, but such coverage would be at a greatly reduced premium.

Fourth, physicians complain about the trend in loss of autonomy. Enterprise liability would probably exacerbate this trend. An argument for autonomy is that it allows providers to use their professional skill and judgment in particularized situations. Outsiders, such as hospitals (or health plan review boards) may not be well positioned to know all the details and considerations evident in a physician-patient interaction. Furthermore, enterprise liability may increase the bargaining power of hospitals and health plans vis-á-vis individual physicians. This may be so, but there is no reason to believe that the current power relationship between hospitals and individual medical staff members is ideal. Physicians have much more autonomy in U.S. hospitals than do their counterparts in most other countries.

Fifth, inpatient care is shrinking as a share of the total personal health care dollar. More care is being delivered on an ambulatory basis. So, as Danzon writes, "It is increasingly anachronistic to view the hospital as the focus of care and hence as the best locus of liability."[57] But this concern disregards another trend. Hospital-provided ambulatory care is growing, and hospital enterprise liability would encompass care at all sites at which the hospital organization or system provides care.

Bottom Line on Advantages and Disadvantages of Enterprise Liability

Enterprise liability, despite its drawbacks, addresses many aspects of the malpractice crisis, including patient safety. A major barrier is that a political constituency for enterprise liability is lacking at both federal and state levels. Health care consumers are not well organized. Providers appear to be concerned about the "deep pockets" argument as well as potential loss of autonomy, and at the same time hospitals and health plans apparently see no evidence that assuming liability for physicians and other providers would make them more attractive in the marketplace.[58]

Incentives to Encourage Adoption of Enterprise Insurance or Enterprise Liability

Given that existing market forces have not led to adoption of either enterprise insurance or enterprise liability, what types of specific policy interventions may be implemented to encourage its adoption by hospitals and their medical staffs?

As already noted, legislation is needed for enterprise liability to exist. Presumably legislation could also contain a provision forcing physicians to participate in at least one hospital's program. Another compulsory approach would be for Medicare to require participating hospitals to have patient safety programs which would include enterprise insurance as a component.

Rather than use the stick to promote enterprise liability, there are also carrots. One approach would be to offer public reinsurance to hospitals with insurance plans that satisfy certain criteria. Hospitals with qualified plans could be granted the option of offering no-fault plans as an alternative to tort. Abraham and Weiler contend that implementation of enterprise liability may be a stepping-stone on the road to no-fault.[59] What they seem to have in mind as an ultimate goal is a universal no-fault of the type that has been implemented in a few countries. However, recognizing the difficulty in moving to a mandatory strict medical liability system, they propose an elective version of no-fault.[60] What is proposed here follows the same premise—a voluntary plan offered as an alternative to tort by individual hospitals.

Reforms Possibly Linked to Provision of Enterprise Insurance and/or Enterpriase Liability

Public Reinsurance/Excess Insurance

Public reinsurance or excess insurance (when applied to hospitals) plans have worked well when premiums have been set on an actuarial basis with loss reserving by policy year rather than on a pay-as-you-go basis, thresholds for coverage are indexed for inflation, and there is experience rating of reinsurance premiums (chapter 10). A rationale for public provision is that (1) high premiums on private reinsurance contracts reflect a high cost of risk bearing and (2) there are cycles in availability and premiums that can be very disruptive to primary insurers.

Although provision of publicly subsidized excess insurance would be attractive to hospitals, it may be difficult to offer coverage at actuarially fair premiums that are *appreciably* below premiums prevailing in the private reinsurance market, given that a public program would face risk of catastrophic loss similar to that of its private counterparts. However, public monies could be used to fund a pool to cover possible shortfalls. This public expenditure could be limited by restricting availability of public coverage to those hospitals with qualified enterprise insurance plans. To the extent that PCFs reduce volatility of availability and premiums in the reinsurance/excess insurance market, volatility in the overall market for medical malpractice insurance would be reduced.[61]

Voluntary No-Fault

No-fault insurance has several attractive features relative to tort: in particular, low administrative expense and speedier payment. Coverage of monetary losses may be broader, while payment for nonmonetary loss is likely to be more restricted. The hospital could be allowed to charge patients a premium if they opt for the no-fault plan. This premium would be a net savings to the institution from eliminating tort claims.

A hospital with a good patient safety record may find it advantageous to offer no-fault insurance. The very fact that such insurance is being offered may be taken as a signal that the hospital/medical staff have confidence in the safety record of the hospital. It would be expected that hospitals would be open about events that led to injury. However, it would be counterproductive to impose an obligation of disclosure on such plans absent a claim, unless it was in the business interest of the hospital to do so.

It is important, however, that coverage extend to a large number of conditions. Exclusions from coverage would need to be broad and easily understood by patients. Very narrow thresholds, such as those in existence in Florida and Virginia, are difficult for patients to assess in advance of injuries. A few very costly procedures may be excluded from coverage, but it would be important that these be listed and described in understandable terms in advance.

Patients would contract for no-fault coverage well in advance of receiving care at the hospital, thus avoiding situations in which they have an active health condition and face immediately at point of service, which could be interpreted in legal terminology as an adhesion contract.[62] For employer-sponsored plans, it would be a simple matter for an employee to designate whether or not he or she wishes to substitute no-fault for tort. The employee would select a plan for services and receive services from the specific hospital with which that plan contracts. Surcharges for no-fault (if surcharges are imposed on patients) would then be built into the premium charged. Or, alternatively, payment (presumably a higher one) could be made at the time the employees/families present at the hospital for care.

In the case of voluntary no-fault, since insured patients would agree not to sue under tort, the savings in tort payments would offset at least part of the cost of the no-fault plan. Other options, such as for the use of alternative dispute resolution mechanisms, could also be made on this basis.

No-fault plans would require prior regulatory approval, depending on the applicable regulatory authority. Regulators would pay attention to the method of enrolling persons into the plan, pricing, and issues bearing on plan solvency.

This type of voluntary no-fault program would offer several important advantages to hospitals and their medical staffs. First, it would relieve providers of the threat of tort. Second, offering no-fault benefits would be a signal that the hospital has an effective patient safety program and low rates of medical errors and injuries. Third, to the extent that injury victims value quick payments with little involvement of attorneys, this should increase demand for the hospital's services as well.

A universal compulsory no-fault program is infeasible in the United States. Unlike the countries that have adopted no-fault for medical injuries, the United States lacks universal health insurance coverage. It seems improbable that the United States would give such priority to persons with ioatrogenic injuries over all other possible reasons for obtaining medical care.

Reforming Determination of Liability and Damages

Health Courts

The rationale for health courts—that lay juries and even judges lack the extensive technical background needed to understand complex evidence—is part of a much larger issue about the use of scientific evidence in the courts more generally. Health courts represent only one of several nonmutually exclusive alternatives for addressing this issue. These alternatives include (1) use of court-appointed experts, (2) bifurcated trials, (3) use of special masters, (4) specially convened expert panels, (5) blue ribbon juries, and (6) alternative dispute resolution.[63]

Under trial bifurcation, the court tries liability and damages at separate stages of litigation. Bifurcation helps to limit the number of issues that a judge or jury must consider in a single trial. Special masters may be appointed at any stage in the trial process. They possess special expertise in the issues at hand, and can aid the court in assessing important technical issues. Court-appointed experts or expert panels can be used to present evidence in a more neutral fashion than experts appointed by the litigants who have an incentive to present one side of the evidence. Unfortunately, with this method, the other side of the evidence may not be revealed during cross examination either because the cross examining attorney lacks the expertise to effectively probe into narrow technical issues or because the expert simply stonewalls. Blue-ribbon juries might be drawn from a pool of experts on a given topic.

For example, in assessing liability and damages in a case involving a brain-damaged infant, the jury might be composed of obstetricians, pediatricians, special educators, psychologists, social workers, clergy, and others who have professional and practical experience in dealing with individuals (and families) with such injuries. By contrast, a blue-ribbon jury for a failure to diagnose cancer case might include a radiologist, a pathologist, a sonographer, and a risk communication expert.

States might consider health courts as an option. Nevertheless, we are reluctant to give this option our enthusiastic endorsement. Preserving juries in some form, even if they are blue-ribbon juries, would provide broader representation of perspectives and values than would sole reliance on a narrow group of professionals to make judgments on specific cases. Even a judge with health expertise will not be able to be expert on the full range of issues health courts are likely to confront. In the end, as Mehlman acknowledges, it is important that any health court be viewed as legitimate by plaintiffs as well as defendants.[64] If the court consists entirely of or is dominated by physicians and other health professionals, buy-in by plaintiffs seems highly improbable.

Scheduled Damages

There is widespread concern about the variability and unpredictability of damages, especially for nonmonetary loss. Although only a very small fraction of legal disputes ever reach verdict, results at verdict presumably guide settlement negotiations. The major public policy response of the states has been to impose a cap on nonmonetary damages or on total damages.

Such caps have two virtues. First, they are simple to administer. Second, there is empirical evidence that imposing caps reduces payments for damages and for administrative expense (chapter 5), which is plausibly the reason that they have received so much political support.

Caps are flawed because they assume that unjustifiable variability and unpredictability are much more common for severe injuries, a premise for which empirical support is lacking. Also, the vast majority of caps are not indexed for inflation. Thus, unless states explicitly change the statutes, over time the real value of the cap will approach zero. This approach amounts to taking away individuals' access to recovery through tort via the back door. A more direct (and honest) approach would be to legislate an end to recovery on grounds of medical malpractice.

As explained in chapter 5, there is some academic support for the view that there should be no payment for nonmonetary loss, but there is also substantial academic support for the position that such payments should be made. Whatever the intellectual arguments are, explicitly eliminating payment for nonmonetary loss is not an achievable reform. And there is a long history of paying for nonmonetary loss in the United Stated, at least back to the late nineteenth century, when Civil War veterans were paid pensions based in part on such loss. Achieving this goal by the back door—that is, specifying caps in nominal terms and not updating them— seems to be feasible. A cap fixed in nominal dollars is not a policy that the advocates of such damage caps would like to be applied to themselves.

The U.S. Congress could hypothetically decide to freeze physicians' fees paid by Medicare for reasons of simplicity and cost containment. Such a policy would be vehemently opposed by the advocates of nominal caps on damages, such as California's, which have not been increased since 1975. All told, if variability, predictability, and accuracy of loss determination are to be improved, this goal should be accomplished in a way other than flat caps fixed in nominal dollars.

Several approaches for achieving this goal, in particular with regard to nonmonetary damages, have been proposed.[65] None of them have been implemented to date.

At one extreme, all proposals for scheduling damages will be opposed by the organized trial bar on grounds that they limit jury discretion in awarding damages. There is a trade-off between complete

individualization of awards and reducing volatility and increasing predictability of awards. At the other extreme, groups representing defendants will object to proposed alternatives to the present system, including
flat caps, on grounds that they are needlessly complex. These same
groups, however, tend to have no problem with complexity when their
reimbursement is involved.

Rather than select among the various proposals that have been published or among many others that might be developed, it is the notion
of scheduling and its feasibility that is endorsed here. States should carefully examine the options, listening to experts on all sides. No system
for scheduling nonmonetary loss can be perfect, and states are likely to
differ in their assessments of the importance of various advantages and
deficiencies.

In any event, total loss should not be scheduled or capped. However,
it would be appropriate for states to review the instructions that are
provided to juries in order to assess whether guidelines for determination
of monetary loss should be developed. Cost-benefit and cost-effectiveness
analysis are becoming more widely used, and some developments in these
fields may be usefully applied to damage assessment in medical
malpractice.

Contracts for Services

Service contracts, described in chapter 5, represent a missed opportunity
for organizations that are sufficiently vertically integrated, and can add
some additional integration, to offer care on a comprehensive basis to
persons with severe medical injuries. Large academic health centers
(AHCs) are such organizations. The contracts combine service provision
and insurance functions. An AHC would at most very rarely have an
affiliation with an insurer. AHCs could find insurer partners and market
such contracts as a joint venture. Being involved in such contracting
would provide potential teaching and research opportunities as well.

The two small no-fault programs in Florida and Virginia have gained
experience with managing the care of severely impaired children over the
life course (to date only the first part of the life course). Admittedly, such
contracting is a great idea in principle, but in practice, AHCs may not
be ready for this. However, as cost containment pressures from payers,

including Medicare, continue to build, this type of program may look increasingly attractive.

Final Word

In a very readable and useful book, Tom Baker exposes the myths of medical malpractice.[66] By contrast, the present book has described only a few of these myths. Perhaps the myths have had the positive effect of alerting the public and their elected representatives to the medical malpractice issue. The myths and the name calling have had the unfortunate consequence of leading to adoption of both ineffective and often misguided public policies. In particular, there is a missed opportunity in not aligning the financial incentives for patient safety with the rhetoric that medical care is unsafe and considering medical malpractice as something to be limited rather than reformed in a way that it could be more effective in achieving its deterrence function. In sum, we should and can do better.

Notes

Chapter 1

1. This is discussed in chapter 4.

2. Chapter 12 addresses the prospects for medical malpractice to have a productive role in injury prevention.

3. Kersh (2006).

4. It is helpful to outline the functions and goals of the tort system both generally and in relation to medical malpractice. These points are explained much more fully in textbooks on tort law and on law and economics. See, e.g., Shapo (2003) and Micelli (2004). To begin with, medical malpractice is a cause of action within the law of torts. Torts are neither criminal nor contractual in nature, although some torts are also crimes punishable by imprisonment. In a civil action for tort, the plaintiff attempts to hold the defendant liable for causing harm to his or her person or property, whether or not the defendant's actions were deliberate or simply careless. If the plaintiff is successful, the court shifts the plaintiff's loss to the defendant by granting either monetary compensation or an equitable remedy. Tort doctrines are largely in the state domain and have evolved over centuries from both common and statutory law.

In tort, an injury is not enough to obtain damages. The plaintiff must prove four elements for a successful claim in medical malpractice tort cases. These elements do not apply to all tort actions. There are three different categories of tort—intentional, negligent, and strict liability—each with different requirements for proof of liability. The vast majority of medical malpractice cases are negligent torts. However, battery is a type of intentional tort that has been used in medical malpractice cases. Usually a battery case involves lack of informed consent or failure to respect an advance directive, and requires a showing of voluntary intentional action, not negligence.

Those who cannot demonstrate each element receive no compensation. These elements are (1) the defendant owed a duty of care (duty), (2) he or she failed to conform to the required standard of care (breach of duty), (3) this failure was the proximate cause of the plaintiff's injury (causation), and (4) the plaintiff suffered either pecuniary or emotional damages (damages). Most medical malpractice lawsuits are filed as negligent tort actions, as opposed to strict liability, or as an intentional tort. To prove negligence, plaintiffs must present evidence that is convincing to a jury on three criteria: an injury occurred; an action or inaction of the defendant caused the injury; and the action or inaction represents a failure to exercise due care. Nevertheless, even when a plaintiff is successful in proving the negligence of the defendant, if the plaintiff suffered only a minor injury, he or she should not expect much compensation.

5. Dram shop statutes make alcohol servers liable for subsequent accidents caused by persons who drank in their establishment or were under the legal drinking age (Sloan, Stout, Whetten-Goldstein, et al. 2000).

6. White (2004).

7. Sturgis (1995, p. 8). Whether compensation can be provided at a lower cost and more equitably through public and private insurance systems is a point of contention, and will be discussed at length later in this book.

8. This is discussed further in chapter 3.

9. This is discussed further in chapter 6.

10. State of Maryland (2004, p. 24).

11. Vidmar (1998, 2004).

12. Sloan, Bovbjerg, and Githens (1991).

13. Abraham (2001).

14. See, e.g., Mello and Studdert (2006); Sloan (1990).

15. Experience rating is discussed further in chapter 3.

16. Schwartz and Mendelson (1989).

17. See, e.g., Shavell (1980).

18. See, e.g., Perssons and Tabillini (2002); Sloan and Hsieh (1990).

19. E.g., Becker (1983); Posner (1976); Stigler (1971).

20. This is discussed in more detail in chapter 10.

21. Hickson et al. (1992, 1994, 2002); Sloan and Hsieh (1995); Farber and White (1991); Nalebuff (1987); Nalebuff and Scharfstein (1987); May and Stengel (1990); Sieg (2000).

22. Weiler et al. (1993); Mills, Boyden, and Rubsamen (1977).

23. E.g., Danzon and Lillard (1983); Sloan and Hsieh (1990).

24. Sloan et al. (1993).

25. Ibid.

26. Sloan, Whetten-Goldstein, et al. (1998).

27. Bovbjerg and Sloan (1998).

28. Vidmar (1995, 2003).

29. Helland and Taborrok (2003).

30. Bovbjerg (1991).

31. See, e.g., Doherty, Lamm-Tennant, and Starks (2003); Doherty and Posey (1997); Nye and Hofflander (1987); Lai et al. (2000); Winter (1988, 1994).

32. Shavell (1987).

33. E.g., Fournier and McInnes (2001); Ellis, Gallup, and McGuire (1990); Sloan and Hassan (1990).

34. Sloan (1990).

35. Schwartz and Mendelson (1989).

36. Sloan, Bovbjerg, and Githens (1991).

37. Schlesinger and Venezian (1986).

38. Hoerger, Sloan, and Hassan (1990).

39. Danzon (1985, 1994).

40. Danzon, Pauly, and Kingston (1990).

41. Kessler and McClellan (1996); Localio et al. (1993); Sloan, Entman, et al. (1997).

42. Institute of Medicine (2000).

43. Entman, Glass, Hickson, et al. (1994).

44. Sloan, Mergenhagen, Burfield, et al. (1989).

45. Danzon (1994).

46. Sloan, Mergenhagen, and Bovbjerg (1989); Danzon (1986); Zuckerman, Bovbjerg, and Sloan (1990); Born and Viscusi (1994); Born, Viscusin and Carelton (1998); Sloan (1995).

47. Harrington (1994).

48. Sloan, Bovbjerg, and Githens (1991).

49. E.g., Shavell (1987).

50. See, e.g., Tinetti, Bogardus, and Agostini (2004).

51. Discussed in chapter 3.

52. E.g., Abraham (1986).

53. B. L. Smith (1992); Munch and Smallwood (1980); Hay (1996).

54. Both sides must answer questions during the discovery process. Experts on both sides are deposed. During a trial, each witness is examined directly and is subject to cross-examination.

55. Mills, Boyden, and Rubsamen (1977).

56. Weiler et al. (1993).

57. This is discussed further in chapter 8.

58. Studdert, Mello, and Brennan (2004).

59. See chapter 8 for further discussion.

60. Sieg (2000).

61. Hoerger, Sloan, and Hassan (1990).

Chapter 2

1. Underwriting standards are the criteria insurers use for deciding whether or not to insure an individual or an organization.

2. There are some differences in dating of the cycles. For example, some would start the cycle of the mid-1970s in 1974. See graphs at http://www.iii.org/media/facts/statsbyissue/pcinscycle/ (accessed July 21, 2006).

3. See, e.g., T. Baker (2005b).

4. Discussed in chapter 7.

5. See chapter 6.

6. Keynesian economics is based on the ideas of the twentieth-century British economist John Maynard Keynes. Keynesian economics promotes a mixed economy in which both the state and the private sector play an important role; more specifically, it advocates monetary and fiscal programs run by the government to increase employment and spending. Keynesian economics is in contrast with laissez-faire economics, an economic theory based on the belief that markets and the private sector can operate well on their own, without state intervention (Doherty and Posey 1987).

7. Sloan, Bovbjerg, and Githens (1991).

8. See chapter 10 for a discussion on reinsurance.

9. Health insurance is a type of first-party insurance. It provides coverage for losses the individual himself or herself incurs. For instance, if a car hits a fence while backing out of the garage, automobile collision insurance covers the loss. The threshold of evidence required for payment tends to be much lower for first-party than for third-party insurance. For the former, it is only necessary to show that an accident and loss co-occurred. Complex causation and negligence issues are avoided. For this reason, the overhead of such insurance tends to be far lower than for third-party insurance.

10. Rosenblatt (2004).

11. Sloan, Bovbjerg, and Githens (1991).

12. This may be somewhat of an overestimate, since these estimates seem to start with the date the injury occurred, and the vast majority of policies sold since the 1970s are sold on a claims-made basis.

13. Some medical malpractice insurers invest heavily in stocks (see Percy 2004), but these are in the minority.

14. Kaufman and Ryan (2000, p. 3); Best (1998).

15. See chapter 10 for a detailed discussion of reinsurance.

16. Market risk is risk that the value of the security will fall; credit risk is the risk that the company will be unable to pay its fixed obligations to investors.

17. Danzon (1985) suggests that the increase in medical malpractice premiums during the 1970s may have reflected an increase in the correlation between investment and underwriting returns, the latter reflecting the difference between premium income and expenses attributable to payments to claimants, legal expense, and other administrative expense associated with issuing insurance policies. Insurers not only derive cash flow from investments but, to the extent that returns on investments have no relationship to or are negatively related to underwriting returns, investing provides a method of diversifying away risk. If returns become more positively correlated, the diversification advantage of investments diminishes. As a consequence, one would expect premiums to rise. There is no good evidence that the correlation has been changing or, if it has, in which direction the change has occurred.

18. This time interval is far too short for insurers to have learned anything material about loss development during that policy year.

19. According to the U.S. General Accounting Office (June 2003, p. 15), after adjusting for inflation, the mean annual increase in paid losses was about 3.0 percent between 1988 and 1997, but for 1998–2001, the mean annual rate of increase in paid losses was 8.2 percent. This rate of increase was plausibly reflected in higher initial incurred losses after 2000.

20. In much of the latter part of the twentieth century, and to a lesser extent at the beginning of the twenty-first, economists studying both firm and consumer behavior have typically assumed that firms are rational. Some financial models applied to insurance pricing build on the rational expectations hypothesis. That is, insurers combine all available information on future expected losses and administrative expense to form informationally efficient predictors of future losses (Fairley 1979; Moridaira, Urrutia, and Witt 1992; Kraus and Ross 1982; Myers and Cohn 1987; Hill 1979). Further, the standard assumption is that there are no "agency" problems. That is, insiders in the firm act to maximize the value of their employing organizations.

   However, both earlier and more recent studies relax these assumptions, allowing for nonrational behavior and agency problems. Assumptions of rationality and lack of agency problems are sometimes made for convenience.

21. Nye and Hofflander (1987, p. 502).

22. The word is derived from the Greek for "few sellers." Because the decisions of one firm influence and are influenced by the decisions of other firms, oligopolistic markets and industries are at the highest risk for collusion.

23. For simplicity, firm objectives are often assumed to be unitary in economic analysis. That is, the firm has a clear objective, such as profit maximization, which it pursues continually.

24. This type of argument is also made by Alice Rosenblatt (2004), an actuary, in explaining cycles in the context of health insurance.

25. Nye and Hofflander (1987, p. 502) provide empirical support for the loss extrapolation hypothesis for some, but not all, lines of property-liability insurance they investigated. They did not include medical malpractice insurance in their study.

26. See Sloan, Bovbjerg, and Githens (1991) for a discussion of such behavior.

27. United States General Accounting Office (June 2003).

28. Nye et al. (1988); United States General Accounting Office (June 2003).

29. Cummins and Outreville (1987).

30. However, the presence of these internal conflicts substantially complicates formal modeling of insurer behavior.

31. An example of behavior counter to the rational expectations hypothesis is setting premiums based on past losses (Venezian 1985).

32. Surowiecki (2004).

33. Interest rates not adjusted for inflation rates.

34. Mankiw (2007, p. 542).

35. United States Department of Commerce (2006, table 706).

36. Such as the discounted cash flow and the capital asset pricing models.

37. See, e.g., Myers and Cohn (1987).

38. E.g., Doherty and Garven (1995); Gron (1994b); Gron and Lucas (1998); Winter (1988, 1991, 1994).

39. Priest (1987).

40. Or, in another property-casualty insurance context, to a series of hurricanes.

41. Fung, Lai, Peterson, et al. (1998) report that surplus changes relate to premiums, but with a lag of from three to five years after the shock to surplus occurred. These authors also find interest rate effects on premiums, but again with a lag. An earlier study based on aggregate time series data from the property-casualty insurance industry for 1949–1990 by Gron (1994b) finds that the difference between the price of insurance and noncapital costs, referred to as the price-payment margin (PPM), varies with surplus (net assets), but with a lag, and increases and decreases in surplus have different effects on PPM.

42. Sloan, Bovbjerg, and Githens (1991).

43. Gron (1994a).

Chapter 3

1. State of Florida (2003, p. iii).

2. Ibid. (p. vi).

3. Ibid.

4. http://www/usatoday.com/news/washington/2005-01-05-bush-tort_x.htm, (accessed July 7, 2006).

5. Danzon, Pauly, and Kingston (1990, p. 122).

6. See, e.g., United States General Accounting Office (1995); United States Congress, Office of Technology Assessment (1994).

7. Microeconomics studies how individuals, households, and firms make decisions to allocate limited resources, typically in markets where goods or services are being bought and sold.

8. All economic models are abstractions. Economists evaluate the performance of a model not on the assumptions, which are inherently unrealistic, but on the accuracy of the predictions. The assumption of profit maximization has worked well in predicting responses to changes in factors exogenous to individual physicians, such as insurers' change in payment rates on physicians' fees and physicians' decisions to accept the insurers' payments as payment in full (see, e.g., Sloan, Cromwell, and Mitchell 1978). More complex models can incorporate more realism, but greater generality usually comes at a loss of the model's predictive ability.

9. United States Government Accountability Office (2005).

10. See, in particular, McGuire (2000); McGuire and Pauly (1991).

11. Bovbjerg and Berenson (2006, p. 223).

12. Sloan and Bovbjerg (1989); Sloan, Bovbjerg, and Githens (1991); Thorpe (2004).

13. See, for example, commentary by Thomas Young, MD, in his presidential address to the South Atlantic Association of Obstetrics and Gynecology in January 2005. He complains that reimbursement has seriously lagged increases in practice cost in general and the increases in medical malpractice premiums in particular. Young (2005).

14. Rodwin, Chang, and Clausen (2006).

15. Ibid.

16. United States Department of Commerce (2006).

17. See, e.g., Blumenthal (2004).

18. See, e.g., Fuchs (1978); E. F. Hughes et al. (1972).

19. See, e.g., Newhouse et al. (1982a, 1982b); Schwartz et al. (1980) and articles referenced therein.

20. Mello et al. (2005).

21. Brooks et al. (2005).

22. Sloan, Mergenhagen, et al. (1989).

23. Mello, Kelly, Studdert, et al. (2003, p. 227).

24. New Jersey Hospital Association (2002).

25. Luft (1980); Luft, Bunker, and Enthoven (1979).

26. A loading factor represents a dollar amount added to the expected loss in arriving at a premium.

27. Chapters 4 and 5.

28. United States General Accounting Office (June 2003, August 2003).

29. Mello, Studdert, and Brennan (2003).

30. United States General Accounting Office (June 2003, p. 5).

31. Sloan (1990).

32. United States Congress, Office of Technology Assessment (1994, p. 13).

33. Ibid. (p. 42).

34. Web of Science, http://scientific.thomson.com/products/wos (accessed September 15, 2005).

35. Kessler and McClellan (1996).

36. Caps on damages are statutorily set limits on the amount of compensation that can be awarded to the plaintiff for monetary and nonmonetary damages.

37. Punitive damages may be awarded when the defendant's action is found to have deliberately harmed the patient or to have represented conduct not befitting a professional. A few states have abolished punitive damages in medical malpractice cases (punitive damages are rarely paid in the context of medical malpractice).

38. Prejudgment interest refers to interest payments on the loss between the date of injury or date a lawsuit is filed, and the date the verdict is reached. Limits on prejudgment interest reduce such interest payments.

39. The common law allows the plaintiff to collect damages on elements of loss for which he or she has received payment from other sources. Statutory changes enacted by some states either have required that juries be informed of payments from collateral sources before they assess compensation for monetary loss, or that payments from collateral sources be deducted from compensation.

40. Caps on contingency fees limit a plaintiff's attorney's fees to a fixed percentage of the award or allow for judicial review of the proposed fee and approval of the fee depending on the outcome of the review.

41. Rather than pay damages as a lump sum, under periodic payments for future damages, payment is made only as long as the defendant lives or suffers from the injury.

42. Under the common-law joint and several liability rule, individual defendants in a tort suit can be held liable for the total amount of damages, irrespective of their actual share of liability. Under joint and several liability reform, states have limited an individual defendant's liability to his or her share of total liability.

43. A patient compensation fund (PCF) is a government-operated mechanism that pays the loss in excess of a statutorily determined amount. In one state, Pennsylvania, the dollar ceiling on payments by the PCF is so low that the PCF

has in effect provided a middle layer of coverage in recent years (see Sloan, Eesley, Conover, et al. 2005).

44. United States General Accounting Office (1993).

45. The lag may be relevant for claims frequency and premiums since there is a delay from the date of injury to the date the claim is filed, and the constitutionality of some reforms may be subsequently challenged. However, practice patterns are likely to respond much more quickly to such statutory changes.

46. The rationale for a three-year lag is less clear than for claims frequency and for premiums. When separate variables were defined for direct and indirect reforms, neither had statistically significant effects on recordkeeping, diagnostic tests, referrals for consultation, or time spent with patients. It is not clear that less recordkeeping and time spent with patients would be desired by most well-informed patients.

47. Sloan, Githen, Clayton, et al. (1993).

48. Localio et al. (1993).

49. Danzon (1994). Our review of the literature revealed no more recent studies.

50. Studdert, Mello, Sage, et al. (2005) report such statements. This type of study is subject to the same deficiencies mentioned during the discussion of physician supply.

51. In an otherwise excellent review, Danzon (2000, pp. 1370–1371) is not cautious about extrapolating these insignificant findings. She writes: "The point estimate is negative but not statistically significant. Taking this point estimate at face value and extrapolating would imply that tort liability reduced the rate of negligent injuries per admission by 29 percent (from 1.25 with no liability to 0.89 with the current system) and reduced the overall rate of medical injuries per admission by 11 percent (from 3.7 to 3.3). The failure to find significant effects may be influenced by the small sample (forty-nine hospitals) and imperfect instruments available. Moreover, at best these data would estimate the marginal effect of changes in liability over the limited range of variation in the New York sample. Considering these intrinsic limitations that bias against finding significant effects, together with other evidence that physicians do perceive a significant risk of suit and change their behavior in response to liability, Weiler et al. conclude that liability plausibly does have a significant deterrent effect.

This empirical evidence on deterrence benefits is consistent with the rough calculations by Danzon (1985): that under quite generous assumptions about the costs of defensive medicine, the malpractice system would pay for itself (yield positive net benefits) if it reduced negligent injury rates by at least 20 percent, ignoring such intangible benefits."

These conclusions push these statistically insignificant findings too far.

52. According to Mello and Brennan (2002): "Recognizing the limitations of the initial HMPS (Harvard Medical Practice Study), a different subgroup of

investigators later took a second stab at modeling deterrence. One of the investigators had done some additional work on constructing measures of deterrence, and we hoped that a more sophisticated model might yield more conclusive findings than the initial models had. Over a three-year period in the mid-1990s, several researchers in a variety of disciplines debated the proper specification of these models, often clashing over suggested approaches. The number of different models proliferated; by the conclusion of the project, the team had run models with four different measures of malpractice risk, two different outcome measures, and two different estimation strategies. In the end, we were unable to agree that any one model was correctly specified, and also could not agree on how to interpret the group of findings as a whole. As a result, we did not submit our findings for publication" (p. 1611). The outcome measures were the theoretically appropriate variables described in the text.

53. The survey data were also used in Hickson, Clayton, Entman, et al. (1994), described earlier.

54. There were several underlying actions/inactions used: for instance, substandard documentation and failure to counsel the patient about events or future risk appropriately. In addition, errors could be coincidental and unassociated with the outcome; associated with the adverse outcome but not related to either cause or preventability of the outcome; or to the outcome in such a way that the error may have caused or contributed to the adverse outcome; or missed the opportunity to prevent it.

55. Danzon (1994, 1985); Shavell (1980).

Chapter 4

1. See, e.g., Dao (2005) for states' responses to the most recent crisis: "The impending battles over malpractice costs have in some states been wrapped in the broader cloak of 'tort reform,' intended to restrict the civil liability of many types of businesses. They also come at a time when President Bush has pledged to push for federal restrictions on medical malpractice lawsuits. But in most of the states, soaring malpractice premiums have been the driving force for the campaigns—in part because compelling stories about doctors and their patients have put human faces on the larger issue."

2. See, e.g., Majoribanks et al. (1996).

3. Using data from interviews of physicians and attorneys, Peeples, Harris, and Metzloff (2000) report that most physicians who were sued did not believe that they were liable, and expressed a desire for vindication. The authors explain that there is a distinct cultural difference between law and medicine. At the risk of overgeneralizing, for lawyers, settlement is neutral and does not have a negative connotation. For physicians, settlement implies fault.

4. Danzon (2000).

5. *Ad damnum* clauses are used in a complaint to set a maximum amount of money that a plaintiff can recover under a default judgment if the defendant fails to appear in court. An *ad damnum* clause can also set an absolute limit on the amount of damages recoverable in the case, regardless of how much loss the plaintiff is able to prove at trial. The reasoning is that a defendant should not be exposed to liability greater than the *ad damnum* solely because he or she does not come to court and defend himself or herself. In most states and in the federal courts, a plaintiff can collect money damages in excess of the *ad damnum* if proof can be presented at trial to support the higher amount. http://www.answers.com/topic/ad-damnum (accessed October 2, 2006).

6. Barker (1992).

7. Both of these statutory changes are discussed in detail in chapter 6.

8. Bovbjerg (1995).

9. Both PCFs and JUAs are described in considerable detail in chapters 8 and 10.

10. In the late 1980s, Robert Rabin, a highly respected legal scholar of tort, concluded that the "time for a substantive reform of tort doctrine has largely passed. There is no turning back to the harsh world of wholesale exemptions from fault responsibility. Correlatively, there is no persuasive indication of a substantial move 'beyond' fault. . . . If modest improvements in the system are to be effected, the would-be reformer must look elsewhere than substantive doctrine" (Rabin 1988, p. 39).

11. Kinney (1995).

12. Scheduling damages is discussed in detail in chapter 5.

13. Generally, ADR is made up of any means of settling disputes outside of the courtroom. The two most frequently used forms are mediation and arbitration. Arbitration is basically a simplified version of litigation—without discovery and with simpler rules of evidence. In mediation an impartial third party facilitates an agreement in the common interest of all the parties involved.

14. There are many advantages, as well as several disadvantages, to arbitration. Some advantages are that its cost can be cheaper, the proceedings are generally private, there is more flexibility than in a court, and that when the subject of dispute is highly technical, arbitrators with the appropriate degree of expertise can be appointed. Two disadvantages are that the parties have to pay for the arbitrators, which adds an extra layer of legal expense, and that the rule of applicable law is not binding.

15. Mediation is different from arbitration in that mediation sessions are not decided in favor of one party or another. The mediator facilitates the negotiation process between the parties. In addition, the parties are not bound to resolve their dispute, and may pursue litigation if they are dissatisfied with the results of mediation.

16. See chapter 11 for a discussion of no-fault.

17. See chapter 6 for further discussion of this and related proposals.

18. Enterprise liability is discussed in greater detail in chapter 12.

19. Weiler (1991); Abraham and Weiler (1994).

20. Epstein (1978); Havighurst (1995).

21. If contracts are set at the group level, they may reflect preferences of the median group member, but there is likely to be substantial heterogeneity within the group, which would be lost in establishing a single standard for the group as a whole. Furthermore, as Danzon (2000, p. 1382) points out, if a provider tried to restrict care at the level of the individual patient in return for a lower fee, courts may view this as a contract of adhesion because it is patient-specific; the reasoning would be that an asymmetric power relationship exists between a physician and an individual patient.

22. Kinney (1995); United States General Accounting Office (1993).

23. Kinney cites a president of the American Medical Association who stated that no-fault approaches are "anti-professional" because they are "freeing physicians from the consequences of their actions" (Kinney 1995, p. 123).

24. Abraham and Weiler (1994).

25. The U.S. Congress has become involved in tort reform from time to time, but to date no important legislation has been enacted.

26. Whiteman (1985); Ray (1982); Kingdon (1981); Songer et al. (1985); Songer (1988).

27. Songer (1988).

28. Spiller and Vanden Bergh (2003). Not only are they common, but for some states, amendments are frequent. Louisiana's tenth constitution, adopted in 1921, was amended over 530 times before being replaced by a new constitution in 1972, which has subsequently been amended over fifty times (Tarr 1998). In 1998, eighteen states required only a simple majority to ratify an amendment (Tarr 1998).

29. There have been only twenty-seven successful amendments to the U.S. Constitution in 220 years.

30. Witt (2005).

31. The United States uses a common-law system as opposed to a civil-law system (used in Europe, Latin America, Quebec, and the state of Louisiana). In a civil-law system, judges look solely to statutes and written legal codes as the basis for their decisions. This is in contrast with a common-law system, where the judiciary does not rest its authority upon any express or positive statute or other written declaration, but upon statements of principles found in the decisions of courts. Some courts have defined common law as a law of necessity, to be applied only in the absence of explicit, controlling statutory law. See *Metropolitan Life Ins. Co. v. Strnad*, 255 Kan. 657 (1994); *State v. Lawrence*,

98 Idaho 399 (1977). In practice, most courts make rulings using legislation, written legal codes, and constitutions. However, these rulings are heavily informed by prior judicial decisions. For a detailed analysis of the difference between the two legal systems, and their developments, see Zweigert and Kötz (1987).

32. The benefit of a common-law system is that the common law is not static; it is dynamic and has an inherent capacity for growth and change. As described in *American Jurisprudence*: "It is to be derived from the interstices of prior opinions and a well-considered judgment of what is best for the community. Its development is informed by the application of reason and common sense to the changing conditions of society, or to the social needs of the community which it serves. It is constantly expanding and developing in keeping with advancing civilization and the new conditions and progress of society, and adapting itself to the gradual change of trade, commerce, arts, inventions, and the needs of the country. It is said that public policy is the dominant factor in the molding and remolding of common-law principles to the end that they may soundly serve the public welfare and the true interests of justice. The fact that no case remotely resembling the one at issue is uncovered does not paralyze the common-law system, which is endowed with judicial inventiveness to meet new situations." (Thomas 2006)

33. V. E. Schwartz, Behrens, and Lorber (2000). For an in-depth discussion of the politics of electoral accountability, see Tarr (2005).

34. Coolidge (1905, p. 213).

35. Statutes of repose, like statutes of limitation, place limits on how long after an injury a suit may be brought. However, repose statutes begin at the time of the negligent injury, not at the tie of discovery. Statutes of repose establish an outer limit for when a suit may be brought. This prevents doctors from being sued decades after a procedure is performed.

36. Krumlauf (2005). There were other changes in the law as well, which are not included in the list in the text. See Am. Sub. H.B. 350, 21st Leg., Reg. Sess. (Ohio 1996).

37. *State ex rel. Ohio Academy of Trial Lawyers v. Sheward*, 86 Ohio St. 3d 451; 1999 Ohio 123; 715 N.E.2d 1062.

38. The constitutionality of damage caps is explored separately in chapter 5.

39. The court cited the one-subject rule as the basis for declaring the statute unconstitutional. Provisions in legislation must unite to form a single subject for purposes of Section 15(D), Article II, of the Ohio Constitution. However, in a 1991 case the court held that a bill may contain more than one topic, so long as there is a common purpose or relationship between the topics. (See *Hoover*, 19 Ohio St. 3d at 6; 19 Ohio B. Rep. at 5; 482 N.E.2d at 580.) This bill affected eighteen different titles, thirty-eight different chapters, and over one hundred different sections of the Revised Code, as well as procedural and evidentiary rules and hitherto uncodified common law.

40. The constitution vests the legislative power of the state in the General Assembly (Section 1, Article II, Ohio Constitution), the executive power in the governor (Section 5, Article III, Ohio Constitution), and the judicial power in the courts (Section 1, Article IV, Ohio Constitution). The constitution also specifies that "the general assembly shall [not] . . . exercise any judicial power, not herein expressly conferred" (Section 32, Article II, Ohio Constitution; *State ex rel. Ohio Academy of Trial Lawyers v. Sheward*, 86 Ohio St. 3d 451; 1999 Ohio 123; 715 N.E.2d 1062). In 2005, the Arkansas Supreme Court challenged the constitutionality of its tort reform altering the statute of limitations (*Davis v. Parham*, 2005 Ark. LEXIS 300). But using the rational basis test, the court ruled the statute had a rational relationship between the burden of proof required and a legitimate government objective. Similarly, a 1981 case in the Alabama Supreme court challenged the statute of limitations in the tort reform act (*Reese v. Rankin Fite Memorial Hospital*, 403 So. 2d 158; 1981 Ala. LEXIS 3630). The court upheld the statute, saying, ". . . we cannot substitute our judgment for that of the legislative branch, whose enactments come to us clothed with a presumption of validity."

41. Krumlauf (2005).

42. Ohio courts have consistently held that challenges to legislation should be brought in an action in the Court of Common Pleas rather than an extraordinary writ to the Supreme Court. See *State ex rel. Gaydosh v. Twinsburg* (2001), 93 Ohio St.3d 576, 579; 2001 Ohio 1613; 757 N.E.2d 357; and *Rammage v. Saros*, 97 Ohio St.3d 430, 431; 2002 Ohio 6669, at P11; 780 N.E.2d 278.

43. *Strahler v. St. Luke's Hosp.*, 706 S.W.2d 7; 1986 Mo. LEXIS 248; 62 A.L.R.4th 735.

44. § 516.105 R.S.Mo. (2006).

45. Missouri Constitution, Art. I, §14.

46. See *Reese v. Rankin Fite Memorial Hospital*, 403 So.2d 158 (Ala. 1981); *Eastin v. Broomfield*, 116 Ariz. 576 (1977); *Gay v. Rabon*, 652 S.W.2d 836 (1983); *Lacy v. Green*, Del. Super., 428 A.2d 1171 (1981); *Pinillos v. Cedars of Lebanon Hospital Corporation*, 403 So.2d 365 (Fla. 1981); *LePelley v. Grefenson*, 614 P.2d 962 (1980); *Anderson v. Wagner*, 402 N.E.2d 560, *appeal dismissed* 449 U.S. 807, (1979); *Johnson v. St. Vincent Hospital, Inc.*, 404 N.E.2d 585 (1980); *Rudolph v. Iowa Methodist Medical Center*, 293 N.W.2d 550 (Iowa 1980); *Stephens v. Snyder Clinic Association*, 631 P.2d 222 (1981); *Everett v. Goldman*, 359 So.2d 1256 (La. 1978); *Attorney General v. Johnson*, 385 A.2d 57, *appeal dismissed* 439 U.S. 805 (1978); *Paro v. Longwood Hospital*, 369 N.E.2d 985 (1977); *Linder v. Smith*, 629 P.2d 1187 (Mont. 1981); *Prendergast v. Nelson*, 256 N.W.2d 657 (1977); *Perna v. Pirozzi*, 457 A.2d (1983); *Armijo v. Tandysh*, 646 P.2d 1245 (1981), *overruled by Roberts v. Southwest Community Health Servs.*, 837 P.2d 442 (1992); *Comiskey v. Arlen*, 390 N.Y.S.2d 122 (1976); *Roberts v. Durham County Hospital Corporation*, 289 S.E.2d 875 (1982), *aff'd*, 298 S.E.2d 384 (1983); *Beatty v. Akron City Hospital*, 424 N.

E.2d 586 (1981); *Allen v. Intermountain Health Care, Inc.*, 635 P.2d 30 (1981); *Duffy v. King Chiropractic Clinic*, 565 P.2d 435 (1977); *State ex rel. Strykowski v. Wilkie*, 261 N.W.2d 434 (1978); *Woods v. Holy Cross Hospital*, 591 F.2d 1164 (5th Cir. 1979); *DiAntonio v. Northampton-Accomack Memorial Hospital*, 628 F.2d 287, 291–292 (4th Cir. 1980); *Fitz v. Dolyak*, 712 F.2d 330 (8th Cir. 1983). The California Supreme Court held that its statutory provision regarding periodic payment of future damages was constitutional because it did not deny due process, equal protection, or trial by jury. *American Bank and Trust Company v. Community Hospital of Los Gatos-Saratoga, Inc.*, 683 P.2d 670 (1984).

47. *Strahler v. St. Luke's Hosp.*, 706 S.W.2d 7 (Mo. Ganc 1986). The *Lochner* era is a period in American legal history (1890–1937) during which the U.S. Supreme Court struck down many economic regulations. Many criticize the *Lochner* era as a regrettable period in U.S. jurisprudence; this view is embodied by the term "to Lochnerize," which connotes fundamental judicial error (Cloud 1996). *Lochner v. New York*, 198 U.S. 45 (1905).

48. U.S. Congressional Budget Office (2004, pp. 8–9).

49. These summaries have been prepared by the Council of State Governments, the National Governors' Association, the National Conference of State Legislatures, the U.S. General Accounting Office, and the Office of Technology Assessment of the U.S. Congress (now defunct). At one time, the Robert Wood Johnson Foundation had a program dedicated to the study of medical malpractice and its reform. More recently, the Pew Charitable Trusts invested in such research and evaluation. With very few exceptions, such as New York State's involvement in the Harvard Medical Practice Study (Weiler, Hiatt, Newhouse, et al. 1993), states have not been involved in conducting such research or in sponsoring the work of others.

50. See chapter 1 for a discussion of the participants in this market.

51. Nathanson (2004).

52. Shmanske and Stevens (1986).

53. U.S. Congressional Budget Office (2004); U.S. Congress, Office of Technology Assessment (1994). See e.g., Bovbjerg (1995); Danzon (2000); Saxton (2003); Studdert, Yang, and Mello (2004); U.S. Congressional Budget Office (2003).

54. But not earlier evidence. See Sloan (1985).

55. Sloan, Bovbjerg, and Githens (1991).

56. It is likely that this reform was evaluated in some studies in preliminary analysis, but the reform was dropped from the results that were reported. One cannot know this for sure, although it seems unlikely that in terms of savings, periodic payments have anywhere near the cost-saving potential of caps.

57. They are discussed in greater detail in chapter 8.

58. Also see Gunnar (2004).

59. Sloan, Bovbjerg, and Githens (1991).

60. Encinosa and Hellinger use the county as the observational unit.

61. Sloan, Bovbjerg, and Githens (1991).

62. The Task Force devoted three pages to an innovative medical no-fault program it had implemented over a decade before the report was written.

63. Thorpe (2004, p. W4-27).

64. See Danzon (2000, p. 1396) for further discussion of this point.

Chapter 5

1. Glassman (2004); Kelly and Mello (2005).

2. Danzon (1984); Zuckerman, Bovbjerg, and Sloan (1990).

3. Born and Viscusi (1994); Born, Viscusi, and Carleton (1998); Sloan, Mergenhagen, and Bovbjerg (1989); Thorpe (2004); Zuckerman, Bovbjerg, and Sloan (1990).

4. Sloan (1985).

5. Glassman (2004).

6. See, e.g., Browne and Wells (1999).

7. Kelly and Mello (2005).

8. Ibid.

9. The research cited in this chapter's first paragraph evaluated the effects of limits on damages in medical malpractice cases in general and did not focus on California. Nor did this research—or, to our knowledge, most research by others (exceptions being Pace, Golinelli, and Zakaras 2004; and Studdert, Yang, and Mello 2004)—assess the other policy changes that California has implemented that may account for the relative stability in premiums in that state.

10. This topic was discussed more extensively in chapter 4.

11. E.g., Croley and Hanson (1995, p. 1803).

12. The function of insurance is to transfer money from the healthy to the sick, but money is not a perfect substitute for irreplaceable loss (Cook and Graham 1977; Danzon 2000, p. 1372).

13. For the United Kingdom, see the *Ogden Tables*, 5th ed. (London: Government Actuary's Department 2004). http://gad.gov.uk/publications/docs/ogdentables5thed.pdf (accessed June 20. 2007).

14. See, e.g., Rustad (1992).

15. Kelly and Mello (2005).

16. Bovbjerg (1991, p. 467).

17. See chapter 11.

18. E.g., Gan et al. (2001).

19. As explained below, economic theory offers a prediction of when an individual would and would not want to purchase insurance in excess of anticipated monetary loss.

20. See, e.g., Croley and Hanson (1995, pp. 1837–1841).

21. Croley and Hanson (1995). Theoretically, the amount people are willing to pay for insurance depends on the value of an extra dollar in the healthy versus the sick or injured state. Conclusive evidence on the marginal utility in healthy versus sick states is lacking (see e.g., Viscusi and Evans 1990).

22. Viscusi (1979, 1992).

23. See chapter 6 for discussion of lawyer compensation issues.

24. Calfee and Winston (1993).

25. Of course, strong advocates for tort reform could argue the opposite. If we had binding limits on lawyers' contingent fees, then pressures to compensate injury victims for nonmonetary loss would diminish.

26. Treaster (2003).

27. Pace, Golinelli, and Zakaras (2004).

28. Campion (2003).

29. The discussion of constitutional challenges draws extensively on Kelly and Mello's (2005) comprehensive analysis of this issue.

30. California's law was challenged on this basis, but the court concluded that there was no inherent right to collect an unlimited amount of tort damages.

31. Hallinan (2004); Niemeyer (2004).

32. Peeples and Harris (2005).

33. Vidmar, Gross, and Rose (1998).

34. See, e.g., Sieg (2000) for data on the percent of trials won by medical malpractice plaintiffs in Florida; and Vidmar, Robinson, and MacKillop (2006).

35. McCaffrey, Kahneman, and Spitzer (1995).

36. Helland and Tabarrok (2003).

37. Bovbjerg, Sloan, Dor, et al. (1991).

38. On undercompensation of medical injuries by tort, see the discussion later in this chapter.

39. There is no sound empirical evidence linking an outlier award on the high side to subsequent payments, either settlements or awards at verdict. However, the conventional wisdom is that such a link exists and is important. For example, in a brief critique of Hyman and Silver (2006), Ted Frank discusses a "problem of outlier cases, with disproportionate damages that have a disproportionate effect on the system" (2006).

40. Precedent-setting applies much less to jury trials since common practice is not to inform jurors about previous awards. Nor is it likely that even the judge has this type of information.

41. Abraham (2001).

42. See chapter 2 for discussion of this point.

43. An example of a jury instruction on damages: "The purpose of the law of damages is to award, as far as possible, just and fair compensation for the loss, if any, which resulted from the defendant's violation of the plaintiff's rights. If you find that the defendant is liable on the claims, as I have explained them, then you must award the plaintiff sufficient damages to compensate him or her for any injury proximately caused by the defendant's conduct.... A prevailing plaintiff is entitled to compensatory damages for the physical injury, pain and suffering, mental anguish, shock and discomfort that he or she has suffered because of a defendant's conduct.... The damages that you award must be fair and reasonable, neither inadequate nor excessive." Section 77-3, Sand, Siffert, Loughlin, et al. (2005).

44. Bovbjerg, Sloan, and Blumstein (1989).

45. Sloan, Githens, Clayton, et al. (1993).

46. See chapter 4; and Studdert, Yang, and Mello (2004).

47. Pace, Golinelli, and Zakaras (2004) quantify the effect of not allowing the California cap to rise with increases in overall prices. Some other states that implemented caps did not duplicate the effects in California (Mogel 2003). In Indiana, which combines a limit on total damages with a patient compensation fund (PCF), the mean payment for large medical malpractice claims was substantially higher than the mean payment for similar claims in Michigan and Ohio, states without PCFs and caps (Bovbjerg 1991; Gronfein and Kinney 1991). Although this result most likely reflects idiosyncrasies of the PCF-total caps combination in Indiana and mainly policies of the PCF, it serves as a reminder that context and interactions between caps and other policy changes are critically important to consider. Even though caps reduce payments on average, for cases that would otherwise settle for much less than the cap, plaintiffs may base their expected values of payment on the amount of the cap, thus forming unrealistic expectations and reducing the probability of settlement (Pogarsky and Babcock 2001).

48. Hertzka (2003).

49. Pogarsky and Babcock (2001).

50. Chupkovich (1993).

51. For example, a North Dakota court found the state's damage cap ceiling in violation of the state equal protection guarantee. The statute benefited physicians but denied adequate compensation to plaintiffs with proven meritorious claims, and did nothing toward the elimination of nonmeritorious claims (de Sa e Silva 1988).

52. See, e.g., Bovbjerg (1991).

53. This lack of information applies to all tort cases, not just medical malpractice. Gash (2005) proposed a national punitive damages registry to address a

problem particularly applicable to product liability, namely, that a defendant who has allegedly injured multiple plaintiffs by a single action or a course of conduct, faces multiple punitive damages for that conduct.

54. Having state registries based on jury verdicts (admittedly the minority of claims) linked to a national registry would provide valuable data not only on findings relative to liability but, most important, on the rationale for awards at verdict. The following items might be recorded by the registry: (1) nature and extent of injuries; (2) findings on each element of monetary loss, including losses in wages; medical, custodial, and special education costs, both past and projected, with the discount rate used and an explicit account of future inflation underlying the calculation of future loss; (3) identification of the types of non-monetary losses and compensation levels for each; and (4) adjustments made for comparative negligence, prior settlements by other defendants, collateral sources, joint and several liability, and/or other factors.

55. This argument have been made by others as well. See, e.g., Studdert, Yang, and Mello (2004).

56. Scheduled damages have been advocated by the following scholars, among others: Bovbjerg, Sloan, and Blumstein (1989); Corrigan, Greiner, and Erickson (2002); Mello and Brennan (2002).

57. See, e.g., Viscusi (1993).

58. European tables may provide some guidance, but they should not be adopted uncritically.

59. Gold et al. (1996).

60. Bovbjerg, Sloan, and Blumstein (1989); Sloan and Hsieh (1990).

61. These values would be indexed by the Consumer Price Index.

62. Juries might indicate that the case involved less pain and suffering than one scenario but more than another. Then the pain and suffering might be reduced or increased to the midpoint of the dollar values associated with each of the scenarios in the notebook.

63. See, e.g., Schuck (1991). The premise that jury awards for nonmonetary loss are seriously flawed is not a generally accepted proposition. For example, Cohen and Miller (2003) examine juries' "willingness to award" nonmonetary damages in over 1,200 cases of consumer product-related injuries and intentional assaults by a third party. Based on data on awards for injuries with out-of-pocket losses sustained by the plaintiff, the authors computed implicit values of a statistical life from jury awards for nonfatal injuries. They found that jury awards are predictable (using regression analysis), but there is a high degree of variability. There is also substantial variability in the circumstances leading to the awards. The implied values of a statistical life from the jury award data range from $1.4 to $3.8 million, well within the range independently derived from wage-risk studies (see e.g., Viscusi 1993). In spite of their results, the authors state that they favor scheduling awards for nonmonetary loss.

64. He suggests that juries assess damages from an ex ante perspective that asks how much a reasonable person would have paid to eliminate the risk that caused the nonmonetary loss. Such willingness to pay would reflect both the probability of the loss and the value of the loss, given that a loss occurred. He also proposes that juries be asked to assume a specific probability that the injury would occur. Then, based on their responses, one could assign values to the loss, given that it occurred.

65. Alberini, Hunt, and Markandya (2006); Perreira and Sloan (2002); Sloan, Viscusi, Chesson, et al. (1998); Viscusi and Evans (1990).

66. There are several possible ways to deal with this problem. One is to use a Delphi technique. Jurors would get feedback on the mean responses in the first round as well as the high and low values. They then would be asked to repeat the valuation exercise. Perhaps by the second or third round, there would be some convergence in responses. Alternatively, the court could employ a panel of citizens who would be asked to perform the valuation task. Since the valuations would have to be done in person, this could be an expensive exercise. On the other hand, the cost would be low relative to the awards being contemplated in some cases.

67. Avraham (2006, p. 103).

68. Blumstein, Bovbjerg, and Sloan (1991).

69. Farber and Bazerman (1986); Stern, Rehmus, Lowenberg (1975).

70. Würdemann Vanderbilt (1912, p. 884).

Chapter 6

1. See, e.g. Kritzer (1997).

2. Kritzer (2002) presents data on litigation rates by country which place the United States fifth after Germany, Sweden, Israel, and Austria. The issues for which the lawsuits are brought vary among countries.

3. Brickman (2003, p. 658).

4. Lesser et al. (2004). Lester Brickman (2003, p. 657) argues that by "pursuing anticompetitive strategies including erecting barriers to competition from outside the profession and promulgating ethical rules restricting price competition within the profession, contingent-fee lawyers have not only flouted ethical rules and fiducial protections but have also imposed substantial rents on tort claimants as a price for tort claiming." A deficiency of this criticism is that to the extent it applies to contingent-fee lawyers, it applies to lawyers in general.

5. See, e.g., Olson (1991, p. 45).

6. See Tabarrok and Helland (2005, p. 11).

7. Daniels and Martin (2006).

8. Formal Opinion 94–389, Contingent Fees, December 5, 1994.

9. W. K. Davis (1999).

10. *Taylor v. Bemiss*, 110 U.S. 42 (1884).

11. W. K. Davis (1999).

12. Plaintiffs are risk-averse and attorneys are risk-neutral. (Danzon 1983). Whatever law firms' risk preferences, members of a firm can diversify away some risk by taking on many cases (Garoupa and Gomez-Pomar 2002).

13. Inselbuch (2001).

14. Dana and Spier (1993); Danzon (1983); Hay (1996).

15. Hay (1997).

16. Some have argued that contingent fee arrangements are more appropriate when there is asymmetric information between attorneys and their clients, the former knowing more about their own ability, and clients, at least initially, knowing more about the merits of the case (Dana and Spier 1993; Rubinfeld and Scotchmer 1993). When there is asymmetric information, contingent fees can allow clients to signal the quality of their cases and attorneys to signal the quality of their advice. A client who thinks he or she has a high-quality case should be willing to pay a high hourly fee and a low contingent fee percentage, while an attorney would signal high quality by offering services at a relatively high contingent fee percentage. A problem with the use of contingent fees as a signaling device is that variation in such fee percentages is quite small—mostly in the range of 33 to 40 percent (Sloan, Githens, Clayton, et al. 1993).

17. These are called "agency problems" in economics.

18. A theoretical paper by Choi (2003) argues that leaving the lawyer in charge of the litigation and guaranteeing him or her a large amount of the rent can increase the plaintiff's return from a settlement.

19. In a theoretical study, Emons (2000) shows that fixed contingent fees may lead to insufficient attorney effort, and paying the attorney by the task performed always implements efficient behavior.

20. L. A. Baker (2001–2002).

21. Sieg (2000).

22. Miceli (1994).

23. L. A. Baker (2001–2002).

24. Dana and Spier (1993).

25. Brickman (2003, p. 655).

26. We have updated his estimates to 2004 dollars.

27. Kritzer (2004, p. 188).

28. Responses to the survey also indicated that tort reform public relations campaigns and decisions of the Texas Supreme Court, rather than the statutory changes themselves, were perceived as having the greatest negative impact on the lawyers' practices. Public relations campaigns were seen as influencing juror

attitudes; following campaigns, there was a widespread perception among jurors that the system was out of control. Not only did public relations campaigns, judicial decisions, and legislative changes affect attitudes, but there was also a decline in automobile liability caseload.

29. Kakalik, Hensler, McCaffrey, et al. (1998).

30. The same Wisconsin survey revealed that most lawyers in the study, 60 percent, charged a fixed 33 percent contingent fee; 31 percent employed a variable fee. For variable fees, the most common pattern was a fee of 25 percent if there was no substantial trial preparation, rising to 40 percent if the case resulted in an appeal. There were sometimes reductions in fees below the rate specified in the retention agreement. Kritzer concludes that "At least in Wisconsin, the assertion by contingency fee critics that there is a uniform contingency fee is clearly false" (2004, p. 39). But, as Brickman notes, relative to many, if not most, states, Wisconsin is not a litigious state; as a result, data from this state may be unrepresentative of contingent fee practices in more litigious states (2003, p. 685).

31. Kritzer (1997).

32. Kritzer (2004, pp. 68, 71).

33. Brickman (2003, p. 697).

34. Ibid. (pp. 698, 734). Brickman cites *Burnett v. Commissioner* as evidence of this. In *Burnett,* the plaintiff taxpayer, an attorney, attempted to deduct advances made to his clients which were only to be repaid only if there was recovery for the client. In this case, the court stated: "Here there was a close correlation between the conditions of reimbursement and the primary criterion employed by petitioner to select clients to receive financial assistance, e.g., although reimbursement was tied to the recovery of a client's claim, assistance was granted only to those whose claims would in all probability be successfully concluded. Moreover, petitioner experienced a high rate of return on the advances, evidenced by the fact that during the five-year period ending in 1961 in which petitioner's conditional advances were made, only $4,417 out of approximately $290,000 of them became worthless. These factors clearly indicate that the advances were intended to, and did, operate as loans, i.e., advances virtually certain of repayment, to petitioner's clients" 356 F.2d 755, 760 (5th Cir. 1966).

35. Kritzer (2004, p. 39).

36. Brickman (2003, p. 685).

37. Hawaii Rev. Stat. §607-15.5 (1986).

38. Pa. Stat. Ann. Tit. 40 §1301.604

39. *Heller v. Frankston,* 475 A.2d 1291, 1296 (Pa. 1984).

40. Or. Rev. Stat. §752.150 (1975).

41. Or. Rev. Stat. §18.540 (1987).

42. Idaho Code §39-4213

43. N.H. Rev. Stat. Ann. §507–C:8

44. *Carson v. Maurer*, 424 A.2d 825, 839 (N.H. 1980).

45. Ibid.

46. Fla. Stat. §768.56 (1980).

47. Florida Constitution, Art. I, §26 (2005).

48. Ibid. This amount is exclusive of reasonable and customary costs and does not take into account the number of defendants.

49. *In re Amendments to the Rules Regulating the Fla. Bar*, 933 So.2d 417 (Fla. 2006).

50. T. Baker (2005b, p. 185).

51. Charles Silver states the perceived problem: "Unsophisticated laypersons cannot shop for legal services intelligently . . ." (2002, p. 2088).

52. California (Cal. Bus. & Prof. Code §6146); Connecticut (Conn. Gen. Stat. §52–251c); Delaware (Del. Code Ann. Tit. 18 §6865); Florida (Florida Code of Professional Responsibility, Disciplinary Rule 2-106 and Fla. Stat. §768.595); Illinois (Ill. Rev. Stat. ch. 110, §2–1114); Maine (Me. Rev. Stat. Ann. Tit. 24, §2961); Massachusetts (Mass. Gen. Laws Ann. ch. 231, §60I); New Jersey (New Jersey Court Rules §1:21-7); New York (N.Y. Jud. Law §474a); Wisconsin (Wis. Stat. §655.013); Wyoming (Ct. Rules Governing Contingent Fees R.5).

53. Arizona (Ariz. Rev. Stat. Ann. §12-568); Hawaii (Hawaii Rev. Stat. §607-15.5); Iowa (Iowa Code §147.138; Kansas (Kan. Stat. Ann. §7-121b); Maryland (Md. Cts. & Jud. Proc. §3-2A-07); Nebraska (Neb. Rev. Stat. §44-2834); New Hampshire (N.H. Rev. Stat. Ann. §508:4-e); Tennessee (Tenn. Code Ann. §29-26-120); Washington (Wash. Rev. Code §7.70.070); Wyoming (Ct. Rules Governing Contingent Fees, R.6).

54. Florida (Fla. Stat. §§766.207, 766.209); Indiana (Ind. Code §16-9.5-5-1); Massachusetts (Mass. Gen. Laws Ann. ch. 231, §60I); Michigan (Michigan Court Rules, Rule 8.121(B)); Oklahoma (Okla. Stat. Tit. 5, §7); Tennessee (Tenn. Code Ann. §29-26-120); Utah (Utah Code Ann. §78-14-7.5).

55. While both court review and sliding-scale statutes have been enacted in ten states, some of the statutes under the court review category are not mandatory; rather, it is at the discretion of the court or upon the request of the parties to review attorney fees.

56. For particulars, see chapter 11.

57. These data are from the 1992 Civil Justice Survey of State Courts.

58. These data were obtained from closed medical malpractice insurance claims from the Department of Insurance for the State of Florida.

59. Helland and Tabarrok (2003, p. 54).

60. Sloan and Hoerger (1991).

61. Di Pietro and Carns (1996); Stanley (2003); Vargo (1993). The description here does not do full justice to the historical facts surrounding this issue. There were many other factors in play, such as animosity toward lawyers, heavy restrictions on attorneys' fees if they could collect them, and the use of attorneys during this time period.

62. Vargo (1993).

63. *Canter v. American Ins. Co.*, 28 U.S. 307 (1830).

64. Vargo (1993).

65. Di Pietro and Carns (1996).

66. Alaska R. Civ. Proc. 82.

67. Ibid.

68. Di Pietro and Carns (1996).

69. Snyder and Hughes (1990); J. W. Hughes and Snyder (1995).

70. J. W. Hughes and Snyder (1995).

71. Ibid.

72. Di Pietro and Carns (1996).

73. Ibid.; Stanley (2003).

74. O'Connell and Bryan (2000–2001).

75. Ibid.

76. Copland (2004).

77. Sloan, Githens, Clayton, et al. (1993).

78. Ibid.

79. In re: Petition for Rulemaking to Revise the Ethical Standards Relating to Contingency Fees, Utah Supreme Court Advisory Committee on Rules of Professional Conduct (2004, p. 76).

80. The origins of legal insurance have been traced back to ancient Rome. However, this lengthy history and development are extraneous to this discussion. Instead, we list the years in which specific legal insurance policies were created or offered. The following countries have had LEI since the year listed: Austria, 1955; Greece, 1971; Great Britain, 1975; Luxembourg, 1969; Sweden, Norway, and Denmark, 1960s (Pfennigstorf 1986).

81. This capture of the market is due to uninsured loss recovery, which forms the most significant part of the market. Uninsured loss recovery is the pursuit, after a car accident, of the uninsured losses for which the insured is involved but not at fault. (Kilian 2003).

82. Ibid.

83. Ibid.

84. Ibid.

85. Ibid.

86. Ibid.

87. Ibid.

88. Ibid.

89. Maute (2001).

90. Costich (1994).

91. 377 U.S. 1 (1964). The brotherhood's activities also met resistance in Illinois (1932), Ohio (1933), California (1941), New York (1933), Tennessee (1952), and Missouri (1960). See also Riedmueller (1973–1974).

92. Maute (2001).

93. This is not to suggest that there were not many other criticisms and points of opposition; rather, this was one area where a lot of debate and reform centered.

94. Heid and Misulovin (2000).

95. Pfenningstorf (1975).

96. Ibid.

97. Kilian (2003).

98. Kritzer (2004, p. 254).

99. See Lerman (1999).

100. Haltom and McCann (2004, p. 136).

Chapter 7

1. See, e.g., Developments in the Law: Confronting the New Challenges of Scientific Evidence (1995); and Helland and Tabarrok (2000).

2. Dann (2002).

3. These criticisms of juries are found in many articles. See, for example, Vidmar (1994a).

4. But not Vidmar (1994b), whose work supports juries. He mentions that others had alleged race and gender bias.

5. Procedures differ across states in terms of the presentation of arguments involving punitive damages. In some states, there are separate trials for hearing evidence and deciding on punitive damages. In others, this is done at the same trial at which liability and compensatory damages are determined (Priest 2002, p. 10).

6. Ellsworth and Reifman (2000).

7. Vidmar and Rose (2001); Viscusi and Born (2005).

8. Zimmerman and Oster (2002, p. A1).

9. MacCoun (1993, p. 138).

10. Vidmar, Gross, and Rose (1998).

11. Moller, Pace, and Carroll (1999).

12. Grisham (1996).

13. Vidmar (1994a).

14. Cohen and Smith (2004).

15. Vidmar (1994a).

16. 174 Cal. App. 3d 831 (1985).

17. Sugarman (1990).

18. Taragin, Willett, Wilczek, et al. (1992).

19. Ibid. (p. 780).

20. Farber and White (1991).

21. Sloan, Githens, Clayton, et al. (1993).

22. Studdert, Mello, Gawande, et al. (2006).

23. See chapter 5 for a description.

24. The authors acknowledge in their discussion of limitations that not blinding the physician reviewers as to the case outcomes may have caused hindsight bias. They argue that if hindsight bias existed, it would have led the reviewers to overestimate the prevalence and costs of claims not associated with medical error. But more important, hindsight bias could lead one to reject the myth that claims outcomes are random. However, reviewers *were* blinded as to outcome in the third study discussed in the text. Although blinding would have been preferable, it seems doubtful that the results would be overturned if reviewers had not known whether or not payment was in fact made.

25. Studdert, Mello, and Brennan (2004)l; Weiler (1993); Weiler, Hiatt, Newhouse, et al. (1993).

26. Farber and White (1991); Hoerger, Sloan, and Hassan (1990).

27. Lichtenstein, Slovic, Fischhoff, et al. (1978); Morgan, Granger, Brodsky, et al. (1983); Viscusi (2002b, pp. 182–183).

28. Tversky and Kahneman (1973). One of the issues in mock jury research is that individuals seem to be sensitive to the magnitude of the plaintiff's initial demand for compensation (sometimes called the "ask") or for demands by the plaintiff's attorney in closing argument at trial. However, as Vidmar (2004a) noted, such experiments are unrealistic in that jurors would be exposed to counterarguments in the defendant's attorney's closing statement. Presumably the argument would be that compensation should be much lower, even if the jury found liability.

29. Sunstein (2003); Galanter (1993, p. 84).

30. MacCoun (1993, p. 162).

31. Lempert (1993, p. 192).

32. A common technique in empirical research on juries is to obtain responses to hypothetical questions from persons who are asked to assume that they are jurors ("mock jurors").

33. The framing of questions is the subject of a literature in its own right, as is whether or not the questions asked of mock jurors are those that jurors would be asked to answer in the real world. For example, Vidmar (1999) criticizes prior research comparing judge and jury decision-making on grounds that the experiments ask jurors to make decisions about law—decisions that are exclusively the responsibility of the judge.

34. Lempert (1999).

35. Viscusi (2002b).

36. Vidmar and Rice (1993).

37. Vidmar (1993).

38. Sunstein, Schkade, and Kahneman (2000).

39. Sunstein, Schkade, and Kahneman (2002, pp. 132, 141).

40. Viscusi (2002a, p. 207; 2001).

41. Sunstein (2002a, p. 257).

42. Vidmar (2004).

43. Sloan, Githens, Clayton, et al. (1993).

44. Polinsky and Shavell (1998, p. 870).

45. Rustad (1992).

46. Moller, Pace, and Carroll (1999) analyze jury verdicts reached in 1985 through 1994 from California; New York; Cook County, Illinois; Harris County, Texas; and the St. Louis metropolitan area. Out of 5,238 verdicts, punitive damages were awarded in 28 of these cases (0.5 percent of total verdicts or 1.7 percent of plaintiff verdicts). In a sample of 1,156 medical malpractice verdicts in the seventy-five largest counties, punitive damages were awarded in only seven cases (0.6 percent of total medical malpractice verdicts). Medical malpractice cases were 9.7 percent of all tort, contract, and real property cases in the sample (Cohen and Smith 2004). Awards for punitive damages were 9.5 percent of total awards for punitive damages in all of the cases. In Vidmar (2004, p. 1367), 12 out of 270 jury verdicts that were examined were medical malpractice cases. The median punitive damage award was $1 million in 1999 dollars; the median compensatory award was 2.5 times higher. Moreover, relative to the other case types, compensatory awards were substantially higher relative to punitive damage awards in medical malpractice.

47. Sunstein (2002a, p. 75).

48. Priest (2002, pp. 2–4).

49. Tabarrok and Helland (1999).

50. Tabarrok and Helland (1999). Eisenberg, LaFountain, Ostrom et al. (2002) report that controlling for other factors, there were no differences between judges

and juries in the rate at which punitive damages were awarded and in the amounts, conditional on a punitive damage award being awarded, but there was greater variability in the magnitude of punitive awards in jury trials than in judge trials. However, the greater range of punitive damage awards in jury trials yielded very few awards that were higher than what judges might have awarded in similar cases. Without controlling for other factors, punitive damage awards were far higher when awarded by juries than by judges, which is consistent with the conventional wisdom and stories in the media that do not account for other factors.

51. Proponents suggest that the establishment of uniform and consistent standards, as well as improved communication, will facilitate patient safety, although it is unclear how effective this would be in practice.

52. At the time this book was written in 2006, despite concerns, it was the reform of choice for many legislatures, including Congress. Proposals in the U.S. House and Senate authorize the Secretary of Health and Human Services (HHS) to award demonstration grants to the states for the development, implementation, and evaluation of health courts. In addition to existing proposals, Senator John Cornyn, a Republican from Texas, advocated health court pilot projects which would shift resolution of claims from state courts to administrative courts maintained by the HHS (Kyl 2006). Common Good was working in partnership with the Harvard School of Public Health on a model "compatible with the U.S. health care and legal environment" (Saltus 2005).

53. In the AMA proposal, a patient has to take his or her claim before a reviewer, two sets of physician peer reviewers, and finally an administrative law judge called a hearing examiner. After all of this, the parties may still appeal to the highest court in the state. See (American Medical Association 1988).

54. The AMA proposal, introduced in 1988, contains several features absent from the more recent Common Good proposal. The AMA's model is multitiered, using two levels of independent review before reaching judicial review. First, a claim is assessed in a prehearing stage. During this stage, reviewers evaluate the merit of the claim, using testimony and medical records. In the absence of an early settlement offer, the reviewer must determine if the claim is nonmeritorious and, if so, recommend dismissal. If the claim is determined to be meritorious, it is further evaluated at the next level by an expert in the same field as the health care provider. If the expert agrees that the claim has merit, the case is sent to a hearings examiner. At this stage, should the claim be determined to have no merit, it is given to a second expert for review.

For cases passing the prehearing and expert reviews, the claimant appears before the hearings examiner in a triallike hearing, with both sides represented by counsel. The examiner serves a judicial function akin to an administrative law judge. The AMA proposal gives the claimant an appointed staff attorney, but allows for private legal representation at the claimant's option. When the hearing process begins, blind settlement offers are required from both parties. The examiner may call witnesses of his or her choosing and must issue a written opinion within ninety days after conclusion of the hearing. In this written opinion, the hearing examiner is not only responsible for determining the defendant's liability, but also must assess damages.

Decisions from the hearing examiner can be appealed to the Medical Board, which is responsible for making a full, independent determination regarding the provider's liability. The Medical Board will be made up of three members, all of whom are selected by the governor upon advice of a nominating committee. The state's intermediate appellate court hears appeals from the Medical Board's decisions. The board would oversee the administrative process, review appeals, and oversee continuing medical education. The AMA hoped that the board would eventually restore consistency in damage awards, resolve claims more quickly, and develop rules and substantive guidelines to complement existing statutory standards.

In spite of the many hoops claimants must jump through before their claim reaches judgment—which even many neutral observers would regard as a negative feature—the AMA proposal contains a few novel concepts. First, the plan requires blind offers during the prehearing stage. If the submitted offers are incompatible (e.g., the plaintiff's offer is higher than the defendant's), the offers are rejected, and the claim continues with the administrative judge. If the defendant's offer is greater than or equal to the claimant's demand, the case is settled at the claimant's amount, with payment required within thirty days. To discourage bad-faith offers, a party may face sanctions should the outcome of the hearing not be an improvement over the blind offer.

A very intriguing aspect of the proposal is the provision of free legal representation to claimants. Current proposals assume health courts will be navigable for the injured party without an attorney. Or, alternatively, injured patients can readily obtain counsel should they need it. However, it is questionable whether attorneys would be willing to accept cases when the damages are scheduled or when there is a 20 percent cap on contingency fees. Attorneys who regularly charge contingency fees of 33–40 percent will not take cases that have a probability of a low damage award, even if some recovery is likely. Appointing a public defender-type lawyer for injured patients solves this problem, but it also shifts the costs from the litigants to taxpayers. However, as discussed below, both tax courts and family courts are accessible to litigants who represent themselves ("pro se" litigants), and they make up a large number of the plaintiffs appearing before these courts.

Investigation of medical records, interviews with providers, and consultations with and the hiring of experts are all costs currently borne by the plaintiff and defendant, but would be shifted to the state. To the extent that the new system increased claims frequency, this would add to cost as well. On the other hand, the dispute resolution process could be much shorter than the current tort system, with many medical malpractice claims being resolved in months rather than in several years, which could reduce cost appreciably.

55. Medical no-fault is discussed more in chapter 11. Very few no-fault systems operating in other countries are truly "no-fault"; rather, they use modified versions of liability—such as avoidable events.

56. Udell and Kendall (2005).

57. United States Constitution, Art. I, Sec. 8, Clause 3. Under principles of state sovereignty and federalism, the constitutionality of federal regulation is questionable. The constitution grants the federal government certain enumerated powers, such as the right to regulate interstate commerce and the power to pass any law that is necessary and proper for the execution of its enumerated powers. Powers that the constitution does not grant to the federal government or forbid to the states are reserved exclusively to the states. Should the U.S. Congress enact a law creating and regulating health courts, it is uncertain whether it would be upheld; the Supreme Court did not invalidate any federal statute as exceeding the states' enumerated powers from 1938 until 1995. These powers historically have been interpreted liberally but, in recent years, reviewed with a more critical eye.

58. Kyl (2006). While the Supreme Court has incorporated most of the Bill of Rights to the states, they have not incorporated the Seventh Amendment. This means that the constitutional protection of jury trials in civil cases applies only to federal courts.

59. Chapter 1's discussion of myth 1.

60. See Danzon (1986).

61. McCoid (1991).

62. P. Davis, Lay-Yee, Scott, et al. (2003).

63. In 2000 President Clinton signed a bill authorizing $10 million a year for a period of four years to support the creation of up to 100 mental health courts. (H. J. Stedman, Davidson, and Brown 2001).

64. The juvenile court system in the U.S. began in 1899 in Chicago, and family courts were first developed in 1914, in response to a perceived societal need for improved court performance in family matters (Babb 1998).

65. For example, a recent study showed that 40 percent of families that appear in court for child abuse, neglect, delinquency, or divorce have been to court previously for another family-related matter (Developments in the Law 2003). Keeping family law issues in the general court system was seen as wasteful because of duplicative judicial attention to the same family in different courts by different judges.

66. The act was sponsored by the U.S. Children's Bureau in collaboration with the National Probation and Parole Association and the National Council of Juvenile Court Judges.

67. Babb (1998, p. 480).

68. Permissive family court systems give litigants the choice of forum. They may file in the family court or in the general court, giving at least two sets of courts jurisdiction over family law claims. Mandatory systems shift all family law cases

from the general court to the specialized family court. Only the family court has jurisdiction, and no other courts are allowed to hear cases dealing with domestic relations. Currently, only a minority of states continue to process family law cases as part of the general civil docket (Babb 1998). And none of the states that have implemented family courts have returned to adjudicating family law cases within the general docket (Kosanovich 2006).

69. Fields (2006).

70. Rottman (2000). For example, a judge may determine in an abuse case that the father had sexually abused his daughter, while a second judge during divorce proceedings excludes evidence of the sexual abuse and grants the father visitation rights (Williams 1995). In contrast, family courts aim to have centralized case files and rulings, giving judges and social services access to all relevant information about the parties before them. In the context of medical malpractice, some physicians are sued repeatedly. Consolidating these cases and coordination with other quality-assurance systems, such as state licensure boards and health insurers, may be more efficient.

71. Forum shopping occurs when the plaintiff searches among jurisdictions or courts to identify the most favorable outcome for plaintiffs due to differences in judges, laws, rules of evidence, and rules of the court, among other things.

72. A U.S. Department of Justice study reports that as of 1995, domestic issues accounted for 40 percent of all civil filings, while tort cases accounted for only 10 percent (S.K. Smith, DeFrances, Langan, et al. 1995). Of the tort cases, medical malpractice cases made up 5 percent (0.5 percent of total filings). In addition to making up such a large part of the docket, domestic filings were not stagnant; between 1984 and 2000, domestic relations filings increased 79 percent (Developments in the Law 2003). On top of the dramatic increase in family law cases, criminal dockets were getting bigger, discovery in civil cases was mounting, and commercial cases were becoming more complex. These factors created an atmosphere where judges were increasingly unable to devote sufficient time to the nuances of family law (Folberg 1999). Attorneys and some pro-se litigants took advantage of the court's disorganization by judge shopping and repetition of judicial efforts (Folberg 1999).

73. For example, in 2002 the District of Columbia created a unified family court (Geraghty and Myniec 2002). Prior to this, there was a family division in place within the court of general jurisdiction. The legislation created a one judge and one family system separate from the general court, changed the judicial rotation from one year to three, and added new judges and judge-magistrates (Geraghty and Myniec 2002). The legislature appropriated $18 million for the transition, though court officials estimated it would take $46 million to hire judges and staff and to build courtrooms (Leonning 2001).

74. Kondo (2001).

75. Domitrovich (1998).

76. Ibid.

77. Judges may burn out quickly through having to deal with the same difficult, emotionally charged family cases every day. This can be detrimental not only for a judge, but also for the parties before him. See Geraghty and Myniec (2002) for a brief discussion of this issue.

78. Babb (1998); Geraghty and Myniec (2002).

79. Babb (1998).

80. Schepard (2002).

81. Judges are responsible for adjudicating custody disputes, child support, divorces, domestic violence charges, juvenile delinquency, all phases of abuse, neglect, and dependency cases, adoption, and guardianship (Kosanovich 2006).

82. See U.S. Constitution, Art. I, Sec. 8, Clause 4.

83. Laro (1995). In addition, over 95 percent of tax cases are brought before the tax court.

84. See Laro (1995) for a discussion of the arguments for and against government bias in tax courts. Proponents suggest there are multiple factors that account for this large percentage, none of which include government bias.

85. The trend toward specialization is not limited to courts. For instance, there are few "general practice" physicians or attorneys left; rapid and complex developments in both medicine and law make it difficult for professionals to remain versed and competent in many areas of practice. Specialty courts are a reflection of this trend.

86. See chapter 11.

87. Sage (1997).

88. The average caseload for a New York Family Court judge is 2,500 cases (Schepard 2002).

89. "In Suits at common law, where the value in controversy shall exceed twenty dollars, the right of trial by jury shall be preserved, and no fact tried by a jury shall be otherwise re-examined in any Court of the United States, than according to the rules of the common law" (Constitution of the United States, Amendment 7).

90. Leonning (2001).

91. Federal Rule of Evidence 702 codified and superseded *Daubert v. Merrell Dow Pharms., Inc.*, 113 S. Ct. 2786 (1993). However, *Daubert's* standard of review is the basis for determining the admissibility of an expert witness's testimony and continues to be used at both the federal and state levels (See, e.g., *United States v. Parra*, 402 F.3d 752, 758 (7th Cir. 2005); *United States v. Mahone*, 453 F.3d 68 (1st Cir. 2006); *United States v. Frabizio*, 2006 U.S. Dist. LEXIS 56327 (D. Mass. 2006); *Alves v. Mazda Motor of Am., Inc.*, 2006 U.S. Dist. LEXIS 65465 (D. Mass. 2006); *Palandjian v. Foster*, 446 Mass. 100 (Mass. 2006); *State v. Abner*, 2006 Ohio 4510 (Ohio Ct. App. 2006). Federal Rule of Evidence 702 states, "If scientific, technical, or other specialized knowledge will

assist the trier of fact to understand the evidence or to determine a fact in issue, a witness qualified as an expert by knowledge, skill, experience, training, or education, may testify thereto in the form of an opinion or otherwise, if (1) the testimony is based upon sufficient facts or data, (2) the testimony is the product of reliable principles and methods, and (3) the witness has applied the principles and methods reliably to the facts of the case."

Chapter 8

1. See chapter 3 in particular for a discussion of defensive medicine.

2. Hyman and Silver (2005).

3. Ibid.

4. Sloan Mergenhagen, Burfield, et al. (1989).

5. Brennan and Mello (2003).

6. Hyman and Silver (2005).

7. Ibid.

8. United States General Accounting Office (1987).

9. See, e.g., Breyer (1982) for a discussion of this rationale for health and safety regulation.

10. Those goods that can be evaluated in terms of their prices and characteristics in advance of the purchase are called "search goods." "Experience goods" are those for which the characteristics can be adequately evaluated only some period after consumption is commenced. Physician visits for routine care are plausibly experience goods. Visits to the emergency room are more likely to be credence goods.

11. In general, such differences in the risk of adverse outcomes (e.g., mechanical failures attributable to how vehicles are used) are overlooked in making comparisons of repair frequency; however, insurers do charge different premiums for automobile insurance based on a particular vehicle's history of frequency of accidents. No insurer, to our knowledge, bases health insurance premiums on the frequency of medical errors at particular facilities or of particular physicians.

12. Making a more reliable product may require more redundancy at various stages of the production process or more durable materials. These additional costs will be incurred by a profit-seeking enterprise if they yield additional revenue at least equal to such extra cost.

13. Manufacturers are also subject to product regulation, which specifies minimum levels of safety equipment and requires that some characteristics, such as fuel consumption, be prominently displayed on the automobile at the time of initial sale. There is also a role for tort liability, as seen recently in the case of the Ford Explorers, which tended to flip over at a seemingly unacceptable rate,

a problem that has been remedied in later models, presumably in part to avoid being sued. Even so, no one assigns the principal role of automobile quality assurance to tort.

14. A cottage industry consists of many small firms.

15. Mello and Brennan (2002).

16. The methodology is described in Brennan, Leape, Laird, et al. (1991).

17. Leape, Brennan, Laird, et al. (1991).

18. Mello and Brennan (2002).

19. A case in point is the IOM report that followed *To Err Is Human*, titled *The Quality Chasm*. At the 2001 press conference at which *Quality Chasm* was released, IOM committee members emphasized that their inquiry into patient safety had sidestepped medical malpractice issues (http://www.iom.edu/ CMS/8089/5432.aspx, accessed July 3, 2006).

20. A national system for reporting medication errors or interactions, the Medication Errors Reporting Program (MER), created by the Institute for Safe Medication Practice, had been in place since 1991. Though it enjoyed some success, the drug error information submitted to the MER program is not fully protected; information may be shared with the FDA and the pharmaceutical companies mentioned in the reports. This lack of confidentiality has significantly inhibited the use of MER. As a result, the system was largely replaced in 1998 by a new anonymous Internet reporting system, MedMARx. Hospitals can subscribe to the program, and providers can report errors through the MedMARx Web site with the assurance that the information will remain confidential. Information from the MedMARx program is not reported to the FDA, and hospitals may obtain data for their facilities and comparative information from other facilities, but the identities are not revealed. Anonymity has proven efficacious; according to the U.S. Pharmacopeia Web site, between 1999 and 2003 nearly 600,000 drug errors were reported to MedMARx (http://www.usp.org/products/medMarx, accessed June 15, 2006).

21. *Err* encourages the U.S. Food and Drug Administration to increase its efforts in monitoring safe use of drugs, both pre and post marketing, by implementing higher standards in drug packaging and labeling, requiring pharmaceutical companies to test potential drug names for confusion with similarly named drugs, and to work directly with physicians, pharmacists, and consumers to establish responses to identified problems. The report notes that during 1997 and 1998, five drugs were removed from the market—but not before almost 20 million people had been exposed to their risks. Some of these drugs were removed by the pharmaceutical companies themselves following reports of adverse outcomes. *Err* hopes to prevent this from reoccurring with more vigorous monitoring.

22. A survey conducted after release of *Err* finds that the mean hospital's annual patient safety budget is $1.9 million, with a range from $50,000 to $15 million (Devers, Pham, and Liu 2004).

23. In the United States, the only national administrative data are Medicare claims data, which predominantly reflect care delivered to persons over the age of sixty-five. In a country with universal health insurance, entire populations are covered. For example, in the Canadian province of Manitoba, claims data are being used for monitoring negligent adverse events (Bruce, Prior, Katz, et al. 2006).

24. In July 2003, the Accreditation Committee on Graduate Medical Education (ACGME) fully implemented modest regulations limiting resident work hours to a maximum of eighty per week or thirty hours per shift, in part a response to studies showing a link between resident physician fatigue and poor performance (D. Weinstein 2002). Despite the ACGME's good intentions, implementation and regulation of this policy have been difficult for many hospitals, and the ACGME's resources for investigating violations are limited. The fundamental problem with regulation of hours is that it is not easy for residents to report violations. Many fear the repercussions of being the whistle-blower or, even worse, causing their residency program to lose its accreditation. As a result, hour violations are difficult for program directors to detect. However, resident hours and fatigue are not the only factors contributing to resident errors. Surveys of residents have revealed other factors that may adversely affect patient safety, including inadequate supervision, problems with handoffs, lack of knowledge, too many other tasks, and a large patient load (Jagsi, Kitch, Weinstein, et al. 2005; Wu, Folkman, McPhee, et al. 2003).

25. Public goods have the property that individual A's consumption does not reduce individual B's consumption of the good. In this context, hospital A's use of a report on errors does not diminish hospital B's ability to consume this information. By contrast, for a private good such as a peanut butter sandwich, if individual A eats it, the same sandwich cannot be eaten by individual B.

26. The Joint Commission on Accreditation of Healthcare Organizations (JCAHO) and the National Quality Forum (NQF) have developed a system to collect and classify data from all existing systems (Wood and Nash 2005). With the intent of making national comparisons of adverse event reports, the JCAHO and NQF plan to standardize data collected from state reporting systems using a "Patient Safety Event Taxonomy" system. The hope is that by providing an amalgamation of information, hospitals can learn from the mistakes of their peers nationally, instead of relying on data restricted to their state or individual hospital (Wood and Nash 2005).

27. For example, a mixed-up X-ray may have been discovered before an adverse outcome actually occurred, but this should be seen as a fortuitous circumstance. Pennsylvania, followed by Florida and Maryland, corrected this problem in 2002 by adding near-miss events to the definition of adverse event (Wood and Nash 2005). As of 2004, only twenty-four states had implemented mandatory reporting systems (Weinberg, Hilborne, and Ngyuen, 2005).

28. Marchev, Rosenthal, and Booth (2003).

29. Flowers and Riley (2001).

30. Institute of Medicine (2000); United States Census Bureau (2000).

31. Wright and Katz (2005).

32. The cost of compliance for the U.S. Food and Drug Administration, drug wholesalers, and manufacturers was estimated to be $5.1 million, and $680 million for hospitals (Warburton 2005). Advocates of the system estimate savings of $3.9 billion annually from reductions in hospitalization days attributable to medication errors (Warburton 2005), but these savings do not accrue to hospitals which receive more revenue when there are more hospital days.

33. In its favor, the use of bar codes is a simple process; a physician's electronic order is sent directly to the pharmacy, where a bar code specific to the patient is generated. The pharmacist proceeds to verify the order, apply the bar code to the medicine, and send it to the appropriate floor, where nurses can compare the bar codes of the patient and the medicine, using a scanner (Wright and Katz 2005).

34. Wright and Katz (2005).

35. Partners Healthcare deemed this to be a worthwhile expenditure. Partners includes community hospitals in Boston, two academic medical centers, specialty facilities, and community health centers. The cost for Partners to implement a bar-coding system was $10 million, with an additional $1 million in annual operating cost (Wright and Katz 2005). However, Brigham and Women's Hospital, one of Partners' two founding academic medical centers, reported a 50 percent decrease in drug errors, which it estimated as the prevention of twenty dispensing errors per day at $4,700 per event (Wright and Katz 2005).

36. Critics point to the human error inevitably involved in the system. For instance, a patient without diabetes almost received a large dose of insulin after his bar-coded wristband had been inadvertently switched with that of another patient who had diabetes (Koppel, Metlay, Cohen, et al. 2005; McDonald 2006; Wachter 2006).

37. Birkmeyer (2003).

38. Koppel, Metlay, Cohen, et al. (2005).

39. For cost estimates, see Bates, Leape, Cullen, et al. (1998).

40. The annual operating cost is high because the system must be continuously updated to achieve its potential. A CPOE system, however, need not incorporate all the bells and whistles. Even a modest CPOE system can provide great error reduction so long as it provides for dose selection, a simple process for checking orders against allergies and drug interactions, and a method for physicians to clearly mark the frequency of the drug dosages (Bates, Leape, Cullen, et al. 1998). In addition to error reduction, CPOE results in improved documentation, since the only way the physician can place an order is through the computer system. Also, the system provides a detailed log of all patient orders, which may be useful in tort litigation defense.

41. A randomized, controlled clinical trial showed a connection between a comprehensive electric medical record system and a 12.7 percent reduction in charges per admission (Kaushal, Shojania, and Bates 2003). Cutler, Feldman, and Horwitz (2005) report that for-profit hospitals were the least likely to invest in CPOE systems and government hospitals (excluding federally owned hospitals) were the most likely to do so. Apparently, the view that CPOE reduces cost is not shared by for-profit hospitals.

42. One study found a threefold increase in mortality of critically ill children after the installation of commercially sold CPOEs (Han, Carcillo, Venkataraman, et al. 2005; Wachter 2006). User error accounts for much of this; in a survey 72 percent of house staff reported "difficulty in viewing all the medications on one screen," causing uncertainty about medications and dosages (Koppel, Metlay, Cohen, et al. 2005). Other serious problems found with use of CPOE include failure to provide for suspension of medication post surgery, sending medication to the wrong room, and inflexible ordering screens that result in prescription of incorrect medications.

43. Koppel, Metlay, Cohen, et al. (2005). One hospital reported a 20 to 40 percent loss of efficiency with the use of CPOEs (Poon, Blumenthal, Jaggi, et al. 2004).

44. One study found that more than 80 percent of malpractice suits are due to communication problems between treating physicians (Levinson 1994). Another major source of discontinuity exists with the use of a call system, which requires residents to cover other teams' patients during a twenty-four-hour period. The handoff between the on-call resident and the patient's regular resident is where communications may fail. X-rays and test results may be lost or misdated, thus preventing coordination between the physicians of the patient's diagnosis and care (Ghandi 2005). Unsurprisingly, one study found an association between potentially preventable adverse events and a cross-coverage system where every four days patients are seen by the on-call resident instead of their usual resident (Petersen, Brennan, O'Neil, et al. 1994). In addition, a typical primary care physician may have to review up to 800 data elements from chemistry and hematology reports per week, spending more than seventy minutes per day on test result management (Poon, Blumenthal, Jaggi, et al. 2004). Confronted with this information overload, it is difficult for a primary care physician to adequately communicate and follow up with other physicians caring for the patient in the inpatient setting.

In the United States, patients' physicians typically follow them into the hospital. This is unlike most countries, where hospital-based physicians work independently of community physicians (Ajdari and Fein 1998; Wachter and Goldman 1996). Quite independently of *Err* and in spite of custom, a new specialty has emerged which alters inpatient care. Hospitalists, who care for and coordinate the care of hospitalized patients, have grown in number since their emergence in the early 1990s; currently there are 10,000 hospitalist physicians with a professional society of 5,000 members (Freese 1999; Wachter 2004). There have been numerous studies regarding the effect of hospitalists on patient safety, and they have several findings in common.

Most of the studies found that hospitalists reduced the average length of hospital stay and lowered costs (Wachter and Goldman 2002). Diamond, Goldberg, and Janosky (1998) find that the readmission rate at a community teaching hospital was reduced by almost 50 percent after the introduction of hospitalists. It appears from the data that improvements in cost and outcomes increase with time. A study done by Meltzer, Manning, Morrison, et al. (2002) demonstrated an 8 percent reduction in length of hospital stay, 4.6 percent lower costs, an 18 percent reduction in risk for thirty-day mortality, and a 14 percent reduction in risk for six-day mortality with the care of hospitalists, but only after their second year of service. This same study also showed a $780 savings in adjusted costs for the hospitalists' second year of service. A more recent study (Kaboli, Barnett, and Rosenthal 2004) echoed these findings. Another profession consists of intensivists who focus their work in the ICU (Wachter and Goldman 1996). Twenty-two percent of hospitals have fully implemented the use of intensivists (Devers, Pham, and Liu 2004).

Even though hospitalists may improve coordination of care for hospitalized patients, there has been some concern in the medical community regarding the negative impact of a hospitalist system. A central and reoccurring concern is not only the discontinuity in care during hospital admission and discharge, but also increased costs for the hospital, and the effect on the relationship between patients and their primary care physician (Showstack, Katz, and Weber 1999; Wachter 2004). The hospitalist program at Kaiser Permanente Medical Center in Santa Clara, California, faced the most resistance from internists reluctant to hand over their inpatient responsibilities (Craig, Hartka, Likosky, et al. 1999). To allay these fears, successful hospitalist systems have implemented procedures to continue communication between the hospitalists and the primary care physicians. A few of these measures are calling the primary care physician at both admission and discharge, faxing daily progress notes, and encouraging the involvement of the primary care physician through hospital visits or phone calls to the patient (Wachter and Goldman 2002). After introduction of hospitalists in 1994, Park Nicollet Hospital in Minnesota found that 89 percent of their internists and family practitioners felt the hospitalist system was better or much better than before; it had improved the care of patients, their call schedules, and communication with colleagues (Freese 1999). However, some evidence shows that when patients are seen by hospitalists during the week and see traditional general medicine attendings over the weekend, the discontinuity of care eliminates any savings a hospitalist may have accumulated during the week (Meltzer 2001).

45. Institute of Medicine (2000).

46. Marchev, Rosenthal, and Booth (2003).

47. The Act also requires that hospital peer review groups report any disciplinary actions against medical staff to the National Practitioner Data Bank (42

USCS §11132). Such reports may be accessed by other hospitals considering a physician for membership on their medical staff. The HCQIA was designed to allow the removal of incompetent doctors by peer review committees without fear of lawsuit from the physician in question; it was not designed to protect information from discovery by malpractice plaintiffs or the public more generally.

The court in *Johnson v. Nyack* stated, "The HCQIA gave qualified immunity from suit to officials who conduct peer reviews that meet the standards outlined in the statute. Yet Congress, in providing protection for those involved in peer review, did not establish a privilege for most documents created in that process" 169 F.R.D. 550, 560 (1996 SD NY). Another court went so far as to say, "The Health Care Quality Improvement Act of 1986 is a clear congressional statement that no general medical peer review privilege exists in federal law" (*Mattice v Mem'l Hosp. of S. Bend* 203 FRD 381 (N.D. Ind. 2001).

48. Marchev (2003).

49. Weinberg, Hilborne, and Ngyuen (2005).

50. They state: "Reluctance to embrace [physician clinical performance assessment] PCPA initiatives on grounds that they will be used as evidence against physicians in malpractice litigation reflects perceptions of the law rather than realities. The bar for admission of such evidence in malpractice litigation is high and the possibility that PCPA data will reach this bar seems remote, at least for the vast majority of injury types that prompt litigation. However, PCPA measures may be used against physicians in other medicolegal circumstances. Their exclusion in litigation does not necessarily extend, for example, to proceedings by state licensure boards, hospital review committees, and other adjudicatory bodies with more relaxed rules of evidence" (Kesselheim, Ferris, and Studdert 2006 pp. 1833–1834).

51. Longo, Hewett, Ge, et al. (2005).

52. Wood and Nash (2005).

53. These are similar to the MedMARx system. See above.

54. Jacobson and Bloche (2005); Wood and Nash (2005).

55. Daly (2005).

56. State governments, irrespective of hospital responses in their states, support public release of this information; a majority of the states with reporting systems, fourteen of twenty-one, felt it would be useful to release it to the public. In 2003, these states issued periodic reports or planned to (Marchev, Rosenthal, and Booth 2003).

57. Sage (2003); White (1994).

58. These theories are discussed in greater detail in chapter 9.

59. Continuing medical education requirements may be imposed, but basically physicians, unlike drivers, whose licenses require periodic reexaminations, are

licensed for life (with the exception of delicensure from disciplinary proceedings).

60. Sloan, Mergenhagen, Burfield, et al. (1989).

61. Ameringer (1999). Bovbjerg, Aliaga, and Gittler (2006) document that medical boards are experimenting with some promising alternatives to conventional processes.

62. The American Medical Association is attempting to remedy these inconsistencies through a voluntary accreditation program which measures individual physicians against national standards and peer performance (Viswanathan and Salmon 2000).

63. Blumstein and Sloan (1988).

64. Newton (2001). A sampling of the variability of these statutes: in 1999, forty-seven states had immunity statutes, forty-eight states had peer review statutes, and thirty-one states required confidentiality and gave privilege to information obtained during peer review (Scheutzow 1999). Of these thirty-one states, only eight imposed civil or criminal penalties for breach of confidentiality; of the forty-eight states granting privilege, only ten granted full protection to any parties in a civil action involving the provider under review without requiring release of that information to the state licensing board (Scheutzow 1999).

65. As of the late 1990s, forty-four states used evaluations from the Joint Commission on Accreditation of Healthcare Organizations (JCAHO) as a requirement for licensure, with 85 percent of hospitals accredited. Health plans are evaluated in a similar fashion, with accreditation a component in obtaining licensure (Institute of Medicine 2000).

66. Devers, Pham, and Liu (2004). To address patient safety issues in ambulatory care, Schaffer, Feldman, Fleischer, et al. (2005) suggest that all physicians be accredited by a hospital, including performing a minimum number of procedures per year. However, there is some evidence suggesting that stricter licensing and credentialing laws may not improve outpatient safety. Based on a study of reported adverse events in office settings in Florida during 2000–2004, Coldiron, Fisher, Adelman, et al. (2005) report that 94 percent of the physicians reporting adverse events were board certified, and 97 percent had hospital privileges.

Some states and professional organizations, including Pennsylvania, Rhode Island, Florida, California, Georgia, Texas, the American Society of Plastic Surgeons, and the American Society of Aesthetic Plastic Surgeons, require accreditation from an outside agency (Coldiron, Fisher, Adelman, et al. 2005; Franko 2001). In addition, the JCAHO has recently taken the initiative to reduce errors from patient handoffs. For the first time, they are requiring hospitals to establish standards for communications during handoffs (Landro 2006).

67. Bradley, Herrin, Elbel, et al. (2006). E.g., beta-blocker use at admission and discharge, aspirin use at admission and discharge, and angiotensin-converting enzyme (ACE) indicator use.

68. Heart attack.

69. Hyman and Silver (2005).

70. Ibid. Physicians in other specialties have also recognized that they have a positive role to play in improving patient safety in their practices. For example, Attarian and Vail (2005) suggest to their colleagues that every surgeon document and demonstrate four elements in the care of each patient: (1) technical knowledge of the procedure; (2) competence in performance; (3) carefulness in evaluation and diagnosis; and (4) care in the treatment of patients using informed consent, professional skill and attention to the patient's surgery, postoperative care, and complications. The authors conclude that following this standard of care will make proving liability nearly impossible, while improving patient safety.

71. Thirty-nine states have introduced legislation, and six have passed laws (R. Weinstein, Siegel, and Brennan 2005).

72. Marchev, Rosenthal, and Booth (2003).

73. Marchev (2003). Nineteen of the twenty-one states enacted legislation designed to protect the reported data. Methods included de-identification of data, to protect facility confidentiality, and anonymous reporting, to reduce the risk of increased litigation. Though helpful in encouraging providers' participation, both of these methods limit the value of the data for individual consumer choice.

74. Marchev, Rosenthal, and Booth (2003).

75. Dranove, Kessler, McClellan, et al. (2003).

76. Jin and Leslie (2003).

77. Coldiron, Fisher, Adelman, et al. (2005).

78. Texas includes all outpatient facilities owned or run by a hospital in its mandatory reporting requirements (Texas Health and Safety Code Sec.241.202 (2003). However, many states extend the duty only to outpatient surgical facilities (National Academy for State Health Policy 2006). See Pennsylvania (Pa. Stat. Ann. tit. 40, §1303.301–1303.315 (2003)); Nevada (Nev. Rev. Stat. Ann. §439.800–439.890 (2006)); and Connecticut (Conn. Gen. Stat. §19a-127n (2006).

79. See chapter 3 for a more detailed discussion of this issue.

80. Lemaire (1985).

81. Moore and Viscusi (1989); also see chapter 10.

82. Topel (1984).

83. Sloan, Stout, Whetten-Goldstein, et al. (2000).

84. Enterprise liability is discussed in depth in chapter 12.

85. Havighurst (1997). Danzon (2000), however, cautions that the saving in litigation cost would be minor. Individual physicians would still be called to testify to describe the course of events leading to the injury. In addition,

she notes that as long as the liability rule includes negligence, individuals may be asked to describe the facts leading to a conclusion of negligent or non-negligent acts.

86. The case for health plans as the enterprise is as follows. They are well-capitalized; the managed health plans may have the capacity to balance quality and cost in their product offerings, and can incorporate alternative dispute resolution into contractual provisions (Sage and Jorling 1994). Managed health plans presumably are actively involved in managing care and eliminating care that is not cost-effective. Thus, shifting liability to them seems to be a practical alternative.

Several health plans have willingly embraced enterprise liability without any compulsion from statutes or regulation. Kaiser-Permanente, Sharp Health Care, the Public Health Service, the Department of Defense, the Veterans Administration, the Indian Health Service, and the Bureau of Prisons all expressly assume liability for the medical errors of their staff physicians (Sage and Jorling 1994). Having responsibility for the actions of physicians with which health plans have contractual arrangements creates incentives for health plans to be more cautious in their screening of providers (Jacobi and Huberfeld 2001).

But having health plans be the enterprises also has several important disadvantages. And the disadvantages are substantial enough to largely eliminate health plan enterprise liability as a major alternative to the present system.

Unlike hospitals, health plans are typically not located where the medical care is delivered. Except in closed staff managed care organizations, such as Kaiser, most physicians have contractual arrangements with several health plans. It becomes difficult to abide by various protocols of different health plans and, often, even to know what the protocols are. There is considerable turnover in the ownership of health plans. During the course of a single tort case, health plan ownership may change several times. Much of employer-provided health insurance in the United States is self-insured. It seems doubtful that many employers would desire to take on being potentially liable for medical malpractice. Nor would they likely be efficient in performing this role. Given the managed care backlash and physician opposition to many health plans, this would amount to moving physicians from the frying pan, the existing situation, into the fire, enterprise liability with health plans the enterprise of choice. Finally, some personal health care services may not be covered by enterprise liability. Services such as lasik surgery or home health or nursing home care, may not be covered by the health plan. In principle, such services could be excluded from coverage under the enterprise liability program, and force providers to continue to obtain medical malpractice insurance as they do currently.

87. Mello and Brennan (2002).

88. Danzon (1985).

89. Sloan (1990). Of fourteen medical malpractice insurers, three multiple-line, commercial stock and eleven single-line physician-sponsored mutuals or reciprocals specializing in medical malpractice insurance surveyed in 1987–1988 by

colleagues and the first author, often fewer than 1 percent of physician insureds paid more than standard rates because of adverse prior claims experience. Among these, only recent claims were counted against the physician since insurers believed that old claims have little predictive value. None of the surcharges exceeded 200 percent of standard rates.

The survey revealed several reasons that medical malpractice insurers were reluctant to engage in experience rating. Some national medical organizations and their physician constituents opposed it. Surcharged physicians often left the company because they were able to secure lower premiums from competing insurers. This occurred because each insurer used only its own experience in setting premiums. Experience rating was seen as infeasible in medical malpractice insurance markets in which competition prevailed, since physicians could always find a lower-priced alternative. Some insurers indicated that experience rating is inappropriate for a line with low claims frequency, such as medical malpractice insurance.

90. Sloan, Bovbjerg, and Githens (1991). In some cases, physicians with adverse records find that their coverage is not renewed and they must seek coverage from surplus line insurers (W. B. Schwartz and Mendelson 1989) or joint underwriting associations (see chapter 9).

91. Both insurers of physicians and self-insuring hospitals frequently purchase reinsurance coverage (see chapter 9).

92. The Poisson process, named after the French mathematician Siméon-Denis Poisson (1781–1840), is a stochastic process which is defined in terms of the occurrences of events (Ellis, Gallup, and McGuire 1990; Rolph 1981; Nye and Hofflander 1988). (http://en.wikipedia.org/wiki/Poisson_process, accessed June 20, 2007).

93. Sloan and Hassan (1990).

94. In Soviet history and iconography, a Stakhanovite follows the example of Aleksei Grigorievich Stakhanov, employing hard work to overachieve on the job Stakhanovite workers were honored and rewarded for exceptional diligence in increasing production (Wren and Bedeian 2004). http://en.wikipedia.org/wiki/Stakhanovite (accessed June 20, 2007).

95. Mello, Kelly, Studdert, et al. (2003).

Chapter 9

1. Danzon (1985).

2. Sloan (1990).

3. Sloan, Bovbjerg, and Githens (1991).

4. A Lloyd's association is like a reciprocal (see below) in that the organization issues no policies. Rather, it serves as a mechanism whereby members insure themselves and others. A Lloyd's association insures outsiders, whereas in a

reciprocal, members insure each other. In the malpractice insurance field, the Lloyd's form is used only for reinsurance.

5. Greene (1976).

6. Klein (1995); Sloan, Bovbjerg, and Githens (1991).

7. Sloan and Hsieh (1990).

8. Klein (1995).

9. Harrington (2002).

10. Cummins and Danzon (1991).

11. See chapter 2 for further discussion of this point.

12. Blackmon and Zeckhauser (1991); Grabowski, Viscusi, and Evans (1989).

13. Yelen (1993).

14. Hart, Shleifer, and Vishny (1997).

15. The Risk Retention Act was first passed by the U.S. Congress in 1981 to assist individuals or organizations seeking product liability coverage (P.L. 97–45). It responded to specific concerns about manufacturers' ability to purchase coverage even prior to the crisis of the mid-1980s. In 1986, the coverage was expanded to include liability coverage in general, including medical malpractice insurance (P.L. 99–563).

16. States without mandatory insurance use other mechanisms to accomplish the same objective.

17. According to Schwartz and Mendelson (1989a), in the 1980s, about 900 physicians in the United States lost coverage from a standard insurer and were able to gain coverage through a JUA.

18. Schwartz and Mendelson (1989b).

19. Sloan, Bovbjerg, and Githens (1991, p. 177).

20. In a theoretical study, Shavell (1987) shows that insurance does not necessarily interfere with the deterrence function of malpractice liability if premiums are perfectly experience rated. In contrast to medical malpractice, experience rating is common in other lines, e.g., automobile insurance or workers' compensation.

21. Sloan (1990).

22. Hickson, Clayton, Githens, et al. (2002); Sloan, Mergenhagen, Burfield, et al. (1989).

23. For example, New York State required that its Department of Insurance institute merit rating in the mid-1980s. Merit rating is a system of surcharges and credits based on an individual insured's history of liability claims relative to the average insured in his or her specialty and geographic area, and on disciplinary actions by hospitals or licensing boards against the insured. Based on this experience, James P. Corcoran, Superintendent of Insurance of New York State concludes: "Physicians are unalterably opposed to merit rating. It is unrealistic

to apply a merit rating plan, or any individual risk rating plan, to a low-frequency, high-severity coverage. Due to the length of time claims are open, it is difficult to have enough meaningful data for merit rating of medical malpractice. A merit rating plan is not intended to be used to remove poor doctors by pricing them out of business" (1997, p. 2). An experience review plan was proposed in Massachusetts, but in the face of political opposition from physicians, the plan was never adopted (Sloan, Mergenhagen, Burfield, et al. 1989). Other programs implemented by individual insurers have not been evaluated (Sloan, Bovbjerg, and Githens 1991, pp. 173–176). Of the thirteen out of the fourteen insurers that had previously implemented some form of experience rating among the insurers surveyed in 1987–1988, most had completely abandoned the program as of the survey date or continued a program in a very limited form (Sloan, Bovbjerg, and Githens 1991, p. 177).

24. Sloan and Hassan (1990).

25. Nutter (1985).

26. Council of State Governments (2003); New York Department of Insurance (1997); Robinson (1986).

27. Morton (2003).

28. Sutter (2002).

29. Council of State Governments (2003); New York Department of Insurance (1997); Robinson (1986).

30. Kenney (1988).

31. Sloan, Bovbjerg, and Githens (1991).

32. Nutter (1985).

33. Hospital and Healthsystem Association of Pennsylvania (2002b).

34. Bovbjerg and Bartow (2003).

35. Hospital and Healthsystem Association of Pennsylvania (2002a). These increases occurred even though coverage from the JUA tends to be relatively expensive (Eskin 2003; Mello, Kelly, Studdert, et al. 2003).

36. State of Florida (2003).

37. One exception is legislation introduced in Missouri requiring the JUA administrator to formulate, implement, and monitor a risk management program for all policyholders (State of Missouri 2002, 2003).

38. Pennsylvania Professional Liability Joint Underwriting Association Manual. http://www.pajua.com/images/200309%20U-W%20Manual.pdf.

39. Downs and Sommer (1999).

40. Sloan, Bovbjerg, and Githens (1991, pp. 55–56).

41. Lee, Mayers, and Smith (1997).

42. Hofflander and Nettesham (2001).

43. Cummins (1988); Lee, Mayers, and Smith (1997).

44. Downs and Sommer (1999). On the other hand, a guaranty fund may induce insurers to monitor each other and alert regulators when a competitor takes on too much risk (Hall, Cummins, Laderman, et al. 1988).

45. See, e.g., Sloan (2004).

46. Gron (1990, 1994a).

47. Gron (1994b).

48. E.g., Breyer (1982); Peltzman (1976); Posner (1974); Stigler (1971).

49. Schneiberg and Bartley (2001).

50. Meier (1988).

51. Grabowski, Viscusi, and Evans (1989) investigated the effects of state automobile insurance regulation on price and availability of insurance. Earlier studies on these outcomes had produced mixed results, in part because there was little variation in state regulatory practices in the sample. Grabowski and coauthors used a sample of thirty states for the period 1974 to 1981 and a sample of eleven states that had deregulated such insurance. They report that regulation reduced the auto insurance premiums relative to losses, but also increased the size of the involuntary market in these states by 17 percent. The involuntary market consisted of JUA and assigned-risk plans. The disadvantage of the involuntary market is the extensive subsidy of unsafe drivers, which not only is inequitable but also increase the risk of driving to the public at large.

52. Munch and Smallwood (1980).

53. Above, we used the example of a 0.4–0.5 percent insolvency risk. A lower insolvency risk would require higher initial capitalization. Perhaps some consumers are willing to tolerate a 0.4–0.5 percent insolvency risk per year. By setting the initial capitalization standard too high, these persons are made worse off. Also, some firms may be undesirable in terms of their insolvency risk, but may offer other products with attributes that some consumers desire. Also, elimination of competition from small firms may result in higher premiums being charged by those firms that are able to gain entry into the market. Winter (1988, 1991) warns that insurance regulators who use the premium-to-surplus ratio to gauge insolvency risk may view increases in ratio as an unfavorable development. If regulators act on this evidence to restrict the supply of insurance during downturns in the insurance cycle, they may exacerbate the cycle by reducing availability of coverage. Winter does not present any direct empirical evidence that regulation has actually had this effect.

54. Sloan, Bovbjerg, and Githens (1991).

55. Born, Viscusi, and Baker (2006).

56. Viscusi and Born (1995).

57. Viscusi and Born (2005).

58. Born (2001, p. 212).

59. Goldstein (2003).

60. Darragh (2002b).

61. Goldstein (2003).

62. Ibid.

63. Darragh (2002a).

64. Goldstein (2003).

65. McLeod (2002).

66. Darragh (2002b).

67. Ibid.

68. McLeod (2002).

69. Ibid.

70. Goldstein (2003).

71. Ibid.

72. St. Paul stopped accepting new clients and refused to renew the policies of its current policyholders in 2000.

73. In 1991 NORCAL acquired the assets and liabilities of the Medical Indemnity Corporation of Alaska (MICA), and in 1994 it acquired a portion of Premier Alliance Insurance Company's business located in Rhode Island. NORCAL then opened offices in Anchorage and Providence. A few years later, NORCAL entered into a jointly owned venture with the Medical Mutual Liability Insurance Society of Maryland (Med Mutual). Its portion of this venture began with the start of an insurance holding company, Medical Group Holdings, Inc. (MGH). In 2000, NORCAL acquired 100 percent ownership of MGH from Med Mutual. Also during this time period, NORCAL acquired the majority interest in Pennsylvania Medical Society Liability Insurance Company (PMSLIC). Four years later, MGH acquired the ownership of PMSLIC, giving NORCAL 100 percent ownership and making PMSLIC a subsidiary of NORCAL.

74. Darmiento (2005).

75. Ibid.

76. Cebula (1995); Grossman (1992); Keeley (1990); Wheelock and Wilson (1995).

77. Grossman (1992).

78. Keeley (1990).

79. Wheelock and Wilson (1995).

80. Cebula (1995).

Chapter 10

1. Sloan, Bovbjerg, and Githens (1991).

2. Klein (1998, p. 176).

3. Kunreuther (1998, p. 47).

4. Medical malpractice insurers have solved the problem of the lag between the date of injury and the date of claim filing by switching to claims-made coverage from occurrence coverage. Under claims made, the insurer covers losses from all claims filed during the policy year. Under an occurrence policy, the insurer covers losses from injuries occurring during the policy year.

5. Sloan, Eesley, Conover, et al. (2004).

6. Kunreuther, Pauly, and Russell (2004); Michel-Kerjan and Marcellis-Warin (2006).

7. According to Doherty and Smetters (2005), there is more monitoring when the primary insurer and reinsurer are affiliates than when they are unaffiliated, presumably because affiliations reduce monitoring cost.

8. In Pennsylvania, a PCF provides what is essentially a middle layer of medical malpractice insurance coverage for hospitals. Thus, since there is no corridor between the maximum loss covered by the primary insurer and the point at which the middle layer attaches to the PCF plan, the incentive that the primary insurer has to defend claims is reduced. It is often easier for a primary insurer to close a case when the settlement offer rises to an amount covered by the PCF than to fight for a lower settlement at a level below which the PCF is obligated to pay part of the claim.

9. Hoerger, Sloan, and Hassan (1990).

10. A survey of hospital administrators conducted in 2004 by the first author and Duke University colleagues revealed that hospitals choose to purchase excess coverage to eliminate/reduce total excess loss, to spread the risk of catastrophic loss over time, and to address trustee concerns (Sloan, Eesley, Conover, et al. 2004). Some might argue that medical malpractice expense is a small percentage of total hospital revenue—3.9 percent for physicians, 1 percent for hospitals (United States General Accounting Office 1995; United States Government Accountability Office 2005, p. 5). However, to the extent that raising hospital prices is precluded, increases in premiums directly reduce profits so that premium increases as a share of profits are likely to be substantially higher. Factors such as market competitiveness and hospital ownership influence the ability of hospitals to shift costs by increasing prices. The extent of this cost-shifting to consumers appears to be stable over time (Zwanziger, Melnick, and Bamezai 2000).

11. Given that bankruptcy is not costless, even an insurer not averse to risk (risk-neutral insurer) would demand reinsurance. In analyzing decisions of firms, economists typically assume that the firm is risk neutral. An alternative is to assume that the firm is risk averse. While this complicates the analyses, in general, the more complex assumption of risk aversion does not yield important additional insights.

12. See chapter 2 for further discussion of insurer constraints.

13. Froot (2001) This information was obtained from Guy Carpenter & Company, a reinsurance subsidiary of Marsh McLennan and by far the largest at-risk intermediary in the United States.

14. Ibid. (p. 541).

15. Weiss and Chung (2004).

16. See chapter 9 for a discussion of adequacy of primary medical malpractice premiums for which the requisite data are available.

17. A common misconception is that insurers can just increase premiums in response to previous losses. Such patterns are observed, but for a different reason. Premium increases following the occurrence of a catastrophic event may be attributable to probability updating by insurers (future events seem more likely) and not to repayment of losses from prior claims (Froot and O'Connell 1997; Michel-Kerjan and Marcellis-Warin 2006; Weiss and Chung 2004).

There may also be updating by potential insurance purchasers. There is empirical evidence in other contexts (e.g., flood insurance and terrorism insurance) that consumers tend to cancel their policies after a period during which an event did not occur. After an event occurred, their beliefs and demand for insurance change dramatically. See a summary of evidence in Kunreuther, Pauly, and Russell (2004) and Kunreuther (2006).

18. Kunreuther, Pauly, and Russell (2004).

19. Moral hazard is an issue for insurance more generally. According to Kunreuther (2006), "If the insurer reduced the Lowes' [a hypothetical family] homeowners' premium by $275, would the family invest in the mitigation measure? Empirical evidence on individuals' decision processes with respect to adoption of protective measures suggests that they would not."

20. The cedent.

21. Froot lists two other possible explanations that are even more speculative than the others, and therefore are not discussed here. In the end, he calls for more empirical evidence and does not reach definitive conclusions among the various explanations he proposes. Overall, the high cost of externally supplied equity capital seems to be the most compelling of the above explanations. Subsequent research by Weiss and Chung (2004) finds empirical support for this explanation.

22. Nordman, Cermak, and McDaniel (2004).

23. See further discussion of this issue in chapter 2.

24. Doherty, Lamm-Tennant, and Starks (2003); Bovbjerg and Bartow (2003, p. 21).

25. Venezian (1985). These shocks can be due to factors that affect property-casualty insurance in general (Doherty, Lamm-Tennant, and Starks 2003; Gron 1994a; Winter 1988).

26. Froot and O'Connell (1997).

27. Sloan, Bovbjerg, and Githens (1991), using data on medical malpractice coverage for the years 1975–1985, conclude that profitability of primary medical malpractice insurers on a risk-adjusted basis was about at the level one would expect in a competitive industry. This analysis is based on income and balance sheets (convention statements), which are routinely filed with state departments of insurance. However, given the lack of regulation of reinsurers by these same departments, a parallel analysis cannot be conducted for reinsurance.

28. Even self-insured hospitals pay "premiums" for excess coverage in terms of their loss experience plus overhead costs of running a captive or risk retention group (RRG). Regulators also require self-insured entities to hire a "fronting" insurer licensed in the state to assure payment of claims (Bovbjerg and Bartow 2003). Despite the increase in premiums, 20 percent of hospitals in a Duke study reported they had had difficulties collecting payments from their excess carrier since 2000, and 33 percent reported difficulties in collecting payments from their PCF (Sloan 2004).

Theory suggests two ways for high premiums or lack of availability of coverage to affect hospitals. First, hospitals unable to purchase coverage may cease provision of services that are most likely to produce malpractice claims as a way of reducing their exposure to risk. Second, if coverage is purchased at a high price, hospital cash flow could be compromised. Five of the twenty-one hospitals in the Duke University study reported closing services (obstetrics, for example) or failing to open a service as a result of concerns about excess coverage (Sloan and Eesley 2006). In addition, lack of excess insurance or high premiums had affected hospital operations in the past for 40 percent of hospitals surveyed. Many hospitals surveyed said that fewer dollars were available for expansion of services due to high premium expenses.

29. Blumberg and Holahan (2004).

30. Katherine Swartz (2006) proposes that the federal government provide a reinsurance program for health insurance that would take responsibility for persons in the highest 1 percent of medical expenses but would be limited to persons who were in the individual and small-group insurance markets. She estimates that such a program would reduce health insurance premiums for such coverage by 20–40 percent, with the caveat that the savings would depend on how the reinsurance programs were structured. She argues that such a program would have the advantage of reducing insurers' incentives to select against high-cost individuals which exists currently.

31. Admittedly, for equity reasons, the change in identity may be social welfare-enhancing.

32. Insurers that sell medical liability insurance but no other type of coverage.

33. Sloan, Bovbjerg, and Githens (1991, p. 123).

34. Sloan, Bovbjerg, and Githens (1991).

35. Sloan, Eesley, and Conover (2005, fig. 2).

36. Bovbjerg and Bartow (2003).

37. Hoerger, Sloan, and Hassan (1990).

38. Pinnacle Actuarial Resources (2003).

39. Philadelphia juries, for example, in recent years have often awarded amounts in medical malpractice cases in excess of $1 million (Bovbjerg and Bartow 2003). In Pennsylvania, the presence of a PCF has not eliminated hospital demand for private excess coverage (Hospital and Healthsystem Association of Pennsylvania 2002a).

40. See the classic article by Rothschild and Stiglitz (1976), which led to the authors receiving a Nobel Prize in economics.

41. All PCFs except those in Pennsylvania and New York now use the reserving for anticipated losses mechanism. Pennsylvania still uses pay-as-you-go financing even though several state PCFs have decided to drop it (Hofflander, Nye, and Nettesheim 2001).

42. Kansas, New Mexico, Wisconsin, and Louisiana have used loss-reserving in funding their PCFs (Kansas Health Care Stabilization Fund 2002; Louisiana Patient Compensation Fund, http://www.lapcf.state.la.us; New Mexico Public Regulation Commission 2001; Wisconsin Patient Compensation Fund, http://oci .wi.gov/pcf/htm). Still, choosing to hold reserves in and of itself does not assure adequate financing. Though the reasons may differ, public and private insurers which have actuarial evaluations performed do not always follow their recommendations (Sloan, Bovbjerg, and Githens 1991, p. 157). Additionally, reserves are vulnerable to utilization for unrelated purposes, as has occurred in Wisconsin (Wisconsin Insurance Report 2001, http://oci.wi.gov/ann_rpt/bus_2001/anrpttoc .htm; Wisconsin Hospital Association 2003).

43. Sloan, Bovbjerg, and Githens (1991, pp. 123–144).

44. Albert (2003) tells the story of one physician's decision to move from Pennsylvania to Wisconsin based on the different medical malpractice environments in each state.

45. Sutter (2002). The New Mexico Department of Insurance completed an actuarial study concluding that the state's PCF was underfunded by $9 million, but the state medical society recommended no increase in physician contributions.

46. Sloan, Bovbjerg, and Githens (1991).

47. In Wisconsin, a state in which the PCF does maintain reserves at a relatively high level (Wisconsin Insurance Report 2001), the governor proposed to tap $200 million from the fund in order to subsidize Medicaid (Wisconsin Hospital Association 2003).

48. For further discussion of this issue, see chapters 5 and 7.

49. Hofflander, Nye, and Nettesheim (2001).

50. In South Carolina, which historically appeared to underreserve as a matter of policy, health care providers could be sued individually for the

full amount claimed if the PCF's funds were insufficient to pay its obligations. The state's PCF and its consulting actuary considered the PCF a risk pool rather than an insurance company, and therefore saw no need for regulatory oversight or standard loss-reserving practices (South Carolina Legislative Audit 2000).

51. Margolis (1982); Musgrave (1957).

52. During the course of research on this report, the first author requested unpublished material from several state agencies. In many cases, the material was sent. In other cases, however, data could not be obtained. In at least one case, an employee volunteered to work overtime, for an overtime wage, to photocopy financial documents. Apparently no records were publicly available, nor was production of the documents seen as an appropriate function of the public agency.

53. Anderson (1976).

54. Insurance is available to residents only after their community has completed the requirements. The area must be declared flood prone by FEMA, and the community must file an application with the NFIP within one year (R. Stedman 2003). After completing a thorough application process requiring approval of flood hazard maps and the institution of new community ordinances, the community becomes part of the Emergency Program, making it eligible for limited flood insurance (R. Stedman 2003).

55. http://www.insurancescrawl.com/archives/2005/11/stranded_withou.html.

56. http://www.fema.gov/pdf/nfip/market_pen.pdf.

57. United States Congressional Budget Office (2002).

58. http://www.insurancescrawl.com/archives/2005/11/stranded_withou.html.

59. Chu (2005).

60. United States Congressional Budget Office (2002).

61. Available at www.citizensfla.com.

62. Kunreuther (2006).

63. Doherty and Smetters (2002); United States Congressional Budget Office (2002, Box B-1, p. 45); Varian (2001).

64. United States Congressional Budget Office (2002).

65. Varian (2001); Doherty and Smetters (2002).

Chapter 11

1. See, e.g., Danzon (1991).

2. Danzon (1994).

3. Danzon (1991).

4. Weiler, Hiatt, Newhouse, et al. (1993); Bovbjerg and Sloan (1998); Studdert and Brennan (2001).

5. Weiler, Hiatt, Newhouse, et al. (1993).

6. (Weiler 1993); Weiler, Hiatt, Newhouse, et al. (1993, p. 146).

7. Studdert and Brennan (2001).

8. See, e.g., Weiler, Hiatt, Newhouse, et al. (1993).

9. Joint Legislative Audit and Review Commission of the Virginia General Assembly (2002, p. 4).

10. Ibid. (p. 83).

11. State of Florida (2003).

12. Sloan, Whetten-Goldstein, Kulas, et al. (1999).

13. Freeman and Freeman (1989).

14. Sloan et al. (1997).

15. Studdert, Fritz, and Brennan (2000).

16. Blair and Stanley (1988); Nelson and Ellenberg (1986).

17. Sloan, Whetten-Goldstein, Entman, et al. (1997).

18. Failure to give adequate notice is understandable, in that few expectant mothers want to contemplate life with a child with cerebral palsy before the fact, and this outcome has a low probability of occurring.

19. Studdert, Fritz, and Brennan (2000, p. 523).

20. Ibid. (p. 524).

21. Bovbjerg and Sloan (1998, p. 112).

22. Joint Legislative Audit and Review Commission of the Virginia General Assembly (2002, p. vi).

23. Ibid. (p. 25). Unlike Florida, where closed medical malpractice claims are publicly available and can be compared with no-fault, there are no claims in the public domain in Virginia. Thus there is no way to perform an independent comparison.

24. Sloan, Whetten-Goldstein, Entman, et al. (1997).

25. Joint Legislative Audit and Review Commission of the Virginia General Assembly (2002, p. 9) In comparison, the tort system overhead is approximately 50 percent (Kakalik and Pace 1986).

26. Bovbjerg and Sloan (1998).

27. Hay (1996); Danzon (1983); B. L. Smith (1992).

28. Joint Legislative Audit and Review Commission of the Virginia General Assembly (2002, p. 16).

29. Ibid. (p. xv).

30. Ibid. (p. 8).

31. Norton (1997); Bovbjerg and Sloan (1998).

32. Joint Legislative Audit and Review Commission of the Virginia General Assembly (2002, pp. 37–38).

33. State of Florida (2003, p. 306).

34. Joint Legislative Audit and Review Commission of the Virginia General Assembly (2002, p. 49).

35. Ibid. (p. v).

36. NICA reserved $3 million per covered child on average (State of Florida 2003).

37. Sloan, Whetten-Goldstein, Entman, et al. (1997); Sloan, Whetten-Goldstein, Stout, et al. (1998).

38. Sloan, Whetten-Goldstein, Entman, et al. (1997).

39. Bovbjerg and Sloan (1998, p. 117).

40. Lloyd-Puryear, Ball, and Benor (1998).

41. http://www.hrsa.gov/vaccinecompensation. Influenza and hepatitis A vaccines have recently been added to the program.

42. http://www.hrsa.gov/vaccinecompensation/statistics_report.htm#post_1988.

43. Ibid.

44. Advisory Commission on Childhood Vaccines (2003).

45. http://www.hrsa.gov/vaccinecompensation/statistics_report.htm#post_1988.

46. Evans (1998).

47. Sloan, Berman, Rosenbaum, et al. (2004).

48. Finkelstein (2004).

49. Advisory Commission on Childhood Vaccines (2004).

50. Ridgway (1999).

51. Evans (1998, p. 8).

52. During the discovery phase of the proceedings, respondents have produced 92,268 documents related to thimerosal. The Department of Justice believes the excessive number of documents is delaying the proceedings and runs counter to the intent of the no-fault program. The U.S. Food and Drug Administration was asked to determine which documents may be relevant. The petitions appear to be leveling off, but the number of thimerosal claims, about ten times the number of nonthimerosal claims between 2002 and 2004, resulted in a need for additional funding to process all of the petitions. Since 1996, the appropriations to staff the VICP program have stayed flat. However, the president's budget for FY 2005 sought an increase of $2,305,000 (50 percent of the past appropriations) to handle the growth in vaccine injury claims caused by thimerosal-related claims (Keisler 2004).

53. Institute of Medicine (2004).

54. *Holder v. Abbott Laboratories Inc.* (2006). 444 F.3d 383; see also W. Davis (2006).

55. Finkelstein (2003, p. 5).

56. These changes include the addition of chronic arthritis from rubella vaccines, the removal of certain disorders for the DTP vaccine, and a clarification of the definition of encephalopathy in 1995. In 1997, modifications of the table included the addition of brachial neuritis and removal of encephalopathy for tetanus-containing vaccines, as well a number of other modifications. In 1998 rotavirus vaccine was added to the table. August 2002 brought a second category of rotavirus along with an additional injury for that vaccine, addition of pneumococcal conjugate vaccines with no condition specified, and removal of early-onset Hib disease and residual seizure disorder from the table (Health Resources and Services Administration 2006).

57. Ridgway (1999, p. 69).

58. Ibid. (p. 71).

59. Ibid. One solution may be to extend the statute of limitations so that the scientific literature has more time to catch up to the legal reality of decisions that need to be made. However, the problem is that while the scientific literature is coming to a consensus, there are unknown numbers of people who are incurring and having to pay large medical bills for real injuries. The VICP addresses this potential problem with a long retroactive window once a change is made. If an injury or a new vaccine is added to the table, petitioners have two years from the effective date of the table change to file a claim for a vaccine-related injury or death that occurred up to eight years before the effective date of the table change (Advisory Commission on Childhood Vaccines 2004).

60. An important issue not discussed in the text relates to patient safety. There are issues regarding how safety concerns are being communicated to vaccine manufacturers and what they are actually doing about them. Do manufacturers have to spend too much to comply with erroneous adverse events (this may be happening with thimerosal), resulting in a costly tax on more beneficial innovations? Or are they spending too little to expeditiously correct legitimate safety issues? If the option of tort is eliminated, where is the manufacturer's incentive to correct and prevent the (admittedly rare) problems caused by the vaccines? Isn't genetic testing or altering the vaccine possible to prevent some of these side effects?

Part of the answer is that there are four ways vaccine safety is monitored (Institute of Medicine 1997). One question for a broader medical no-fault program is whether it would require implementation of a similar safety monitoring system to be able to update Tables of Injuries for a wide variety of medical procedures and pharmaceuticals. For vaccines, the four monitoring systems are the Vaccine Adverse Event Reporting System (VAERS), the Vaccine Safety Datalink (VSD), monitoring by vaccine manufacturers themselves, and monitoring by the FDA.

VAERS was set up in 1990 and is administered by the Centers for Disease Control and Prevention and the FDA. Health care providers are required to report to VAERS serious adverse events occurring within thirty days of vaccination. However, the number of doses actually given from each lot is not known, so interpretation of VAERS data is uncertain. Five adverse events have a very different meaning if they are the result of twenty doses given from a lot as compared to two million doses having been given.

Actively capturing more complete and detailed information from Oregon, Washington, and California, the Vaccine Safety Datalink (VSD) helps to determine whether an event is linked with a vaccine or with some other cause. The VSD can test and evaluate signals of potential problems spotted by the VAERS system.

Food and Drug Administration monitoring is accomplished via review of VAERS and the manufacturer's data. Manufacturers form the largest percentage of contributors to VAERS, so this monitoring represents some built-in duplication. The National Childhood Vaccine Injury Act of 1986 mandates that manufacturers report adverse events to the Department of Health and Human Services.

61. Advisory Commission on Childhood Vaccines (2003).

62. Freeman and Freeman (1989).

63. Fishback and Kantor (1998b, p. 305).

64. But employees in nonunionized settings paid for the added benefits in the form of reduced wages (Arnould and Nichols 1983; Dorsey and Walzer 1983; Fishback and Kantor 1998a, 1998b; Gruber and Krueger 1991).

65. Fishback and Kantor (1998b, p. 326).

66. Ibid. (especially p. 326).

67. Ibid. (p. 325).

68. Ibid. (p. 327).

69. R. Smith (1990).

70. Ruser (1998).

71. Biddle, Roberts, Rosenman, and Welch (1998).

72. Leigh and Robbins (2004).

73. Rhodes and Ohlsson (1997, pp. 5–6 and 5–7).

74. This has been documented by Ruser (1998) and Campolieti and Hyatt (2006).

75. Moore and Viscusi (1989).

76. Library (2004, p. 1), see http:www.igs.berkeley.edu/library/htWorkersCompensation.htm (accessed December 30, 2004).

77. Bovbjerg, Tancredi, and Gaylin (1991).

78. Joost (1992, chapter 7).

79. Sloan and Githens (1994).

80. Landes (1982); Kochanowski and Young (1985); and Lund and Zador (1986).

81. Sloan, Reilly, and Schenzler (1994, 1995).

82. Brown (1985).

83. Cohen and Dehejia (2003); Cummins, Phillips, and Weiss (2001).

84. Loughran (2001).

85. Gaudry (1986); Devlin (1990).

86. Lemstra and Olszynski (2005).

87. Gellhorn (1988); E. Cohen and Korper (1976); Palmer (1979); Rosenthal (1988).

88. Fallberg and Borgenhammar (1997).

89. Essinger (2005).

90. Danzon (1994).

91. Fallberg and Borgenhammar (1997).

92. Danzon (1994).

93. Ibid.

94. Ibid.; Studdert and Brennan (2001).

95. Espersson (2000).

96. Ibid.

97. Danzon (1994).

98. Compensability is available for treatment-related infections only. Examples of uncompensable infections are postsurgical infections of the intestines, trachea, and tissue of diminished vitality. Also, infection from prolonged catheterization or drainage is not compensable.

99. Danzon (1994).

100. Ibid.; Fallberg and Borgenhammar (1997); Studdert and Brennan (2001); Espersson (2005).

101. Sappideen (1993).

102. This is also referred to as the Patient Claims Panel. Claimants may skip this step and proceed directly to a court of general jurisdiction, though it is in their interest to have their claim evaluated by a panel of experts before proceeding to a costly judicial process (Espersson 2000).

103. Danzon (1994).

104. Ibid.; Studdert and Brennan (2001).

105. Fallberg and Borgenhammar (1997).

106. Danzon (1994).

107. Ibid.; Fallberg and Borgenhammar (1997).

108. Espersson (2000).

109. Ibid.

110. Swedish Medical Association (2003).

111. Physician involvement includes alerting patients to possible medical injuries, referring patients to social workers, and aiding patients in the filing of their complaint (Studdert and Brennan 2001).

112. Danzon (1994).

113. Studdert and Brennan (2001).

114. Ibid.

115. Ibid.

116. Danzon (1994).

117. Ibid.

118. (Miller 1993). Justice Woodhouse was also involved in the formation of Australia's no-fault system. Australia's Northern Territory has used a no-fault system for compensating motor vehicle injuries since 1979. During the early 1970s, Justice Woodhouse performed an inquiry and wrote a comprehensive report for Australia regarding a possible national compensation scheme (O'Connell and Partlett 1988). Woodhouse, who helped New Zealand develop its system, recommended a scheme for compensating victims of both accidents and illnesses. His report also suggested that Australia abolish concurrent access to the tort system and institute more funding and better structures for accident prevention (O'Connell and Partlett 1988). Legislation to adopt the report was submitted to the Parliament and quickly passed in the House of Representatives. However, approval from the Senate was also necessary. The legislation was submitted to the Senate and was immediately sent to committee; it was not introduced for vote until several years later, at which point the governor prorogued Parliament and the bill lapsed (O'Connell and Partlett 1988). In recent years, Australia has been reconsidering implementing a medical malpractice no-fault system similar to New Zealand's.

119. New Zealand has had a no-fault system for workers' compensation since the 1900s. In 1928 a no-fault automobile program was added, and in 1972, the no-fault scheme was expanded to include all personal injuries.

120. Hitzhusen (2005); Weiss (2004); Flood (2000).

121. Bismark and Paterson (2006).

122. Lowes (2003).

123. Studdert, Thomas, Zbar, et al. (1997). Only a few years after the 1992 reform, the Accident Rehabilitation and Compensation Insurance Act was repealed and replaced with the Accident Insurance Act of 1998. The substance of the revised no-fault program remained mostly unchanged, except for its partial privatization (Todd 2000). Employers and self-employed persons were now allowed to purchase insurance from either private companies or the state-owned

company, eliminating the monopoly of the Accident Compensation Corporation (ACC). After the 1992 and 1998 reforms, only a small percentage of injury victims who might have been eligible for compensation actually applied for coverage (Todd 2000). However, most of the claims filed were identified as adverse events and assessed by the ACC to be compensable (P. Davis, Lay-Yee, Fitzjohn, et al. 2002).

124. Studdert and Brennan (2001).

125. Weiss (2004).

126. Ferguson (2003).

127. Hitzhusen (2005).

128. Bismark and Paterson (2006).

129. Paterson (2004).

130. Bismark, Dauer, Paterson, et al. (2006).

131. Ibid.

132. P. Davis, Lay-Yee, Scott, et al. (2003).

133. Hitzhusen (2005). This was not always so. Accident victims were placed ahead of those with illness for compensation, in order to encourage a fast recovery which would allow them to return to work more quickly. This lengthened the wait for those filing claims under illness (Flood 2000).

134. Cunningham (2004b, p.5).

135. Ibid.

136. Cunningham (2004a, p. 2).

137. Rosenthal (1988).

138. Kupeli (1996).

139. Danzon (2000, p. 1394).

Chapter 12

1. Symposium on Medical Malpractice (1975, p. 1177).

2. The chapters in parentheses in this chapter refer to chapters in this book.

3. Arlen (2006); Havighurst (1995).

4. T. Baker (2005b, p. 172).

5. Danzon (1986).

6. Abraham and Weiler (1994); Bovbjerg and Berenson (2006).

7. E.g., Sharkey (2006).

8. See, e.g., Kersh (2006).

9. Mechanic (1975, p. 1195).

10. Mehlman (2006) makes this point.

11. Several promising opportunities are discussed in chapter 8.

12. See chapter 9 for further discussion of alternative ownership forms.

13. This is also a reason that physicians often object to talking to managed care personnel on the telephone, seeking permission to perform a test or admit a patient to the hospital.

14. These points are made by Abraham and Weiler (1994, p. 400), among others.

15. At least to our knowledge, he is the first to use this term (T. Baker 2006).

16. Some borderline coverage issues might arise. For example, a physician may have misdiagnosed a condition in his or her office, which led to an error while the same patient was hospitalized. This type of error should be assigned to the enterprise, since the hospital has a duty to implement safeguards to identify the possibility of such errors before they occur.

17. The United States General Accounting Office (1987) reports that about 80 percent of the claims closed in 1984 involved an injury that occurred in a hospital.

18. For example, the Risk Management Foundation has covered Harvard medical institutions and physicians since 1976. Medical malpractice insurance coverage is provided by Controlled Risk Insurance Company, Ltd. (CRICO) and Controlled Risk Insurance Company of Vermont, a risk retention group (www.rmf.harvard.edu/company/about-us.aspx, accessed August 14, 2006). Abraham and Weiler (1994) describe CRICO's scrutinizing of cases that had generated suits and payments arising from anesthesia procedures in the 1980s. Initially, the new standards that were introduced were opposed by some physicians as "cook-book" medicine. But Harvard hospitals' administrators required implementation of standards which resulted in reductions of anesthesia-related mishaps and claims.

19. The simulations were performed by Sloan and Hassan (1990).

20. McCarran-Ferguson Act, 15 USCS §1012.

21. Liability Risk Retention Act, 15 USCS §3902. Risk retention groups are discussed further below.

22. T. Baker (2006, p. 287).

23. Starr (1982).

24. For example, is it not strange that a person brought to an emergency room where he or she receives many diagnostic tests would be billed separately by the hospital and by the physicians who interpret the tests? This is a common practice at most hospitals in the U.S. In most cases, the patient will have had no direct contact with the test interpreters. They are "retained" only in the sense that the patient may have agreed that the tests be performed.

25. Sloan and Hassan (1990).

26. This point is made by Bovbjerg and Berenson (2006, p. 240).

27. Based on several citations provided in the article, Mello, Kelly, Studdert, et al. (2003) conclude that at the time the article was published, there were 100 hospital captives operating in the United States.

28. Christopherson (1996).

29. Koviak (2004).

30. Christopherson (1996).

31. Of the 3,400 captives created worldwide, nearly 1,850 have a U.S. sponsor (ibid.).

32. Ibid.

33. P.L. 97–45.

34. The Risk Retention Amendments of 1986.

35. Congress provides some protection to group members by giving U.S. district courts the authority to enjoin risk retention groups from the business of insurance upon finding the group in a financially hazardous condition. 15 U.S. Code §3906.

The rationale for relaxing regulatory requirements was that the groups do not sell insurance to consumers, but only to their own members, and regulatory oversight by a single state is likely to be sufficient for this reason. Members of the risk groups must be related to each other, similar to businesses being in common through related trade, product, services, premises, or operation. Groups cannot exclude anyone from membership solely in order to gain a competitive advantage (Geiger 1997; Sloan, Bovbjerg, and Githens 1991).

36. Sloan, Bovbjerg, and Githens (1991).

37. Sage, Hastings, and Berenson (1994).

38. In 1995 the Court of Appeals for the District of Arizona held that even if a hospital cannot be liable under *respondeat superior*, it may still be liable under ostensible agency (*Joslin v. Yuma Regional Medical Ctr.*, 1995 U.S. App. LEXIS 31614).

39. For example, in *Menzie v. Windham Community Memorial Hospital*, the court recognized an apparent agency cause of action, but granted summary judgment for the defendant because the plaintiff could not establish his reliance on the apparent agency relationship with the physician (774 F. Supp. 91, D. Conn. 1991).

40. See *Simmons v. St. Clair Memorial Hospital*, 332 Pa. Super. 444 (1984); *Sword v. NKC Hospitals, Inc.*, 714 N.E. 2d 142 (Ind. 1999); *Leconche v. Elligers*, 1991 Conn. Super. LEXIS 1693. A recent case in Arizona has criticized the position that merely providing care is sufficient to establish an apparent agency relationship. The court held that some action of the principal is required; having staff privileges alone is not enough. *Henry v. Flagstaff Med. Ctr.*, 132 P.3d 304 (Ariz. Ct. App. 2006).

41. Abraham and Weiler (1994, pp. 390–391). In Colorado, courts decided the contrary; physicians are the principal and the hospital is the agent, leaving the

physician liable for the acts of nurses and staff below him or her. *Krane v. St. Anthony Hospital Systems*, 738 P.2d 75 (Colo. Ct. App. 1987).

42. Tappan (2005).

43. Abraham and Weiler (1994).

44. Ibid.

45. *Thompson v. Nason Hospital*, 591 A.2d 703 (Pa. 1991), followed by *Welsh v. Bulger*, 698 A.2d 581 (Pa. 1997). See also *Johnson v. Misericordia Community Hospital*, 99 Wis. 2d 708, 735 (Wis. 1981).

46. In U.S. hospitals, before a physician can secure admitting privileges, the medical staff of the hospital is charged with reviewing the physician's credentials and other qualifications.

47. Beginning with *Darling v. Charleston Community Memorial Hosp.*, 211 N.E.2d 253 (Ill. 1965), courts have held hospitals directly liable for failing to supervise or credential physicians. Later courts have added to the duties, including failure to ensure the safety and availability of facilities and equipment, setting policies that interfere with a physician's independent medical judgment, and failing to monitor and oversee the treatment both prescribed and administered by its physicians. *Humana Medical Corp. v. Traffanstedt*, 597 So. 2d 667 (Ala. 1992); *Muse v. Charter Hosp.*, 117 N.C. App. 468, 474 (N.C. Ct. App. 1995); *Pedroza v. Bryant*, 101 Wn.2d 226 (Wash. 1984).

48. *Graham v. Barolat*, 2004 U.S. Dist. LEXIS 23567 (E.D. Pa. Nov. 17, 2004).

49. Abraham and Weiler (1994).

50. Steves (1976, pp. 1324–1325).

51. Sage (1997).

52. *Thornton v. Ware County Hosp. Auth.*, 215 Ga. App. 276 (1994).

53. *Schleier v. Kaiser Foundation Health Plan of the Mid-Atlantic States, Inc.*, 876 F.2d 174 (1989), holding an HMO liable for the actions of one of its physicians, despite the fact the physician was contracted and not employed by the hospital.

54. Sage (1997, p. 169).

55. Tappan (2005).

56. Sage, Hastings, and Berenson (1994).

57. Danzon (2000, p. 1378).

58. See, e.g., Mello and Brennan (2002).

59. Abraham and Weiler (1994).

60. Ibid. (p. 427).

61. Sloan and Eesley (2006).

62. An adhesion contract is typically a standard form or boilerplate contract

entered into by parties with unequal bargaining power. For example, a consumer renting a car must sign the contract as is; the only other option is to find another car rental agency that offers more favorable terms. In most cases, the industry (e.g., airlines, credit cards, banks) utilizes standard contracts, giving the consumer no choice as to the terms and no option to negotiate. The consumer may be able to go to another car rental agency, but the likelihood that the terms of the contract would be different is small. Courts treat these contracts as they treat any other contract, and the contract is upheld unless it is determined to be unconscionable. This has been interpreted as the "absence of meaningful choice on the part of one party due to one-sided contract provisions, together with terms which are so oppressive that no reasonable person would make them and no fair and honest person would accept them." *Fanning v. Fritz's Pontiac-Cadillac-Buick*, 322 S.C. 399, 403 (S.C. 1996).

63. Developments in the Law (1995). Readers should consult this article for a much more detailed discussion of these issues.

64. Mehlman (2006).

65. See chapter 5.

66. T. Baker (2005b).

References

Abraham, Kenneth S. 1986. *Distributing Risk: Insurance, Legal Theory, and Public Policy*. New Haven, CT: Yale University Press.

———. 2001. The Trouble with Negligence. *Vanderbilt Law Review* 54 (3): 1187–1224.

Abraham, Kenneth S., and Paul C. Weiler. 1994. Enterprise Medical Liability and the Evolution of the American Health Care System. *Harvard Law Review* 108: 381–436.

Advisory Commission on Childhood Vaccines. 2003. 54th Meeting of the Advisory Commission on Childhood Vaccines (ACCV) and conference call (Mar. 5).

———. 2004. 56th Meeting of the Advisory Commission on Childhood Vaccines (ACCV) and conference call (Mar. 16).

Ajdari, Zohreh, and Oliver Fein. 1998. Primary Care in the United Kingdom and the United States. *Archives of Family Medicine* 7: 311–314.

Alberini, A., A. Hunt, and A. Markandya. 2006. Willingness to Pay to Reduce Mortality Risks: Evidence from a Three-Country Contingent Valuation Study. *Environmental & Resource Economics* 33 (2): 251–264.

Albert, Tanya. 2003. A Tale of Two States. *American Medical News* 46 (18): 9–10.

American Medical Association, Specialty Society Medical Liability Project. 1988. A Proposed Alternative to the Civil Justice System for Resolving Medical Liability Disputes: A Fault-Based Administrative System. *Connecticut Medicine* 52 (6): 347–350.

Ameringer, Carl F. 1999. *State Medical Boards and the Politics of Public Protection*. Baltimore: Johns Hopkins University Press.

Anderson, Dan R. 1976. All Risks Rating Within a Catastrophe Insurance System. *Journal of Risk and Insurance* 43 (4): 629–651.

Aranson, Allison F. 1992. The United States Percentage Contingent Fee System: Ridicule and Reform from an International Perspective. *Texas International Law Journal* 27: 755–794.

Arlen, Jennifer. 2006. Private Contractual Alternatives to Malpractice Liability. In *Medical Malpractice and the U.S. Health Care System*, edited by William M. Sage and Rogan Kersh. Cambridge: Cambridge University Press.

Arnould, Richard J., and Len M. Nichols. 1983. Wage-Risk Premiums and Workers' Compensation: A Refinement of Estimates of Compensating Wage Differential. *Journal of Political Economy* 91 (2): 332–340.

Attarian, D. E., and T. P. Vail. 2005. Medicolegal Aspects of Hip and Knee Arthroplasty. *Clinical Orthopedics and Related Research* 433: 72–76.

Avraham, R. 2006. Putting a Price on Pain-and-Suffering Damages: A Critique of the Current Approaches and a Preliminary Proposal for Change. *Northwestern University Law Review* 100 (1): 87–119.

Babb, B. A. 1998. Fashioning an Interdisciplinary Framework for Court Reform in Family Law: A Blueprint to Construct a Unified Family Court. *Southern California Law Review* 71 (3): 469–546.

Baicker, Katherine, and Amitabh Chandra. 2004. *The Effect of Malpractice Liability on the Delivery of Health Care*. NBER Working Paper no. 10709. Cambridge, MA: NBER. Available at http://www.nber.org/papers/w10709. (accessed June 22, 2007).

Baker, L. A. 2001–2002. Facts About Fees: Lessons for Legal Ethics. *Texas Law Review* 80: 1985–1995.

Baker, T. 2005a. Medical Malpractice and the Insurance Underwriting Cycle. *DePaul Law Review* 54: 393–438.

———. 2005b. *The Medical Malpractice Myth*. Chicago: University of Chicago Press.

———. 2006. Medical Malpractice Insurance Reform: "Enterprise Insurance" and Some Alternatives. In *Medical Malpractice and the U.S. Health Care System*, edited by William M. Sage and Rogan Kersh. Cambridge: Cambridge University Press.

Barker, Drucilla K. 1992. The Effects of Tort Reform on Medical Malpractice Insurance Markets: An Empirical Analysis. *Journal of Health, Politics, Policy and Law* 17 (1): 143–161.

Barry, John E., and Bert W. Rein. 1999. *The Case for Abolishing Contingent Fee Arrangements Working Paper*. Washington, DC: Washington Legal Foundation.

Bates, David W., Lucian L. Leape, David J. Cullen, Nan Laird, Laura A. Petersen, Jonathan M. Teich, Elizabeth Burdick, Mairead Hickey, Sharon Kleesfield, Brian Shea, Martha Vander Vliet, and Diane L. Sieger. 1998. Effect of Computerized Physician Order Entry and a Team Intervention on Prevention of Serious Medication Errors. *Journal of the American Medical Association* 280 (15): 1311–1316.

Becker, G. S. 1983. Theory of Competition Among Pressure Groups for Political Influence. *Quarterly Journal of Economics* 98: 371–400.

Beider, P., and S. Hagen. 2004. *Limiting Tort Liability for Medical Malpractice.* Congressional Budget Office. Available at http://www.cbo.gov/showdoc.cfm? index=4968&sequence=0 (accessed June 21, 2007).

Best, A. M. 1998. *Best's Aggregates & Averages: Property-Casualty.* Oldwick, NJ: A.M. Best.

Biddle, Jeff, Karen Roberts, Kenneth D. Rosenman, and Edward M. Welch. 1998. What Percentage of Workers with Work-Related Illnesses Receive Workers' Compensation Benefits? *Journal of Occupational and Environmental Medicine* 40 (4): 325–331.

Birkmeyer, J. D. 2003. The Leapfrog Group's Patient Safety Practices: The Potential Benefits of Universal Adoption. Available at http://www.leapfroggroup .org/media/file/Leapfrog-Birkmeyer.pdf (accessed June 22, 2007).

Bismark, Marie, Edward Dauer, Ron Paterson, and David Studdert. 2006. Accountability Sought by Patients Following Adverse Events from Medical Care: The New Zealand Experience. *Canadian Medical Association Journal* 175 (8): 889–894.

Bismark, Marie, and Ron Paterson. 2006. No-Fault Compensation in New Zealand: Harmonizing Injury Compensation, Provider Accountability, and Patient Safety. *Health Affairs* 25 (1): 278–283.

Blackmon, B. G., and R. Zeckhauser. 1991. Mispriced Equity—Regulated Rates for Auto Insurance in Massachusetts. *American Economic Review* 81 (2): 65–69.

Blair, E., and F. J. Stanley. 1988. Cerebral Palsy in Low-Birthweight Infants. *Developmental Medicine & Child Neurology* 30 (4): 550–552.

Blumberg, L. J., and J. Holahan. 2004. Government as Reinsurer: Potential Impacts on Public and Private Spending. *Inquiry* 41: 130–143.

Blumenthal, D. 2004. New Steam from an Old Cauldron: The Physician-Supply Debate. *New England Journal of Medicine* 350 (17): 1780–1787.

Blumstein, J., and F. A. Sloan. 1988. Antitrust and Hospital Peer Review. *Law and Contemporary Problems* 51: 7–92.

Blumstein, J., F., Randall R. Bovbjerg, and F. A. Sloan. 1991. Beyond Tort Reform: Developing Better Tools for Assessing Damages for Personal Injury. *Yale Journal of Regulation* 8 (1): 171–212.

Born, P., and W. K. Viscusi. 1994. Insurance Market Responses to the 1980s Liability Reforms: An Analysis of Firm-Level Data. *Journal of Risk and Insurance* 61 (2): 192–218.

Born, P. H., W. Kip Viscusi, and D. W. Carleton. 1998. The Distribution of the Insurance Market Effects on Tort Liability Reforms. *Brookings Papers on Economic Activity*: 1998: 55–105.

Born, Patricia, W. Kip Viscusi, and Tom Baker. 2006. The Effects of Tort Reform on Medical Malpractice Insurers' Ultimate Losses. *Harvard Law and*

Economics Discussion Paper No. 554. Available at SSRN: http://ssrn.com/abstract=921441 (accessed June 22, 2007).

Born, Patricia H. 2001. Insurer Profitability in Different Regulatory and Legal Environments. *Journal of Regulatory Economics* 19 (3): 211–237.

Bovbjerg, R. R. 1991. Lessons for Tort Reform from Indiana. *Journal of Health Politics, Policy, and Law* 16 (3): 465–482.

Bovbjerg, R. R., F. A. Sloan, and J. F. Blumstein. 1989. Valuing Life and Limb in Tort: Scheduling Pain and Suffering. *Northwestern University Law Review* 83 (4): 908–976.

Bovbjerg, R. R., L. R. Tancredi, and D. S. Gaylin. 1991. Obstetrics and Malpractice: Evidence on the Performance of a Selective No-Fault System. *Journal of the American Medical Association* 265 (21): 2836–2843.

Bovbjerg, Randall. 1989. Legislation on Medical Malpractice: Further Developments and a Preliminary Report Card. *University of California-Davis Law Review* 22 (2): 499–556.

———. 1991. Lessons for Tort Reform from Indiana. *Journal of Health Politics, Policy, and Law* 16 (3): 465–483.

———. 1995. *Medical Malpractice: Problems & Reforms.* Washington, DC: Urban Institute.

Bovbjerg, Randall R., Pablo Aliaga, and Josephine Gittler. 2006. State Discipline of Physicians: Assessing State Medical Boards Through Case Studies. Washington, DC: Urban Institute.

Bovbjerg, Randall R., and Anna Bartow. 2003. Understanding Pennsylvania's Medical Malpractice Crisis: Facts About Liability Insurance, the Legal System, and Health Care in Pennsylvania. In *The Project on Medical Liability in Pennsylvania for the Pew Charitable Trusts.* New York: Columbia University.

Bovbjerg, Randall R., and Robert A. Berenson. 2006. Enterprise Liability in the 21st Century. In *Medical Malpractice and the U.S. Health Care System*, edited by William M. Sage and Rogan Kersh. Cambridge: Cambridge University Press.

Bovbjerg, R. R., and F. A. Sloan. 1998. No-Fault for Medical Injury. *University of Cincinnati Law Review* 67: 53–123.

Bovbjerg, R. R., F. A. Sloan, A. Dor, and C. R. Hsieh. 1991. Juries and Justice: Are Malpractice and Other Personal Injuries Created Equal? *Law and Contemporary Problems* 54: 5–42.

Bradley, E. W., J. Herrin, B. Elbel, R. J. McNamara, D. J. Magid, B. K. Nallamoutu, Y. Wang, S. L. T. Normand, J. A. Spertus, and H. M. Krumholz. 2006. Hospital Quality for Acute Myocardial Infarction: Correlation Among Process Measures and Relationship with Short-Term Mortality. *Journal of the American Medical Association* 296 (1): 72–78.

Brennan, T. A., Lucian L. Leape, N. M. Laird, L. Hebert, R. Localio, A. G. Lawters, J. P. Newhouse, P. C. Weiler, and H. H. Hiatt. 1991. Incidence of Adverse Events and Negligence in Hospitalized Patients. *New England Journal of Medicine* 324 (8): 370–376.

Brennan, Troyen A., and Michelle M. Mello. 2003. Patient Safety and Medical Malpractice: A Case Study. *Annals of Internal Medicine* 139 (4): 267–273.

Breyer, S. 1982. *Regulation and Its Reform.* Cambridge, MA: Harvard University Press.

Brickman, Lester. 1989. Contingent Fees Without Contingencies: Hamlet Without the Prince of Denmark? *University of California-Los Angeles Law Review* 37: 29–138.

———. 1996. ABA Regulation of Contingency Fees: Money Talks, Ethics Walks. *Fordham Law Review* 65: 247–336.

———. 2003. Effective Hourly Rates of Contingency-Fee Lawyers: Competing Data and Non-Competitive Fees. *Washington University Law Quarterly* 81 (3): 653–669.

Brooks, R. G., N. Menachemi, A. Clawson, and L. Beitsch. 2005. Availability of Physician Services in Florida, Revisited: The Effect of the Professional Liability Insurance Market on Access to Health Care. *Archives of Internal Medicine* 165 (18): 2136–2141.

Brown, C. 1985. Deterrence in Tort and No-Fault: The New Zealand Experience. *California Law Review* 73: 976–1002.

Browne, Mark J., and Brenda P. Wells. 1999. Claims Adjudication in the Personal Automobile Insurance Residual Market. *Journal of Risk and Insurance* 66 (2): 275–290.

Bruce, S., H. Prior, A. Katz, M. Taylor, S. Latosinsky, P. Martens, C. De Coster, M. Brownell, R, Soodeen, and C. Steinbach. 2006. *Application of Patient Safety Indicators in Manitoba: A First Look.* Manitoba Centre for Health Policy.

Calfee, J. E., C. Winston, and K. Viscusi. 1993. The Consumer Welfare Effects of Liability for Pain and Suffering: An Exploratory Analysis. *Brookings Papers on Economic Activity, Microeconomics* 1993 (1): 133–196.

Campion, E. W. 2003. Death at Duke. *New England Journal of Medicine* 348 (12): 1083–1084.

Campolieti, M., and D. E. Hyatt. 2006. Further Evidence on the "Monday Effect" in Workers' Compensation. *Industrial & Labor Relations Review* 59 (3): 438–450.

Cebula, Richard J. 1995. The Impact of Federal Deposit Insurance on Savings and Loan Failures: Reply [to Ira S. Saltz]. *Southern Economic Journal* 62 (1): 256–259. (Saltz on p. 253.)

Choi, Albert. 2003. Allocating Settlement Authority Under a Contingent-Fee Arrangement. *Journal of Legal Studies* 32: 585–610.

Choi, Seungmook, Don Hardigree, and Paul D. Thistle. 2002. The Property/Liability Insurance Cycle: A Comparison of Alternative Models. *Southern Economic Journal* 68 (3): 530–548.

Christopherson, J. A. 1996. The Captive Medical Malpractice Insurance Company. *Annals of Health Law* 5: 121–143.

Chu, K. 2005. FEMA Halts Flood Insurance Payments. *USA Today*, Nov. 17.

Chupkovich, Patricia J. 1993. Statutory Caps: An Involuntary Contribution to the Medical Malpractice Insurance Crisis or a Reasonable Mechanism for Obtaining Affordable Health Care? *Jounal of Contemporary Health Law Policy* 9: 337–376.

Cloud, Morgan. 1996. The Fourth Amendment During the Lochner Era: Privacy, Property, and Liberty in Constitutional Theory. *Stanford Law Review* 48 (3): 555–631.

Cohen, Alma, and Dehejia, Rajeev. 2003. The Effect of Automobile Insurance and Accident Liability Laws on Traffic Fatalities.

Cohen, Eva D., and Samuel P. Korper. 1976. The Swedish No-Fault Patient Compensation Program: Provisions and Preliminary Findings. *Insurance Law Journal* 637: 70.

Cohen, M. A., and T. R. Miller. 2003. "Willingness to Award" Nonmonetary Damages and the Implied Value of Life from Jury Awards. *International Review of Law and Economics* 23: 165–181.

Cohen, Thomas H., and Steven K. Smith. 2004. *Civil Trial Cases and Verdicts in Large Counties, 2001*. Washington, D.C.: A.S. Department of Justice, Office of Justice Programs, Bureau of Justice Statistics.

Coldiron, B., A. H. Fisher, E. Adelman, C. B. Yelverton, R. Balkirshnan, M. A. Feldman, and S. R. Feldman. 2005. Adverse Event Reporting: Lessons Learned from Four Years of Florida Office Data. *Dermatologic Surgery* 31 (9): 1079–1093.

Cook, Phillip J., and Daniel A. Graham. 1977. The Demand for Insurance and Protection: The Case of Irreplaceable Commodities. *Quarterly Journal of Economics* 91 (1): 143–156.

Coolidge, Thomas Jefferson. 1905. *Jefferson in His Family*. Vol. 15 of *The Writings of Thomas Jefferson*. Edited by A. Lipscomb and A. Bergh. Washington, DC: Thomas Jefferson Memorial Association of the United States.

Copland, James R. 2004. *Contingency Fees: Format, Links Down*. Available at http://www.pointoflaw.com/feature/fee_ding_frenzy.php. (cited Sept. 25, 2006).

Corrigan, Janet, Ann Greiner, and Shari M. Erickson, eds. 2002. *Fostering Rapid Advances in Health Care: Learning from System Demonstrations*. Washington, D.C.: National Academics Press. Also available at http://www.nap.edu/books/0309087074/html. (accessed June 22, 2007).

Costich, J. F. 1994. Joint State-Federal Regulation of Lawyers: The Case of Group Legal Services under ERISA. *Kentucky Law Journal* 82: 627–659.

Council of State Governments. 2003. Medical Malpractice Crisis. *Trends Alert*. Lexington: The Council.

Craig, Diane E. , Liz Hartka, William H. Likosky, William M. Caplan, Paul Litsky, and Jannalee Smithey. 1999. Implementation of a Hospitalist System in a Large Health Maintenance Organization: The Kaiser Permanente Experience. *Annals of Internal Medicine* 130 (4): 355–359.

Croley, Steven P., and Jon D. Hanson. 1995. The Nonpecuniary Costs of Accidents: Pain-and-Suffering Damages in Tort Law. *Harvard Law Review* 108 (8): 1785–1898.

Cummins, J. David. 1988. Incorporating Risk in Insurance Guaranty Fund Premiums. In *Workers' Compensation Insurance Pricing: Current Programs and Proposed Reforms*, edited by P. S. Borba and D. Appel. Dordrecht: Kluwer Academic.

Cummins, J. David, and Patricia M. Danzon. 1991. Price Shocks and Capital Flows in Liability Insurance. In *Cycles and Crises in Property/Casualty Insurance: Causes and Implications for Public Policy*, edited by J. D. Cummins, S. E. Harrington, and R. W. Klein. Kansas City, MO: National Association of Insurance Commissioners.

Cummins, J. David, and J. Francois Outreville. 1987. An International Analysis of Underwriting Cycles. *Journal of Risk and Insurance* 54 (2): 246–262.

Cummins, J. David, Richard D. Phillips, and Mary A. Weiss. 2001. The Incentive Effects of No-Fault Automobile Insurance. *Journal of Law and Economics* 44 (2): 427–464.

Cunningham, Wayne. 2004a. The Medical Complaints and Disciplinary Process in New Zealand: Doctors' Suggestions for Change. *Journal of the New Zealand Medical Association* 117 (1198): 1–9.

———. 2004b. New Zealand Doctors' Attitudes Towards the Complaints and Disciplinary Process. *Journal of the New Zealand Medical Association* 117 (1198): 1–9.

Cutler, David M. , N. E. Feldman, and J. R. Horwitz. 2005. U.S. Adoption of Computerized Physician Order Entry System. *Health Affairs* 24 (6): 1654–1664.

D'Arcy, Stephen P. 1986. Legislative Reform of the Medical Malpractice Tort System in Illinois. *Journal of Risk and Insurance* 53 (3): 538–550.

Daly, R. 2005. Voluntary System to Collect Medical-Error Data. *American Psychiatric Association* 40 (17): 11.

Dana, James D., and Kathryn E. Spier. 1993. Expertise and Contingent Fees: The Role of Asymmetric Information in Attorney Compensation. *Journal of Law, Economics, and Organization* 9 (2): 349–367.

Daniels, Stephen, and Joanne Martin. 2002. It Was the Best of Times, It Was the Worst of Times: The Precarious Nature of Plaintiffs' Practice in Texas. *Texas Law Review* 80: 1781–1828.

———. 2006. Plaintiffs' Lawyers, Specialization, and Medical Malpractice. *Vanderbilt Law Review* 59 (4): 1051–1073.

Dann, B. M. 2002. Jurors as Beneficiaries of Proposals to Objectify Proof of Standard of Care in Medical Malpractice Cases. *Wake Forest Law Review* 37: 943–952.

Danzon, P. M. 1984. Tort Reform and the Role of Government in Private Insurance Markets. *Journal of Legal Studies* 13 (3): 517–549.

———. 1985. Liability and Liability Insurance for Medical Malpractice. *Journal of Health Economics* 4: 309–331.

———. 1986. The Frequency and Severity of Medical Malpractice Claims: New Evidence. *Law and Contemporary Problems* 49 (2): 57–84.

———. 2000. Liability for Medical Malpractice. In *Handbook of Health Economics*, edited by A. J. Culyer and J. P. Newhouse. Amsterdam: Elsevier.

Danzon, P. M., M. V. Pauly, and R. Kingston. 1990. The Effects of Malpractice Litigation on Physicians' Fees and Incomes. *American Economic Review* 80: 122–127.

Danzon, Patricia M. 1994. Alternative Liability Regimes for Medical Injuries: Evidence from Simulation Analysis. *Journal of Risk and Insurance* 61 (2): 219–244.

Danzon, Patricia, and Lee A. Lillard. 1983. Settlement out of Court: The Disposition of Medical Malpractice Claims. *Journal of Legal Studies* 12: 345–377.

Danzon, Patricia M. 1991. Liability for Medical Malpractice. *Journal of Economic Perspectives* 5 (3): 51–69.

———. 1994. The Swedish Patient Compensation System: Myths and Realities. *International Review of Law and Economics* 14: 453–466.

Danzon, Patricia M. 1983. Contingent Fees for Personal Injury Litigation. *Bell Journal of Economics* 14 (1): 213–224.

Dao, James. 2005. G. O. P. Push in States to Curb Malpractice Costs. *The New York Times*, Jan. 14, p. 1.

Darmiento, L. 2005. California Keeps Malpractice Rates in Check. *Los Angeles Business Journal*, Feb. 14, p. 12.

Darragh, T. 2002a. Medical Malpractice Insurers Struggle in Pennsylvania. *The Morning Call*, Allentown, PA, Apr. 21.

———. 2002b. Risky Insurance Company Move Also Fuels Pa. Malpractice Crisis. *The Morning Call*, Allentown, PA, Apr. 21.

Davis, Peter, Roy Lay-Yee, Julie Fitzjohn, Phil Hider, Robin Briant, and Stephan Schug. 2002. Compensation for Medical Injury in New Zealand: Does

"No-Fault" Increase the Level of Claims Making and Reduce Social and Clinical Selectivity? *Journal of Health Politics, Policy, and Law* 27 (5): 833–854.

Davis, Peter, Roy Lay-Yee, Alastair Scott, Robin Briant, and Stephan Schug. 2003. Acknowledgement of "No Fault" Medical Injury: Review of Patients' Hospital Records in New Zealand. *British Medical Journal* 326 (7380): 79–80.

Davis, W. Kent. 1999. The International View of Attorney Fees in Civil Suits: Why Is the United States the "Odd Man Out" in How It Pays Its Lawyers? *Arizona Journal of International and Comparative Law* 16: 361–436.

Davis, W. N. 2003. Special Problems for Specialty Courts: Clients Get Needed Treatment Rather Than Jail Time, but Prosecutors and Defense Lawyers Alike Worry About Compromising Their Roles as Advocates. *American Bar Association Journal* 89: 32–37.

———. 2006. No Longer Immune?: Court Opens Door to Cases Claiming Link Between Autism and Vaccine Preservative. *American Bar Association Journal* 92: 19, 43.

de Sa e Silva, Marco. 1988. Constitutional Challenges to Washington's Limit on Noneconomic Damages in Cases of Personal Injury and Death. *Washington Law Review* 63 (3): 653–675.

Developments in the Law: Confronting the New Challenges of Scientific Evidence. 1995. *Harvard Law Review* 108 (7): 1481–1605.

Developments in the Law: VI. Unified Family Courts and the Child Protection Dilemma. 2003. *Harvard Law Review* 116 (7): 2099–2122.

Devers, Kelly J., Hoangmai H. Pham, and Gigi Liu. 2004. What Is Driving Hospitals' Patient-Safety Efforts? *Health Affairs* 23 (2): 103–114.

Devlin, R. A. 1990. Some Welfare Implications of No-Fault Automobile Insurance. *International Review of Law and Economics* 10: 193–205.

Di Pietro, S., and T. W. Carns. 1996. Alaska's English Rule: Attorney's Fee Shifting in Civil Cases. *Alaska Law Review* 13: 33–96.

Diamond, Herbert S., Elliot Goldberg, and Janine E. Janosky. 1998. The Effect of Full-Time Faculty Hospitalists on the Efficiency of Care at a Community Teaching Hospital. *Annals of Internal Medicine* 129 (3): 197–203.

Doherty, N. A., and J. R. Garven. 1995. Insurance Cycles: Interest-Rates and the Capacity Constraint Model. *Journal of Business* 68 (3): 383–404.

Doherty, N. A., and L. Posey. 1997. Availability Crises in Insurance Markets: Optimal Contracts with Asymmetric Information and Capacity Constraints. *Journal of Risk and Uncertainty* 15 (1): 55–80.

Doherty, N. A., and K. Smetters. 2005. Moral Hazard in Reinsurance Markets. *Journal of Risk and Insurance* 72 (3): 375–391.

Doherty, Neil A., Joan Lamm-Tennant, and Laura T. Starks. 2003. Insuring September 11th: Market Recovery and Transparency. *Journal of Risk and Uncertainty* 26 (2/3): 179–199.

Domitrovich, S. 1998. Utilizing an Effective Economic Approach to Family Court: A Proposal for a Statutory Unified Family Court in Pennsylvania. *Duquesne University Law Review* 37 (1): 1–66.

Dorsey, S., and N. Walzer. 1983. Workers' Compensation, Job Hazards, and Wages. *Industrial and Labor Relations Review* 36 (4): 642–654.

Downs, David H., and David W. Sommer. 1999. Monitoring, Ownership, and Risk-Taking: The Impact of Guaranty Funds. *The Journal of Risk and Insurance* 66 (3): 477–497.

Dranove, David, and Anne Gron. 2005. Has the Malpractice Crisis in Florida Really Affected Access to Care? *working paper*. Northwestern University.

Dranove, David, Daniel Kessler, Mark McClellan, and Mark Satterthwaite. 2003. Is More Information Better? The Effects of "Report Cards" on Health Care Providers. *Journal of Political Economy* 111 (3): 555–588.

Dubay, Lisa, Robert Kaestner, and Timothy Waidmann. 1999. The Impact of Malpractice Fears on Cesarean Section Rates. *Journal of Health Economics* 18 (4): 491.

Dubner, Stephen, and Steven D. Levitt. 2006. Freakonomics: Selling Soap. *The New York Times*, Sept. 24.

Eisenberg, Theodore, John Goerdt, Brian Ostrom, David Rottman, and Martin T. Wells. 1997. The Predictability of Punitive Damages. *Journal of Legal Studies* 26: 623–661.

Eisenberg, Theodore, Neil LaFountain, Brian Ostrom, David Rottman, and Martin T. Wells. 2002. Juries, Judges, and Punitive Damages: An Empirical Study. *Cornell Law Review* 87: 743–782.

Ellis, Randall P., Cynthia L. Gallup, and Thomas G. McGuire. 1990. Should Medical Professional Liability Insurance Be Experience Rated? *Journal of Risk and Insurance* 57 (1): 66–78.

Ellsworth, Phoebe C., and Alan Reifman. 2000. Juror Comprehension and Public Policy: Perceived Problems and Proposed Solutions. *Psychology, Public Policy, and Law* 6 (3): 788–821.

Emons, Winand. 2000. Expertise, Contingent Fees, and Insufficient Attorney Effort. *International Review of Law and Economics* 20: 21–33.

Encinosa, William E., and Fred J. Hellinger. 2005. Have State Caps on Malpractice Awards Increased the Supply of Physicians? *Health Affairs* 24 (Web Exclusives): 250–258. Available at: http://content.healthaffairs.org/webexclusives/index .dtl?year=2005 (accessed June 22, 2007).

Entman, S. S., C. A. Glass, G. B. Hickson, P. B. Githens, K. Whetten-Goldstein, and F. A. Sloan. 1994. The Relationship Between Malpractice Claims History and Subsequent Obstetric Care. *Journal of the American Medical Association* 272 (20): 1588–1591.

Epstein, R. 1978. Medical Malpractice: Its Cause and Cure. In *The Economics of Medical Malpractice*, edited by S. Rottenberg. Washington, DC: American Enterprise Institute Press.

Eskin, David J. 2003. Prepared Witness Testimony, Hearing Before the U.S. House Committee on Energy and Commerce (Feb. 10). Abington, PA: Abington Memorial Hospital.

Espersson, Carl. 2000. The Patient Injury Act: A Comment by Carl Espersson. Available at http://www.patientforsakring.se/infoglueDeliverLive/digital Assets/2129_Engelska_comments.pdf.

———. 2005. The Swedish Patient Injury Act. Transcript by Federal News Service, Washington, DC 2005. Available at www.patientforsakring.se/infoglue DeliverLive/digitalAssets/2129_Engelska_comments.pdf.

Essinger, K. 2005. The Regions' Mutual Insurance Company for Patient Injuries (LOF). at. Available http://www.patientforsakring.se/infoglueDeliverLive/ digitalAssets/2129_Engelska_comments.pdf.

Evans, G. 1998. Vaccine Liability and Safety Revisited. *Archives of Pediatric and Adolescent Medicine* 152: 7–10.

Fairley, W. B. 1979. Investment Income and Profit Margins in Property-Liability Insurance: Theory and Empirical Results. *Bell Journal of Economics* 10: 192–210.

Fallberg, L. H., and E. Borgenhammar. 1997. The Swedish No Fault Patient Insurance Scheme. *European Journal of Health Law* 4: 279–286.

Farber, Henry S., and Max Bazerman. 1986. The General Basis of Arbitrator Behavior: An Empirical Analysis of Conventional and Final-Offer Arbitration. *Econometrica* 54 (4): 819–844.

Farber, Henry S., and Michelle J. White. 1991. Medical Malpractice: An Empirical Examination of the Litigation Process. *Rand Journal of Economics* 22: 199–217.

Ferguson, J. 2003. Medical Misadventure Under Accident Compensation: Diagnosis and Treatment of a Problem. *New Zealand Law Review* part IV: 485.

Fielding, Stephen L. 1990. The Social Construction of the Medical Malpractice Crisis: A Case Study of Massachusetts Physicians. *Sociological Forum* 5 (2): 279–295.

Fields, G. 2006. In Brooklyn Court, a Route Out of Jail for the Mentally Ill. *Wall Street Journal*, Aug. 21, pp. A1, A8.

Finkelstein, Amy. 2004. Static and Dynamic Effects of Health Policy: Evidence from the Vaccine Industry. *Quarterly Journal of Economics* 119 (2): 527.

Finkelstein, Joel B. 2003. Frist Bill Further Safeguards Doctors from Vaccine Lawsuits. *American Medical News* 46 (16): 5.

Fishback, P. V., and S. E. Kantor. 1998a. The Political Economy of Workers' Compensation Benefit Levels, 1910–1930. *Explorations in Economic History* 35 (2): 109–139.

———. 1998b. The Adoption of Workers' Compensation in the United States, 1900–1930. *Journal of Law and Economics* 41 (2): 305–341.

Fitzpatrick, Sean M. 2003–2004. Fear Is the Key: A Behavioral Guide to Underwriting Cycles. *Connecticut Insurance Law Journal* 10 (2): 255.

Flood, Colleen M. 2000. New Zealand's No-Fault Accident Compensation Scheme: Paradise or Panacea? *Health Law Review* 8 (3): 1–9.

Flowers, Lynda, and Trish Riley. 2001. *State-Based Mandatory Reporting of Medical Errors: An Analysis of the Legal and Policy Issues.* Portland, ME: National Academy for State Health Policy.

Folberg, J. 1999. Family Courts: Assessing the Trade-offs. *Family and Conciliation Courts Review* 37 (4): 448–453.

Fournier, Gary M., and Melayne Morgan McInnes. 2001. The Case for Experience Rating in Medical Malpractice Insurance: An Empirical Evaluation. *The Journal of Risk and Insurance* 68 (2): 255–276.

Frank, Ted. 2006. Hyman and Silver: "Medical Malpractice Litigation and Tort Reform: It's the Incentives, Stupid." Available at http://www.pointoflaw.com/archives/003181.php (cited December 20, 2006).

Franko, Frederick P. 2001. State Laws and Regulations for Office-Based Surgery. *Association of Operating Room Nurses* 73 (4): 843–846.

Freeman, Andrew D., and John M. Freeman. 1989. No-Fault Cerebral Palsy Insurance: An Alternative to the Obstetrical Malpractice Lottery. *Journal of Health Politics, Policy, and Law* 14 (4): 707–718.

Freese, Robert B. 1999. The Park Nicollet Experience in Establishing a Hospitalist System. *Annals of Internal Medicine* 130: 350–354.

Froot, Kenneth A. 2001. The Market for Catastrophe Risk: A Clinical Examination. *Journal of Financial Economics* 60 (2): 529–571.

Froot, Kenneth, and Paul G. J. O'Connell. 1997. The Pricing of U.S. Catastrophe Reinsurance. In *National Bureau of Economic Research Working Paper* 6043. Cambridge, MA: NBER, pp. 1–36.

Fuchs, V. R. 1978. Supply of Surgeons and Demand for Operations. *Journal of Human Resources* 13: 35–56.

Fung, Hung-Gay, Gene C. Lai, Gary A. Patterson, and Robert C. Witt. 1998. Underwriting Cycles in Property and Liability Insurance: An Empirical Analysis of Industry and By-line Data. *Journal of Risk and Insurance* 65 (4): 539–561.

Galanter, Marc. 1993. The Regulatory Function of the Civil Jury. In *Verdict: Assessing the Civil Jury System*, edited by R. E. Litan. Washington, DC: The Brookings Institution.

Gan, T. J., F. Sloan, G. D. Dear, H. E. El-Moalem, and D. A. Lubarsky. 2001. How Much Are Patients Willing to Pay to Avoid Postoperative Nausea and Vomiting? *Anesthesia and Analgesia* 92 (2): 393–400.

Garoupa, Nuno, and Fernando Gomez-Pomar. 2002. Cashing by the Hour: Why Large Law Firms Prefer Hourly Fees over Contingent Fees. UPF Working Paper No. 639. Available at SSRN: http://ssrn.com/abstract=394305 (accessed June 22, 2007).

Gash, J. 2005. Solving the Multiple Punishments Problem: A Call for a National Punitive Damages Registry. *Northwestern University Law Review* 99 (4): 1613–1686.

Gaudry, M. 1986. Measuring the Effects of the 1978 Quebec Automobile Insurance Act and the DRAG Model. Montreal: Dept. of Economics, University of Montreal, Publication #493, Sept. Mimeo.

Geiger, R. S. *Risk Retention Groups: Preemption of State Law* 1997. Available at: http://library.findlaw.com/1997/Dec/1/126440.html (accessed Aug. 16, 2006).

Geistfeld, M. 1995. Placing a Price on Pain and Suffering: A Method for Helping Juries Determine Tort Damages for Nonmonetary Damages. *California Law Review* 83: 773–852.

Gellhorn, Walter. 1988. Medical Malpractice Litigation (U.S.)—Medical Mishap Compensation (N.Z.). *Cornell Law Review* 73 (2): 170–212.

Geraghty, A. H., and W. J. Myniec. 2002. Unified Family Courts: Tempering Enthusiasm with Caution. *Family Court Review* 40 (4): 435–452.

Ghandi, Tejal K. 2005. Fumbled Handoffs: One Dropped Ball After Another. *Annals of Internal Medicine* 142 (5): 352–358.

Glassman, Adam D. 2004. The Imposition of Federal Caps in Medical Malpractice Liability Actions: Will They Cure the Current Crisis in Health Care? *Akron Law Review* 37: 417.

Gold, M. R., J. E. Siegel, L. B. Russell, and Milton C. Weinstein, eds. 1996. *Cost-Effectiveness in Health and Medicine.* New York: Oxford University Press.

Goldstein, J. 2003. Collapse Spreads Misery. *The Philadelphia Inquirer*, Mar. 2, Section E, page 1.

Grabowski, H., W. K. Viscusi, and W. N. Evans. 1989. Price and Availability Tradeoffs of Automobile Insurance Regulation. *Journal of Risk and Insurance* 56 (2): 275–299.

Greene, Mark R. 1976. The Government as an Insurer. *Journal of Risk and Uncertainty* 43 (3): 393–407.

Grisham, John. 1996. *The Runaway Jury.* New York: Doubleday.

Gron, Anne. 1990. Property-Casualty Insurance Cycles, Capacity Constraints, and Empirical Results Ph. D. dissertation. Department of Economics. MIT, Cambridge, MA.

———. 1994a. Capacity Constraints and Cycles in Property-Casualty Insurance Markets. *Rand Journal of Economics* 25 (1): 110–127.

———. 1994b. Evidence of Capacity Constraints in Insurance Markets. *Journal of Law & Economics* 37: 349.

Gron, Anne, and Deborah Lucas. 1998. External Financing and Insurance Cycles. In *The Economics of Property-Casualty Insurance*, edited by D. F. Bradford. Chicago: University of Chicago Press.

Gronfein, William P., and Eleanor DeArman Kinney. 1991. Controlling Large Malpractice Claims: The Unexpected Impact of Damage Caps. *Journal of Health Politics, Policy, and Law* 16 (3): 465–483.

Grossman, Richard S. 1992. Deposit Insurance, Regulation, and Moral Hazard in the Thrift Industry: Evidence from the 1930's. *American Economic Review* 82 (4): 800–822.

Gruber, J., and Alan Krueger. 1991. *Tax Policy and the Economy*. Cambridge, MA: MIT Press.

Gunnar, William P. 2004. Is There an Acceptable Answer to Rising Medical Malpractice Premiums? *Annals of Health Law* 13: 465.

Hall, Bronwyn-H., Clint Cummins, Elizabeth S. Laderman, and Joy Mundy. 1988. The R&D Master File Documentation. *NBER Technical Working Paper* 0072. Cambridge, MA: NBER.

Hallinan, Joseph T. 2004. In Malpractice Trials, Juries Rarely Have the Last Word. *Wall Street Journal*, Nov. 30.

Haltom, William, and Michael W. McCann. 2004. *Distorting the Law: Politics, Media, and the Litigation Crisis*. Chicago: University of Chicago Press.

Han, Yong Y., Joseph A. Carcillo, Shekhar T. Venkataraman, Robert S. B. Clark, R. Scott Watson, Trung C. Nguyen, Hulya Bayir, and Richard A. Orr. 2005. Unexpected Increased Mortality After Implementation of a Commercially Sold Computerized Physician Order Entry System. *Pediatrics* 116 (6): 1506–1512.

Harrington, Scott E. 1994. State Decisions to Limit Tort Liability: An Empirical Analysis of No-Fault Automobile Insurance Laws. *Journal of Risk and Insurance* 61 (2): 276–294.

———. 2002. Repairing Insurance Markets. *Regulation* 25 (2): 58–63.

Harrington, Scott E., and Robert E. Litan. 1988. Causes of the Liability Insurance Crisis. *Science* 239: 737–741.

Hart, O., A. Shleifer, and R. W. Vishny. 1997. The Proper Scope of Government: Theory and an Application to Prisons. *Quarterly Journal of Economics* 112 (4): 1127–1161.

Havighurst, C. C. 1995. *Health Care Choices: Private Contracts as Instruments of Health Reform*. Washington, DC: American Enterprise Institute Press.

Havighurst, Clark C. 1997. Making Health Plans Accountable for the Quality of Care. *Georgia Law Review* 31: 587–649.

Hay, Bruce L. 1996. Contingent Fees and Agency Costs. *Journal of Legal Studies* 25 (2): 503–533.

———. 1997. Optimal Contingent Fees in a World of Settlement. *Journal of Legal Studies* 26: 259–278.

Health Resources and Services Administration. 2006. Vaccine Injury Table. Available at http://www.hrsa.gov/vaccinecompensation/table.htm (accessed Sept. 2006).

Heid, B., and E. Misulovin. 2000. The Group Legal Plan Revolution: Bright Horizon or Dark Future? *Hofstra Labor and Employment Law Journal* 18: 335–365.

Helland, Eric, and Alexander Taborrok. 2000. Runaway Judges? Selection Effects and the Jury. *Journal of Law, Economics, and Organization* 16 (2): 306–333.

———. 2003. Race, Poverty, and American Tort Awards. *Journal of Legal Studies* 32: 27–58.

Hellinger, Fred J., and William E. Encinosa. 2003. The Impact of State Laws Limiting Malpractice Awards on the Geographic Distribution of Physicians. Washington, DC: U.S. Department of Health and Human Services.

Hersch, Joni, and W. Kip Viscusi. 2004. Punitive Damages: How Judges and Juries Perform. *Journal of Legal Studies* 33: 1–29.

Hertzka, Robert E. 2003. State Medical-Malpractice Law Works. *The San Diego Union-Tribune*, B7.

Hickson, G. B., E. W. Clayton, S. S. Entman, C. S. Miller, P. B. Githens, K. Whetten-Goldstein, and F. A. Sloan. 1994. Obstetricians' Prior Malpractice Experience and Patients' Satisfaction with Care. *Journal of the American Medical Association* 272 (20): 1583–1587.

Hickson, G. B., E. W. Clayton, P. B. Githens, and F. A. Sloan. 1992. Factors That Prompted Families to File Medical Malpractice Claims Following Perinatal Injuries. *Journal of the American Medical Association* 267 (10): 1359–1363.

Hickson, Gerald B., Charles F. Federspiel, James W. Pichert, Cynthia S. Miller, Jean Gauld-Jaeger, and Preston Bost. 2002. Patient Complaints and Malpractice Risk. *Journal of the American Medical Association* 287 (22): 2951–2957.

Hill, R. D. 1979. Profit Regulation in Property-Liability Insurance. *Bell Journal of Economics* 10: 172–191.

Hitzhusen, M. 2005. Crisis and Reform: Is New Zealand's No-Fault Compensation System a Reasonable Alternative to the Medical Malpractice Crisis in the United States? *Arizona Journal of International and Comparative Law* 22: 649–689.

Hoerger, T., F. A. Sloan, and M. Hassan. 1990. Loss Volatility, Bankruptcy, and Insurer Demand for Reinsurance. *Journal of Risk and Uncertainty* 3: 221–245.

Hofflander, Alfred E., and Blaine F. Nye. 1985. *Medical Malpractice Insurance in Pennsylvania.* Menlo Park, CA: MAC Group.

Hofflander, Alfred E., and Jane D. Nettesham. 2001. *Report on the Medical Malpractice Insurance Delivery System in Pennsylvania.* Redwood City, CA: Standford Consulting Group.

Hospital and Healthsystem Association of Pennsylvania. 2002a. *Survey of Professional Liability Coverage: Findings of Statewide Survey.* Harrisburg, PA: Health and Hospital Association of Pennsylvania.

———. 2002b. *Professional Liability Coverage in Pennsylvania: Findings of a Statewide Survey.* Harrisburge, PA: Health and Hospital Association of Pennsylvania.

Hughes, E. F., V. R. Fuchs, J. E. Jacoby, and E. M. Lewit. 1972. Surgical Work Loads in a Community Practice. *Surgery* 71 (3): 315–327.

Hughes, James W., and Edward A. Snyder. 1995. Litigation and Settlement Under the English and American Rules: Theory and Evidence. *Journal of Law and Economics* 38 (1): 225–250.

Hyman, David A., and Charles Silver. 2005. The Poor State of Health Care Quality in the U.S.: Is Malpractice Liability Part of the Problem or Part of the Solution? *Cornell Law Review* 90 (4): 893–994.

———. 2006. Medical Malpractice Litigation and Tort Reform: It's the Incentives, Stupid. *Vanderbilt Law Review* 59 (4): 1085–1136.

Inselbuch, Elihu. 2001. Contingent Fees and Tort Reform: A Reassessment and Reality Check. *Law and Contemporary Problems* 64 (Spring/Summer): 175–196.

Institute of Medicine. 1997. Board on Health Promotion and Disease Prevention: Vaccine Safety Forum, Summaries of Two Workshops.

———. 2000. *To Err is Human: Building a Safer Health System.* Washington, DC: National Academies Press.

———. 2004. Immunization Safety Review: Vaccines and Autism. Washington, DC: National Academy Press. Also available at http://books.nap.edu/catalog/10997.html.

———. 2001. *Crossing the Quality Chasm: A New Health System for the 21st Century.* Washington, D.C.: National Academy Press.

Institute of Medicine, Janet Corrigan, Ann Greiner, and Shari M. Erickson. 2002. *Fostering Rapid Advances in Health Care Learning from System Demonstrations.* Washington, DC: National Academies Press.

Jacobi, John V., and Nicole Huberfeld. 2001. Quality Control, Enterprise Liability, and Disintermediation in Managed Care. *Journal of Law, Medicine and Ethics* 29 (3/4): 305–322.

Jacobson, Peter D., and M. Gregg Bloche. 2005. Improving Relations Between Attorneys and Physicians. *Journal of the American Medical Association* 294 (16): 2083–2085.

Jagsi, Reshma, Barrett T. Kitch, Debra F. Weinstein, Eric G. Campbell, Matthew Hutter, and Joel S. Weissman. 2005. Residents Report on Adverse Events and Their Causes. *Archives of Internal Medicine* 165 (22): 2607–2613.

Jin, Ginger Zhe, and Phillip Leslie. 2003. The Effect of Information on Product Quality: Evidence from Restaurant Hygiene Grade Cards. *Quarterly Journal of Economics* 118 (2): 409–451.

Joint Legislative Audit and Review Commission of the Virginia General Assembly. 2002. Review of the Virginia Birth-Related Neurological Injury Compensation Program. Richmond: Common wealth of Virginia.

Joost, Robert H. 1992. *Automobile Insurance and No-Fault Law*. 2nd ed. West Publishing Co. Deerfield, IL. Clark Boardman Callaghan.

Kaboli, Peter J., Mitchell J. Barnett, and Gary E. Rosenthal. 2004. Associations with Reduced Length of Stay and Costs on an Academic Hospitalist Service. *American Journal of Managed Care* 10 (8): 561–568.

Kagan, Robert A. 2001. *Adversarial Legalism: The American Way of Law*. Cambridge, MA: Harvard University Press.

Kakalik, J. S., D. R. Hensler, D. McCaffrey, M. Oshiro, N. M. Pace, and M. E. Valana. 1998. *Discovery Management: Further Analysis of the Civil Justice Reform Act Evaluation Data*. Santa Monica, CA: Rand Corporation.

Kakalik, J. S., and Nicholas M. Pace. 1986. *Costs and Compensation Paid in Tort Litigation*. Santa Monica, CA: RAND Corporation.

Karpoff, Jonathan M., and John R. Lott. 1999. On the Determinants and Importance of Punitive Damage Awards. *Journal of Law and Economics* 42: 527–572.

Kaufman, Allan M., and Thomas A. Ryan. 2000. Strategic Asset Allocation for Multi-Line Insurers Using Dynamic Financial Analysis. *Casualty Actuarial Society Forum: Dynamic Financial Analysis Call Papers*, 1–20 Available at http://www.casact.org/pubs/forum/00sforum/00sf001.pdf (accessed Jan. 20, 2005).

Kaushal, R., K. G. Shojania, and D. W. Bates. 2003. Effects of Computerized Physician Order Entry and Clinical Decision Support Systems on Medication Safety. *Archives of Internal Medicine* 163: 1409–1416.

Keeley, Michael C. 1990. Deposit Insurance, Risk, and Market Power in Banking. *American Economic Review* 80 (5): 1183–1200.

Keisler, Peter D. 2004. Statement Before the Subcommittee on Commercial and Administrative Law, Committee on the Judiciary, on Budget and Resource Needs of the Justice Department Civil Division for Fiscal Year 2005. United States House of Representatives, Mar. 9. Available at http://www.house.gov/judiciary/keisler030904.htm (accessed Dec. 21, 2004).

Kelly, C. N., and M. M. Mello. 2005. Are Medical Malpractice Damages Caps Constitutional? An overview of state litigation. *Journal of Law, Medicine and Ethics* 33 (3): 515–534.

Kenney, Roger K. 1988. *Financial Condition of Medical Malpractice JUAs.* Schaumburg, IL: Alliance of American Insurers.

Kersh, R. 2006. Medical Malpractice and the New Politics of Health Care. In *Medical Malpractice and the U.S. Health Care System*, edited by W. M. Sage and R. Kersh. Cambridge: Cambridge University Press.

Kesselheim, A. S., T. G. Ferris, and D. M. Studdert. 2006. Will Physician-Level Measures of Clinical Performance Be Used in Medical Malpractice Litigation? *Journal of the American Medical Association* 295 (15): 1831–1834.

Kessler, D. P., W. M. Sage, and D. J. Becker. 2005. Impact of Malpractice Reforms on the Supply of Physician Services. *Journal of the American Medical Association* 293 (21): 2618–2625.

Kessler, Daniel, and Mark McClellan. 1996. Do Doctors Practice Defensive Medicine? *The Quarterly Journal of Economics* 111 (2): 353–390.

Kessler, Daniel P., and Mark McClellan. 1997. The Effects of Malpractice Pressure and Liability Reforms on Physicians' Perceptions of Medical Care. *Law and Contemporary Problems* 60 (1): 81–106.

Kilian, M. 2003. Alternatives to Public Provision. The Role of Legal Expenses Insurance in Broadening Access to Justice: The German Experience. *Journal of Law and Society* 30 (1): 31–48.

Kingdon, John. 1981. *Congressmen's Voting Decisions*, 2nd ed. New York: Harper & Row.

Kinney, Eleanor D. 1995. Malpractice Reform in the 1990's: Past Disappointments, Future Success? *Journal of Health Politics, Policy, and Law* 20 (1): 109–135.

Klein, Robert W. 1995. Insurance Regulation in Transition. *Journal of Risk and Insurance* 62 (3): 363–404.

———. 1998. Regulation and Catastrophe Insurance. In *Paying the Price: The Status and Role of Insurance Against Natural Disasters in the United States*, edited by H. Kunreuther and R. J. Roth, Sr. Washington, DC: Joseph Henry Press.

Klick, Jonathan, and Thomas Stratmann. 2003. Does Medical Malpractice Reform Help States Retain Physicians and Does It Matter? Working paper under review by *Journal of Legal Studies*.

Kochanowski, Paul S., and Madelyn V. Young. 1985. Deterrent Aspects of No-Fault Automobile Insurance: Some Empirical Findings. *Journal of Risk and Insurance* 52 (20): 269.

Kondo, LeRoy L. 2001. Advocacy of the Establishment of Mental Health Specialty Courts in the Provision of Therapeutic Justice for Mentally Ill Offenders. *American Journal of Criminal Law* 28 (3): 255–336.

Koppel, R., J. P. Metlay, A. Cohen, B. Abaluck, A. R. Localio, S. E. Kimmel, and B. L. Strom. 2005. Role of Computerized Physician Order Entry Systems in Facilitating Medication Errors. *Journal of the American Medical Association* 293 (10): 1197–1203.

Kosanovich, A. 2006. One Family in Two Courts: Coordination for Families in Illinois Juvenile and Domestic Relations Courts. *Loyola University Chicago Law Journal* 37 (3): 571–616.

Koviak, N. W. 2004. An Insurance Perspective on the Medical Malpractice Crisis. *Annals of Health Law* 13 (2): 607–616.

Kraus, Alan, and Stephen A. Ross. 1982. The Determination of Fair Profits for the Property-Liability Insurance Firm. *Journal of Finance* 37 (4): 1015–1028.

Kritzer, Herbert M. 1997. Contingency Fee Lawyers as Gatekeepers in the American Civil Justice System. *Judicature* 81 (1): 22–29.

———. 2002. Lawyer Fees and Lawyer Behavior in Litigation: What Does the Empirical Literature Really Say? *Texas Law Review* 80: 1943–1983.

———. 2004. *Risks, Reputations, and Rewards: Contingency Fee Legal Practice in the United States.* Stanford, CA: Stanford University Press (Stanford Law and Politics).

Krumlauf, Clare Elizabeth. 2005. Ohio's New Modified Joint and Several Liability Laws: A Fair Compromise for Competing Parties and Public Policy Interests. *Cleveland State Law Review* 53 (2): 333–358.

Kunreuther, Howard. 1998. Insurability Conditions and the Supply of Coverage. In *Paying the Price: The Status and Role of Insurance Against Natural Disasters in the United States*, edited by H. Kunreuther and R. J. Roth, Sr. Washington, DC: Joseph Henry Press.

Kunreuther, Howard, M. Pauly, and T. Russell. 2004. Demand and Supply Side Anomalies in Catastrophe Insurance Markets: The Role of the Public and Private Sectors. Paper prepared for the *MIT/LSE/Cornell Conference on Behavioral Economics*, London, May 2004.

Kunreuther, Howard C. 2006. Has the Time Come for Comprehensive Natural Disaster Insurance? In *On Risk and Disaster: Lessons from Hurricane Katrina*, edited by R. Daniels, D. F. Kettl, and H. C. Kunreuther. Philadelphia: University of Pennsylvania Press.

Kupeli, M. A. 1996. Tort Law = No Fault Compensation: An Unrealistic Elixir to the Medical Malpractice Ailment. *Suffolk Transnational Law Review* 19: 559–572.

Kyl, J. 2006. Meaningful Health Care Reform Begins with Health Courts. Washington, D.C.: Republican Policy Committee.

Lai, Gene C., Robert C. Witt, Hung-Gay Fung, Richard D. MacMinn, and Patrick L. Brockett. 2000. Great (and Not So Great) Expectations: An Endogenous Economic Explication of Insurance Cycles and Liability Crises. *Journal of Risk and Insurance* 67 (4): 617–652.

Landes, Elisabeth M. 1982. Insurance, Liability, and Accidents: A Theoretical and Empirical Investigation of the Effect of No-Fault Accidents. *Journal of Law and Economics* 25 (1): 49–65.

Landro, Laura. 2006. Hospitals Combat Errors at the 'Hand-Off'. *The Wall Street Journal*, June 28, pp. D1–D2.

Laro, D. 1995. The Evolution of the Tax Court as an Independent Tribunal. *University of Illinois Law Review* 1995 (1): 17–29.

Leape, Lucian L., T. A. Brennan, N. Laird, A. G. Lawthers, A. R. Localio, B. A. Barnes, L. Hebert, J. P. Newhouse, P. C. Weiler, and H. Hiatt. 1991. The Nature of Adverse Events in Hospitalized Patients: Results of the Harvard Medical Practice Study II. *New England Journal of Medicine* 324 (6): 377–384.

Lee, Soon-Jae, David Mayers, and Clifford W. Smith. 1997. Guaranty Funds and Risk-taking Evidence from the Insurance Industry. *Journal of Financial Economics* 44 (1): 3–24.

Leigh, J. Paul, and John A. Robbins. 2004. Occupational Disease and Workers' Compensation: Coverage, Costs, and Consequences. *The Milbank Quarterly* 82 (4): 689–721.

Lemaire, Jean. 1985. *Automobile Insurance: Actuarial Models*. Boston: Kluwer-Nijhoff.

Lempert, Richard. 1993. Civil Juries and Complex Cases: Taking Stock After Twelve Years. In *Verdict: Assessing the Civil Jury System*, edited by R. E. Litan. Washington, DC: The Brookings Institution.

———. 1999. Juries, Hindsight, and Punitive Damage Awards: Failures of a Social Science Case for Change. *DePaul Law Review* 48: 867.

Lemstra, M., and W. P. Olszynski. 2005. The Influence of Motor Vehicle Legislation on Injury Claim Incidence. *Canadian Journal of Public Health* 96 (1): 65–68.

Leonning, C. D. 2001. D. C. Family Court Funding Splits Officials: Norton, DeLay Say Budget Request to Congress Was Inadequate, Mishandled. *The Washington Post*, Sept. 22, p. B2.

Lerman, Lisa G. 1999. Blue-Chip Bilking: Regulation of Billing and Expense Fraud by Lawyers. *Georgetown Journal of Legal Ethics* 12: 205–366.

Lesser, Steven B., Edward R. Blumberg, Janice P. Brown, Michael V. Ciresi, Thomas A. Demetrio, Lewis H. Goldfarb, Michael S. Hull, Perry K. Huntington, Robert Johnson, Daniel M. Klein, Marc S. Moller, Charles M. Silver, Patrick E. Longan, and D. Christopher Wells. 2004. *Report on Contingent Fees in Medical Malpractice Litigation*. American Bar Association.

Levinson, W., D. L. Roter, J. P. Mullooly, V. T. Dull, and R. M. Frankel. 1997. Physician-Patient Communication: The Relationship with Malpractice Claims Among Primary Care Physicians and Surgeons. *Journal of the American Medical Association* 277 (7): 553–559.

Levinson, Wendy. 1994. Physician-Patient Communication: A Key to Malpractice Prevention. *Journal of the American Medical Association* 272 (20): 1619–1620.

Library, Institute of Governmental Studies, University of California. 2004. *Workers' Compensation in California 2004*. Available at http://www. igs.berkeley.edu/library/htWorkersCompensation.htm (accessed Dec. 30, 2004).

Lichtenstein, Sarah, Paul Slovic, Baruch Fischhoff, Mark Layman, and Barbara Combs. 1978. Judged Frequency of Lethal Events. *Journal of Experimental Psychology: Human Learning and Memory* 4 (6): 551–581.

Lloyd-Puryear, Michele A., Leslie K. Ball, and David Benor. 1998. Should the Vaccine Injury Compensation Program Be Expanded to Cover Adults? *Public Health Reports* 113: 236–242.

Localio, A. R., A. G. Lawthers, J. M. Bengtson, L. E. Hebert, S. L. Weaver, T. A. Brennan, and J. R. Landis. 1993. Relationship Between Malpractice Claims and Cesarean Delivery. *Journal of the American Medical Association* 269 (3): 366–373.

Longo, Daniel R., John F. Hewett, Bin Ge, and Shari Schubert. 2005. The Long Road to Patient Safety: A Status Report on Patient Safety Systems. *Journal of the American Medical Association* 294 (22): 2858–2865.

Loughran, David S. 2001. *The Effect of No-Fault Automobile Insurance on Driver Behavior and Automobile Accidents in the United States*. Santa Monica, CA: RAND Institute for Civil Justice.

Lowes, Robert. 2003. Malpractice: Do Other Countries Hold the Key? *Medical Economics* 80 (14): 58–60.

Luft, H. S. 1980. The Relation Between Surgical Volume and Mortality: An Exploration of Causal Factors and Alternative Models. *Medical Care* 18 (9): 940–959.

Luft, H. S., J. P. Bunker, and A. C. Enthoven. 1979. Should Operations Be Regionalized: Empirical Relation Between Surgical Volume and Mortality. *New England Journal of Medicine* 301 (25): 1364–1369.

Lund, Adrian, and Paul Zador. 1986. Re-Analyses of the Effects of No-Fault Auto Insurance on Fatal Crashes. *Journal of Risk and Insurance* 53: 226–342.

MacCoun, Robert. 1993. Inside the Black Box: What Empirical Research Tells Us About Decisionmaking by Civil Juries. In *Verdict: Assessing the Civil Jury System*, edited by R. E. Litan. Washington, DC: The Brookings Institution.

Mankiw, N. Gregory. 2007. *Principles of Economics*, 4th ed. Mason, OH: Thomson South-Western.

Marchev, Mimi. 2003. *Medical Malpractice and Medical Error Disclosure: Balancing Facts and Fears*. Portland, ME: National Academy for State Health Policy.

Marchev, Mimi, J. Rosenthal, and M. Booth. 2003. *How States Report Medical Errors to the Public: Issues and Barriers*. Portland, ME: National Academy for State Health Policy.

Margolis, Howard. 1982. A Thought Experiment on Demand-Revealing Mechanisms. *Public Choice* 38 (1): 87–91.

Marjoribanks, Timothy, Mary-Jo Delvecchio Good, Ann G. Lawthers, and Lynn M. Peterson. 1996. Physicians' Discourses on Malpractice and the Meaning of Medical Malpractice. *Journal of Health and Social Behavior* 37 (2): 163–178.

Matsa, D. 2007. Does Liability Keep the Doctor Away? Evidence from Tort Reform Damage Caps. *Journal of Legal Studies* 36.

Maute, Judith L. 2001. Pre-Paid and Group Legal Services: Thirty Years After the Storm. *Fordham Law Review* 70: 915–944.

May, M. L., and D. B. Stengel. 1990. Who Sues Their Doctors? *Law and Society Review* 24: 105–120.

McCaffery, Edward J., Daniel J. Kahneman, and Matthew L. Spitzer. 1995. Framing the Jury: Cognitive Perspectives on Pain and Suffering Awards. *Virginia Law Review* 81 (5): 1341–1420.

McCoid, J. C. II. 1991. Right to Jury Trial in Bankruptcy: *Granfinanciera, S. A. v. Nordberg*. *American Bankruptcy Law Journal* 65 (1): 15–42.

McDonald, C. J. 2006. Computerization Can Create Safety Hazards: A Bar-Coding Near Miss. *Annals of Internal Medicine* 144 (7): 510–516.

McGuire, P. 2000. Futurology as Further Ideology: Reflections on Pryor's Millennium Survey of Economists. *American Journal of Economics and Sociology* 59 (1): 35–38.

McGuire, T. G., and M. V. Pauly. 1991. Physician Response to Fee Changes with Multiple Payers. *Journal of Health Economics* 10 (4): 385–410.

McLeod, D. 2002. PHICO Execs Deny Fault for Insolvency. *Business Insurance* 36 (1): 3–5.

Mechanic, D. 1975. Some Social Aspects of the Medical Malpractice Dilemma. *Duke Law Journal* 1975 (6): 1179–1196.

Mehlman, Maxwell J. 2006. The Shame of Medical Malpractice. *Journal of Legal Medicine* 27: 17–32.

Meier, Kenneth J. 1988. *The Political Economy of Regulation: The Case of Insurance*. Albany: SUNY Press.

Mello, M. M., and D. M. Studdert. 2006. The Medical Malpractice System: Structure and Performance. In *Medical Malpractice and the U.S. Health Care System*, edited by W. M. Sage and R. Kersh. Cambridge: Cambridge University Press.

Mello, M. M., D. M. Studdert, C. M. DesRoches, J. Peugh, K. Zapert, T. A. Brennan, and W. M. Sage. 2005. Effects of a Malpractice Crisis on Specialist Supply and Patient Access to Care. *Annals of Surgery* 242 (5): 621–628.

Mello, Michelle M., and Troyen A. Brennan. 2002. Deterrence of Medical Errors: Theory and Evidence for Malpractice Reform. *Texas Law Review* 80 (7): 1595–1637.

Mello, Michelle M., Carly N. Kelly, David M. Studdert, Troyen A. Brennan, and William M. Sage. 2003. Hospitals' Behavior in a Tort Crisis: Observations from Pennsylvania. *Health Affairs* 22 (6): 225–233.

Mello, Michelle M., David M. Studdert, and Troyen A. Brennan. 2003. The New Medical Malpractice Crisis. *New England Journal of Medicine* 348 (23): 2281–2284.

Meltzer, David. 2001. Hospitalists and the Doctor-Patient Relationship. *Journal of Legal Studies* 30 (1): 589–606.

Meltzer, David, W. G. Manning, J. Morrison, M. N. Shah, L. Jin, T. Guth, and W. Levinson. 2002. Effects of Physician Experience on Costs and Outcomes on an Academic General Medicine Service: Results of a Trial of Hospitalists. *Annals of Internal Medicine* 137 (11): 866–875.

Miceli, Thomas J. 2004. *The Economic Approach to Law.* Stanford, CA: Stanford University Press.

———. 1994. Do Contingent Fees Promote Excessive Litigation? *Legal Studies* 23: 211–224.

Michel-Kerjan, Erwann, and Nathalie de Marcellis-Warin. 2006. Public-Private Programs for Covering Extreme Events: The Impact of Information Distribution on Risk-Sharing. *Asia-Pacific Journal of Risk and Insurance* 1 (2): 21–49.

Miller, Richard S. 1993. An Analysis and Critique of the 1992 Changes to New Zealand's Accident Compensation Scheme. *Maryland Law Review* 52: 1070–1092.

Mills, D. H., J. S. Boyden, and D. S. Rubsamen. 1977. *California Medical Association Medical Insurance Feasibility Study.* San Francisco: Sutter Publications.

Mogel, Gary S. 2003. Damage Caps Tied to Lower Loss Costs: Milliman. *National Underwriter Property and Casualty-Risk and Benefits Management* 107 (17): 22–24.

Moller, Erik K., Nicholas M. Pace, and Stephen J. Carroll. 1999. Punitive Damages in Financial Injury Jury Verdicts. *Journal of Legal Studies* 28: 283–339.

Moore, Michael J., and W. Kip Viscusi. 1989. Promoting Safety Through Workers' Compensation: The Efficacy and Net Wage Costs of Injury Insurance. *Rand Journal of Economics* 20 (4): 499–515.

Morgan, M. Granger, S. F. Brodsky, D. A. Butler, D. W. Ditz, L. I. Ezekoye, H. K. Florig, D. F. Geisler, D. J. Morgan, J. D. Moteff, K. A. Perusich, S. R. Rod, M. S. Sandilya, M. B. H. Weiss, C. F. Wiecha, B. P. Wise, L. A. Wojcik, and H. R. Zane. 1983. On Judging the Frequency of Lethal Events: A Replication. *Risk Analysis* 3 (1): 11–16.

Moridaira, Soichiro, Jorge L. Urrutia, and Robert C. Witt. 1992. The Equilibrium Insurance Price and Underwriting Return in a Capital Market Setting. *Journal of Risk and Insurance* 59 (2): 291–300.

Morton, Tom. 2003. Panel Dumps State Malpractice Insurance Idea. *The Casper Star Tribune*, October 29.

Munch, P., and D. Smallwood. 1980. Solvency Regulation in the Property/Casualty Insurance Industry. *Bell Journal of Economics* 11: 261–279.

Musgrave, R. 1957. Review of an Expenditure Tax. *American Economic Review* 47: 200–205.

Myers, Stewart C., and Richard A. Cohn. 1987. A Discounted Cash Flow Approach to Property-Liability Insurance: Theory and Empirical Results. In *Fair Rate of Return in Property-Liability Insurance*, edited by David Cummins and Scott E. Harrington. Boston: Kluwer Academic.

Nalebuff, B. 1987. Credible Pretrial Negotiation. *Rand Journal of Economics* 18: 198–210.

Nalebuff, B., and D. Scharfstein. 1987. Testing in Models of Asymmetric Information. *Review of Economics and Statistics* 54: 265–277.

Nathanson, Mitchell J. 2004. It's the Economy (and Combined Ratio), Stupid: Examining the Medical Malpractice Litigation Crisis Myth and the Factors Critical to Reform. *Pennsylvania State Law Review* 108: 1077.

National Association of Insurance Commissioners. 1980. *Malpractice Claims: Final Compilation*, edited by M. P. Sowka.

Nelson, K. B., and J. H. Ellenberg. 1986. Antecedents of Cerebral Palsy: Multivariate Analysis of Risk. *New England Journal of Medicine* 315 (2): 81–86.

New Jersey Hospital Association. 2002. Hospitals Share Stories of Doctors Leaving and Patients' Access to Care Threatened; NJHA Calls for Relief from Medical Malpractice Crisis. *Press Release*.

New South Wales Law Reform Commission. 1984. *Accident Compensation Final Report: Transport Accidents Scheme for New South Wales*, report 43. New South Wales Government Printer, Sydney.

New York Department of Insurance. 1997. *The Status of the Primary and Excess Medical Malpractice Market and the Future Need for the Medical Malpractice Insurance Association*. Albany: New York Department of Insurance.

Newhouse, J. P., A. P. Williams, B. W. Bennett, and W. B. Schwartz. 1982a. Does the Geographical Distribution of Physicians Reflect Market Failure? *Bell Journal of Economics* 13: 493–505.

———. 1982b. Where Have All the Doctors Gone? *Journal of the American Medical Association* 247 (17): 2392–2396.

Newton, G. E. 2001. Maintaining the Balance: Reconciling the Social and Judicial Costs of Medical Peer Review Protection. *Alabama Law Review* 52 (2): 723–742.

Niemeyer, Paul V. 2004. Awards for Pain and Suffering: The Irrational Center-piece of Our Tort System. *Virginia Law Review* 90: 1401–1422.

Nordman, E., D. Cermak, and K. McDaniel. 2004. *Medical Malpractice Insurance Report: A Study of Market Conditions and Potential Solutions to the Recent Crisis.* National Association of Insurance Commissioners: Kansas City, KS.

Norton, Stephen A. 1997. The Medical Malpractice Premium Costs of Obstetrics. *Inquiry* 34 (1): 62–69.

Nutter, Franklin W. 1985. The Second Time Around. *Best's Review* 86 (4): 22.

Nye, Blaine F., and Alfred E. Hofflander. 1987. Economics of Oligopoly: Medical Malpractice Insurance as a Classic Illustration. *Journal of Risk and Insurance* 54 (3): 502–519.

———. 1988. Experience Rating in Medical Professional Liability Insurance. *Journal of Risk and Insurance* 55 (1): 150–157.

Nye, David J., Donald G. Gifford, Bernard L. Webb, and Marvin A. Dewar. 1988. The Causes of the Medical Malpractice Crisis: An Analysis of Claims Data and Insurance Company Finances. *Georgetown Law Journal* 76: 1495–1561.

O'Connell, J. 1979. *The Lawsuit Lottery: Only the Lawyers Win.* New York: Free Press.

O'Connell, J., and P. B. Bryan. 2000–2001. More Hippocrates, Less Hipocracy: "Early Offers" as a Means of Implementing the Institute of Medicine's Recommendations on Malpractice Law. *Journal of Law and Health* 15: 23–52.

O'Connell, Jeffrey. 1982. Offers That Can't Be Refused: Foreclosure of Personal Injury Claims by Defendants' Prompt Tender of Claimants' Net Economic Losses. *Northwestern University Law Review* 77: 589–632.

O'Connell, Jeffrey, and D. F. Partlett. 1988. An America's Cup for Tort Reform? Australia and America Compared. *University of Michigan Journal of Law and Reform* 21: 443–487.

Office of the Governor for the State of California. 2004. Governor Schwarzenegger Signs Workers' Compensation Legislation. Available at http://gov.ca.gov/index.php?/press-release/3109/ (April 14, 2004; accessed Sept. 26, 2006).

Olson, Walter K. 1991. *The Litigation Explosion: What Happened When America Unleashed the Lawsuit.* New York: Truman Talley BooksDutton.

———. 2003. *The Rule of Lawyers: How the New Litigation Elite Threatens America's Rule of Law.* New York: St. Martin's Press.

Pace, Nicholas M., Daniela Golinelli, and Laura Zakaras. 2004. *Capping Non-economic Awards in Medical Malpractice Trials : California Jury Verdicts Under MICRA.* Santa Monica, CA: RAND Institute for Social Justice.

Palmer, Geoffrey. 1979. *Compensation for Incapacity.* Wellington, NZ: Oxford University Press.

———. 1994. New Zealand's Accident Compensation Scheme: Twenty Years On. *University of Toronto Law Journal* 44 (3): 223–273.

Paterson, Ron. 2004. Complaints and Quality: Handle with Care! *Journal of the New Zealand Medical Association* 117 (1198): 1–9.

Patient Safety Toolbox for States. 2006. National Academy for State Health Policy. Available at http://www.pstoolbox.org/ (accessed June 22, 2007).

Pauly, M. V. 2002. Is Medical Care Different? In *Competition in the Health Care Sector: Past, Present, and Future*, edited by W. Greenberg. Washington, DC: Beard Books.

———. 2006. Who Pays When Malpractice Premiums Rise? In *Medical Malpractice and the U.S. Health Care System*, edited by W. M. Sage and R. Kersh. Cambridge: Cambridge University Press.

Peeples, R., and C. T. Harris. 2005. Learning to Crawl: The Use of Voluntary Caps on Damages in Medical Malpractice Litigation. *Catholic University Law Review* 54 (3): 703–746.

Peeples, Ralph, Catherine T. Harris, and Thomas B. Metzloff. 2000. Settlement Has Many Faces: Physicians, Attorneys and Medical Malpractice. *Journal of Health and Social Behavior* 41 (3): 333–346.

Peltzman, Sam. 1976. *Toward a More General Theory of Regulation*, NBER Technical Working Paper 133. Cambridge, MA: National Bureau of Economic Research.

Percy, E. Farish. 2004. Checking Up on the Medical Malpractice Liability Insurance Crisis in Mississippi: Are Additional Tort Reforms the Cure? *Mississippi Law Journal* 73: 1001.

Perreira, K. M., and F. A. Sloan. 2002. Living Healthy and Living Long: Valuing the Nonpecuniary Loss from Disability and Death. *Journal of Risk and Uncertainty* 24 (1): 5–29.

Persson, Torsten, and Guido Tabillini. 2002. Political Economics and Public Finance. In *Handbook of Public Economics*, edited by A. J. Auerbach and M. Feldstein. Amsterdam: Elsevier Science.

Petersen, Laura A., Troyen A. Brennan, Anne C. O'Neil, E. Francis Cook, and Thomas H. Lee. 1994. Does Housestaff Discontinuity of Care Increase the Risk for Preventable Adverse Events? *Annals of Internal Medicine* 121 (11): 866–872.

Pfenningstorf, W., and Alec M. Schwartz, eds. 1986. *Legal Protection Insurance: American and European Approaches*. Chicago: American Bar Foundation, American Prepaid Legal Services Institute.

Pfenningstorf, Werner. 1975. *Legal Expense Insurance: The European Experience in Financing Legal Services*. Chicago: American Bar Association.

Pinnacle Actuarial Resources. 2003. *Final Report on the Feasibility of an Ohio Patient Compensation Fund*. Available at http://www.ohioinsurance.gov/Documents/05-01-03FinalReport.pdf (accessed June 22, 2007).

Pogarsky, G., and L. Babcock. 2001. Damage Caps, Motivated Anchoring, and Bargaining Impasse. *Journal of Legal Studies* 30 (1): 143–159.

Polinsky, A. M., and S. Shavell. 1998. Punitive Damages: An Economic Analysis. *Harvard Law Review* 111 (4): 869–962.

Poon, E. G., D. Blumenthal, T. Jaggi, M. M. Honour, D. W. Bates, and R. Kaushal. 2004. Overcoming Barriers to Adopting and Implementing Computerized Physician Order Entry Systems in U.S. Hospitals. *Health Affairs* 23 (4): 184–190.

Posner, R. A. 1974. Theories of Economic Regulation. *Bell Journal of Economics and Management Science* 5 (2): 335–358.

———. 1976. Toward a More General Theory of Regulation. *Journal of Law and Economics* 19: 211–240.

Priest, George L. 1987. The Current Insurance Crisis and Modern Tort Law. *Yale Law Journal* 96: 1521–1590.

———. 2002. Introduction: The Problem and Efforts to Understand It. In *Punitive Damages: How Juries Decide*, edited by C. R. Sunstein, R. Hastie, J. W. Payne, D. A. Schkade, and W. K. Viscusi. Chicago: University of Chicago Press.

Rabin, Robert L. 1988. Some Reflections on the Process of Tort Reform. *San Diego Law Review* 25: 13–48.

Ray, David. 1982. The Sources of Voting Cues in Three State Legislatures. *Journal of Politics* 44: 1074–1087.

Reynolds, R. A., J. A. Rizzo, and M. L. Gonzalez. 1987. The Cost of Medical Professional Liability. *Journal of the American Medical Association* 257 (20): 2776–2781.

Rhodes, M. S., and G. L. Ohlsson. 1997. *Workers' Compensation Answer Book.* New York: Panel Publishers.

Ridgway, Derry. 1999. No-Fault Vaccine Insurance: Lessons from the National Vaccine Injury Compensation Program. *Journal of Health Politics, Policy and Law* 24 (1): 59–90.

Riedmueller, N. J. 1973–1974. Group Legal Services and the Organized Bar. *Columbia Journal of Law and Social Problems* 10: 228–263.

Robinson, Glen O. 1986. The Medical Malpractice crisis of the 1970's: A Retrospective. *Law and Contemporary Problems* 49 (2): 5–35.

Rodwin, M. A., H. J. Chang, and J. Clausen. 2006. MARKETWATCH. Malpractice Premiums and Physicians' Income: Perceptions of a Crisis Conflict with Empirical Evidence. *Health Affairs* 25 (3): 750–758.

Rolph, J. E. 1981. Some Statistical Evidence on Merit Rating in Medical Malpractice Insurance. *Journal of Risk and Insurance* 48 (2): 247–260.

Rosenblatt, A. 2004. The Underwriting Cycle: The Rule of Six. *Health Affairs* 23 (6): 103–106.

Rosenthal, Marilynn M. 1988. *Dealing with Medical Malpractice: The British and Swedish Experience*. Durham, NC: Duke University Press.

Rothschild, Michael, and Joseph E. Stiglitz. 1976. Equilibrium in Competitive Insurance Markets: An Essay on the Economics of Imperfect Information. *Quarterly Journal of Economics* 90 (4): 630–649.

Rottman, David. 2000. Does Effective Therapeutic Jurisprudence Require Specialized Courts (and Do Specialized Courts Imply Specialist Judges?). *Court Review* 37: 22–27.

Rubinfeld, Daniel L., and Suzanne Scotchmer. 1993. Contingent Fees for Attorneys: An Economic Analysis. *Rand Journal of Economics* 24 (3): 343–356.

Ruser, John W. 1998. Does Workers' Compensation Encourage Hard to Diagnose Injuries? *Journal of Risk and Insurance* 65 (1): 101–124.

Rustad, Michael. 1992. In Defense of Punitive Damages in Products Liability: Testing Tort Anecdotes with Empirical Data. *Iowa Law Review* 78: 1–88.

Sage, W. M. 1997. Enterprise Liability and the Emerging Managed Health Care System. *Law and Contemporary Problems* 60 (2): 159–210.

Sage, W. M., K. E. Hastings, and R. A. Berenson. 1994. Enterprise Liability for Medical Malpractice and Health Care Quality Improvement. *American Journal of Law and Medicine* 20 (1–2): 1–28.

Sage, William M. 2003. Medical Liability and Patient Safety. *Health Affairs* 22 (4): 26–36.

Sage, William M., and James M. Jorling. 1994. A World That Won't Stand Still: Enterprise Liability by Private Contract. *DePaul Law Review* 43: 1007–1043.

Saks, Michael J. 1992. Do We Really Know Anything About the Behavior of the Tort Litigation System—and Why Not? *University of Pennsylvania Law Review* 140: 1147–1292.

Saltus, R. 2005. *Ending Malpractice Roulette: Do Health Courts Offer a Fairer Way to Settle Patients' Injury Claims?* Available at http://www.hsph.harvard.edu/review/review_fall_05/rvwfall05_malpractice.html (accessed June 22, 2007).

Sand, Leonard B., John S. Siffert, Walter P. Loughlin, Steven A. Reiss, and Nancy Batterman. 2005. *General Civil Instructions*. Edited by Matthew Bender and Company. 3rd ed. Vol. 4, *Modern Federal Jury Instructions*: Matthew Bender. Original edition, 1984.

Sappideen, C. 1993. No-Fault Compensation for Medical Misadventure—Australian Expression of Interest. *Journal of Contemporary Health Law and Policy* 9: 311–322.

Saxton, Jim. 2003. *Liability for Medical Malpractice: Issues and Evidence*. Washington, DC: Joint Economic Committee, United States Congress.

Schaffer, C. L., S. R. Feldman, A. B. Fleischer, M. J. Huether, and G. J. Chen. 2005. The Cutaneous Surgery Experience of Multiple Specialties in the Medicare

Population. *Journal of the American Academy of Dermatology* 52 (6): 1045–1048.

Schepard, A. 2002. Law Schools and Family Court Reform. *Family Court Review* 40 (4): 460–472.

Scheutzow, Susan O. 1999. State Medical Peer Review: High Cost but No Benefit—Is it Time for a Change? *American Journal of Law and Medicine* 25 (1): 7–60.

Schlesinger, H., and E. Venezian. 1986. Insurance Markets with Loss-Prevention Activity Profits, Market Structure, and Consumer Welfare. *Rand Journal of Economics* 17 (2): 227–238.

Schneiberg, M., and T. Bartley. 2001. Regulating American Industries: Markets, Politics, and the Institutional Determinants of Fire Insurance Regulation. *American Journal of Sociology* 107 (1): 101–146.

Schuck, Peter H. 1991. Scheduled Damages and Insurance Contracts for Future Services: A Comment on Blumstein, Bovbjerg, and Sloan. *Yale Journal of Regulation* 8 (1): 213–221.

Schwartz, Victor E., Mark A. Behrens, and Leah Lorber. 2000. Tort Reform Past, Present, and Future: Solving Old Problems and Dealing with "New Style" Litigation. *William Mitchell Law Review* 27 (1): 237–269.

Schwartz, W. B., and D. N. Mendelson. 1989a. Physicians Who Have Lost Their Malpractice Insurance: Their Demographic Characteristics and the Surplus-Lines Companies That Insure Them. *Journal of the American Medical Association* 262 (10): 1335–1341.

Schwartz, W. B., and D. N. Mendelson. 1989b. The Role of Physician-Owned Insurance Companies in the Detection and Deterrence of Negligence. *Journal of the American Medical Association* 262 (10): 1342.

Schwartz, W. B., J. P. Newhouse, B. W. Bennett, and A. P. Williams. 1980. The Changing Geographic Distribution of Board-Certified Physicians. *New England Journal of Medicine* 303 (18): 1032–1038.

Shapo, Marshall S. 2003. *Tort Law and Culture*. Durham, NC: Carolina Academic Press.

Sharkey, C. M. 2006. Caps and the Construction of Damages in Medical Malpractice Cases. In *Medical Malpractice and the U.S. Health Care System*, edited by William M. Sage and Rogan Kersh. Cambridge: Cambridge University Press.

Shavell, S. 1980. Strict Liability vs. Negligence. *Journal of Legal Studies* 9 (1): 1–25.

———. 1987. *Economic Analysis of Accident Law*. Cambridge, MA: Harvard University Press.

Shmanske, Stephen, and Tina Stevens. 1986. The Performance of Medical Malpractice Review Panels. *Journal of Health Politics, Policy, and Law* 11 (3): 525–535.

Showstack, Jonathan, Patricia P. Katz, and Ellen Weber. 1999. Evaluating the Impact of Hospitalists. *Annals of Internal Medicine* 130 (4): 376–381.

Sieg, H. 2000. Estimating a Bargaining Model with Asymmetric Information: Evidence from Medical Malpractice Disputes. *Journal of Political Economy* 108: 1006–1021.

Silver, Charles. 2002. Does Civil Justice Cost Too Much? *Texas Law Review* 80: 2073–2113.

Sloan, F. A., S. Berman, S. Rosenbaum, R. A. Chalk, and R. B. Giffin. 2004. The Fragility of the US Vaccine Supply. *New England Journal of Medicine* 351 (23): 2443–2447.

Sloan, F. A., and Randall R. Bovbjerg. 1989. *Medical Malpractice: Crises, Response, and Effects.* Washington, DC: Health Insurance Association of America Research Bulletino.

Sloan, F. A., S. S. Entman, B. A. Reilly, C. A. Glass, G. B. Hickson, and H. H. Zhang. 1997. Tort Liability and Obstetricians' Care Levels. *International Review of Law and Economics* 17 (2): 245–260.

Sloan, F. A., P. B. Githens, E. W. Clayton, G. B. Hickson, D. A. Gentile, and D. F. Partlett. 1993. *Suing for Medical Malpractice.* Chicago: University of Chicago Press.

Sloan, F. A., and M. Hassan. 1990. Equity and Accuracy in Medical Malpractice Insurance Pricing. *Journal of Health Economics* 9: 289–319.

Sloan, F. A., and C. R. Hsieh. 1990. Variability in Medical Malpractice Payments. *Law and Society Review* 24: 601–650.

———. 1995. Injury, Liability, and the Decision to File a Medical Malpractice Claim. *Law and Society Review* 29 (3): 413–435.

Sloan, F. A., P. M. Mergenhagen, and R. R. Bovbjerg. 1989. Effects of Tort Reforms on the Value of Closed Medical Malpractice Claims. *Journal of Health Politics, Policy, and Law* 14: 63–89.

Sloan, F. A., P. M. Mergenhagen, W. B. Burfield, R. R. Bovbjerg, and M. Hassan. 1989. Medical Malpractice Experience of Physicians: Predictable or Haphazard? *Journal of the American Medical Association* 262 (23): 3291–3297.

Sloan, F. A., K. Whetten-Goldstein, S. S. Entman, E. D. Kulas, and E. M. Stout. 1997. The Road from Medical Injury to Claims Resolution: How No-Fault and Tort Differ. *Law and Contemporary Problems* 60: 35–70.

Sloan, Frank, Jerry Cromwell, and Janet Mitchell. 1978. *Private Physicians and Public Programs.* Lexington, MA: Lexington Books.

Sloan, Frank A. 1985. State Responses to the Malpractice Insurance "Crisis" of the 1970s: An Empirical Assessment. *Journal of Health Politics, Policy, and Law* 9 (4): 629–646.

———. 1990. Experience Rating: Does it Make Sense for Medical Malpractice Insurance? *American Economic Review* 80 (2): 128–133.

————. 2004. *Public Medical Malpractice Insurance.* Funded by The Project on Medical Liability in Pennsylvania. Pew Charitable Trust. Available at http://www.pewtrusts.org/pdf/medical_malpractice_sloan_030904.pdf (accessed June 22, 2007).

————, ed. 1995. *Valuing Health Care: Costs, Benefits, and Effectiveness of Pharmaceuticals and Other Medical Technologies.* New York: Cambridge University Press.

Sloan, Frank A., Randall R. Bovbjerg, and Penny B. Githens. 1991. *Insuring Medical Malpractice.* New York: Oxford University Press.

Sloan, Frank A., and Charles E. Eesley. 2006. Governments as Insurers in Professional and Hospital Liability Insurance Markets. In *Medical Malpractice and the U.S. Health Care System—New Century, Different Issues,* edited by W. M. Sage and R. Kersh. Cambridge: Cambridge University Press.

Sloan, Frank A., Charles E. Eesley, and Chris J. Conover. 2006. Public Provision of Medical Malpractice Insurance: Pennsylvania's Experience. Working Paper, Duke University Center for Health Policy.

Sloan, Frank A., Charles E. Eesley, Christopher J. Conover, Carrie A. Mathews, and William M. Sage. 2005. Public Medical Malpractice Insurance: An Analysis of State-Oriented Patient Compensation Funds. *DePaul Law Review* 54 (2): 247–276.

Sloan, Frank A., Stephen S. Entman, Bridget A. Reilly, Cheryl A. Glass, Gerald B. Hickson, and Harold H. Zhang. 1997. Tort Liability and Obstetricians' Care Levels. *International Review of Law and Economics* 17 (2): 245–260.

Sloan, Frank A., and Penny B. Githens. 1994. Drinking, Driving, and the Price of Automobile Insurance. *Journal of Risk and Insurance* 61 (1): 33–58.

Sloan, Frank A., and Thomas J. Hoerger. 1991. Uncertainty, Information and Resolution of Medical Malpractice Disputes. *Journal of Risk and Uncertainty* 4: 403–423.

Sloan, Frank A., Bridget A. Reilly, and Christoph Schenzler. 1994. Effects of Prices, Civil and Criminal Sanctions, and Law Enforcement on Alcohol-Related Mortality. *Journal of Studies on Alcohol* 55 (4): 454–466.

————. 1995. Effects of Tort Liability and Insurance on Heavy Drinking and Drinking and Driving. *Journal of Law and Economics* 38 (1): 49–77.

Sloan, Frank A., Emily M. Stout, Kathryn Whetten-Goldstein, and Lan Liang. 2000. *Drinkers, Drivers, and Bartenders: Balancing Private Choices and Public Accountability.* Chicago: University of Chicago Press.

Sloan, Frank A., W. Kip Viscusi, Harrell W. Chesson, Christopher J. Conover, and Kathryn Whetten-Goldstein. 1998. Alternative Approaches to Valuing Intangible Losses: Evidence for Multiple Sclerosis. *Journal of Health Economics* 17 (4): 475–497.

Sloan, Frank A., Kathryn Whetten-Goldstein, Penny B. Githens, and Stephen S. Entman. 1995. Effects of the Threat of Medical Malpractice Litigation and Other Factors on Birth Outcomes. *Medical Care* 33 (7): 700–714.

Sloan, Frank A., K. Whetten-Goldstein, E. Kulas, G. Hickson, and S. Entman. 1999. Compensation for Birth Related Injury: No-Fault Compared to Tort Systems. *Archives of Pediatrics and Adolescent Medicine* 153: 41–48.

Sloan, Frank A., Kathryn Whetten-Goldstein, Emily Stout, Stephen Entman, and Gerald Hickson. 1998. No Fault System of Compensation for Obstetric Injury: Winners and Losers. *Obstetrics and Gynecology* 91 (March): 437–443.

Smarr, Lawrence. 2003. *Medical Malpractice Insurance Myths*: American College of Surgeons.

Smith, B. L. 1992. Three Attorney Fee-Shifting Rules and Contingency Fees. *Michigan Law Review* 90: 2154–2189.

Smith, Robert S. 1990. Mostly on Mondays: Is Worker's Compensation Covering Off-the-Job Injuries? In *Benefits, Costs, and Cycles in Workers' Compensation*, edited by P. S. Borba and D. Appel. Boston: Kluwer Academic.

Smith, Steven K., Carol J. DeFrances, Patrick A. Langan, Bureau of Justice Statistics Statisticians, and John Goerdt. 2006. Tort Cases in Large Counties. Washington, DC: U.S. Department of Justice. Available at http://www.ojp.gov/bjs/pub/ascii/tcilc.txt (accessed Sept. 25, 2006).

Snyder, Edward A., and James W. Hughes. 1990. The English Rule for Allocating Legal Costs: Evidence Confronts Theory. *Journal of Law, Economics, and Organization* 6 (2): 345–380.

Songer, Donald R. 1988. The Influence of Empirical Research: Committee vs. Floor Decision Making. *Legislative Studies Quarterly* 13 (3): 375–392.

Songer, Donald R., James M. Underwood, Sonja G. Dillon, Patricia E. Jameson, and Darla W. Kite. 1985. Voting Cues in Two State Legislatures: A Further Application of the Kingdon Model. *Social Science Quarterly* 66: 983–990.

South Carolina Legislative Audit Council. 2000. *A Review of the Medical Malpractice Patients' Compensation Fund.* Available at http://www.lac.sc.gov/NR/rdonlyres/φE4FφE92-6A69-441φ-AE41-29DE784D58DE/φ/pcf.pdf (assessed June 22, 2007).

Spence, M. 1977. Consumer Misperceptions, Product Failure and Product Liability. *Review of Economic Studies* 64: 561–572.

Spiller, Pablo T., and Richard G. Vanden Bergh. 2003. Toward a Positive Theory of State Supreme Court Decision Making. *Business and Politics* 5 (1): 7–43.

Stanley, R. 2003. *Buckhannon Board and Care Home, Inc. v. West Virginia Department of Health and Human Resources*: To the Prevailing Party Goes the Spoils . . . and the Attorneys' Fees! *Akron Law Review* 36: 363–409.

Starr, P. 1982. *The Social Transformation of American Medicine.* New York: Basic Books.

State of Florida. 2003. *Report of the Governor's Select Task Force on Healthcare Professional Liability Insurance.* Tallahassee: Florida Insurance Council.

State of Maryland. 2004. Governor's Task Force on Medical Malpractice and Health Care Access, Final Report. Available at http://www.governor.maryland.gov/pdfs/medmal_112404.pdf (accessed Jan. 4, 2005).

State of Missouri. 2002. Senate Bill no. 1204.

———. 2003. Senate Bill no. 551.

Stedman, H. J., S. Davidson, and C. Brown. 2001. Mental Health Courts: Their Promise and Unanswered Questions. *Law and Psychiatry* 52 (4): 457–458.

Stedman, Richard R. II. 2003. Of Hurricanes and Airplanes: The Congressional Knee-Jerk Reaction to September 11. *Loyola Law Review* 49 (4): 991–1023.

Stern, J., C. Rehmus, J. Lowenberg, H. Kasper, and B. Dennis. 1975. *Final-Offer Arbitration*. Lexington, MA: Lexington Books.

Steves, Myron F., Jr. 1976. A Proposal to Improve the Cost to Benefit Relationships in the Medical Professional Liability Insurance System. *Duke Law Journal* 1975 (6): 1305–1333.

Stigler, G. J. 1971. Theory of Economic Regulation. *Bell Journal of Economics and Management Science* 2: 3–21.

Studdert, D. M., and T. A. Brennan. 2000. The Problems with Punitive Damages in Lawsuits Against Managed-Care Organizations. *New England Journal of Medicine* 342 (4): 280–284.

Studdert, D. M., M. M. Mello, and T. A. Brennan. 2004. Medical Malpractice. *New England Journal of Medicine* 350: 283–292.

Studdert, D. M., M. M. Mello, A. A. Gawande, T. K. Gandhi, A. Kachalia, C. Yoon, A. L. Puopolo, and T. A. Brennan. 2006. Claims Errors and Compensation Payments in Medical Malpractice Litigation. *New England Journal of Medicine* 354 (19): 2024–2033.

Studdert, D. M., M. M. Mello, W. M. Sage, C. M. DesRoches, J. Peugh, K. Zapert, and T. A. Brennan. 2005. Defensive Medicine Among High-Risk Specialist Physicians in a Volatile Malpractice Environment. *Journal of the American Medical Association* 293 (21): 2609–2617.

Studdert, David M., and Troyen A. Brennan. 2001. No-Fault Compensation for Medical Injuries: The Prospect for Error Prevention. *Journal of the American Medical Association* 286 (2): 217–223.

Studdert, David M., Lori A. Fritz, and Troyen A. Brennan. 2000. The Jury Is Still In: Florida's Birth-Related Neurological Injury Compensation Plan After a Decade. *Journal of Health Politics, Policy and Law* 25 (3): 499–526.

Studdert, David M., Eric J. Thomas, Brett I. W. Zbar, Joseph P. Newhouse, et al. 1997. Can the United States Afford a "No-Fault" System of Compensation for Medical Injury? *Law and Contemporary Problems* 60 (1–2): 1.

Studdert, David M., Y. T. Yang, and Michelle M. Mello. 2004. Are Damages Caps Regressive? A Study of Malpractice Jury Verdicts in California. *Health Affairs* 23 (4): 54–67.

Sturgis, Robert W. 1995. *Tort Cost Trends: An International Perspective*. St. Louis, MO: TillinghastTowers Perrin.

Sugarman, Stephen D. 1990. The Need to Reform Personal Injury Law Leaving Scientific Disputes to Scientists. *Science* 248 (4957): 823–828.

Sunstein, Cass R. 2002a. To Punish or Not? In *Punitive Damages: How Juries Decide*, by C. R. Sunstein, R. Hastie, J. W. Payne, D. A. Schkade, and W. K. Viscusi. Chicago: University of Chicago Press.

———. 2002b. What Should Be Done? In *Punitive Damages: How Juries Decide*, by C. R. Sunstein, R. Hastie, J. W. Payne, D. A. Schkade, and W. K. Viscusi. Chicago: University of Chicago Press.

———. 2003. Terrorism and Probability Neglect. *Journal of Risk and Uncertainty* 26 (2/3): 121–136.

Sunstein, Cass R., David Schkade, and Daniel Kahneman. 2000. Do People Want Optimal Deterrence? *Journal of Legal Studies* 29: 237–253.

———. 2002. Do People Want Optimal Deterrence? In *Punitive Damages: How Juries Decide*, by C. R. Sunstein, R. Hastie, J. W. Payne, D. A. Schkade, and W. K. Viscusi. Chicago: University of Chicago Press.

Surowiecki, J. 2004. *The Wisdom of Crowds*. New York: Doubleday.

Sutter, R. L. 2002. *Kansas Health Care Stabilization Fund, Indicated Liabilities at June 30, 2002: Surcharge Determination for FY2003*. St. Louis, MO: Tillinghast Towers Perrin.

Swartz, Katherine. 2006. *Reinsuring Health: Why More Middle-Class People Are Uninsured and What Government Can Do*. New York: Russell Sage Foundation Press.

Swedish Medical Association, National Board of Health and Welfare. 2003. Working in Sweden: Information for Doctors from EU/EEA Countries. Available at http://www.lg.se/upload/epi/lg/pdf/2005/working_in_sweden.pdf (accessed June 22, 2007).

Symposium on Medical Malpractice: Preface. 1975. *Duke Law Journal* 1975 (6): 1177.

Tabarrok, Alexander, and Eric Helland. 1999. Court Politics: The Political Economy of Tort Awards. *Journal of Law and Economics* 42: 157–188.

———. 2005. *Two Cheers for Contingent Fees*. Washington DC: American Enterprise Institute Press.

Tappan, Kristie. 2005. Medical-Malpractice Reform: Is Enterprise Liability or No-Fault a Better Reform? *Boston College Law Review* 46: 1095–1130.

Taragin, Mark I., Laura R. Willett, Adam P. Wilczek, Richard Trout, and Jeffrey L. Carson. 1992. The Influence of Standard of Care and Severity of Injury on the Resolution of Medical Malpractice Claims. *Annals of Internal Medicine* 117 (9): 780–784.

Tarr, G. Alan. 1998. Interest Groups and Judicial Federalism: Organizational Litigation in State Judiciaries. *Publius* 28 (4): 167–168.

———. 2005. *Judicial Process and Judicial Policymaking.* 4th ed. Belmont, CA: Wadsworth Publishing.

Thomas, Tim A. 2006. *Common Law*, 2d, vol. 15A *of American Jurisprudence*: Thomas West Publishing.

Thorpe, Kenneth E. 2004. The Medical Malpractice "Crisis": Recent Trends and the Impact of State Tort Reforms. *Health Affairs.* Available at http://content. healthaffairs.org/cgi/reprint/hlehaff.w4.20vl?maxtoshow=&HITS=10&hits=10 &RESULTFORMAT=&authorl=thorpe&andorexactfulltext=and&searchid=1 &FIRSTINDEX=0&resourcetype=HWCIT (accessed June 22, 2007).

Tinetti, Mary E., Sidney T. Bogardus, Jr., and Joseph V. Agostini. 2004. Potential Pitfalls of Disease-Specific Guidelines for Patients with Multiple Conditions. *New England Journal of Medicine* 351 (27): 2870–2874.

Todd, S. 2000. International Torts: A Comparative Study. Privitization of Accident Compensation: Policy and Politics in New Zealand. *Washburn Law Journal* 39: 404.

Topel, Robert H. 1984. Experience Rating of Unemployment Insurance and the Incidence of Unemployment. *Journal of Law and Economics* 27 (1): 61–90.

Treaster, Joseph B. 2003. Malpractice Insurance: No Clear or Easy Answers. *The New York Times.* New York, N.Y., March 5, C1.

Tversky, A., and D. Kahneman. 1973. Availability: A Heuristic for Judging Frequency and Probability. *Cognitive Psychology* 5: 207–232.

U.S. Congress, Office of Technology Assessment. 1994. *Defensive Medicine and Medical Malpractice.* OTA-H-602. Washington, DC: U.S. Congress.

U.S. Congressional Budget Office. 2002. *Federal Reinsurance for Disasters.* Washington, DC: U.S. Congress.

———. 2003. *The Economics of U.S. Tort Liability: A Primer.* Washington, DC: U.S. Congress.

———. 2004. *The Effects of Tort Reform: Evidence from the States.* Washington, DC: U.S. Congress.

Udell, Nancy, and David B. Kendall. 2005. *Health Courts: Fair and Reliable Justice for Injured Patients.* Progressive Policy Institute Policy Report (Feb.). Available at http://www.ppionline.org/documents/healthcourts_0217.pdf (accessed June 22, 2007).

United States Census Bureau. 2000. *State and County QuickFacts.* Available at http://quickfacts.census.gov/qfd (accessed Sept. 22, 2006).

United States Department of Commerce. 2006. *Statistical Abstract of the United States: The National Data Book*, 125th ed. Washinton, DC: United States Census Bureau.

United States Government Accountability Office. 2005. *Medicare Physician Fees: Geographic Adjustment Indices Are Valid in Design, but Data and Methods Need Refinement.* Washington, DC: United States General Accountability Office.

United States General Accounting Office. 1987. *VA Health Care, VA's Patient Injury Control Program Not Effective.* Washington, DC: U.S. Government Printing Office.

————. 1993. *Medical Malpractice: Medicare/Medicaid Beneficiaries Account for a Relatively Small Percentage of Malpractice Losses.* Washington, DC: U.S. Government Printing Office.

————. 1995. *Medical Liability: Impact on Hospital and Physician Costs Extends Beyond Insurance.* Washington, DC: U.S. Government Printing Office.

————. May 1993a. *Medical Malpractice: Experience with Efforts to Address Problems.* GAO/T-HRD-93–24 (May).

————. 2003b. *Medical Malpractice Insurance: Multiple Factors Have Contributed to Increased Premium Rates.* Washington, DC: United States General Accounting Office.

————. 2003c. *Medical Malpractice: Implications of Rising Premiums on Access to Health Care.* Washington, DC: United States General Accounting Office (Aug.).

Vargo, John F. 1993. The American Rule on Attorney Fee Allocation: The Injured Person's Access to Justice. *American University Law Review* 42:1567–1636.

Varian, Hal R. 2001. Catastrophe Bonds Could Fill the Gaps in Reinsurance. *New York Times.* New York, N.Y., October 25, C2.

Venezian, Emilio. 1985. Ratemaking Methods and Profit Cycles in Property and Liability Insurance. *Journal of Risk and Insurance* 52: 477–500.

Vidmar, Neil. 1993. Empirical Evidence on the Deep Pockets Hypothesis: Jury Awards and Suffering in Medical Malpractice Cases. *Duke Law Journal* 43 (2): 217–266.

————. 1994a. Are Juries Competent to Decide Liability in Tort Cases Involving Scientific/Medical Issues? Some Data from Medical Malpractice. *Emory Law Journal* 43 (3): 885–911.

————. 1994b. Pap and Circumstance: What Jury Verdict Statistics Can Tell Us About Jury Behavior and the Tort System. *Suffolk University Law Review* 28 (4): 1205–1234.

————. 1995. *Medical Malpractice and the American Jury.* Ann Arbor: University of Michigan Press.

————. 1998. The Performance of the American Civil Jury: An Empirical Perspective. *Arizona Law Review* 40 (3): 849–899.

————. 1999. Juries Don't Make Legal Decisions! And Other Problems: A Critique of Hastie et al. On Punitive Damages. *Law and Human Behavior* 23 (6): 705–714.

————. 2003. Juror Discussions During Civil Trials. *Arizona Law Review* 45: 1–82.

Vidmar, Neil, Felicia Gross, and Mary Rose. 1998. Jury Awards for Medical Malpractice and Post-Verdict Adjustments of Those Awards. *DePaul Law Review* 48: 265–300.

Vidmar, Neil, and Jeffrey J. Rice. 1993. Assessments of Noneconomic Damage Awards in Medical Negligence: A Comparison of Jurors with Legal Professionals. *Iowa Law Review* 78: 883–912.

Vidmar, Neil, Russell M. Robinson III, and Kara MacKillop. 2006. "Judicial Hellholes": Medical Malpractice Claims, Verdicts and the "Doctor Exodus" in Illinois. *Vanderbilt Law Review* 59 (4): 1309–1342.

Vidmar, Neil J. 2004. Experimental Simulations and Tort Reform: Avoidance, Error and Overreaching in Sunstein et al.'s *Punitive Damages*. *Emory Law Journal* 53 (1): 1359–1403.

Vidmar, Neil J., and M. R. Rose. 2001. Punitive Damages by Juries in Florida: In Terrorem and in Reality. *Harvard Journal on Legislation* 38:487–513.

Viscusi, W. K., and W. N. Evans. 1990. Utility Functions That Depend on Health-Status Estimates and Economic Implications. *American Economic Review* 80 (3): 353–374.

Viscusi, W. Kip. 1979. *Employment Hazards: An Investigation of Market Performance*. Cambridge, MA: Harvard University Press.

————. 1992. *Fatal Tradeoffs: Public and Private Responsibilities for Risk*. New York: Oxford University Press.

————. 1993. The Value of Risks to Life and Health. *Journal of Economic Literature*. 31 (4): 1912–1946.

————. 2001. Jurors, Judges, and the Mistreatment of Risk by the Courts. *Journal of Legal Studies* 107: 107–142.

————. 2002a. Corporate Risk Analysis: A Reckless Act? In *Punitive Damages: How Juries Decide*, by C. R. Sunstein, R. Hastie, J. W. Payne, D. A. Schkade and W. K. Viscusi. Chicago: University of Chicago Press.

————. 2002b. Judging Risk and Recklessness. In *Punitive Damages: How Juries Decide*, by C. R. Sunstein, R. Hastie, J. W. Payne, D. A. Schkade, and W. K. Viscusi. Chicago: University of Chicago Press.

Viscusi, W. Kip, Richard J. Zeckhauser, Patricia Born, and Glenn Blackmon. 1993. The Effect of 1980s Tort Reform Legislation on General Liability and Medical Malpractice Insurance. *Journal of Risk and Uncertainty* 6: 165–186.

Viscusi, W. Kip, and P. H. Born. 1995. Medical Malpractice Insurance in the Wake of Liability Reform. *Journal of Legal Studies* 25: 463–490.

———. 2005. Damage Caps, Insurability, and the Performance of Insurance. *Journal of Risk and Insurance* 72 (1): 23–42.

Viswanathan, Hema N., and J. Warren Salmon. 2000. Accrediting Organizations and Quality Improvement. *American Journal of Managed Care* 6 (10): 1117–1130.

Wachter, R. M. 2004. The End of the Beginning: Patient Safety Five Years After "To Err is Human." *Health Affairs* W4-534–W4-545.

———. 2006. Expected and Unanticipated Consequences of the Quality and Information Technology Revolutions. *Journal of the American Medical Association* 295 (23): 2780–2783.

Wachter, Robert M., and Lee Goldman. 1996. The Emerging Role of "Hospitalists" in the American Health Care System. *New England Journal of Medicine* 335: 514–517.

———. 2002. The Hospitalist Movement 5 Years Later. *Journal of the American Medical Association* 287 (4): 487–494.

Warburton, Rebecca Nunn. 2005. Patient Safety—How Much Is Enough? *Health Policy* 71: 223–232.

Weiler, P. C. 1991. *Medical Malpractice on Trial.* Cambridge, MA: Harvard University Press.

———. 1993. The Case for No-Fault Medical Liability. *Maryland Law Review* 52: 908–950.

Weiler, Paul C., Howard H. Hiatt, Joseph P. Newhouse, William G. Johnson, Troyen Brennan, and Lucian L. Leape. 1993. *A Measure of Malpractice: Medical Injury, Malpractice Litigation, and Patient Compensation.* Cambridge, MA: Harvard University Press.

Weinberg, J., L. H. Hilborne, and Q. T. Ngyuen. 2005. Regulation of Health Policy: Patient Safety and the States. *Advances in Patient Safety* 1: 405–422.

Weinstein, Debra F. 2002. Duty Hours for Resident Physicians: Tough Choices for Teaching Hospitals. *New England Journal of Medicine* 347: 1275–1278.

Weinstein, R. A., J. D. Siegel, and T. A. Brennan. 2005. Infection-Control Report Cards: Securing Patient Safety. *New England Journal of Medicine* 353 (3): 225–227.

Weiss, Gail Garfinkel. 2004. Malpractice: Can No-Fault Work? *Medical Economics* 81 (11): 66–71.

Weiss, M. A., and J. H. Chung. 2004. U.S. Reinsurance Prices, Financial Quality, and Global Capacity. *Journal of Risk and Insurance* 71 (3): 437–467.

Wheelock, David C., and Paul W. Wilson. 1995. Explaining Bank Failures: Deposit Insurance, Regulation, and Efficiency. *Review of Economics and Statistics* 77 (4): 689.

White, Michelle J. 1994. The Value of Liability in Medical Malpractice. *Health Affairs* 13 (4): 75–87.

———. 2004. The "Arms Race" on American Roads: The Effect of Sport Utility Vehicles and Pickup Trucks on Traffic Safety. *Journal of Law and Economics* 47 (2): 333–356.

Whiteman, David. 1985. The Fate of Policy Analysis in Congressional Decision Making: Three Types of Use in Committees. *Western Political Quarterly* 38 (2): 294–311.

Williams, P. A. 1995. Children and the Law: A Unified Family Court for Missouri. *University of Missouri Kansas City Law Review* 63 (3): 383–428.

Winter, R. A. 1988. Liability Crisis and the Dynamics of Competitive Insurance Markets. *Yale Journal of Regulation* 5: 455–500.

———. 1991. The Liability Insurance Market. *Journal of Economic Perspectives* 5 (3): 115–136.

———. 1994. Dynamics of Competitive Insurance Markets. *Journal of Financial Intermediation* 3: 379–415.

Winter, Ralph. 1991. Solvency Regulation and the Insurance Cycle. *Economic Inquiry* XXIX (3): 458–472.

Wisconsin Hospital Association. March Inc. 2003. *2003–2005 State Budget: Impacts on Wisconsin Hospitals.* Available at http://www.wha.org/pubArchive/position_Statements/pp2003issuesummary.pdf (accessed June 22, 2007).

Wisconsin Insurance Report. 2001. Madison: State of Wisconsin, Office of the Commissioner of Insurance.

Witt, John Fabian. 2005. The Long History of State Constitutions and American Tort Law. *Rutgers Law Review* 36 (4): 1159–1199.

Wood, Kathryn E., and David B. Nash. 2005. Mandatory State-Based Error-Reporting Systems: Current and Future Prospects. *American Journal of Medical Quality* 20 (6): 297–303.

Wren, Daniel A., and Arthur G. Bedeian. 2004. The Taylorization of Lenin: Rhetoric or Reality? *The International Journal of Social Economics* 31 (3): 87–299.

Wright, A. A., and I. T. Katz. 2005. Bar Coding for Patient Safety. *New England Journal of Medicine* 353 (4): 329–331.

Wu, A. W., S. Folkman, S. J. McPhee, and B. Lo. 2003. Do House Officers Learn from Their Mistakes? *Journal of the American Medical Association* 265: 2089–2094.

Würdemann Vanderbilt, Henry. 1912. *Injuries of the Eye.* Chicago: Cleveland Press.

Yelen, S. 1993. Withdrawal Restrictions in the Automobile Insurance Market. *Yale Law Journal* 102 (6): 1431–1455.

Young, T. 2005. Presidential Address. Human Error, Patient Safety and the Tort Liability Crisis: The Perfect Storm. *American Journal of Obstetrics and Gynecology* 193 (2): 506–511.

Zimmerman, Rachel, and Christopher Oster. 2002. Assigning Liability: Insurers' Missteps Helped Provoke Malpractice "Crisis." *The Wall Street Journal*, June 24, A1, 8.

Zuckerman, Stephen, Randall R. Bovbjerg, and Frank Sloan. 1990. Effects of Tort Reforms and Other Factors on Medical Malpractice Insurance Premiums. *Inquiry* 27: 167–182.

Zwanziger, Jack, Glenn A. Melnick, and Anil Bamezai. 2000. Can Cost Shifting Continue in a Price Competitive Environment? *Health Economics* 9 (3): 211–226.

Zweigert, Konrad, and Heinz Kötz. 1987. *An Introduction to Comparative Law*, 2nd rev. ed. Oxford: Clarendon Press.

Index

Abraham, Kenneth S., 396n18
Academic health centers (AHCs), 334
Access to care
  barriers, 53, 55
  patient travel time and, 70
  physician supply and, 69–71
Accident Compensation Corporation
    (ACC), 300–303, 394–95n123
Adams, Mark L., 13
Adhesion contracts, 398–99n62
Adjusted loss expense, 32, 44
ADR. *See* Alternative dispute
    resolution (ADR)
Adverse outcomes. *See* Errors,
    medical; Injuries, medical
Alaska, 150–51, 152, 383n73
ALE. *See* Adjusted loss expense
Alternative dispute resolution (ADR),
    92, 310
A.M. Best, 47, 242
American Association for
    Accreditation of Ambulatory
    Facilities, 210
American Bar Association, 138
  on prepaid legal services, 157, 158
American Hospital Association, 229
American Medical Association
  on damage caps, 109
  on effects of tort reforms, 76
  on health courts, 177,
    364–65n53–54
  on physicians' incomes, 62

  on physician supply, 69
  premium trends, 58
  on runaway juries, 164
American Society of
    Anesthesiologists, 208
Ameringer, Carl F., 207
Anesthesiologists, 208–9, 224
Anticipated losses, 37, 387n41
Aranson, Allison F., 144
Arbitration, 128–29, 298–99,
    347n13–14
Arizona, 63, 65
Association of British Insurers, 156
Attachment points, reinsurance,
    249–50
Attorneys. *See* Lawyers
Australia, 295, 394n118
Autism, 290, 305
Avraham, R., 124
Awards. *See* Compensation, patient

Baicker, Katherine, 68
Baker, Tom, 36, 86
  on reforms, 316, 318, 319, 335
  on regulation, 239
Balance sheets, insurer's, 33–34
Banking industry, 243–44
Bankruptcy
  courts, 179–80
  hospital, 230
  insurer, 129, 218, 220–21, 239–42,
    384n11